Journeys and Dwellings

Journeys and Dwellings

Indian Ocean Themes in South Asia

Edited by

HELENE BASU

Institute for Ethnology
University of Münster

ORIENT LONGMAN PRIVATE LIMITED

Registered Office
3-6-752 Himayatnagar, Hyderabad 500 029 (A.P.), India
e-mail: orientswan@gmail.com

Other Offices
Bangalore, Bhopal, Bhubaneshwar, Chennai,
Ernakulam, Guwahati, Hyderabad, Jaipur, Kolkata,
Lucknow, Mumbai, New Delhi, Patna

ISBN 13: 978 81 250 3141 3
ISBN 10: 81 250 3141 3

Maps cartographed by
Sangam Books (India) Private Limited, Hyderabad

Typeset in Iowan OldSt BT 10.5/13 *by*
Line Arts, Pondicherry 605 003

Printed at
Graphica Printers
Hyderabad

Published by
Orient Longman Private Limited
3-6-752, Himayatnagar, Hyderabad 500 029
Email: orientswan@gmail.com

Contents

List of Maps

Preface

The present volume originates in an interdisciplinary workshop on 'Western India and the Indian Ocean' held at the Conference of Modern South Asian Studies in Heidelberg in 1999. Since then, the study of Indian Ocean historical and social settings has gained great momentum. Reflecting the demands of the subject, a global network of scholars has emerged sharing an interest in a great diversity of Indian Ocean themes. In this context, the 'Crossing Borders Programme' at the University of Iowa has proved a major impetus for furthering studies in the Indian Ocean region. A generous fellowship granted by the University of Iowa and German Academic Exchange Service made it possible for me to begin with editing the present volume. Some of the original participants of the workshop in Heidelberg had moved on to other areas, while other scholars had embarked on Indian Ocean studies whose contributions are included in the present volume. I wish to express my gratitude especially to Paul Greenough and Jim Giblin from the University of Iowa for their encouragement and the many fruitful discussions we had on the subject. My gratitude also goes to Mary Nooter Roberts, Edward Alpers and Allen Roberts from the University of California in Los Angeles for sharing their ideas in most congenial ways during several meetings.

Ilka Borchardt has contributed greatly to bringing the volume into shape. My final thanks are due to Angelika Malinar for her untiring support of this project.

Abbreviations

AICC	All India Congress Committee
GSB	Gauda Saraswat Brahmins
NAI	National Archives of India, New Delhi
IOR	India Office Records and Library, London
TASU	Tanzania Seamen's Union
ZNA	Zanzibar National Archives

A map of the Indian Ocean

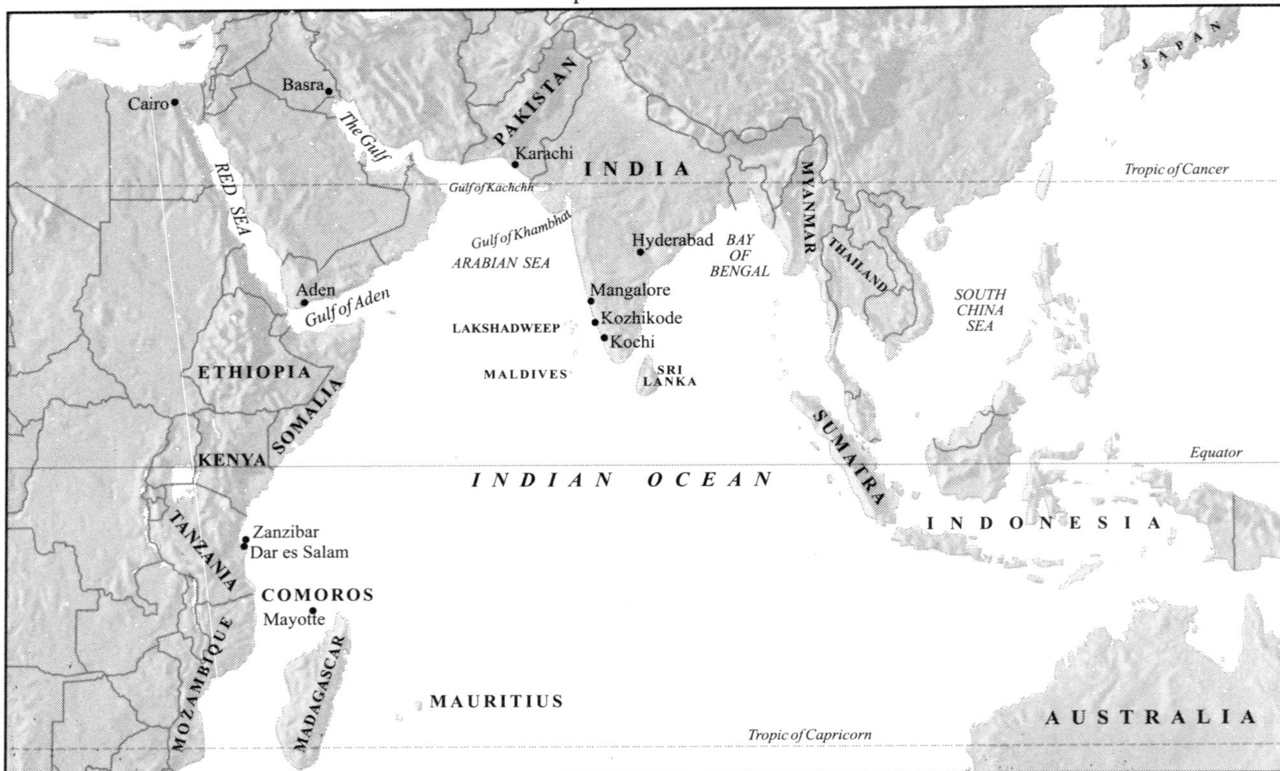

Map 1

Introduction

Helene Basu

The image of the Indian Ocean brings to mind a world linked by transregional movements of goods, people, messages and cultural practices long before the present age of globalisation. In his book *In an Antique Land,* Amitav Ghosh (1992) has opened a window to this world by interweaving several tales that are situated on different layers of time and space: of thirteenth-century travellers, a Jewish trader and his Indian slave sailing across the ocean, from Egypt to Aden to Mangalore and back; and of late-twentieth-century travellers, such as an Indian anthropologist in Egypt or Egyptian villagers journeying to the Gulf to work in the oil fields. By its very form, *In an Antique Land* addresses the problems that scholars are faced with when turning to the Indian Ocean: a 'struggle with history'[1], an erosion of the idea that cultural units are clearly demarcated by geographical boundaries, a shift of perspective from localised 'roots' to movements along 'routes'—and vice versa, from journeys to dwellings. These dimensions constitute the theoretical context in which the present volume is situated.

Anthropologists have come to question the static division of the world into territorially bounded culture areas, a division that seems more reflective of unequal relationships of power and the dominance of Euro-American categories than conducive to critical social analysis (Gupta and Ferguson 1997;

[1] I have borrowed this phrase from the title of a workshop organised by Edward Simpson and Kai Kresse in St. Andrews, Scotland, in April 2004.

Appadurai 2000a). The present volume has grown out of an interdisciplinary workshop that brought together historians and anthropologists interested in going beyond the territorial limitations of area studies and anthropological assumptions regarding clearly bounded culture areas.[2] It was felt that by concentrating on South Asia in relation to the wider Indian Ocean world, new perspectives would emerge that highlight movement, forced and voluntary migration, and travelling actors, cultures and faiths, on the one hand, as well as processes of settlement, cultural relocation, mixture and assimilation, on the other (cf. Clifford 1997). While these processes are more often associated with late-twentieth-century globalisation and West-South relationships (cf. Inda and Rosaldo 2002), the contributors to this volume are directing their attention to historical and contemporary flows of people, ideas and practices across the Indian Ocean region and examining their relocations in South Asia.[3]

A few words are necessary to clarify what is meant by the term 'Indian Ocean'. First of all, it is a cover term for several separately named seas, such as the 'Arabian Sea', the 'Red Sea' the 'Gulf', the 'Bay of Bengal' and the 'South China Sea'. Pearson suggested a useful description of the overall area of sea covered by the Indian Ocean:

> One way to visualise. . .the Indian Ocean proper is to see it as a vast equilateral triangle. The base is the tropic of Capricorn. . . . The two sides go north, the western one then including the Swahili and south Arabian coasts, up to north India, and then down from the apex through Burma, Sumatra and to northwest Australia. The only real problem with this is that it excludes the Gulf and the Red Sea, and these were intricately connected with the Indian Ocean. . . . An

[2] The workshop, entitled "Western India and the Indian Ocean", was organised by Helene Basu and Peter Fluegel, and held in 1999 at the 16th Conference on Modern South Asian Studies in Heidelberg.

[3] Most of the authors are actually concerned with India, but the fact that two contributors focus upon sites elsewhere in the region, namely Sri Lanka and Pakistan, necessitated using the expression 'South Asia'. Therefore no claim is being made to cover the whole of South Asia's involvement with the Indian Ocean. In particular, the eastern part of the region and links with Southeast Asia are not dealt with in this volume.

> alternative. . .is to see it as a vast letter M, with the Red Sea and Gulf on one side, and the Bay of Bengal on the other, divided by India. (Pearson 2003: 15)

The term 'Indian Ocean' is originally a translation of the Arabic *'al-bahr al hindi'*. In Arab usage this could refer to either the Arabian Sea or the more extensive area of the Indian Ocean itself (Wink 1999). These names, given to parts of the ocean by Arabs and Europeans, all reflect locally rooted perspectives from where oceanic regions are mapped. Some of the original Indian terms for the ocean are rather religious in nature instead. From the time of the *Dharmashastras* the ocean was called 'black water' (*kalapani*), a term charged with notions of impurity (Arp 2000). While *kalapani* has not come to be universally used, historians have noted that the term 'Indian Ocean'—like 'Arabian Sea'—seems to privilege unduly certain peoples and sites in the oceanic setting (India, Arabia). Broeze (1989: 3) suggested using the term "the Asian Seas" to refer to "a string of closely related regional systems stretching from east Asia around the continent and across the Indian Ocean to East Africa". Since the designation still excludes East Africa, Pearson suggests "Afrasian Sea" as a more appropriate term (2003: 14). In spite of the problems of mapping and naming, however, no other term has so far achieved acceptance as a suitable substitute for 'Indian Ocean'. In a general sense, this term refers to the peoples living on its littorals as well as to those who use it as a maritime highway and have travelled over the ocean at different times in its history.

The study of the Indian Ocean has very much been a field for historians, one which anthropologists have entered only recently.[4] With regard to India's maritime history, three interrelated areas of research are discernible: (1) merchants and trade, (2) ports and (3) the effects of overseas trade upon economic and political relations in the hinterland (Pearson 1976; Das

[4] Interdisciplinary interactions in regard to the study of the Indian Ocean have been greatly advanced by the conference organised by Edward Alpers and Allen Roberts on Cultural Exchange and Transformation in the Indian Ocean World, University of California, Los Angeles, 5–6 April 2002.

Gupta 1967, 1994a, 1994b; Chaudhuri 1985; Das Gupta and Pearson 1987; Mukherjee and Subramanian 1998; Markovits 2000). Recently, Indian Ocean historians have begun to move beyond an analytical perspective that, while concerned with maritime activities, is still primarily land oriented (McPherson 1993; Pearson 2003). Instead, the ocean itself should become the focus as an arena of economic and political interactions. Thus, present historical research is often guided by one or several of the following analytical propositions:

1) A critique is presented of writing histories that take a land-based view by looking at the sea from the land, instead of focusing upon the ocean itself as a meaningful space of interaction (Pearson 2003: 5).

2) The Indian Ocean is no longer merely perceived as masses of water dividing continents but as the centre of a unified maritime world. This unity has been variously sought and defined in terms of a world economic system (Chaudhuri 1985; Reid 1993; Barendse 1999; 2002), of Islam expanding across a range of diverse economic and socio-cultural regional systems (McPherson 1993; Risso 1995).

3) Trans-oceanic migrations of people and their historic settlement in regions other than their original 'homelands' (e.g. Hadhramis or Baluchis in Zanzibar) are conceptualised in spatial metaphors such as 'space on the move' (e.g. Deutsch and Reinwald 2002; Hartwig 2002).

4) Recent historical studies of the East African slave trade have led to the discovery of an 'African diaspora' dispersed over the islands and littorals of the 'Afrasian Sea' (Alpers 1997, 2003).

The analytical perspectives proposed by historians of the Indian Ocean seem to lend support to anthropologists who are critical of separating and identifying areas in accordance with preconceived notions of bounded cultures. On the other hand, anthropologists face a twofold dilemma: a) in coming to terms with and reconfiguring analytic perspectives developed by historians; b) in terms of methodology: while historians work with archival sources, anthropologists seek their findings through ethnographic fieldwork. Moreover, the proposition of Indian Ocean unity leads to the construction of a new region: the maritime Indian Ocean world. Thus, in order to overcome disciplinary divisions between anthropologists and historians and to avoid the pitfalls of new and artificially constructed regional boundaries, the concept of "process geographies", coined by Appadurai, may serve as a useful point of reference. According to this view, regions become

> significant areas of human organisation as precipitates of various kinds of actions, interaction, and motion–trade, travel, pilgrimage, warfare, proselytisation, colonisation, exile. . . .Regions are best viewed as initial contexts for themes that generate variable geographies, rather than as fixed geographies marked by pre-given themes. (Appadurai 2000b: 7–8)

A thematic understanding of the oceanic region helps to avoid the conceptual closure hovering over the idea of the 'unity' of the Indian Ocean world. Instead, it directs us to the question of the quality of trans-oceanic connectedness, with Pearson asking "whether one finds enough strands to depict a rope which binds together the ocean" (2003: 7). To remain with this metaphor, the historians and anthropologists who have been brought together in this volume are focusing on ends of the rope running through the Afrasian Sea that have become loose and that stick out in South Asia as present signs of past trans-oceanic connections and their historical transformations in specific local contexts. It is on this level that anthropological concerns such as the study of cultural values, hierarchies, symbolic systems and practices can benefit from the global designs of historians and, conversely, ground the latter in the lived realities of people connected to the past and present Indian Ocean world.

Considering the significance accorded to the subcontinent reflected in mappings of the ocean, relatively little is known about the ways in which this maritime world has shaped and is manifested in social settings in South Asian regions that were part of it. On the Swahili coast, for example, the impact exercised by people journeying from Arabia upon the emergence of a blend of African and Arab cultural manifestations is well understood (cf. Middleton 1992; Horton and Middleton 2000). By contrast, not much attention has been paid to the effects of similar impacts on South Asian littoral social settings. How have these been influenced by Indian Ocean histories? And how is the Indian Ocean past encountered in the present? In order to answer these questions, a shift of perspective is called for. Thus, instead of looking at the sea from the land, most of the contributors to this volume focus upon the land as seen from the sea. This necessitates rethinking the construction of boundaries on different levels. While the articles brought together here reflect the diverse analytical perspectives and concerns of their authors, they nevertheless reveal, implicitly or explicitly, an engagement with boundaries, that is, with crossings of empirical, methodological or conceptual boundaries and/or with the reconfiguring of new boundaries.

In this way, an amalgamation of Indian Ocean and South Asian themes comes to the fore. These may be further distinguished, for analytical purposes, into those that constitute a conceptual level, referring to scholarly debates, and those that pertain to a practical level based on empirical observation. Themes that constitute landmarks in the scholarly field of the Indian Ocean world form the broad outlines of the three sections of the book: 1) cosmopolitanism versus parochialism; 2) the social and symbolic effects of the ocean in the formation of regional realities; and 3) the historical dispersal of Africans through the slave trade and/or maritime labour and their settlement in today's India and Pakistan.

One problem that has preoccupied historians for a long time has been the 'unity' of this world in the face of great regional and cultural variations. Searching for what makes the ocean into a 'world', historians have variously emphasised ecological structures, economics (networks of trade), harbours, maritime movements and religion (Islam) (e.g. Chaudhuri 1985; Barendse 1999; Risso 1995). This search for unity, however, carries the danger of creating monolithic constructions that are thoroughly unsuited to dealing with diversity, cross-cultural interactions and cultural transformations through movements that are so characteristic of Indian Ocean settings (cf. Pearson 2003: 7). Reflecting the influence of current debates on globalisation, the search for unity has given way to stressing cosmopolitanism as the most distinctive mark of Indian Ocean sites. For McPherson, a leading proponent of the thesis of cosmopolitanism, the term refers to mutual adaptations of cultural forms and may be usefully employed when denoting "the presence of a variety of confessional, cultural, and racial groups within a single urban setting" (2002: 83). But he also cautions his readers that "in the port cities of the Indian Ocean, cosmopolitanism affected only certain sectors of society in a limited number of ways" (ibid.).

In the present volume, it is in regard to the thesis of cosmopolitanism that different approaches shaping interdisciplinary debates between historians and anthropologists are most strongly expressed. Anthropologists are often critical of sweeping concepts such as unity or cosmopolitanism and tend to emphasise instead the necessity of grounding of such concepts in practices and values. A significant example of such an approach is *Islamic Prayer across the Indian Ocean,* edited by David Parkin and Stephen Headley (2000). Here, the claim made by historians that Islam unified the Indian Ocean world is reconsidered in terms of Islamic practices. Regional Islamic consciousness is shown to have arisen from multiple sources. Islamic influences from beyond the Indian Ocean world are found to be as important as the historical maritime movements of peoples from countries bordering the Indian Ocean rim (Parkin 2000: 2). Local variations in Islamic knowledge and practice extend, for example, from South Asia to Mayotte or from Indonesia to Zanzibar (Lambek 2000; Purpura 2000). Instead of concluding that de-territorialised processes of Islamisation across the Indian Ocean have created cosmopolitan enclaves, the intersections of global processes and local encounters are attended to by analysing the intermingling of Islamic traits with non-Islamic local faiths (Parkin 2000: 3).

The second section of the book deals with local settings along the western coast of India that are shaped by or reflect past and present connectedness with the Indian Ocean. Seafaring, trade and travel were the means by which people and value systems originating in diverse cultural settings came into contact and thus formed a 'seascape' marked by heterogeneity, cultural mixing and trans-local relationships and imaginations. This section demonstrates how empirical Indian Ocean themes such as trading, the spreading of Islam by Sufis, and past and present migration processes became entangled in South Asia with themes of hierarchy, status concerns and indigenous imaginations of the sea and of foreigners.

Embodying an important 'loose end of the rope' that runs through the Indian Ocean world, the third section of the book deals with the descendants of Africans in India and Pakistan, former slaves, soldiers and seamen, who constituted a prominent group of Indian Ocean travellers in the past. In the history of the subcontinent they were known by the names 'Habshi' (from Arabic 'Abyssinia') and 'Sidi'.[5] In the medieval history of India, as in the context of Muslim sovereignty, the term 'Habshi' came to be used as an ethnic label for military slaves from all over East Africa, whereas 'Sidi' was used more often as a title for aristocratic Habshi.[6] 'Sidi', moreover, contains several strands of reference: it was the name of a population of southern Ethiopia (Beachey 1976);[7] in north Africa 'Sidi' is a title given to Sufi saints; in the Indian Ocean maritime context, 'Sidi' (or 'Seedi') referred, at least from the eighteenth century, to black slaves, sailors and dockers (Ewald

[5] The latter designation has been subjected to a wide range of spellings, probably corresponding to local pronunciations, such as Siddhi, Sheedi or Sidi.

[6] In Islamic systems of military slavery, the status of slave did not prevent soldiers from obtaining power, wealth or influential positions at the court (cf. Pipes 1981). Indian medieval history abounds with instances of Habshi obtaining power in Bengal, the Deccan and Gujarat. For a more detailed discussion of African military slaves and aristocratic Habshi in India, see Harris (1971); Pankhurst (2003); and Basu (2001).

[7] In writing of Ethiopian slaves in the thirteenth and fourteenth centuries, Beachey mentions "the Shankalla or Sidi, from the Nilotic group occupying the Blue Nile and Sudan frontier, on Ethiopia's western side" (1976: 148).

2000). Today, people of African origin identify themselves as Sidi in parts of Pakistan (Karachi, Makran coast) and India (Gujarat, Karnataka), whereas in Hyderabad (Andhra Pradesh, India) and other parts of Sindh (Pakistan) they prefer the name 'Habshi'.[8] The presence of Sidis in India has been conceptualised in terms of minority studies (also identified sometimes as 'tribal studies') (Anirudh Gupta 1991; Patel 1991) or, more recently, as 'African diasporas' (Alpers 1997; Jayasuriya and Pankhurst 2003; Catlin-Jairazbhoy and Alpers 2004). In this volume, the focus is shifted to Sidi and Habshi practices and constructions of identity in terms of Indian Ocean themes. In this way, social frames of reference applied by Sidis and Habshis come into view that privilege relationships with other Muslim categories—such as 'Sayyid' or 'Arab'—whose origins lie, like the Sidis' and Habshis', in regions across the ocean, in this case in Arabia.[9] What is so revealed is the close interdependence or fusion between 'Africanness' and 'Arabness', one that also underlies notions of 'Swahili' on the east African coast. In South Asian contexts, traces of 'Swahili' cultures appear to have been refigured in terms of hierarchical values of interdependence.

The range of topics addressed in this volume represents a kaleidoscopic view of Indian Ocean themes in relation to South Asian realities studied by anthropologists who take history into account, and by historians applying anthropological

[8] When I carried out fieldwork in the late 1980s in Gujarat, I found that the Sidi in Gujarat resented being called 'Habshi' because they felt that the term had connotations of slavery. A few years later I met people referred to as Sidi in Pakistan among whom a debate was going on aiming at changing their name to 'Habshi' because 'Sidi' was felt to have pejorative connotations. Similarly, in Hyderabad those referred to as 'Sidi' by outsiders call themselves 'Habshi' because the former term is associated with slavery.

[9] It has sometimes been suggested that the name 'Sidi' is derived from 'Sayyid'. The latter are recognized as descendants of the family of the Prophet and thus command great respect in the Muslim social world. In Gujarat and Sindh, Sidis remember and practise relationships of allegiance to Sayyid Sufi (Pirs) which are of great importance in delineating Sidi selfhood. It therefore seems likely that speculations like those mentioned above are based on a confusion of different levels of identification and overlook the fact that social identities in India are often constructed in relation to significant others.

methods. The first section of the book is concerned with journeys across the Indian Ocean. Acknowledging the importance of movement and travel in the formation of the Indian Ocean region gives rise to a methodological challenge: how do we study these phenomena? This challenge is taken up in the first paper by Ned Bertz, a historian among anthropologists, whose findings on twentieth-century Indian Ocean travellers are based on multi-sited fieldwork and archival research in Tanzania and India. Arguing for an Indian Ocean world constructed from the perspective of travelling individuals and in terms of cosmopolitan encounters, Bertz recognises structures of the *longue durée*.[10] For example, while formerly, the monsoon winds imposed on a sailor a prolonged stay in a distant harbour, today an expired contract may force him to stay on until he finds a new job on a ship. By focusing not only on seamen but on different categories of people journeying to and from India and Africa—such as dancing girls from India in Dar-es-Salaam, students from Tanzania in India, Indian populations in East Africa and finally politicians—Bertz draws attention to modern constructions of boundaries that are continually being eroded by long-established practices of crossing borders. The fact that today's travellers over the Indian Ocean are mostly people who are considered marginal by the standards of the places they come from and go to might itself be taken as symptomatic of the permutations that have turned the Indian Ocean into one of the backwaters of globalisation (cf. Pearson 2003: 249ff.).

Abdul Sheriff places the Arab sailing ship, the *dhow*, at the centre of the historical production of Indian Ocean maritime cultures. Directing the focus to Zanzibar, which used to be an important nodal point of maritime networks, Sheriff explores relationships of a *longue durée* constituted by maritime

[10] Historians have consulted the concept of *longue durée*, originally introduced by Ferdinand Braudel in his study of the Mediterranean, with regard to ecological features of the ocean that framed human activities of seafaring in terms of space and time (cf. Chaudhuri 2003: 21). In this context, the *longue durée* refers to stable, unchanging and stationary components of nature and time, as contrasted with chronological change, random events and changing human actions.

movements between the East African coast, Zanzibar and the Hadhramaut coast in southern Arabia (Oman). The abolition of the slave trade at the end of the nineteenth century intensified rather than lessened ethnic intermingling in these locations. By analysing the journey of a dhow in the early twentieth century in terms of the interactions between captains and passengers, Sheriff highlights the important role the dhow played in bringing about mixed social and cultural forms. Sheriff therefore argues that cosmopolitan littoral cultures were formed in this part of the Indian Ocean on and through the dhow.

That travel and migration can have divisive effects locally just as much as providing trans-local connecting links is shown in the chapter by Edward Simpson. Through an ethnographic study of caste loyalties that extend to sites of migration, Simpson challenges cosmopolitan interpretations made by historians. Simpson is concerned with a caste of sailors in Kachchh called Kharvas, who are divided into Muslim and Hindu sections. The latter are tied in patron-client relationships to the Bhatiyas, a Hindu merchant caste from Kachchh extending to Oman. The Kharvas no longer sail, but they still cross the ocean to Oman as migrant labourers. Contemporary patterns of migration are embedded, Simpson argues, in locally rooted patron-client relationships that provide a powerful incentive for continued identifications with local society in Kachchh. Moreover, the Kharva's historical seafaring role is associated with considerations of status in relation to Kachchi merchant castes such as the Bhatiya. Myths and images of the sea that figure importantly in contemporary ritual constructions of Kharva caste identity are, Simpson shows, effectively merged with Hindu symbols derived from the mythology of Vishnu and the epic of the Ramayana. In this way, an opposition to Muslims who are still actively engaged in crossing the sea is constructed by those (Hindu) Kharvas who no longer sail, thus echoing contemporary political trends in religious exclusivity.

The chapters in the second part of the book look at the presence of the ocean in various locations on the western coastline of the subcontinent and in Sri Lanka. Historians have singled out both trade and Islam as the main agents propelling the integration of the Indian Ocean world. Trade, however, was not confined to Muslims alone. Even today, Gujarati merchants are known as 'Banias' all over the Indian Ocean world (e.g. Gregory 1971). Outside India, this term is applied indiscriminately to a range of Hindu, Jain and sometimes even Muslim communities (e.g. Daudi Bohras in East Africa). Within Gujarat, the term Bania is reserved for Jain merchant castes. Harald Tambs-Lyche, in his study of the regional merchant networks that arose from 1500 to 1800 along the western coast from Gujarat to Malabar, stresses the central position of Banias as bankers and financiers of overseas trade. The period from 1500 to 1800 is considered crucial in both sea- and land-oriented histories of India's relationship with the Indian Ocean world (Das Gupta and Pearson 1987; McPherson 1993). During this period, the Portuguese, followed by the trading companies of other European nations, entered the scene and fought to establish control over the Indian Ocean trading system. For the Portuguese, as later for the British, India proved to be of prime importance in building a colonial empire across the Indian Ocean world. A significant effect of overseas trade, then, was the formation of distinct multi-caste merchant communities corresponding to the emergence of regional divisions of labour in commerce. Thus the Banias cooperated with the Portuguese as they had done before with Arabs and other Indian Ocean traders. Opposition to Portuguese claims to dominance, by contrast, strengthened merchant communities in peripheral regions. Some, like the Bhatiyas in Saurashtra and Kachchh, allied themselves with the European enemies of the Portuguese and subsequently acquired influential economic positions under British colonial rule.

In Sri Lanka, we meet with memories of travelling as the foundation of contemporary social constructions of difference between religious traditions. As Llyn Smith shows in her chapter, in Sri Lankan Muslim discourse, notions of purity of Arab descent are merged with ideas of Islamic orthodoxy exemplified by the foreign traveller, the Sufi and bringer of Islam. A myth telling of the miraculous journey of a founding saint who crossed the ocean in a stone coffin reveals the conceptual strategies applied by Muslims in Sri Lanka. Islam is localised by symbolically merging death with travel, the burial of saints in the earth of Sri Lanka with conversion, and the local rooting of Islam. While the network of Sufi saints described by Smith reflects past Arab-Muslim trading patterns, today it connects Sri Lankan Muslims, on the one hand, with those across the ocean, in South India and the Lakshadweep islands, and on the other hand, with the Islamic heartland in Arabia. Smith bases her analysis upon the tension experienced by Muslims who needed to assert the Islamic religion in the face of Hindu and Buddhist traditions, a tension which has led to the somewhat unusual constellation of local Sufi saints embodying Islamic orthodoxy.

The sea has not only shaped the imagination of those who at some point in history have been travellers or have otherwise come in direct contact with it, but also of people who were socially and spatially removed from the Indian Ocean world. Marine Carrin looks at symbolic representations of the relationship between land and sea in Karnataka. The Tulu are an indigenous people living in the forests of coastal Karnataka. Oppositions between agriculture and trade, forest and coast, people of the land and the sea (foreigners), are mediated through the idiom of sacred spirits, who are divided into spirits of the forest and spirits of the sea. The latter include the foreign spirits of Muslim and Chinese merchants, as well as 'sons of the forest' who had become seafarers. In this way, the ocean has come to stand for outside influences upon Tulu society (overseas trade) that are symbolically worked into an integrated whole of the regional social order represented by the spirit world.

Several papers note that seafaring as a way of deriving a livelihood from the ocean has been replaced in post-colonial times by labour migration to the Gulf. The last chapter of this section explores the effects of these transformations on trans-oceanic connections in Kerala. Since the second half of the twentieth century, oil production in the Gulf has become a primary incentive for labour migration from South Asia across the ocean (cf. Leonard 2002). In Kerala, a region as important as Gujarat and with equally old relationships with the Indian Ocean world, post-colonial labour migration to the oil states in the Middle East has resulted in an intensification of tensions between high and low castes, as well as competition for migration between Hindus and Muslims. Elizabeth Chettur analyses the processes whereby the new wealth and consumerism of migrant labourers belonging to the lower castes or Muslim communities are converted into traditional symbols of high status and prestige. The investments in symbols of status by people who were formerly excluded from their acquisition both challenges and reinforces hierarchical notions of caste. Here, the ocean has lost its meaning of bringing about cultural exchange and mutual cultural adaptations, though this is also a significant, if paradoxical, fact for understanding post-colonial Indian Ocean realities in South Asia.

The chapters in the final section of the book explore African and Arab ritual and musical contributions in different regional settings. Helene Basu draws attention to the absence of women and questions of gender in studies of the Indian Ocean world. Although women have been enslaved throughout history in large numbers, the majority of studies dealing with the enslavement of Africans pay little attention to their experiences. Thus, in Gujarat a female African saint epitomises the journey of African women to India. In many parts of East and North Africa which overlap with former slave-providing regions, relationships between Sufi Islam and African religions of spirit possession have been described as corresponding to a division between male and female ritual actions (Islam/possession). By focusing on ritual practices surrounding the female Sidi saint Mai Mishra in Gujarat, Basu analyses the gendered relationship between Sufi Islam and African religions of possession, of which traces are manifested in modified ways in contemporary Sidi women's ritual agencies. The specific and unique character of Sidi ritual practices connected to an assembly of African Sufi saints empitomised by Bava Gor seems to have been shaped in no small measure by the active involvement of African women.

Significantly, the journey of African-derived cultural practices did not remain confined to the arena of the Sidi, as the chapter by Beheroze Shroff demonstrates. Mai Mishra and Bava Gor have become the foci of ritual practices not only of other Muslim fakirs but also of members of the Parsi community. Shroff carefully delineates the social interactions between a Muslim holy man, follower of the Sidi saint Bava Gor, and members of the Parsi community in Bombay, which resulted in Parsi ritual practices directed at Sidi saints. In this context, Parsi ritual specialists embody Sidi saints in trance and thus mediate between the realms of the divine and the human. Referring to the political and economic changes that affected the Parsis' position after independence, Shroff explores the ways in which the veneration of Sidi saints has become a meaningful way for some Parsi families, at least, to come to terms with individually experienced adversities.

The chapter by Sabir Badalkhan brings us to the coast of Makran and Baluchistan in today's Pakistan. Here, a much larger number of Africans has been absorbed by the regional social system than in Gujarat. Activities of singing, drumming and dancing were closely connected with fishing and sailing, professions that in Baluchistan were often practised by people of African origin. As Badalkhan shows, music formed an important mode of communication in the Indian Ocean world, where people often did not know each others' languages. Thus, when ships from Makran arrived in an east African or Hadhramaut port, the sailors were greeted by people singing and dancing, as was also the case for ships coming to the Makran ports. By focusing upon the embeddedness of African musical practices in maritime activities, Badalkhan's contribution demonstrates that sailors played an important role in maintaining contacts between western India and East Africa until the very recent past. As ships from Makran also sailed to

Gujarat, this may explain the vitality of African-derived musical forms not only in Baluchistan but also in neighbouring Gujarat.

The final chapter, written jointly by Helene Basu, Kerrin von Schwerin and Ababu Minda, shows that the influence of the Indian Ocean world extended far inland into the subcontinent (cf. also G. Campbell 2004). In Hyderabad (Andhra Pradesh), the Chaush, a community of Yemeni and Habshi allies, bear witness to this fact. Referring to a common history in the military at the court of the Nawab of Hyderabad in the nineteenth century, on one level, the Chaush tend to distance themselves from an African past. On another level, however, Habshis do recognise their African ancestry as epitomised by Hazrat Bilal, the blind Abyssinian companion of the Prophet and original caller of *ajhan* (morning prayer) in Mecca, just like Sidis in Gujarat and Sindh (Pakistan). Again, it is music which plays an important, though contested, role in articulating Chaush identity in the context of Muslim social settings in Hyderabad. In relation to the multiple sources of identifications stressed by Chaush, the authors explore the corresponding multiple strands of musical styles that together constitute *daff* music. In Hyderabad, the daff is a circular drum held in the left hand and beaten with a stick in the right. Ironically, while according to Chaush notions they are performing 'Arabness' when playing daff music, in commercial contexts the same music is labelled 'African', in order to appeal to a growing market of consumers of exotic music.

Taken together, the chapters in this volume demonstrate that Indian Ocean themes in South Asia manifest themselves in ways that are as varied and multifaceted as oceanic history itself. Cosmopolitan encounters in one context are not rendered impossible by simultaneous trends of parochialism in another. Sea traffic has contributed greatly to the emergence of socially heterogeneous regional social settings shaped by mutual adaptations. And yet, compared to Zanzibar and the Swahili coast, Indian Ocean settings in South Asia remain scattered enclaves engulfed and always to some extent shaped by values of hierarchical difference.

PART ONE

Cosmopolitanism *versus* Parochialism

Map including the Indian subcontinent's western cc

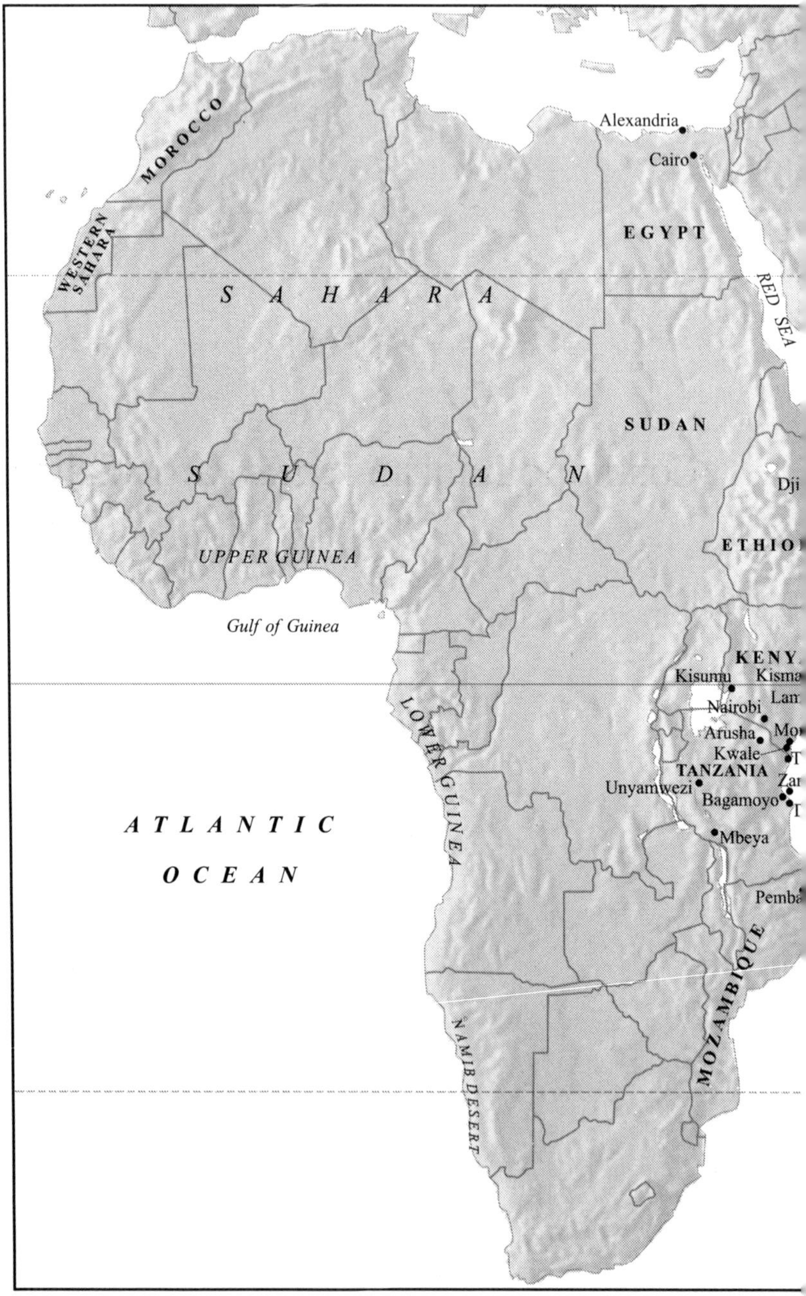

M

Arabian peninsula and the East Coast of Africa

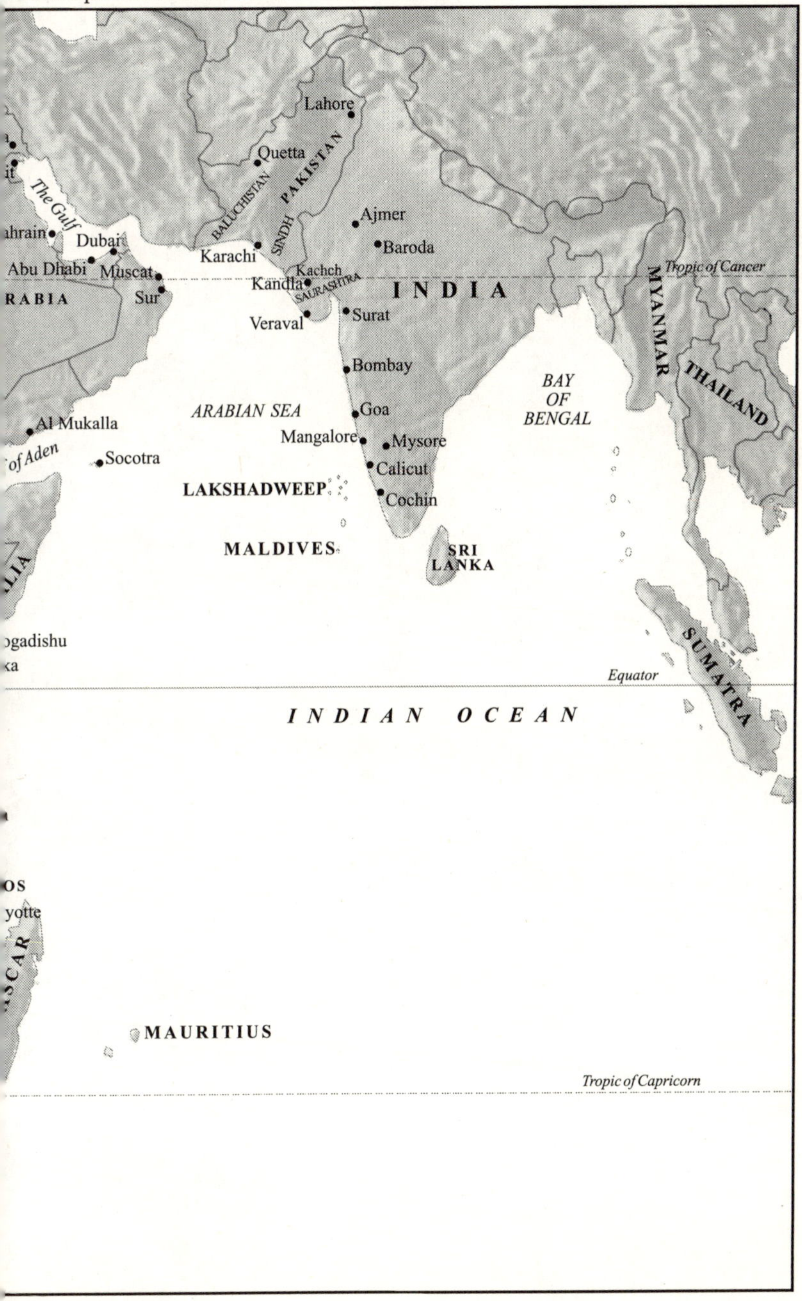

1

*Indian Ocean World Travellers: Moving Models in Multi-Sited Research**

Ned Bertz

Introduction

Showing a nose for frankincense and a penchant for waxing poetic about flying fish skimming the expanse of the great blue yonder, Alan Villiers, a sailor-scholar, published his classic study *The Indian Ocean* in 1952. In it, he somewhat sadly laments the passing of the romantic age of big sailing ships:

> Now no ship sails, upright and graceful, westwards upon the breath of the Indian Ocean trades. No ship storms eastwards before the wild west winds, under close-reefed sails. The monsoon-using dhows survive, from India and Arabia and—to a much less degree—from Persia, and canoes move under sail among the tropic islands.... Such ships still understand the way of the Indian Ocean and its winds and weather; but for some years now all European vessels, which carry the bulk of the vast commerce there, have been driven by power (Villiers 1952: 13).

Whether he meant it or not, Villiers put his salty finger on an issue—power—which would vex the field that he helped initiate, that of Indian Ocean studies. In recent years, this field

* Much material cited here comes from dissertation fieldwork supported by Fulbright-IIE, the American Institute for Indian Studies, the Council of American Overseas Research Centers, and the Graduate College and Department of History at the University of Iowa. This essay will form part of a chapter in my ongoing dissertation project, titled "Race, Nationalism, and the Indian Diaspora of Tanzania in the Twentieth-Century History of the Indian Ocean World". In writing this paper, I acknowledge the intellectual contributions of Jim Giblin, Paul Greenough, Al Roberts, Edward Alpers and Helene Basu, among many others.

has swelled once again, and become a site of academic cross-currents of history, theory and methodology. This paper seeks to navigate within the choppy seas of Indian Ocean World studies, and does so in two discrete parts. First will come a short discussion of the historiographical issues involved in constructing an Indian Ocean World, invoking such questions as boundaries, unity, biases, theory and power. Following, new field research will be brought to bear on the methodology of this academic project. At each stage, the argument laid out here will locate the construction of individual meaning at the level of everyday experience, including both real and imagined encounters.

Indian Ocean World Travellers: Moving Models in Multi-Sited Historiography

The first systematic attempt at a regional history of the Indian Ocean World was published in the early 1960s by the Mauritian historian Auguste Toussaint. He writes about the scholar's problem of perspective: "By what gateway shall we enter the Indian Ocean? What is the most favourable approach for considering it as a whole? [Where are] the best places from which to discover the ocean and, as it were, feel its heartbeat?" (Toussaint 1966: 3) Toussaint, nationalistically and not without some merit, selected his homeland as representative of islands where "we must come to be initiated into the life of the Indian Ocean" (Toussaint 1966: 4). Writing many years later, the theorist Janet Abu-Lughod called the Indian subcontinent, in "medieval times",[1] "on the way to everywhere". She writes that India, in particular the southern stretch, was "both a natural link and a divider in the great sea route," and a "hinge" between separate areas of the Indian Ocean, "that great 'highway' for the migrations of peoples, for cultural dif-

[1] I employ quotation marks around disputed terms of chronology. In particular, I am concerned with the adoption of European divisions of history for the Indian Ocean World. I will use these terms here as reference only, and the assumption is that they say more about European history than that of East Africa or South Asia, for example.

fusion, and for economic exchange" (Abu-Lughod 1989: 261). Writing most recently, Kenneth McPherson argues that "[t]he boundaries of this Indian Ocean World were rarely constant. There was of course a fixed geographic boundary determined by the limits of the Ocean, but in human and economic terms this was a porous frontier. The human and economic limits of the Indian Ocean World constantly fluctuated in response to changing patterns of human activity on land and sea" (McPherson 1993: 5). This paper supports McPherson's analysis, where individual perspective determines the meaning and extent of one's own world, mediated through shifting connections with others in the larger geographic setting heuristically known as the Indian Ocean World. As there is no "heartbeat", no best place from which to view the Indian Ocean, we must strive to see the world through the eyes of its indigenous residents, in all their movement and interregional contact.

This argument does not dilute the importance of world systems theorists like Abu-Lughod for understanding the region under consideration. The name most often invoked for inspiration in this body of literature is Fernand Braudel (Braudel 1972). Subsequent derivations from his Mediterranean model in the Indian Ocean usefully create a "unified" regional history not dominated by the compartmentalisation of national histories, a topic to be discussed later. Toussaint certainly attributes his debt to the French legend in his deployment of the term "geohistory", which he defines as "true retrospective human geography" (Toussaint 1966: 1). Similarly, the geographers Martin Lewis and Karen Wigan rebuke the area studies model of academic institutions (also to be addressed below) as complicit in a harmful historical determinism that is continentally based (Lewis and Wigan 1997). These scholars share Marshall Hodgson's interest in theorising Islam in world history, and his methodological call for "interregional studies" in all their complexity[2] (Hodgson 1993). This essay takes as a point of departure the assumption that people in East Africa and west-

[2] See in particular pp. 288–300 on interregional perspectives. Hodgson makes an important plea for cooperation between scholars in various areas and disciplines, something that I also argue for later in the chapter.

ern India, for example, have a long and varied history of contact of many dimensions—economic as well as cultural—which takes place within a shifting Indian Ocean World constructed by those who live there, and occasionally impinged upon by outside forces from other regions. Thus, to analyse multiple but specific locations and peoples' contact between them over time, rather than viewing the Indian Ocean from one place, and to view these relations within the greater world of the Indian Ocean—this will be the model on which this paper is built.

This brings us to the question of what sort of unity holds the Indian Ocean World together, and how it changes over time. The eminent historian Michael M. Pearson, in his masterfully wideranging but uneven attempt to write the signal book on Indian Ocean studies, dances around the issue of unity (Pearson 2003). He argues that there is a clear distinction to be made between unity and mere connections across the sea, but suggests that at times and in certain wider senses (e.g., through Islam) such a unity might have been possible. Overall, he urges caution, and settles upon the notion of "history *in* the sea" as opposed to writing a "history *of* the sea" (Pearson 2003: 6–9, 249–88). James de Vere Allen more than two decades ago proposed a more specific notion of layers of unity:

> First, there is racial unity of a sort provided by Malay and other migrations; secondly, cultural unity radiating out from the Indian subcontinent; and thirdly, the religious unity provided by Islam, which of all religions has probably been the most successful in subduing, though not necessarily eliminating, political, racial and cultural differences among its adherents. These three layers, as I have called them, were regularly refreshed and reinforced, at least until very recently, by a constant intercourse between most of the lands concerned (Allen 1980: 140).

While I would disagree most strongly with any notions of racial unity, and would not dare to argue that any sort of cultural unity radiates from a specific point, I find Allen's notion of layers of unity useful, and he might be quite accurate in selecting Islam as one of them. It could help ameliorate Pearson's resignation over how to assign meaning to connections when he writes, "Connections go two ways. A Chinese pot will be used in different ways in different places, and may be copied or modified. A Hadhrami preaching Islam will find a different response in Kilwa than in Aceh or Hyderabad, and his words will have different meanings in these two places" (2003: 6). The notions of layers of unity—perhaps better described as (cosmopolitan) layers of connections, to avoid the baggage of "unity"—would also help us get at the regional variation in commerce and culture in the Indian Ocean World, for example amongst the Swahili. Mark Horton and John Middleton argue in their excellent but limited work:

> From the eleventh century onwards maritime trade patterns within the western Indian Ocean become confused.... This confusing picture was exploited in East Africa by the Swahili. Their entrepots might expect a range of visitors arriving on the monsoon from many different places, and they were in a position to play one group off against another. The archaeological evidence suggests variation between towns, as can be gauged from the imported ceramics, with particular ports favouring Gulf, Indian or southern Arabian merchants (Horton and Middleton 2000: 80–1).

In other words, individuals and groups in a multiplicity of encounters with others determined their own practices of cosmopolitan connections, which varied in theme, substance and duration over time. This essay argues the same, likely best represented once again by McPherson:

> To understand the nature of the interlocked world of the Indian Ocean, we need to understand the people who bound it together. The workers of the sea and littoral societies gave the Ocean its human face, and were the agent for the dissemination of cultures and technologies across the Ocean.... People working the Indian Ocean before the coming of Europeans also defined different boundaries for the Indian Ocean world. They perceived different combinations of markets and cultures as part of their particular worldview. Merchants, seamen, fishermen and pilgrims operated within various, and often different, information and cultural networks which set the horizons of their worlds. This world of merchants was defined by various economic, informational and cultural boundaries; for seamen and fishermen by tangible geographic constraints, and for pilgrims by religious boundaries. But for all of

them it was a world dominated by the rhythms of the monsoons (McPherson 1993: 121–2).

For McPherson, the evocative phrase "the rhythms of the monsoons" simply means that the Indian Ocean itself acts as a geographic "highway", as Abu-Lughod asserted, but the question remains in the historiography over how to date its construction and, arguably, dismantling. For this paper, it is sufficient to delve but very briefly into the pre-1800 material. First of all, it must be noted that in the growing field of Indian Ocean studies there is an outstanding bias for the pre-colonial period. This literature has brilliantly shown how long-distance trade began tens of centuries B.C.E., and rose and fell over time based on the variables of technology, trade and inspiration, among many others. Factors such as the spread of Islam and European explorations also affected the development and integration of various parts of the Indian Ocean World, which, according to the literature (ably defined by Chaudhuri, Das Gupta, and Pearson), peaked in the period 1500–1800. Amitav Ghosh, in his magical *In An Antique Land*, which weaves the story of a twelfth-century Jewish merchant of the Indian Ocean World with that of the Indian author's anthropological fieldwork in modern Egypt, captures the earthiness of some of the vast and seemingly unlikely connections forged in this putatively "pre-globalised" world:

> In matters of business, Ben Yiju's networks appear to have been wholly indifferent to many of those boundaries that are today thought to mark social, religious and geographical divisions. Madmun, for instance, is known once to have proposed a joint venture between himself and three traders in Mangalore, each of different social or geographical origins—one a Muslim, one a Gujarati Vania, and the third a member of a landowning caste of Tulunad. Equally, the ships that Ben Yiju and his friends used for transporting their goods were owned by a wide variety of people. . . . The ties forged by trade were so close that Madmun's kinsmen, the nakhuda Mahruz (in a letter written for him by Ben Yiju), once remarked of a ship-owner called "Tinbu," probably of Tamil extraction, that, "between him and me there are bonds of inseparable friendship and brotherhood" (1992: 278–9).

Where the literature starts to concern this essay more seriously is in the handling of the coming of the Europeans. Pearson magnificently argues for a minimal impact in the "early modern period," writing that the effect of the European presence at that time was overall limited in that the newcomers had to accommodate the continuing structures of the Indian Ocean World of which they had a very shallow understanding. However, when the overwhelming political and physical power of colonial rule was introduced, especially by the British, most authors tell the story of the disintegration of the Indian Ocean World as a highway of regional connection. McPherson is not atypical in this regard, although he is likely the most forceful in arguing (along with world systems theorists) for the subordination of the Indian Ocean region to a European-dominated global economy:

> Age-old patterns of communication and interaction across the Indian Ocean were disrupted and destroyed.... In addition to dominating and reshaping indigenous economic activity, Europeans usurped indigenous political authority in much of the Indian Ocean region, and they imposed their own civilisation as the model for behaviour and progress, destroying ancient processes of cultural interaction (McPherson 1993: 199).

This chapter contends that this idea significantly misunderstands the application, resistance, and accommodation of power in the region. First of all, this argument is premised upon the assumption that colonial power sundered the pre-existing unity in the Indian Ocean World, a unity which this paper has already argued is flawed in conception.[3] Second, this argument sees power as only emanating from above, and not from individual everyday experience, and the negative result of its application is the loss from sight of the residents of the Indian Ocean World under the onslaught of colonial and, later, national power. Lastly, this contention entrenches the false dichotomy of the West versus the East, and the triumph of the

[3] One scholar who has briefly agreed with this in print is Sugata Bose (2002: 376).

former in the 'modern' shaping of the latter.[4] As will be shown in the second half of this paper, instead of being 'destroyed' by colonial power, indigenous residents of the Indian Ocean adapted to the new political structures and continued to travel, trade and interact across the sea in altered relationships mediated, but not dominated, by Europeans. Even more resistant to colonial power was the continuation of a certain consciousness of long-standing historical connections. In this, McPherson and other scholars seem to have forgotten their reliance on Braudel's *longue durée* a bit too soon. At the same time, this paper acknowledges the ability of state power—colonial and national—to freeze certain categories of identification, leading to more rigid ways of interacting with others, especially as individuals often had to seek out their way in the Indian Ocean World through prescribed places of entry.

Before moving on to the section on methodological challenges to the conception of an Indian Ocean World, it is useful to include a list of biases that afflict its historiography and theory. Villiers, evocatively as always, clues us into one as he paraphrases the Song of Solomon: "Who is it that cometh out of the wilderness like pillars of smoke, perfumed with myrrh and frankincense, with all the powders of the merchant?" (Villiers 1952: 61) Far and away the largest topic of discussion in Indian Ocean studies tends to be economic linkages, with the most attention given to their representative: the merchant. While undoubtedly important in travelling the Indian Ocean highway to carry goods and ideas from place to place, much gets lost when regional integration is studied purely as an economic function. This overemphasis leads many authors into overreading the collapse of the Indian Ocean World when the European colonial powers come. McPherson writes,

> During the nineteenth century fewer and fewer indigenous maritime merchants travelled the Indian Ocean. An increasing number

[4] Some of these ideas are crystallised in an important article by Dipesh Chakrabarty (1992).

> of them adopted European mercantile principles and organisation and remained landbound.... All of these changes undermined the vitality of ancient merchant communities around the Indian Ocean. While indigenous merchants, artisans and labourers may still have travelled the high seas, they now tended to travel as migrants, moving on a more permanent basis to foreign ports and settlements (McPherson 1993: 241).

However, what is less important about a migrant's connection to a foreign land than a merchant's? In many ways, it is more substantial. Further, were all merchants not at the same time throughout history also migrants in a different way, resting for months in a place to wait for the turning of the monsoon? Looking beyond the purely economic functions of the Indian Ocean travellers—perhaps by usefully invoking Allen's notion of layers—one not only can read a richer world in the past than has been previously described, but can also see its continuation into the present. Usefully, Pearson himself notes a similar historiographical lack in an all too brief look at Hindi films in the region: "So far we can write about the distribution of these movies, or for that matter of Islam or Christianity, but we know little about something even more important, that of their consumption. Certainly Hindi and other Indian movies mean different things to different audiences, in other words are consumed in different ways by different receptors, but this difficult matter has been little studied so far" (Pearson 2003: 281).

The commercial bias in the literature for the connections of merchants has other effects. First, it also leads to an overemphasis on maritime history, with its focus on matters of technology such as sailing, which too easily falls into the trap of tautologically assuming European ascension. Further, the destinations of merchants—the port cities of the Indian Ocean World—become privileged sites in the literature. While I absolutely agree on their crucial role as 'nodal points of change,' as McPherson has effectively shown, a port city cannot be severed from its hinterland (McPherson 2002). Pearson writes effectively of wider littoral societies that run beyond the coastline, but these connections need to be driven much further inland, something to be discussed further in the second section of this paper. For now, we will rely on Ghosh describing his village fieldsite in Egypt, pointing out the endurance of rural travellers in the western Indian Ocean World:

> To me there was something marvellous about the wonder that came into Zaghloul's voice when he talked of travel: for most of his neighbours travel held no surprises at all. The area around Nashawy had never been a rooted kind of place; at times it seemed to be possessed of all the busy restlessness of an airport's transit lounge. Indeed, a long history of travel was recorded in the very names of the area's 'families': they spoke of links with distant parts of the Arab world—cities in the Levant, the Sudan and the Maghreb. That legacy of transience had not ended with their ancestors either: in Zaghloul's own generation dozens of men had been 'outside,' working in the shaikdoms of the Gulf, or Libya, while many others had been to Saudi Arabia on the Hajj, or to the Yemen, as soldiers—some men had passports so thick they opened out like ink-blackened concertinas (Ghosh 1992: 173–4).

Ghosh, strangely unwitting here, points us to yet another problem in the historiographical reliance on merchants: the virtual absence of women. A gendered analysis of travel—something to be considered briefly below—as well as gendered notions of imagination would show the Indian Ocean World to be much more inclusive and diverse than its current history relates.

The historical determinism of European ascendancy in commerce, and conquest in political power, in the Indian Ocean World from the eighteenth century onwards has another, more lasting, negative effect: the power of colonial domination by the Europeans in subjugating older links across the sea is passed uncritically to national polities in the twentieth century. While nationalism is no doubt a hugely important force in shaping people's identities and erecting borders with certain obstacles to pass, it would be wrong to assume cultural and economic exchange withered in its old form and meekly submitted to new structures. Take, for example, Claude Markovits' excellent study of two towns located in the Sindh, in colonial India but partitioned into post-colonial Pakistan

(Markovits 2000). The merchants of these towns locate themselves in "longstanding connections between the 'local' and the 'global,' much antedating the latest developments in the rise of a global capitalist economy" (Markovits 2000: 296). At the same time, Markovits notes that the history of these Sindhi merchants cannot fit into the dominant national histories of Pakistan or India, or even a regional history centered on Sindh. These towns and their merchants ought to be framed by the residents and travellers themselves: where they choose to travel, with whom they trade and marry, and how their everyday experience shapes conceptions of their world.

The question then moves to how to accomplish this complicated objective. Several scholars have proposed ideas that might help us theorise a construction of a range of perspectival Indian Ocean world views. Perhaps the most widely invoked model for a holistic regional approach to people on the move is Paul Gilroy's impressive *The Black Atlantic* (Gilroy 1993). He addresses another layer of experience in an ocean-centred region, that of slavery, a topic very applicable to the Indian Ocean (along with its later extension, indentured labour).[5] In it, he dodges several pitfalls discussed above for the Indian Ocean World: "In opposition to both of these nationalist or ethnically absolute approaches, I want to develop the suggestion that cultural historians could take the Atlantic as one single, complex unit of analysis in their discussions of the modern world and use it to produce an explicitly transnational and intercultural perspective" (Gilroy 1993: 15). While Gilroy could be faulted for creating an artificial 'centre' of the black diaspora in the Atlantic, writing from a North American–European location, his contribution is to innovatively describe one layer of a diasporic experience of people on the move. However, a larger question might be if Gilroy sets a diasporist approach in too rigid contradiction to national histories—this certainly has happened in some histories of parts of the Indian Ocean World, a topic to be discussed below. However, both Clifford

[5] See Hugh Tinker (1993) on this historical process. For a thoughtful look at slavery and identity of a specific place in the wider Indian Ocean World, see Pier M. Larson (2000).

and Alpers try to rescue the useful version of diaspora as conceptualised by Gilroy (Clifford 1997: 261–8). Discussing the understudied African diaspora in the northwest Indian Ocean, Alpers shows how Clifford's 'loosening' of Gilroy's theorisation of diaspora works better than more rigid diasporist approaches that impose a 'collective memory' on a group (Alpers 2003). Quoting Clifford, Alpers writes:

> There is no reason his privileging of the black Atlantic. . .should necessarily silence other diasporic perspectives and that "if diaspora is to be something about which one could write a history. . .it must be something more than the name for a site of the multiple displacements and reconstitutions of identity." It must, like Gilroy's *Black Atlantic*, be "a historically produced social formation" (Alpers 2003: 23).

This useful and complicated approach is also supported by Markovits, who notes that a unitary notion of diaspora, among other things, privileges rootedness over movement, loses sight of class divisions, and assumes that a rise of diasporic nationalism necessarily indicates a sense of diasporic unity (Markovits 2000: 4–7).

In addition to loosening the idea of 'diaspora,' a second counterpoint to theoretical moves toward imposing 'unity' can perhaps be found in the underdefined term of 'cosmopolitanism.' I propose that we can use this concept if we are cautious about what it implies, and also acknowledge the role of imagination in its construction. McPherson points toward a sharpening of its meaning when he writes:

> In Alexandria, Beirut, and Haifa, people did frequently adopt and adapt cultural forms drawn from other confessional or national groups. But in the port cities of the Indian Ocean, cosmopolitanism affected only certain sectors of society in a limited number of ways. If, however, the word is used simply to denote the presence of a variety of confessional, cultural, and racial groups within a single urban setting, then it can readily be applied to the major ports of the Indian Ocean region (McPherson 2002: 83).

While a useful caution, we can expand the sense of 'cosmopolitanism' when we augment it with the inclusion of 'imagination.' While this is most decidedly *not* the approach of Pearson, he does quote an eighteenth-century Persian Indian Ocean traveller who hints at its importance, if read metaphorically: "It is not possible to measure the full extent of that sea except with the eye of fantasy. No one will ever delve to the bottom of that sea except by plunging into the waves of his wildest dreams" (Pearson 2003: 15). A turn to Arjun Appadurai, as does Alpers in his impressive but brief essay "Imagining the Indian Ocean World", helps us think through this question of imagination enormously (Alpers 2002). Appadurai, writing about the new cultural global economy, could also have been speaking about the historic Indian Ocean World when discussing his notion of multiple 'imagined worlds' "that are constituted by the historically situated imaginations of persons and groups spread around the globe." Add to this, his concept of 'ethnoscapes'—"the landscape of persons who constitute the shifting world in which we live" (Appadurai 1996: 33)—and we are pretty close to a better explanation of what we called above the 'cosmopolitan layers of connections' of everyday indigenous experience in the Indian Ocean World.[6] This experience should finally be read as entirely consistent with the active process of 'identification,' as proposed by Cooper and Brubaker in opposition to much less imagined notions of identity (Brubaker and Cooper 2000). Perhaps it is best to conclude this discussion with two somewhat contradictory invocations of Amitav Ghosh, showing varying ways of imagining one's own world. In the end, sometimes it is not the world that people have in common, but their imaginations of it. In the first quote, a community Islamic leader berates an ordinary weaver for asking Ghosh about, of all things, ghosts:

> "What ghosts?" Ustaz Sabry exploded. "These ghosts you talk about. . .they're just products of your own imagination. There are

[6] This approach hopefully also avoids extrapolating methods or theories developed outside of the Indian Ocean World to it, and instead allows for an indigenous explanation of experience.

> no such things, can't you see?... People imagine these things everywhere; in India just as here...and in England and Europe too.... But these things are purely imaginary—no such beings exist."
>
> "Imaginary!" cried the weaver. "What do you mean imaginary? How can something be imaginary if someone sees it with his own eyes, right in front of his face?" (Ghosh 1992: 135)

The second passage comes when the same weaver in a conversation with the anthropologist tries to fathom the inconceivable distance between rural Egypt and urban India:

> "Tell me something, ya doktor," he said. "If I got on to my donkey (if you'll pardon that word) and I rode and rode and rode for days, would I reach your country in the end?" He cocked his head to peer at me, as though the prospect of the journey had already filled him with alarm.
>
> "No, ya Zaghloul," I said, and then thinking of all the reasons why it would not be possible to travel from Egypt to India on a donkey, something caught fire in my imagination and I began to talk as I had never talked before...of visas and quarantines, of the ribbon of war that stretched from Iraq to Afghanistan, of the head of the Dasht-e-Kabir and the height of the Hindu Kush, of the foraging of snow leopards and the hairiness of yaks. No one listened to me more intently than Zaghloul, and for months afterwards, whenever he introduced me to anyone, he would tell them, with a dazzled, wondering lilt in his voice, of how far away my country was, of the deserts and wars and mountains that separated it from Egypt, and of the terrible fate that would befall one if one were to set out for it on a donkey (Ghosh 1992: 173).

It is somewhat fitting that this section, begun on Villiers' frankincense-seeking sailing vessel out on the high sea, ends with a donkey plodding through endless deserts; despite its ability to romance scholars, the Indian Ocean World is a long way from being well understood. In this next section, we turn toward a discussion of the potential of multi-sited methodologies that are necessary to apply the theories discussed here to the swelling wave of historiography of the Indian Ocean World.

Indian Ocean World Travellers: Moving Models in Multi-Sited Fieldwork[7]

Gone seem to be the days when academic researchers plopped down into their field sites—be they small dusty villages, languid regional archives, noisy capital cities, spacious art museums, breezy palm-treed islands, or smelly fish markets—and subsequently produced detailed surveys of local culture, history, politics, sociology, literature or some other social practice, thereby contributing to local, national, regional or area studies. Instead, newer generations of extended fieldwork throw up grand and grandly complicated studies[8] that cast a creative academic gaze on relations between diverse people in disparate places, entangled in worldwide webs of social, cultural, political or economic exchange, and imbricated in overlapping fields of identity, memory and history. In these blossoming projects, a clear focus is often sacrificed at the altar of an ambitious curiosity, but the true victim might be the current epistemological organisation of western universities. In 2002, a conference at the University of California at Los Angeles (UCLA) gathered scholars under the auspice of studying various parts of the same vast and far-flung "region" of the Indian Ocean World. But it seemed that we came together not so much for what we shared but what we lacked: established theoretical and especially methodological (disciplinary?) mod-

[7] A very rough, abbreviated draft of this section was presented to the conference on Cultural Exchange and Transformation in the Indian Ocean World held at the University of California at Los Angeles (UCLA) in April of 2002. Thanks to those in attendance for the discussions.

[8] Admittedly this is an overdrawn comparison between artificial constructs of generational differences in fieldwork, but yet a useful one for analysing the issues before us. Guilty of exaggeration, I will offer here a small sample of titles from the conference to suggest the basis of my claim: "Interrogating Trans-Indian Ocean Dietary Diffusion: The Case of *Ugali, Chapati* and *Pilau* in Kenya and Their Oriental and Arab Origins," (Maurice Y. Amutabi, University of Illinois); "The Ties that Bind: Mecca, Medina and the East African Ulama, ca. 1850–1930," (Anne Bang, University of Bergen); "Consciousness and Migration: The Hadrami Diasporas in Hydrabad (Dekan) and Zanzibar between 1880 and 1968," (Friedhelm Hartwig, Humboldt University); and "Towards a Dualism in Domestic Space: Arab, Red Sea, and Indian Ocean Currents at the Port City of al-Mukha (Mocha) in Yemen," (Nancy Um, Binghamton University).

els for understanding the global flows of people, power, ideas and things that comprise the field-research possibilities of an Indian Ocean World studies agenda. Furthermore, this 'lack' was definitively attributed to growing fissures in the area-studies model of the western academy (Roberts 2002).

M. G. Vassanji, a writer of East African extraction and Indian ethnicity currently practising his craft in Canada, grapples in his work with the confusion of these constantly moving flows, real and imagined. Describing Dar es Salaam, Tanzania, and its Indian Ocean-facing port in his book of short stories called *Uhuru Street*, eerily evoking a modern, land-based version of Villiers' lament of passing quoted above, he muses:[9]

> The ships that pass here no longer carry portents of faraway, impossible worlds. The same harbour, in front of me. The tall-spired cathedral behind me on the right. The pipe fence on which I perch, nervous of pickpockets and the traffic screeching at the back of me; a gust of sea breeze to cool the heat still pulsing in my veins after the long walk. Before me a rolling patch of grass down which I remember as a child doing somersaults. And I remember looking up intently at some ship passing slowly through the narrow channel, at the white-clad passengers leaning out gaily against the railings, waving at us. Strangers whose worlds we had no cravings for at that time, mere curiosity.
>
> All worlds are possible now. Shadowy cargo vessels cheerlessly ply these waters, bringers of unaffordable goods, reminders of deprivation, enticements to get up and go. Silent pipers, whom we follow by jet planes, those who can, and stretch ourselves between lives as contrary as the ends of a cross (Vassanji 1991: 130).

This is amazing stuff, touching on issues of travel and trade, the past and the present, imagination and longing, comings and goings, and stretched-out identities. Much like the narrator in this passage, I too have sat and observed (at the very same harbour) during the period of my fieldwork experience, and have been bewildered and barraged by the constant movement of people, things and ideas through and around my sites

[9] It is appropriate that Vassanji employs ships and the sea in identifying change, as when maritime relations change between different regions in the Indian Ocean World, local conditions inevitably change as well.

of temporary dwelling in Tanzania and India.[10] Departing from this point of confusion, what I would like to attempt in this section is a discussion of key methodological issues relevant to (re-)nascent western academic conceptualisations of an Indian Ocean World.[11]

Naturally, extended fieldwork experiences force reflections on the models—theoretical and methodological—constructed to help study the inhabitants and travellers of the Indian Ocean World. In particular, it has not been methodological challenges to my own project which have prompted these reflections, but rather chance observations of marginal actors on the peripheries of Indian Ocean World societies which have raised questions over how they would fit into existing and evolving academic models. The actors in this are as varied as they are numerous, and include but are not limited to (listed by 'profession'): sailors; smugglers; students; soldiers; slaves; indentured labourers; dancing bar girls; colonial officials, anti-colonial activists and post-colonial diplomats; traders; spirits; and, above all, the everyday local-yet-trans-local woman and man. While this cast of characters could comprise a roll of players in a Bollywood *masala* blockbuster, when transported into academe they represent categories of historical agents who often are ignored for their marginal status, or fall between the cracks of area studies due to their being 'on the move.' So, spurred on by the criticism of area studies which is growing in volume, and seen in the rise of 'crossing borders' and 'ocean

[10] In addition to nearly a year of pre-dissertation research, my fieldwork was conducted between September 2000 and August 2003 in Dar es Salaam, Tanzania, and in New Delhi, Bombay and around the state of Gujarat, India. My project concerns race relations in the Indian Ocean World between Tanzanian Indians and Africans living in and travelling between Dar es Salaam and western India, focusing on histories and memories of everyday encounters from the late colonial period to the present.

[11] This comes with a caveat, of course: this will be not only a far from exhaustive catalogue of important considerations in the process of forming an Indian Ocean World studies category, but also be warned that most examples will be drawn from my areas of specialty: twentieth-century East Africa and western India. However, to establish the same conclusions, many examples could be found much deeper in history, and in a wider geographic spread of territories throughout the Indian Ocean World as well.

area studies' programmes, we have begun to question how academic researchers can analyse better these marginal and mobile populations, along with the things and ideas they carry or exchange.[12] Here, after briefly sketching historical aspects of the various characters mentioned above, we can attempt to put together a critical methodological discussion of the emerging field of Indian Ocean World studies.

Indian Ocean World Travellers: Sailors, Scholars, Soldiers, Slaves, Indentured Labourers, Dance Bar Girls and Politicians

According to the Tanzania Seamen's Union (TASU), there are currently 1200 sailors in the country, the vast majority of whom are stationed not on the lakes but in sea port towns.[13] The sailors are a diverse lot, and although it is estimated that close to 90 per cent are Tanzanian Africans, they come from many places in the country, and adhere to various faiths. The minority is composed of Tanzanians of Arab, Somali and Indian descent, and some women are on board as well.[14] Ports of destination currently range from Tanzania's immediate vicinity in the Indian Ocean to distant harbours across the world, and these journeys feed the country's 'container economy.' TASU has a history that stretches into the colonial period, and we know that similar groups of sailors have come from other eastern African countries as well, part of a many-centuries-old tra-

[12] By now, most readers will be familiar with the thrust of the critique of area studies. For a concise, although far from devastating, summary of them, plus a list of American institutions pursuing crossing borders-style "revitalisation of area studies" initiatives, see this Ford Foundation link: http://www.fordfound.org/publications/recent_articles/crossingborders.cfm. European examples of this trend include the Centre for Modern Oriental Studies in Berlin and the Humboldt University-based Berlin Indian Ocean Research Group.

[13] Interview with Mchafu Ahmed Chakoma, General Secretary of TASU, 28 August 2001, TASU Head Office, Dar es Salaam, Tanzania.

[14] It is not clear how many Tanzanian women work on ships, but their numbers are relatively small. Many are subject to similar discrimination as they face on land, and often are placed in jobs like kitchen work or cleaning. However, it still must be noted that life on transport ships in the Indian Ocean World might not be as much of a man's world as is usually assumed.

dition of Africans manning sailing vessels in the Indian Ocean World.[15] At the same time as in East Africa but beginning earlier, India shipped out organised seafaring bodies of globalised labour which travelled largely to England, including stops in the Persian Gulf and Africa, among other colonial ports.[16] These harbour calls often initiated rather interesting understandings and misunderstandings between sailors and the local population, such as happened when the *Orissa* docked into apartheid South Africa in 1942: when refused service in a seamen's club on account of the colour of their skin, the Indian sailing crew proceeded to trash the bar.[17]

Of course, the movements of sailors are built on historical patterns of trade throughout the Indian Ocean World. The crucial question of how to assess the importance of these moving populations of seafarers arises as they have, in many cases, extended and meaningful contact with overseas countries. In my interviews in Dar es Salaam, one TASU sailor, Ahmad, explained how his first trip from Tanzania to India in 1979–1980 lasted many months.[18] Once in a port like Bombay, it is not unusual that seamen's contracts expire, and thus they are effectively stranded overseas, leaving populations of hundreds of African sailors like Ahmad looking for work in the South Asian subcontinent. However, while cut off from 'home' in Africa, unemployment in exile does open up a new region of opportunity. Ahmad described how, when seeking a job, he simply got on a train from Bombay to New Delhi, and from there went to Lahore and Quetta in Pakistan, and then into

[15] For the best historical account of African sailors in the Indian Ocean maritime world, see Ewald (2000). She lists several sources for pre-1750, despite a focus on 1750–1914.

[16] See, for example, Ahujà (2002), and the forthcoming careful historical work of Michael H. Fisher of Oberlin University (as previewed in his lectures given on 27 February 2002 at Jawaharlal Nehru University in New Delhi and 1 March 2002 at Delhi University in India).

[17] National Archives of India, New Delhi (hereafter NAI), File No. 16–18/42–OS, 1942.

[18] Interview with "Ahmad," 10 October 2001, TASU Branch Office, Kariakoo. Note that this sailor's name and those of his two fellows cited below have been changed here due to the sensitive nature of some of the material.

Iran all the way to Tehran. About a decade later, while again searching for a contract on a boat, he converted his savings to fly from Dar es Salaam to Pakistan, as the demand for seamen was greater there than it was in East Africa. Taking advantage of the experience of his first trip, Ahmad made a similar journey through Central and South Asia, ending in Bombay where he lived for some time before finally reaching Tanzania again. He talks fondly of both trips to India, including grinning about his opportunities to watch cheap Hindi films and to visit Indian prostitutes, who are few in Tanzania.

Another TASU sailor, Musa, started on the boats in the late 1960s.[19] He made his first trip to Bombay in 1973, and also reports going to Delhi, Pakistan and Iran for work. Moreover, he set up several small businesses in and around Bombay, and began to establish a life there, marrying an Indian woman in 1983, fathering a child by her, and building a house for them in a district near Hyderabad. Later, as his ship assignments took him away from India, the connection to his wife and child lapsed to just that of written correspondence, and he took up with an Arab girlfriend who lived in a more regular port of call, Madagascar. A third sailor, Mwijaba, discussed how many of the sailors' grandfathers used to make similar trips on wooden dhows throughout the western Indian Ocean, until steamers slowly began replacing them after their introduction in the nineteenth century.[20] Ironically, despite the onslaught of 'globalisation,' the passenger steamer service linking East Africa to the Gulf and India ended around 1980. While planes might whisk passengers across the Indian Ocean faster, it seems that far fewer people can afford travel post-1980 between India and East Africa. Visa restrictions to India also became more difficult after the 1984 assassination of Indira Gandhi, affectionately referred to as 'Mama Gandhi' by the TASU mariners.[21]

[19] Interview with "Musa," 10 October 2001, TASU Branch Office, Kariakoo.

[20] Interview with "Mwijaba," 10 October 2001, TASU Branch Office, Kariakoo. Regarding steamships, the ascension to supremacy of steam over sails was surprisingly slow. See Gilbert (2002) and Ewald (2000).

[21] Interview with Mr V. Menon, 5 March 2002, Tanzania High Commission, New Delhi, India.

Before then, Tanzanians could enter India without a visa, and Ahmad and Musa both stressed how the Indian Ocean region used to be much more 'free.'[22] Clearly, despite some academic claims that the nation is withering or in the process of extinction in the face of a relentless globalisation, the termination of cheap transport and the introduction of stricter border-crossing regulations seems to indicate that the academic study of nationalism—in parallel with nations' importance in people's everyday lives—will need to be prominent for some time to come.[23]

Due to the relatively short-term nature of contracts in the shipping industry, many seamen have to turn to marginal businesses to survive between jobs. Several members of TASU bleakly reported that it is not unusual to go for months or even years without employment. Thus, it is not surprising that the combination of sailors' mobility and desperation makes them ideal candidates to fall into the drug-running business, one of many smuggling options. This trade primarily runs along the same routes that Ahmad and Musa travelled,[24] from Afghanistan to Pakistan and thereafter into India, with Bombay subsequently being the port from which the drugs are smuggled to points around the world, including through the prominent East African laundering entrepot of Zanzibar.[25] The drugs carried include heroin, opium, cocaine and marijuana, among others.[26] Several informants told me that Tanzanians—many of them arrived as seamen—along with other African nationals

[22] Many factors are at work in this change that the sailors note, some of which will be discussed later in this chapter, including the history of relations between the Government of India and the Indian National Congress with anti-colonial activists in East Africa, and, later, with the independent governments of the new East African states.

[23] It is also not insignificant to note that South Asian nationalism, such as arises from the tension between India and Pakistan, often closes borders as well, further making the Indian Ocean World—once more open to travelling sailors—less "free."

[24] This is *not* to imply that Ahmad and Musa were involved in drug smuggling.

[25] Information corroborated by confidential sources at the US Embassy in Dar es Salaam, Tanzania, in 2001.

[26] For a discussion of drug sellers in Tanzania and opportunities in India, see Moyer 2003.

are very active in the procurement, selling and smuggling of drugs in South Asia, and that many are dying on the dangerous streets of Bombay's underworld.[27] Going by New Delhi and Mumbai newspaper reports as well, a good number of Tanzanians are languishing in Indian prisons after being arrested for possession of drugs or other offences, something confirmed by sources at the High Commission of the Republic of Tanzania in New Delhi.[28]

I argue that these sailors, living lives not only on ships but also in numerous countries in the region, in port cities and even inland from the coast, are but one example of many in the history of contemporary and past Indian Ocean societies constructed through frequent movement and exchange. This entails not just the fulfillment of an economic function, but has important social and cultural residues as well. In a similar example of a population on the move, there has been a long tradition of students travelling throughout the Indian Ocean World in order to obtain higher education.[29] In 1905, two

[27] Some information above comes from interviews in 2002 with Mr B. M. Rayappa, the accountant and assistant manager of the Royal Bombay Seamen's Society, which includes the Mission to Seamen. At the hostel there, Mr Rayappa discussed the reputation of Tanzanian sailors since the 1980s as boisterous, prone to fighting, often incarcerated, and sometime homeless drug peddlers. See also an article on Nigerians and drugs in Bombay, by Pritish Nandy (2002). Many times, however, "Nigerians" conflated for all "Africans" are in fact Tanzanian or Kenyan. My dissertation research in Bombay also included ethnographic experiences with about twenty Tanzanian drug dealers who gather nightly at the Gateway to India to conduct "business"—sometimes small peddling, sometimes carrying large shipments.

[28] Interview with Mr R. C. Kikwabha, Minister Plenipotentiary, Tanzania High Commission, New Delhi, India, 21 December 2001. For a newspaper account, see "Tanzanian Held with Charas," in the Delhi round-up, *The Times of India*, 12 December 2001, which begins: "Police arrested a foreign national near Cama Hotel, Raj Guru Road on Tuesday night and recovered 200 gms of charas from him. The 31-year-old, identified as Antony Juma, has revealed that he was a Tanzanian national but did not possess any documents". *Charas* is hashish, a substance similar to marijuana.

[29] The relevant archival files used in this section are: "Recruitment of Indian Teachers," Tanzania National Archives (hereafter TNA), Secretariat File No. 11558; "Summary of the Vernacular Press, 1960–61," TNA 540/DC 1/68; NAI, Foreign Department, Internal Branch, Part B, File nos. 219–233, March 1906; File nos. 177–178, September 1908; File nos. 252–257, February 1920;

Abyssinian princes, including the 'heir apparent,' were sent to Mayo College in Ajmer, India. In 1908, three sons of a Sultan in Malay were shifted from England to Ajmer, and then in 1919 the Sultan of Zanzibar requested admission to Mayo College for his son. At the same time, there was a demand for school-teachers in the Indian Ocean region, and, for example, the British colonial administration in Dar es Salaam facilitated the recruitment of Indian teachers for government schools from the 1920s.[30] Later on, educational exchanges became formalised, with the 1940s witnessing the Government of India extending scholarships to worthy foreign students throughout the Indian Ocean World. Six places were made available at medical schools in India for South African students, with plans to extend the scheme to East Africa and Mauritius. At least five annual scholarships were initiated in 1947 for East African students pursuing a postgraduate education in India, and this operated alongside similar programmes already in place for Afghan and Iranian students, the latter of whom received 14 paid admissions in that year of Indian independence. The Government of India, justifying this recurrent expenditure, noted that the foreign student scholarship programme was of "urgent importance" to aid in "cultural relations" with friendly countries. By 1960, they were offering 45 scholarships a year to East African students.[31]

There is no doubt that these scholarship programmes propelled more and more people to leave their home shores for opportunities abroad, and the pattern of movement in the region to obtain education, or to find a teaching job, has con-

---

Commonwealth Relations Department, Overseas Branch I, File no. 23–4/45-OS, 1945; Foreign Department, External Affairs, File no. 54(74)-x, 1947.

[30] For a fictionalised account of one teacher in Dar es Salaam, see Vassanji (1996).

[31] Pakistan was extending similar schemes of cooperation. For example, the Tanzanian Kiswahili newspaper *Ngurumo* reported on 28 October 1960 that "Mr. Nyindo of Pare, left in September for five years' training in veterinary science in Pakistan. His studies are financed by the Pakistani Government, while the major part of his fare was found by the Tanganyika Society of Muslim Youth. When leaving he denied that he had any intention of visiting Communist countries." TNA, "Summary of the Vernacular Press, 1960–61," 540/DC 1/68.

tinued. Many Indians in Dar es Salaam also sent their children to India for primary and secondary education because of the 1962 nationalisation of schools shortly after Tanzanian independence. Such educational strategising occurred for a number of reasons: lack of local education in Gujarati; stress on Kiswahili-medium schools instead of English-medium schools; the new government's financial and managerial inability to run successful schools, especially at the secondary level; familial networks in South Asia which offered access to the cheaper Indian educational system; and, finally, racial or religious stereotyping which made Indian parents unwilling to send their children into a school environment with Africans or children of different religious groups. The same trends occurred in higher education as well. By the middle of the 1990s, before a subsequent drop-off, there were more than 600 Tanzanian students in India, and this number paled in comparison to the Kenyans, who totalled several thousand—including more than a hundred students known to currently reside in Indian prisons.[32] As these stays overseas last for several years, the cultural importance of educational exchange in the region needs to be better understood, what with business dealings, marriages, return visits and other social interactions obviously very common. A small example will suffice to show the possibilities of these extended relationships. Fatma Rashid Mohammed, a Zanzibari African Tanzanian woman who obtained a degree from Mysore University in south India in the late 1990s, now spends every Sunday sitting around with her family in Dar es Salaam watching Hindi films. Her cousin who also studied at Mysore married an Indian woman.[33]

In a different way, the Baluchis represent an extraordinary case of an Indian Ocean World population who by nature of their cultural exchange and adaptation, and history of

[32] Interview with Mr R. C. Kikwabha, Minister Plenipotentiary, 21 December 2001, and interview with Mr V. Menon, 5 March 2002, Tanzania High Commission, New Delhi, India.

[33] Series of interviews with Fatma Rashid Mohammed, November 2000 to November 2001, Dar es Salaam.

movement, have sunk into the shadows of academic understandings.[34] Baluchistan today is a province in southwestern Pakistan, but many ethnic Baluchis also live in eastern Iran. At different times in history the region was politically controlled by the Persians, the Mughals or the British, but the Baluchis have a history of movement from the territory. It is known that the Sultan of Oman preferred Baluchi bodyguards and brought many to his court in Muscat. From there, some time early in the second half of the nineteenth century, the Omani Sultanate shipped out Baluchis to be soldiers for its interests in Zanzibar[35] (Sheriff 1987: 215). Subsequently, many Baluchis were given land by the Sultan along the short coastal stretch of German East Africa (later colonial Tanganyika, and then independent Tanzania) controlled by the Omanis, opposite Zanzibar.[36] They became relatively prosperous, farming coconuts and trading along the caravan routes to the interior.[37] According to their descendants, a few Baluchi women were brought along, but largely the male soldiers/farmers/traders intermarried with the people along the coast or even inland. Elders of the Baluchi community in Kaole, just outside Bagamoyo in what now is Tanzania, tell fascinating stories of their history. Due to vibrant trans-territorial links established during the period of caravan trade, a section of the Baluchi community moved to Rujewa village in Mbeya district in the southern Tanzanian highlands, and also set up neighbourhoods in Dar es Salaam. Sheikh Ibrahim Musa Pishuki of Kaole, born in 1932, talked about how his father was a Baluchi, and his mother was from

[34] This obscurity, thankfully, seems to be changing with a number of scholars now looking into Baluchi, and especially Afro-Baluchi, history. For example, see Sabir Badalkhan (2002a, 2002b) of the Istituto Universitario Orientale, Napoli, and Behnaz Mirzai (2002b) of York University, as well as the efforts of a new and very active research group, The African Diaspora in Asia (TADIA), led by Jean-Pierre Angenot and Shihan de Silva Jayasuriya.

[35] Baluchi graves in Kaole, a village south of Bagamoyo in Tanzania, also date to this period.

[36] This section based on an interview with Ibrahim Musa Pishuki, 22 October 2000, Kaole.

[37] For a reference to the famous Baluchi caravan trader Isa bin Husain, one of the first to reach Buganda shortly after 1850, see Sheriff (1987: 184).

Unyamwezi, a central Tanganyikan region, home to an ethnic group very active in the long-distance caravan trade. Pishuki himself married three times, to one woman of mixed Baluchi descent, to a Mnyamwezi and a Mdoe, a people from the Bagamoyo coastal region. He had children with all three wives, and one of his daughters has married an Arab from Tanga and settled in Dar es Salaam, where many Baluchis have intermarried with poorer Muslims of Indian descent.[38]

While the Kaole Baluchis are relatively impoverished since the early-nineteenth-century decline of Bagamoyo as a trading center, some mobile Baluchis in Dar es Salaam today take advantage of their Islamic and Arab connections to do business in places like Muscat, Abu Dhabi and Dubai. Thus, with origins in South Asia, the Persian Gulf and East Africa, and with fluid Muslim identities encompassing Indian, Arab and various African ethnic shades, the Baluchis stand as a prime example of important mobile denizens of the Indian Ocean World. However, despite the fact that they have arrived on the shore of many lands in the region, in the past and the present, they have scarcely arrived in most academic accounts of the history of an Indian Ocean World.[39] One reason for this is

[38] Interview with Ibrahim's aunt, Fatma binti Msafiri, and daughter, Rabia binti Ibrahim, in Magomeni, Dar es Salaam, 7 November 2000. Blandina and James Giblin led the interview.

[39] A population with similar historical themes to the Baluchis is the Sidis, descendants of Africans taken to South Asia, largely as soldier-slaves. However, they have attracted quite a lot of recent scholarly attention, with exciting results. Professors Edward Alpers and Amy Catlin-Jairazbhoy of UCLA, Professor Helene Basu of the Free University, Berlin, James Micklem of the University of Edinburgh, and a University of Iowa team have all conducted fieldwork amongst the Sidis; and see the reference list for several conference papers on the subject. The outstanding book on the subject is by Jayasuriya and Pankhurst (2003). Despite this positive attention paid to the Sidis, one dubious strand of some investigations has been an exoticising search for a lost 'Africanness.' This does not always help the Sidis outside of academics. While aiding a group of Sidi musicians scheduled to tour the UK, I was forced to intervene at the airport when immigration officials persisted in denying the possibility of their Indian citizenship because of the colour of their skin. This encounter was captured in a piece by a *The Times of India* journalist, Naresh Fernandes, and submitted to (but unpublished by) the magazine *Outlook Traveller*. As a final note, I am currently studying archival files from the Maharashtra State Archives (Bombay) which

the lack of methodological and theoretical tools necessary to undertake such a project. Employing notions of overlapping imaginations of cosmopolitan connections on a multi-sited fieldwork project might be the fairest way to begin to describe complicated Baluchi experiences in the Indian Ocean World.

As we have seen, in the studies of the comings and goings of people in the history of the Indian Ocean area, much more is usually known about those who arrive and stay on than on those who return. This is evident in the lack of good histories of the Baluchis, as well for sailors and students in general who travel to diverse places throughout the region, and was noted by Markovits in his study on Sindhi merchants. The same can be said for those transported under what Hugh Tinker called the 'new system of slavery': indentured labour (Tinker 1993). At the tail end of the nineteenth century, the British colonial government in the East Africa Protectorate (later Kenya) imported Indian indentured labour to build the legendary Uganda Railway. Between 1896, when tracks were first laid in the steamy port town of Mombasa, and 1901, when the line finally reached the cool highland shores of Kisumu on Lake Victoria, an estimated 31,983 Indian indentured labourers were brought in to build the railway.[40] A small number, recorded as 6,724, stayed on to live and work in East Africa after the termination of their contracts, not counting the 2,493 who died during the line's construction. These early Indian settlers in Kenya became a spark for further immigration, and, concomitantly, for better or worse, a good amount of academic literature on the South Asian diaspora in East Africa.[41] However, we know

contain narratives of Africans freed in Bombay in the nineteenth century. It is possible that they are ancestors of today's various Sidi populations across South Asia.

[40] The numbers here are drawn from the several works of Robert G. Gregory (especially 1993, 1971). For a critical analysis of the literature on this topic, see Bertz (1998).

[41] Despite the fact that a very small number of South Asians currently living in Kenya descended from indentured labourers, there is still the common myth, that almost all of them had "coolies" as ancestors, partly thanks to the literature, on the construction of the Uganda railway. The academic body of work on South Asians in East Africa will be discussed more thoroughly below.

hardly anything about the vast majority of indentured labourers—well over 20,000, more than two-thirds of the total—who elected to go back to India, or were invalided back due to injury or illness (around 6,454).

A latter-day variation of the indentured labour system, in a much different manifestation, can be found in the movements of Bombay bar girls and their entourages throughout the Indian Ocean World.[42] Following the paths of earlier and contemporary migrations and travels of Indians throughout the area, these *mujra* dancers,[43] as they are known in East Africa, sign up on short-term contracts to dance in locations in the UK, Persian Gulf and East Africa, and perhaps elsewhere. Found in Bombay and in major metros across India, a mujra club (there referred to as a dance bar) normally has a dozen or so young girls who dance, usually wearing saris but occasionally forms of skimpier western dress. While no nudity is involved, mujra patrons can beckon girls over for private flirtation under the pretence of delivering a tip. Some mujra clubs double as high-end prostitution networks as well. As seen in the recent widely acclaimed Bollywood film *Chandni Bar,*[44] many future mujra girls are taken from their villages while still quite young, often against their will or under false promises. Or, they are forced to dance at the clubs to pay back family debts or as another kind of last resort. Bombay is seen as the Indian capital of mujra, and it is from here that just about all

[42] All of the information below is from primary ethnographic research that I have conducted in Dar es Salaam and Bombay over the period of my fieldwork. There is very little secondary academic literature on this topic, but one notable recent exception is by Eileen Moyer (2002) of the University of Amsterdam, and formerly of the University of Iowa.

[43] "Musical performance by a dancing-girl" is the translation from Hindi of mujra (McGregor 1997). It should be noted here that there is a long history of "dancing girls," more commonly known as courtesans or *tawaif*s, as public entertainers in India. This trope is well represented in Hindi films, and subsequently these archetypes are drawn upon by mujra girls in their performances around the world. For a deeper background, see Chandra (1993), and for a good local historical example of the agency of tawaifs, see Oldenburg (1992).

[44] *Chandni Bar* ("The Moonlight Bar"), a 2001 Hindi film by Madhur Bhandarkar, made by Shlok Films, and starring the Hyderabadi actress Tabu.

mujra dancers are exported to cities around the Indian Ocean World.[45]

In Dar es Salaam, the clubs are quite popular, and at any one time there have been up to half a dozen in operation, starting around the early 1990s. The audience is almost completely made up of male Tanzanian Indians, although some Arabs, Africans, travelling Indian nationals and women do attend on occasion. The girls dance from evening until almost sunrise, and are expected to make significant amounts of money in tips that are culled by the owners of the hotels where they dance. The owners also double as the importers, and they make the arrangements with Bombay clubs to secure the girls' services. Given their situation, most of the women are keen to go, since dancing in Africa—there have been clubs in at least Dar es Salaam, Arusha and Nairobi—and the Persian Gulf (where several major trading cities such as Dubai, with substantial immigrant South Asian populations, have mujras), not to mention the UK,[46] is more lucrative than performing in India. Generally, contracts are for three to six months, and compensation for the term of the agreement can range from several hundred dollars per dancer to two thousand. In Dar es Salaam, some clubs' girls are housed and fed together at the owner's expense. And like in India, some Tanzanian mujras double as prostitution rings for wealthier Indians there. The mujra dancers perform almost exclusively to the music of Hindi films, which have historically circulated in the Indian Ocean World since as early as the 1920s and possess wide and diverse audiences across Africa and the Gulf (and far beyond).[47] In some clubs, instead of a sound system, there is a live band comprised of several musicians and singers who travel, on similar short-term contracts, with the dancers to their destinations.

[45] For an article on the estimated 700 dance bars in Bombay, see Dharker (2002).

[46] I have seen clubs in Dubai, and for an account on how London is viewing the presence of mujra as a sign of growing Asian crime, see Tony Thompson (2003).

[47] There is a good and growing amount of literature on the reception to Bollywood films in India and around the world, but very little on them in East Africa. One interesting account is in Fuglesang (1994). My dissertation contains a chapter on Hindi films in Dar es Salaam.

At the termination of the contract, the bar girls usually go back to Bombay before heading out to another overseas destination after some months' time. Sometimes it does not quite come to that, however: in 2002, the Government of Tanzania cracked down on mujra clubs in Dar es Salaam and, upon finding that the dancers had only tourist visas and not work or residence permits, forced the girls to return to India.[48] So, in the Bombay mujra girls, we have another Indian Ocean World population on the move, following earlier and ongoing migrations of people and the exchange of things (Hindi films and music cassettes, for example). There is no doubt that their presence in Dar es Salaam and the Gulf is part of the creation of Indian Ocean World societies, but better academic models are needed in order to analyse how their experiences have historically been constructed, something which will be considered in this chapter's last section.

A final group of Indian Ocean travellers, generally described as politicians, will be used simply to illustrate one aspect of mobility that has hitherto largely been absent in this discussion: the global and regional political and economic frameworks which enable and encourage, or discourage and prevent, flows of people, things and ideas to take place. When thinking about colonial officials, anti-colonial activists and post-colonial diplomats in the Indian Ocean region, one must recognise the primary role political structures play in their travels. How-

[48] One rumour on the streets of Dar es Salaam was that this type of deportation earlier happened in Nairobi, supposedly under direct orders from President Daniel Arap Moi as an attack on the Indian community there. A second rumor in Dar es Salaam and Arusha (but stronger in Kenya) involves the Indian wives of those who attend mujra complaining directly to the government because of the late hours, excessive drinking and money their husbands were frittering away. This supposedly led to the clubs' removal in Arusha and Nairobi earlier, and in Dar es Salaam recently. Another issue in the recent closure of the clubs in Dar es Salaam concerns the evasion of income tax payments, a more likely serious consideration for the government than the girls' immigration status. For a report on the mujra "bust," see the Tanzanian weekly, *The Express*, "Illicit Mujra Cracked," 7 February 2002. Shortly afterwards, *The Express* reported that certain mujra outlets were still activating, illegally. By December of 2002, all the clubs were functioning normally again. Further, a Tanzanian Indian friend told me that by November 2003 a mujra had opened (again?) in Arusha.

ever, in the same way, the changing nature of economic and political relations needs to be considered to frame properly the movement of African slaves, Baluchi soldiers, indentured labourers, students, sailors, smugglers and mujra girls. When the British Empire controlled large parts of the Indian Ocean World, in particular from the late nineteenth century to Indian independence in 1947, colonialism greatly facilitated the transfer of people between British territories. This certainly played a role in the different nature of Indian immigration to the East Africa Protectorate and to German East Africa, as indentured labour was permitted to go to the former but an application was refused for workers to proceed to the latter to help build railways there (Rai 1979: 36). Around the same time, in 1899, the General Consul in Mombasa requested the Government of India to accept long-term African prisoners at the penal colony in the Andaman Islands, and was obliged.[49] Throughout the first several decades of the twentieth century, there were numerous discussions among British colonial officials—on both sides of the Indian Ocean, and in London—about promoting settlement of Indians in East Africa, and even, at a couple of historical moments, of turning Tanganyika into an Indian colony.[50] And not only did colonial officials themselves transfer throughout the British Empire, but they also toured other territories in order to gain ideas as to how best to administer the areas under their control.[51]

Moreover, this system of cross-border colonial administration advice paralleled a unique relationship between the Government of India and what it conceived of as its 'overseas Indians,' built on anti-colonial fault lines. For example, an extraordinary letter from the Secretary of the Indian Overseas

[49] NAI, Home Department, Jails Proceedings, Part A, File nos. 8–9, 1899.

[50] About rewarding German East Africa to Indian colonisation, see the discussion in Gregory (1971: 156–76). For an example of settlement plans, see NAI, Foreign Department, General Branch, Part B, File no. 217, July 1921, "Proposed colonisation of Indian Agriculturists in the TGA territory (GEA): Report of Sir B. Robertson on the subject."

[51] In particular, tried and tested methods of colonial administration in India were applied in Africa. See Gregory (1971) and Mbilinyi (1979: 84–5).

Department of the All Indian Congress Committee (AICC) to Indians everywhere noted that "Only a free India can hope to protect and safeguard the interests of Indians residing abroad."[52] From the 1920s, Indian organisations in South and East Africa regularly petitioned not only their local colonial governments, but also approached the Government of India in order to achieve their political aims. This led to a flurry of governmental deputations to be dispatched in either direction, usually for the purpose of either assessing the condition of Indians in Africa, or to present in person Indian grievances in East Africa to officials in India.[53] Through such travelling linkages, a relationship began to develop between anti-colonial organisations on different shores of the Indian Ocean. Several Indian associations in East Africa joined to create the East Africa Indian National Congress by the 1920s, with similar developments earlier in South Africa. Clear through to 1947, Indians in Africa actively supported the AICC in its drive for independence.[54] Sadly, Partition in South Asia had the effect of exacerbating pre-existing communal tensions among East African South Asians: one Tanzanian Indian recalled wildly celebrating Indian independence as a child in a small village in southern Tanzania, but that, for the first time, the Muslim Indian residents gathered separately to herald the creation of Pakistan.[55] As the colonial and anti-communal frameworks for trans-oceanic cooperation begun to dissolve in 1947, an encompassing anti-colonial nationalism took the place to allow

[52] The letter was dated 25 January 1940, and titled "Our Countrymen Abroad: An Appeal." Nehru Memorial Museum and Library (hereafter NMML), Teen Murti House, New Delhi, AICC OS-40.

[53] For example, a Government of India delegation went to East Africa in 1946 to assess the impact of proposed immigration reform there, and subsequently published a report on their findings. See NAI, Foreign Department, External Branch, File no. 7-x-47, 1947. For an example of travel in the other direction: the East African Indian National Congress sent a delegation in 1929 to present a pamphlet on the "Indian Position in East Africa" to AICC. See AICC FD-8/1929, held at NMML.

[54] A rich collection of letters between Nehru and other members of AICC and various overseas Indians is extant and held at NMML. Also see chapter two in Brennan (2002).

[55] Interview with Mr B. K. Tanna, 6 August 2001, Dar es Salaam, Tanzania.

for the continuation of political exchanges across the Indian Ocean. Prime Minister Jawaharlal Nehru and other Indian politicians vigorously opposed the late imperialist domination of Africa, and on several occasions hosted East African independence leaders in India.[56] This relationship continued after the East African states attained *Uhuru* in the early 1960s, and not only was there sustained high-level cooperation between the new national leaders who were the collaborating anti-colonial nationalists,[57] but this was shadowed by a parade of diplomats and their non-governmental entourages.[58] As discussed in this paper's first section, these powerful relationships cannot be ignored in understanding the nature of individuals' everyday experience in the Indian Ocean World, but at the same time they cannot be assumed to dominate them either. To get at this fine balance, new methodologies of multi-sited research, and more complex theories of exchange and movement, have to be developed.

Moving Models in Multi-Sited Fieldwork: Toward Studying the Indian Ocean World

The Indian Ocean World travellers discussed above have for centuries been part of creating vibrant regional societies based on movement and exchange. However, under the current organisation of area studies at western universities, they have either fallen between the cracks—for their marginal status or their tendency to movement between areas—or been misunderstood. Take, for example, the academic treatment of the South

[56] For example, Bibi Titi Mohammed of the women's wing of the Tanganyika African National Union was interviewed about her visit to India. See Geiger (1997).

[57] One of my favourite pictures of the first president of Tanzania, Julius Nyerere, has him standing in an elegant black overcoat on an obviously chilly day in Agra, unsmilingly posing with the Taj Mahal looming over his shoulder.

[58] See, for example, the establishment of Tanzanian and Indian High Commissions in either country, developmental assistance missions, trade commissions, technical cooperation teams and so on. However, this "special" relationship was not to last forever, and with the death of Indira Gandhi, and the advent of liberalisation in India as well as East Africa, economic relations were prioritised over the quickly fading political ones.

Asian diaspora in East Africa. Despite widely cited calls by such prominent theorists as Arjun Appadurai and James Clifford for border-crossing research, scholars have not yet sufficiently undertaken projects analysing the connections between East Africa and India. This is reflected in the state of the literature on the history of East Africans of Indian descent, which ignores, for example, the ways that Tanzanian Indians and Africans interact with India. Broadly speaking, two bodies of scholarly work exist. The first consists of nationalist histories of Tanzania. These accounts reproduce what Susan Geiger identified as the 'Tanzanian nationalist meta-narrative,' which works in a manner similar to the Indian nationalist master narrative described by Shahid Amin and other members of the Subaltern Studies collective (Amin 1995; Geiger 1997). Adhering to the Tanzanian nationalist meta-narrative, academics' descriptions of nationalism in the late colonial and early post-colonial periods display a narrow, elite-centred focus. The implications of nationalist meta-narratives are profound for the understanding of Indian and African history, in addition to the history of Indian communities in Dar es Salaam. Most obviously, since Tanzanian Indians are not part of the 'imagining' of the nation, they are excluded or disparaged in public discourses that mobilise academic histories of nationalism and nation building in Tanzania for political purposes. Moreover, given the focus on elite politics and socialist economics in Tanzanian nationalist histories, and the commercial activities of prominent trade-oriented Indians, social and cultural interactions between Africans and Indians are not studied, and their relationships are assumed to be antagonistic.[59] This not only ignores a rich history of collaboration, seen in the markets, movie halls and associations of people who come together to consult spirits,[60] but also obfuscates tensions of a

[59] A notable exception is the work of James R. Brennan (2002).

[60] As mentioned earlier, Hindi films in East Africa have historically drawn wide and diverse audiences, and are certainly a cultural medium through which racial, religious, gender, community, national and other identities are negotiated. Further, it should come as no surprise that the belief in spirits, like other trans-Indian Ocean religious idioms such as Islam, is transnational. Linda Giles

social and cultural nature. The second body of literature on the modern history of East African Indians comes from diaspora scholarship, and sympathetically portrays Indians as the victims of African nationalism and, in Tanzania at least, socialism.[61] In this version of history, the Indian nationalist master narrative takes predominance, eliminating individual Africans from view by highlighting Indians' achievements and contributions in the face of an assumedly hostile majority population. This rendering of history still focuses on Indians' estrangement from Africans for political and economic reasons, and refuses to delve into social or cultural interactions. Thus, the importance to race relations in Dar es Salaam of everyday interracial encounters and their overseas manifestations are left out of both nationalist and diasporist approaches. What is now needed is a new kind of scholarship, based on wider apertures and more diverse methods, that will look beyond nationalist rhetoric to examine both sides of a dynamic trans-oceanic historical encounter.

While the academic star of conceptualising an Indian Ocean World shines brightly, there are several dangers yet inherent in the project. One such is that, while looking across borders to study mobile populations, older emigration/immigration models derived from area studies will be reapplied within the new framework of a new area, the Indian Ocean World.[62] It is insufficient to study populations that move across borders and settle without analysing those who return, or those who dwell temporarily, or those who continue to move, in real or imagi-

---

writes, "[S]pirit possession continues to articulate the changing sociocultural universe of the Swahili coast. Spirits are representative of Swahili conceptions of outside groups which have impinged upon Swahili experience throughout their history.... In this way Swahili society constructs the image of the other, but in a dialectical process also constructs the image of the self through opposition" (Giles 1995: 101). A University of Iowa research team conducted interviews with and concerning African, Arab and Indian spirits in Zanzibar in 1997, and spirits in Dar es Salaam will come into my dissertation as well.

[61] Examples of this kind of work are Gregory (1993) and Mangat (1969). Better on this count are the careful local studies of Richa Nagar, as seen in her Ph.D. dissertation (Nagar 1995).

[62] One can see this trouble emerging in some of the expanding studies of Sidis.

nary terms.[63] However, establishing multi-sited fieldwork projects is a methodologically demanding task, especially if instead of two points—traditionally, a 'homeland' and a 'hostland'—a multiplicity of places emerge as crucial to the lives of different Indian Ocean World travellers.[64] Then, the researcher must understand the diverse flows of people, ideas and things much like the wandering narrator did in Amitav Ghosh's gripping ethno-historic novel *In An Antique Land*[65] (1992). Nonetheless, while detailing such transnational movements, one must be very cautious about assuming the ease of border-crossing in a historically globalising world; while borders are illusory in many senses—as the title of Ghosh's undercited *The Shadow Lines* indicates—they can in the name of nationalism also be the source of terrifying violence, forced migrations and barriers to comings and goings, as the text of that novel vividly illustrates (Ghosh 1988). Furthermore, gendered differences in 'border crossing' possibilities produce the academic pitfall of leaving women out while constructing a masculine Indian Ocean World. More groups of women (like the young Indians who exert their limited agency to perform and make a living in overseas mujra clubs) need to be included in this research project, alongside an acknowledgement of the gendered consequences of privileging transnational travellers.

Another caution worries that some notions of an Indian Ocean World—using a body of water as a connection point—foregrounds coastal communities and oceanic linkages over inland ones. It is, for example, as important to see not only the Baluchis' moves from Baluchistan to Muscat to Zanzibar and

[63] For instance, most obviously, this would enrich the study of indentured labourers.

[64] This problem exists in several Indian Ocean projects linking East Africa and India, including my own, which tend to elide the role of the Middle East as an important transit point for people and goods moving between the two continents. Two young scholars who are attempting ambitious multi-sited research projects between East Africa and the Arabian Peninsula are Matthew Hopper, UCLA, and Thomas "Dodie" McDow, Yale University.

[65] Notably, James Clifford (1997) has stressed new types of "fieldwork" along these lines.

the East African mainland coast, but also to view their travels and settlements along caravan routes to the Congo and into villages in the southern highlands of Tanzania. Moreover, in constructing an Indian Ocean World, a related danger lies in reproducing problems inherent in area studies through the process of examining linkages within newer, albeit more accurate, boundaries. When this 'world's' boundaries do not confine East African Indians' relocations to Canada or the United Kingdom, or the ability of Chinese immigrants to establish a Chinatown in Calcutta, one wonders how the study of the Indian Ocean World will successfully analyse its relationship vis-à-vis the 'West,' or with East Asia. A possible solution lies in not only the idea of overlapping geographical worlds, but also in the necessity of understanding that real and imaginary conceptions of the Indian Ocean World intersect and overlap.[66]

As a practical methodological intervention, western academics, who often are not adequately equipped with multiple languages and understandings of the histories and cultures of multiple places, should engage in more long-term, interdisciplinary, collaborative, and mobile fieldwork projects. Several of these have been conducted,[67] but I would suggest that they have failed to be as effective as they could be due to the short-term nature of their visits. Additionally, western academics cannot overlook the rich possibilities of forming partnerships with researchers based in and originally from the Indian Ocean World. Not only does that add 'local' expertise to the study, but even more importantly, it expands academic thinking about the Indian Ocean World: the fact is often ignored that those who have lived and studied in the Indian Ocean World have imagined and analysed it far before the most recent surge of interest in the western academy. Thus, not surprisingly, there are several African Studies Centres in India which are, on average, far older than similar area studies programmes in the

[66] See Edward Alpers (2002) and Allen Roberts (2002). This approach helps us get around the tendency to search out a "centre" for a project: the contradictions inherent in defining an Indian Ocean World help us to overcome struggles over a "centre."

[67] Including several by faculty and students from the University of Iowa.

United States.[68] Moreover, they have long concerned themselves with the study of relations across the Indian Ocean. To not avail of the knowledge and talents of faculty at such established programmes in India and elsewhere will inevitably diminish the chances of western universities to successfully come to terms with understanding the Indian Ocean World.

Finally, as a practical theoretical intervention, I would stress the utility of invoking new, moving models to understand the histories of Indian Ocean World travellers such as those of the sailors, smugglers, soldiers, students and others sketched above. For example:

- The centrality of imaginations of place cannot be overlooked, as seen in the 'India' constructed by the Indians of Dar es Salaam who avidly watch Hindi films by day, and at night stare at mujra girls dancing to the films' tunes (Appadurai 1996). It is also worth noting that gender relations in the Indian diaspora are often structured through the positioning of women as carriers of 'culture.'[69]
- Notions of circuits of exchange are crucial to understanding the region, as exemplified in the fact that a large amount of the national women's dress of East Africa—*kangas*—have historically been produced and designed in India. Collaborative networks function between industrialists (who manufacture the kanga on the same equipment with which they churn out saris), distributors/traders and women from East Africa who suggest patterns and help supply the punchy proverbs that line the garment.[70]

[68] There are outstanding African Studies Centres at Delhi University, University of Mumbai, and Jawaharlal Nehru University in New Delhi, the first of which produces a quarterly journal. There also is a Society of Indian Ocean Studies in New Delhi that publishes the *Journal of Indian Ocean Studies*, and a Centre for Area Studies (Indian Ocean) at Osmania University in Hyderabad.

[69] For a similar phenomenon in India, see Chatterjee (1993).

[70] As part of my dissertation fieldwork, I conducted interviews in Tanzania with the producers and consumers of kangas, with Indian textile company owners and distributors in Bombay, and I also visited a kanga factory in Gujarat. Amazingly, almost all of the kangas that are produced in India come from the rather small town of Jetpur, between Rajkot and Junagadh in the Saurashtra region of Gujarat.

- Grappling with perceiving transnational fields of power, including how formerly 'localised' concepts of colonialism and nationalism overlap and create international linkages, will further assist in understanding the various flows of people, products and ideas throughout the Indian Ocean World. An example rests in the development of notions of a 'Greater India' across the Indian Ocean, and the role it plays in anti-colonial movements in South Asia and Africa.[71]
- Invoking models of active webs between diverse people in disparate places, and their concomitant identities, as Vassanji wrote, stretched "between lives as contrary as the ends of a cross," aids in the conceptualisation of multi-sited, mobile fieldwork. This can be used to analyse, for example, the layers of experience discussed above, such as those of the sailors of the Tanzania Seamen's Union, or the Gujarati families that strategically scatter between Arabia, Africa and India, each of whom tread paths and establish multiple 'homes' throughout the spread of the Indian Ocean World.
- Similarly, while using Appadurai's theory of 'process geographies' to fuse an Indian Ocean World from the parts of a dismantled area studies organisation, we need to further strive to establish 'process historiographies'[72] to understand how this Indian Ocean has evolved and changed over time and linked its residents in various types of cosmopolitan connections.

Only by applying such new, flexible theoretical and methodological innovations will we be able to do adequate academic justice to the complex lives of people like *The Shadow Lines*' narrator's grandmother, for whom the distinction between 'comings and goings' inextricably blurs.[73] Or to our renderings of

[71] See James R. Brennan's work, for example (1999).

[72] Thanks to Paul Greenough for the phrase. On "process geographies", see Appadurai (2000b).

[73] This poignant moment occurs when the grandmother considers going (or coming?) "home" as a foreign (Indian) citizen to Dhaka, reinvented as the capital of

the mobile lives, in reality and imagination, of many other historical and contemporary Indian Ocean World travellers, be they sailors, smugglers, students, soldiers, slaves, indentured labourers, dancing bar girls, colonial officials, anti-colonial activists, post-colonial diplomats, traders, spirits or, above all, the everyday local-yet-trans-local woman and man.

East Pakistan, years after Partition forced her to flee the town of her birth. (Ghosh 1988: 152–3).

2

*The Dhow Culture of the Western Indian Ocean**

Abdul Sheriff

Introduction: The Sea is not the End of the World

Water covers more than two-thirds of the earth's surface, and more than half the world's population lives within 80 kilometres of the sea. Yet, most histories are peculiarly continental, introverted and landlocked in their orientation. To many, the oceans are merely voids that separate the continents, and they are looked at with awe and apprehension. Human development is interpreted as a result of interaction between people and their environment—but that environment is often very narrowly interpreted in terms of land. Human societies are categorised as hunters and gatherers, pastoralists and farmers, often forgetting fish trappers and beachcombers, sea nomads and fishermen, who also rationally exploit their marine environment. In short, we often ignore people's intimate connection with the sea. But for coastal people, such as the Swahili of the East African coast, the maritime Arabs of southern Arabia and the Persian Gulf, or coastal people of India and the Indonesian archipelago, the sea is not the end of the world. It is the beginning of a whole new world of subsistence, resources and opportunities.

The sea permeates all aspects of their lives. A large number are engaged in fishing, sailing, or derive their income from

* The paper is based on a presentation at the Wissenschaftskolleg zu Berlin on 3 June 2003. I would like to thank the institute for the fellowship that enabled me to reflect upon and write on this subject.

maritime activities, such as mangrove cutting and dhow building. They spend their leisure hours near the waterfront. Children play with toy boats, and their parents may build dhows or models for tourists. When Prins asked school children in Lamu, Kenya, to draw whatever came into their heads, the vast majority drew maritime scenes. Many of the myths of the coastal peoples are centred on the sea, including their maritime patron saints (Prins 1965: 5). Nautical similes are abundant in their language and poetry—even the BBC Swahili Service closes its daily programme by "dropping the anchor."

These littoral people are strategically located at the confluence between the continental and maritime environments, able to exploit both economically to diversify and maximise their productivity, and be fashioned by them socially and culturally—thus the dual nature of these maritime societies. Pearson argues that littoral societies can best be understood in terms of a continuum between land and sea that are intertwined in complex and various ways. It is therefore a distortion to see them as either purely land-based or totally maritime (Pearson 1985). For thousands of years they have been exploiting not only the land for its foods and fruits, but also maritime resources to obtain their livelihood and shelter—fish and molluscs from the bountiful sea; mangrove poles from the abundant tropical swamps; and coral stones used in the construction of their durable habitations.

The sea, moreover, is a medium of transport, exchange and intercourse. It provides opportunities for communication, uniting people socially and culturally. With the development of appropriate technology and harnessing of the wind system, they could establish links with other communities across the ocean. They could thus share in the diversity of the world to obtain new plants and animals, and create larger social and cultural unities centred on the ocean. As Braudel has emphasised, it is not the sea as such, but the movement of people, the routes they follow, and the relationships they forge that create unities in human history (Braudel 1972, 1). Much as in the Mediterranean world, all around the Indian Ocean a melange of peoples and cultures has developed. Whatever colour one may use to paint the different continents surrounding it, only a multicoloured ribbon can begin to explain the complex societies of the littoral around its rim that have developed as a result of millennia of trans-oceanic interactions. It refers not merely to the rainbow colours of its mixed populations, but more importantly, their cosmopolitan cultures. As Anirudha Gupta has put it, "where boats ply, commerce generally follows." In the Indian Ocean before the coming of the Europeans, and in some cases long afterwards, "cooperation, not conquest was at the root of maritime prosperity of the coast" (Gupta 1991: ix, xii–xiii). Seafaring commerce is built upon exchanges between peoples of different ecologies and cultures, and calls for a continuous expansion of inter-community relations between the "native" and the "foreigner". It has given rise to a distinctive "maritime culture" (Prins 1965: 263–75). As the primary vehicle for the historical emergence of Indian Ocean maritime culture has been the Indian Ocean sailing ship (dhow), this paper explores (a) the routes taken by dhows, (b) historical transformations in the use of dhows, and (c) those who travelled by dhows.

The Indian Ocean Connected By Dhows

The Indian Ocean is larger than the Mediterranean Sea but still a very compact expanse of water, covering one-fifth of the world's total sea surface. Unlike the Atlantic or the Pacific Oceans, it is enclosed, by Africa to the west, the Asian landmass to the north, and a chain of islands and peninsulas of South-East Asia and Australia to the east, with India forming its fulcrum and giving it its name. It is surrounded by the most populous continents and civilisations, and its rim is today inhabited by one-third of the world's population.

The overall long coastline, the deep gulfs of the Red Sea and the Persian Gulf that penetrate into the Afro-Asian heartland, the broad bays of the Arabian Sea and the Bay of Bengal, and the intricate network of islands and peninsulas along the rim of the Indian Ocean, provides a comfortable maritime environment. The ocean has historically facilitated communication between various communities around its rim. It has therefore enjoyed a considerable degree of economic, social and cultural cohesion over hundreds of years. As Mollat has put it:

> A zone of encounters and contacts, crossed in all directions by the axes of circulation, center for all types of exchanges and sensitive to the most diverse and distant influences, the Indian Ocean, more than many other oceans and seas, is a privileged crossroads of culture (Mollat 1980: 2).

If there is one natural phenomenon that defines an essential feature of the Indian Ocean, it is the monsoons.[1] They played a crucial role in the economy and life of the people around its rim, integrating them into a vast maritime cultural complex. The monsoon winds defined the climate not only in the provision of the vital rainwater for agricultural production around the basin, but also in supplying the motive power for communication over the broad ocean to redistribute the products, agricultural or otherwise, and its people.

In the western Indian Ocean, dhows used the northerly monsoon from November to February to sail to the East African coast or the west coast of India, and returned to the north with the southerly monsoon from April to August, though there was a break in June and July when the seas are too rough for the dhows and many ports were closed altogether. What is important for the social as well as economic history of the Indian Ocean is that the monsoon system imposed a regime that not only facilitated regular seasonal movement across the ocean, but also restricted it in one sense, requiring dhows to spend a long time between the monsoons in their ports of destination. This provided a great potential for social interaction between visiting sailors and the local people.

[1] The latitudinal bands of land and sea, the alternate cooling and heating of the vast Asian landmass in winter and summer, and its juxtaposition with an equally vast warm ocean to the south of it, give rise to a regular seasonal reversal of the winds over the Indian Ocean basin, known by almost identical names from the Swahili coast all the way to Malaysia. In many parts around the basin, the rhythm of economic life is set by the recurrent annual cycle of the monsoons.

The climatic system also created quite varied and complementary environments around the Indian Ocean basin that stimulated communication between them. With Kirk three complementary zones may be identified, each with its own potentialities and external land and sea contacts (Kirk 1962: 265):

1. The Tropical Forest-and-Sea Region of eastern Africa produces some valuable timber, including the termite-resistant mangrove poles that have been used for more than a thousand years in construction of multi-storied stone houses, and as fuel. However, the narrow continental shelf off the East African coast is not as rich in fisheries, and the Swahili coast has therefore provided a ready market for dried fish brought in by the monsoon traders from the north.

2. The Desert-and-Sea Region of the Middle East, with the Red Sea and the Persian Gulf penetrating deep into the Middle East, has a long frontage on the sea, providing a natural environment for the development of a maritime economy and culture. Moreover, the up-welling of cold waters off the south Arabian coast makes it one of the most productive fishing grounds in the world. Fish was used not only for subsistence, as fertilisers and cattle-feed, but was also dried and salted for export on a large scale. Nevertheless, the region is deficient in timber, and is marginal in food production, both of which had to be imported from the neighbouring forest regions. It has also been unable to sustain its population, and its history has been marked by a constant outflow of its surplus population to eastern Africa, India and South-East Asia.

3. The Tropical Forest-and-Sea Region of the west coast of India contains valuable timber, especially sandalwood, mahogany and teak, which have been exported for several millennia to build dhows and houses in the desert region. It also provided suitable conditions for the production of spices for which the Malabar Coast has been famous. Moreover, the west coast of India, especially Gujarat, has also been a major manufacturing region, producing textiles for export from very early times. Thus environmental contrast between the three zones, and especially that between the two tropical forest regions and

the intervening desert region, created an enormous potential for lively trade between them.

Trade was the raison d'etre of communication in the western Indian Ocean, but it was not merely an economic activity. As Polanyi has argued, the economy is embedded in the society (Polanyi, Arensberg and H. Pearson 1957). The commodities exchanged had considerable social and cultural as well as economic significance for the societies between which they were being exchanged. Dates, for example, were a mundane item of subsistence for the Arabs of the desert, but they have assumed a social and even spiritual importance that has been carried to all the Muslim communities around the Indian Ocean and beyond. To have to break the fast during the month of Ramadan in tropical forest regions of Zanzibar or Indonesia without dates would be considered a serious deprivation, and may even destabilise a government.

A characteristic of the dhow trade was that it was typically a peddler trade.[2] Dhows had to wait for the change of the monsoons at one of the Swahili or Indian ports, multiplying possibilities of social interaction between the monsoon visitors and the local populations. Trade, moreover, was bound to exercise considerable influence on the architecture and social tastes of the communities involved in the exchange. One of the main items of export on these dhows from East Africa and the west coast of India was timber, and mangrove poles were the cheapest and strongest wood for house construction. Since mangrove poles are normally only three to four metres long, they determined the width of the rooms and thus the architecture of many medieval towns in the Persian Gulf as well as along the Swahili coast.[3] Apart from these articles of mass consump-

[2] The great Dutch historian van Leur had thus dismissed it as archaic. Trade routes, he said, ran from port to port, exchanging luxuries and raw materials rather than items of mass consumption, and involving a large number of traders (Leur 1955). Some historians have undertaken an economic refutation of this conception of "oriental trade", but what is also serious is the total lack of understanding of the social context and consequences of this type of trading.

[3] The dhow in which Villiers sailed from the Swahili coast to the Persian Gulf in 1938–9 still picked up 600 poles which were sold at Bahrain to an agent of King Saud of Arabia who was then building a palace in Riyadh (Villiers 1940: 320).

tion, sailors and private merchants on the dhows also carried a great variety of commodities for which they could find a market: colourful *sarongs* (loin cloth) from Indonesia which have become part of the dress of people all around the Indian Ocean; small straw fans from Mukalla for hot and humid Mombasa and Zanzibar; and Indian cloth ("harem veils") that were popular with Somali women (Villiers 1940: 146–48).

Villiers has noted considerable historical continuities between the list of goods imported into the northern Somali ports in the first century AD (as recorded in the *Periplus of the Erythraean Sea,* a Greek commercial guide), such as wheat, rice, *ghee,* cotton cloth and sugar, and those brought by the dhow in which he sailed in 1938 (Casson 1989: 61; Villiers 1940: 98). Rather than proving an unchanging East this shows the *longue duree* character of trade across the Indian Ocean. And yet, several valuable items that had been traded in the past were absent in more recent accounts. This is particularly valid for slaves. In the eighth and ninth centuries, and again in the eighteenth and nineteenth, slaves had formed part of the outward cargo of dhows from East Africa, but the Zanj revolt in southern Iraq in the ninth century, and the abolition of the slave trade during the nineteenth put an end to this trade. Medieval Arab writers were also voluble about gold that used to come from Zimbabwe via Sofala and Kilwa; and in the tenth century the Arab traveller Masudi talked at length about ivory which was transported from East Africa via Oman to India and China, a trade that continued into the nineteenth century (Freeman-Grenville 1962: 1, 15). Competition in the nineteenth century from American and European sail ships, and later steamships, deprived dhows of most of the valuable cargoes, such as ivory and cloves. By the late 1950s, steamships were encroaching even into the mangrove trade. By then dhows were carrying only a tenth of the total trade of Zanzibar.[4]

While the volume of trade in the Indian Ocean was undoubtedly augmented by the entry of Europeans into the Indian Ocean, and its commodity structure was transformed by the

[4] Zanzibar National Archives (hereafter ZNA): AK 4–35; BA 36–1–25.

Industrial Revolution to supply its demand for raw materials and take away its manufactured goods, the total number of dhows sailing in the western Indian Ocean did not necessarily diminish. While we do not have very accurate statistics for the nineteenth century, before the threat of steamships or even European sail-ships had begun to erode its comparative advantage, there were said to be about 85 larger Arab dhows ranging from 30 to 160 tons and 150 smaller *bedens* (Omani small dhows) of between 15 and 25 tons arriving at Zanzibar annually. By 1856 the total from Arabia and India was said to have risen to 300 (Nicholls 1971: 352). The numbers do not appear to have declined despite the imposition of colonial rule and the introduction of steamships. According to Martin's research, an average of 200 foreign dhows came into Mombasa annually between 1907 and 1915, while the average between the two world wars, dominated by the Great Depression, was 166 per annum. During the 1907–8 season a total of 345 dhows arrived at Mombasa, the largest number that was not surpassed until 1945 (Martin and Martin 1978: 44). A similar number of dhows entered Zanzibar in 1945 despite the threat of Japanese and German submarines which had sunk several dhows during the Second World War.

Dhow traffic has also remained important along the west coast of India. In the middle of the nineteenth century, an average of more than 800 dhows entered the port of Bombay. However, according to Martin, the numbers had declined to an average of only 168 foreign dhows between 1900s and the 1930s (E. B. Martin 1982: 105). This is perhaps not surprising since Bombay is a major modern port where competition from steamships would have been most intense. Moreover, these figures may be referring only to foreign vessels and excluded Indian sea-going dhows as well as the large number of coastal dhows. It was estimated in the 1940s that about 500 dhows were employed along the west coast of India ranging from ten to above a hundred tons. Vaidya, a well-informed dhow agent in Bombay, estimated that 90 per cent of these dhows were able to sail out to sea, including what he describes as the Arabian-type ships (*baghalas, sambuk, bum* and *ghanja* of 100–150 tons but some of 250 to 500 tons) and the Cutch-Kathiawar and Sindh types (*kotia, ghanja,* and *dhangi* of 50–100 and even up to 200 tons) which sailed westwards to the Persian Gulf and even as far as the East African coast. During the Second World War, dhows were able to take some advantage of the dangers of submarine warfare directed primarily against the larger steamships. Vaidya argued at length about the advantages of dhows for the national economy of India, including the fact that it carried 40 per cent of the total cargo and gave employment to 4000 sailors as well as others in shipbuilding and related subsidiary industries. This is one reason why the Indian government still encourages the use of dhows which moreover also conserve on the consumption of oil (Vaidya 1945: 3, 6).

Although the dhow trade had already declined considerably by the mid twentieth century, there were still more than 300

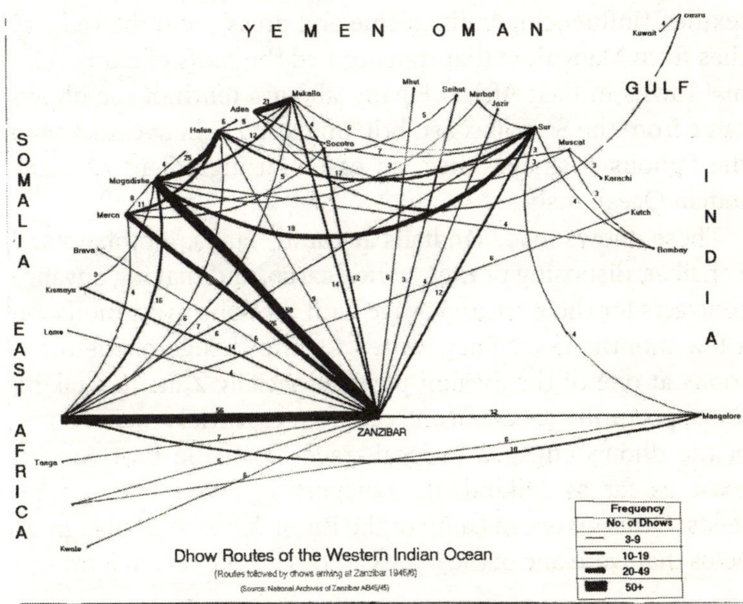

Map 3: Routes followed by dhows arriving at Zanzibar. ZNA, AB 45/45.

monsoon dhows that entered Zanzibar in 1945–6. Tracing the origin and routes of these ancient crafts on a map describes a dense web of intercommunication over the western Indian Ocean, with substantial ramifications on the societies and cultures of the region. Of these, less than a fifth sailed directly from their port of origin to their destination. The rest made more than 400 landfalls at intermediate ports along the coasts of south Arabia, Somalia and East Africa before arriving finally at Zanzibar, and some went beyond to Mozambique, the Comoro islands and Madagascar.

The largest number, more than two-fifths, came from Oman, and especially from the famous dhow port of Sur. Many of them first sailed to Basra at the head of the Gulf to pick up cargoes of dates, sometimes returning to their home ports to collect dried fish and salt. They then sailed to India or Aden to unload part of their cargoes and take on other commodities for the Swahili coast. About an eighth of the dhows originated from the Indian subcontinent, bringing foodstuffs, spices and textiles (influencing both cuisine and dress), and the red clay tiles from Mangalore that transformed the roofs of many colonial towns in East Africa. Finally, about a tenth of the dhows came from the Somali coast, bringing dried fish, livestock, and the famous Kismayu ghee, an essential ingredient of many Indian Ocean dishes.

These dhows made landfalls at Lamu, Tanga, Mombasa and Zanzibar, disposing of their varied cargo, and making advance contracts for their return voyage with the southwest monsoon a few months later. They waited for the change of the monsoons at one of the Swahili ports, especially Zanzibar, taking the opportunity to careen and carry out essential repairs. Some of the dhows engaged in local trade along the East African coast as far as Mikindani, transporting millet and sesame seeds. Others went to Lamu or the Rufiji delta to cut mangrove poles that were one of the main cargoes for the return journey.[5]

[5] As Villiers put it, "the dimensions of many an Arab room are fixed on the beach at Lamu" (Villiers 1940: 164).

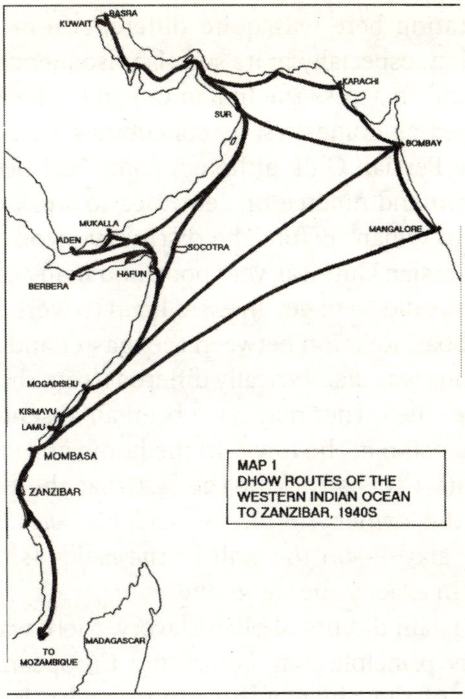

Map 4: Dhow routes of the western Indian Ocean to Zanzibar (1940s).

The Fallout from Slave Trade

Slaves had been a commodity in the dhow trade until the nineteenth century. However, there was plenty of evidence of the fallout of the past slave trade in the dhows of the Indian Ocean into the twentieth century. A high proportion of Kuwaiti and Suri sailors were of African origin, and on the dhow on which Villiers sailed, the captain's mate and the *muadhin* (caller to prayers) were of slave origin too. Racial intermingling and integration had reached quite high levels in the society that seemed to surprise Villiers. Many of the captains were very dark, and at a feast in Kuwait many guests were "almost pure Negro", but Villiers was assured that they were all Arab (Villiers 1940: 360).

The contrasting attitude to slavery and race by Villiers and his Arab hosts can be explained by the fact that the system of slavery operating here was quite different from that in the Atlantic region, especially in its social consequences. A majority of slaves taken across the Indian Ocean to the Middle East were absorbed as domestics, as concubines, or as divers for pearls in the Persian Gulf, although some had been taken in the eighteenth and nineteenth centuries to work on the date plantations in Oman. Before the discovery of oil, the society around the Persian Gulf was very poor, and many of those who acquired slaves did so to get an extra hand to work with on the farm or the boat. Relation between the master and the slave in such situations was diametrically different from those on plantations where the owner may have been an absentee landlord living in a mansion in the town. In the home of a former dhow captain in Sur, I was struck by the fact that the three photographs—of the owner, his dhow, and his *khadim* (servant, freedman or slave)—on the wall in the *majlis* (sitting room) were placed in exactly the same line.

Although Islam did not abolish slavery, there was a built-in emancipatory principle long before the European emancipation decrees of the nineteenth century, and a large class of freedmen was a normal feature in Islamic societies. There are nineteen references to slaves in the Qur'an, and more than half of them enjoin Muslims to free their slaves for various spiritual rewards. Secondly, Islam recognised and regulated the prevalent intercourse between masters and their female slaves as a legal institution with two important consequences. A slave wife or "concubine" who bore her master a child could not thereafter be sold, and automatically became free on the death of her master. Secondly, children born of such unions were fully legitimate and free, with equal status and inheritance rights to those born of free mothers. Thus, all the children of the Sultan of Zanzibar in the nineteenth century had slave mothers, and in due course many of them became sultans. Islam thus provided a window of upward social mobility, what Ali Mazrui has termed "ascending miscegenation" where both the mother and her children became free, in contrast to American slavery where such unions were equally widespread without changing the social status of either the slave woman or her offspring, who all became "black" and slave (Mazrui 1997).

The system had a significant influence on social integration in Muslim societies. Throughout the nineteenth century there are indications of substantial populations of African origin all around the Persian Gulf of whom at least a third were free long before the British-inspired emancipations in the twentieth century. It was reported in 1831 that about a third of the slaves from Mombasa "or their descendants", who were pearl divers or fishermen, were free and received a share of the pearls they fished.[6] A survey of the Persian Gulf region by Lorimer at the beginning of the twentieth century gives a very interesting portrait of an Indian Ocean ethnic melting pot. He makes a distinction between free(d) Africans and slaves living separately from their masters for whom he gives statistics, and those slaves living with their masters who he says cannot be distinguished from the clans of their masters. Thus, in a population of about 60,000 on Bahrain Island, he found 5,000 free Africans, 6,000 slaves and an uncertain number living with their masters. In some cases the slave was married to a free woman with whom his master had no concern; but in others the master provided the slave with a slave wife. In Kuwait, there were 4,000 Africans in a population of 35,000 of whom one-third were *ma'tuq* (emancipated), while two-thirds were *mamluk* (slaves). In Qatar there were 2,000 free Africans and 4,000 slaves out of a population of 27,000, not counting those living with their owners. Many of them depended almost entirely on pearl diving in the Persian Gulf. On the so-called Trucial Coast in what is now the United Arab Emirates, African slaves were said to be "exceptionally numerous in the coast towns." At Sharjah there was "a large negro community", many of whom still spoke Swahili. At Ras al-Khaima, the population was described as "a mongrel race" known as *Ahl Ras al-Khaima* (people of Ras al-Khaima). On the Persian coast a similar "hybrid race" is described at Bandar Abbas which included a mixture of Iranians, Baluchis, Arabs as well as Africans, collec-

[6] Wilson to Norris, 28.1.1831, Maharashtra State Archives, Mumbai, vol. 1/1830–31.

tively called Abbasis, and the lower classes spoke a local dialect or pidgin which was a compound of Persian, Baluchi, Arabic and Swahili ingredients. With the suppression of the slave trade, the proportion was constantly shifting in the direction of the free. By the beginning of the twentieth century the proportion between the two sections at Manama, the Bahraini capital, had reversed and the African population did no longer remain a separate entity.[7]

Dhow Captains and Passengers

The movement of people had a long-lasting impact on the social and cultural history of the Indian Ocean region. Its ports were places of lively interactions between people from all over the Indian Ocean rim. In a description that could have been repeated almost verbatim for many other Indian Ocean ports, Villiers says of Mukalla on the Hadhrami coast:

> the streets of Mukalla teemed with strange human beings dressed in all the colourful costumes of the East—Banyan merchants in their flappy diaphanous trousers and little black hats, Yemenites in sarongs and turbans, Beduins in black and indigo,. . .Persian, Somali, Kuwaiti, Suri, Batini sailors and nakhodas, wandering half-castes with blood from all the East in them, half-Malays, half-Turks, half-African, half-Egyptians, half-Baluchi, half-Balinese. The Hadhrami wanders far and takes his women where he finds them, bringing back the male offspring to his native land, and the blood of the whole East pulses in those busy Mukalla streets (Villiers 1940: 61).

Even the Sultan of Mukalla seemed to Villiers more Indian than Arab, and the *na'ib* or ruler of Shihr chewed betel nuts and leaves very much as Indians or some Swahili do (Villiers 1940: 63, 69).

The dhow traffic involved a very large floating population. Several categories of people moved in these dhows across the ocean, some more often than others, as the captains *(nakhodas)* of the dhows and their crews as well as merchant passengers.

[7] Lorimer 1908–15: 7, 10, 26, 241, 276, 343–34, 667, 750, 1008, 1051–53, 1098, 1160–61, 1226, 1436–37, 1531–32, 1762, 1782.

Dhows were commanded and manned by people who, through a long experience of life over the common sea, had developed a sense of community not only among themselves but also with the various maritime communities they visited on their annual voyages. The crew of a dhow belonged to different sects of Islam, and many were of slave origin, but such distinctions seemed to be of little importance at sea. People consumed the same type of food and the same quantities of it (Villiers 1940: 56, 177, 185). When in 1938 Villiers sailed in a dhow from Aden to Zanzibar and then back to Kuwait, he was was impressed by what he called "brotherhood of the sea."

> The friendship of these nakhodas from the same home port was a very real thing and they formed a united band. They were prepared at any time to assist another's vessel in any circumstance, to perform risky feats of salvage without payment, to lend one another a carpenter, a dozen seamen, a cook, or a bale of carpets, or anything else that might be needed. In case of distress, they were prepared to carry another crew for thousands of miles. They carried one another's junior officers, sent here and there to collect long-due debts: and for none of these things did they accept payment.... Theirs was a real brotherhood of the sea (Villiers 1940: 301).

At all the ports they entertained each other. At Shihr on the south Arabian coast, the nakhoda of Villiers' dhow gave a feast to which every other nakhoda in port, all the port officials, all the passenger agents and half their clients, a group of Suri and Mahra people, a Yemeni Sayyid (descendant of the Prophet) and several merchants were invited, and carpets and musicians were borrowed from other dhows in the harbour.

Dhows tended to carry a very large number of crew members in relation to their tonnage. In 1945–6, more than 300 foreign dhows put in at Zanzibar which carried more than 6,000 sailors. Economic historians may consider this number uneconomic, but what is important for the history of the Indian Ocean is the social impact of this substantial movement of people to and fro, year in and year out.[8] The dhow sailors were

[8] For the sake of comparison, many large steamers, each with a tonnage of several tens of dhows, put into East African ports these days with small crews of Kore-

no mere flotsam, especially in view of the fact that the monsoon system imposed on them a long period of stay in East Africa or India until the winds changed to enable them to return to their home countries. Racial intermingling and integration reached quite high levels in these maritime communities. Since women formed only a tiny monority of dhow travellers, many of the Arab men married local women, giving rise to a rainbow population and a very cosmopolitan culture.[9] The absence of women on the sea thus had important implications for social and cultural as well as racial integration in the western Indian Ocean (Villiers 1940: 142, 207, 301, 360).[10]

After the long voyage, sailors on Villiers' dhow often talked of *bebes* (ladies) and *bints* (girls) for which Lamu and Zanzibar had been historically famous. As a result of polygamy, Arab and other Muslim captains and sailors had established liaisons with local women and a "plurality of domiciles" at many of the places they regularly visited. Sindbad seemed to have found a wife in nearly every port, and Ibn Battuta married at almost every landfall in the Indian Ocean (Severin 1982: 130; Battuta 1994: 820, 823–24, 836). Thus family bonds were forged that stretched across the ocean. Evidence from the beginning of the twentieth century shows many nakhodas establishing second and third homes along the Somali and Swahili coasts, in the Comoro islands and northern Madagascar. Thirty proprietors from the pre-eminent Omani dhow port of Sur were operating along the eastern seaboard of Africa where they claimed residence and had families in the French colonies from Djibouti to

---

ans, Taiwanese or Greeks, and they spend a couple of days on shore while the cargo is being unloaded by cranes. They may scatter a few wild oats, but their social impact on the local people, or of the local people on them, is minimal.

[9] Arab women were always scarce overseas. Thus, even in 1945 women formed only 1 per cent of the 2,654 passengers who landed at Mombasa (Martin and Martin 1978: 48–50, 70).

[10] Such cultural interaction and miscegenation has been going on at least since the first century A.D. As the *Periplus* noted: "The merchants of Muza [on the south Arabian coast] send out to [the East African coast] merchant craft that they staff mostly with Arab skippers and agents who, through continual intercourse and intermarriage, are familiar with the area and its language" (Casson 1989: 61).

Madagascar.[11] At least a quarter of the population of Sur (about 10,000) had such trans-oceanic connections.[12]

Suris were trading and settling not only in the French colonies but in the British and German colonies in East Africa as well. They saw no contradiction in being citizens of convenience of several European colonial states at the same time in their undivided world of the Indian Ocean. One nakhoda from Sur, for example, had one son by a woman from Pemba, another by a Comorian, and a daughter by a *suria* (secondary slave wife) from the African interior. Another captain had been trading between Arabia and East Africa. He had established one home in Mombasa where one son was born and settled, and another at Lamu where another son was born by a Swahili woman. The latter in turn married a Lamu woman, and from his inheritance he bought a dhow, two houses and a piece of land on the island. These Suris were not merely trading to far-flung ports of the Indian Ocean. Some who had prospered in East Africa preferred to retire to their ports of origin, but others were also acquiring immovable properties at their ports of call, intermarrying, and giving birth to children of the Indian Ocean. Europeans, bound by ideas of monogamy and the nation state, were thoroughly bewildered by the sailors of the Indian Ocean who appeared to them to "divide their favours, connubial and commercial, between their ports of origin and their ports of adoption."[13]

I conducted interviews at the dhow port of Sur in 1997 which confirmed that this pattern of social interaction persisted into the late twentieth century, leaving a rich residue of social and cultural relations several decades after the dhow trade itself had almost come to an end. The composition of my host family was probably typical. The old captain had an Arab

[11] They owned a total of 56 dhows between them with a crew of 160. They also owned the right to use the French tricolour.

[12] Case on behalf of His Majesty's Government, India Office Library and Records, London (hereafter IOR), R/15/1/406.

[13] British Consul, Muscat to Resident, Persian Gulf, 26.6.1912 & 8.8.1912, IOR, R/15/1/426. By trying to box them into neat nationalities, the British were trying to impose their conceptions in place of the global unity of the Indian Ocean world.

wife in Sur, another in Zanzibar, and the third was an African in the interior of Tanzania. I often witnessed such "rainbow families" with all shades of brown and black. No social distinctions seemed to divide them internally. Many people of Sur were children of Suri fathers who had married slave or free African women. The children of such unions had equal rights of inheritance regardless of the complexion or social status of the mother. Others were more obviously of slave origin. Today, they are all Arabic-speaking and have adopted the local surnames of Arab "tribes". As Saleh b. Yusuf, my host, said, four generations of his family were born in Sur, but the fifth was from Africa. "All the people here were from Africa", he said with some exaggeration. "After two or three generations they were considered Omani; even half the government was African. The mother was African and the father was Omani. But all are Arab."

In almost every case, sailors from Sur had gone to sea in their mid-teens as *walad* (lads) working as apprentices, or as nakhodas in their early twenties. Many knew at least a little bit of Kiswahili, but this was entirely because of trade connections with the East African coast long after the abolition of the slave trade. Almost all of them retain a very nostalgic image of Zanzibar as "the island of dreams" (Jarwan 1985: 201).[14] They remember it as a peaceful place where one could sleep anywhere in safety, and where food was cheap. Some of them still like to visit East Africa, although they no longer sail but fly in these days.[15]

The ninety-year old Jum'a b. Khamis, belonging to the Bani Bu Ali tribe of Aijeh across the creek from Sur, was a nakhoda as his father had been. He said they were like fish, spending nearly ten months of the year at sea. He had spent seven years at Zanzibar where his uncle had a house, and he had almost

[14] Zanzibar was the terminus of the monsoon dhows before the Zanzibar Revolution of 1964.

[15] One of the most knowledgeable nakhodas in Sur, Said b. Hamed, came to East Africa in 1987. It is significant that he spent two weeks each in the old dhow ports of Zanzibar and Mombasa, and only four days in the new colonial port of Dar es Salaam, and only because one of the old dhow agents then lived there.

forgotten Arabic when he returned. He was referred to by his nephew by the Swahili honorific title *mzee* (gentleman or old man). He himself told me with a twinkle in his ancient eyes that he had learnt all his Kiswahili from the women of Zanzibar, and was very proud of the fact that he could identify dialectical variations in Kiswahili. His brother Subeit b. Khamis, who still builds dhows and is a famous drummer playing the *msondo* drum of Swahili origin, still remembers fondly a Swahili lady who used to sell local foods in the Funguni quarter of Zanzibar which was the stronghold of the dhow population during the monsoon season. Their nephew, an engineer working on dhow engines, had lived at Zanzibar, Mombasa, Tanga and Lamu. He had a house at Kismayu on the Somali coast where he had married a Bajuni woman.

Although the dhow traffic with the Swahili coast has now ended, the social link between Sur and Zanzibar has not snapped. Sur still retains the atmosphere of a cosmopolitan dhow port where memories and social realities remind one of former connections by dhows across the Indian Ocean. A remarkably large number of people of Sur can still speak Kiswahili. In recent times, their numbers have been augmented by the return of many Suris or their children who returned from East Africa because of the political and economic upheavals there and the almost simultaneous improvement in the conditions in Oman.

The situation that had prevailed on the East African coast was also reproduced on the west coast of India where Arab sailors had been making landfalls and interacted with the local people for centuries. As a result of this ancient maritime commercial connection, a wealthy mercantile *pardesi* (foreign) and a vibrant local Mappila Muslim community had grown up on the Malabar coast which merged over the centuries. According to Barbosa writing at the beginning of the sixteenth century, the Mappila constituted nearly 20 per cent of the population, a proportion that seems to have been maintained into the twentieth century. In the the vicinity of Calicut, one of the most important medieval entrepots on the coast of southwestern

India, their numbers even rise to 50 per cent. Mappilas played an important role in the economy and politics of Kerala, and their networks stretched as far as Arabia. Not surprisingly, Malayalam, the language of Keralites, like Kiswahili, is liberally peppered with Arabic and Persian words (Dale 1980).[16] Thus, Sur's other maritime arm that extended to the west coast of India has remained strong partly because of the continuing commercial relations and recent labour migration from India. Many of the carpenters working at present on dhows in Sur and elsewhere in the Gulf region are in fact Indians from the Malabar coast, working under the supervision of the old Suri dhow builders (Ibid.).

Apart from the sailors who were typically birds of passage even though some of them did tarry for long periods at their ports of call or even settled down, the dhows also carried passengers who included seasonal traders as well as longer-term migrants. When the northeast monsoon set in, very mixed groups of passengers boarded dhows from Arabia for the East African coast or the west coast of India. They included merchants, hawkers, migrants, porters, children, musicians and beggars—and even a few women. Apparently only a small number of the passengers returned. For example, in 1945 a total of 2,654 Arabs landed at Mombasa, and the following year more than a thousand passengers disembarked at Zanzibar. To give an impression of the range of people travelling on dhows even in the first half of the twentieth century, I refer to the passenger list of the dhow in which Villiers sailed in 1938 from Aden to Zanzibar and back to Kuwait. The dhow had taken on board 118 passengers from the Hadhrami ports of Mukalla and Shihr. These were the last Arab ports before

[16] There was tomb of the Raja of Cranganore in Malabar who had allegedly converted to Islam at the beginning of 3rd AH/10th AD and was buried in Dhofar. In the mid nineteenth century, the Hadhrami Seyyid Fadl the Moplah, who had settled on the Malabar coast, was exiled by the British to Arabia, and he tried unsuccessfully to set up his own state in Dhofar. Lorimer 1908–15: 21–22. List of Arabic and Persian loanwords in Malayalam compiled by Gayatri Devi, and subsequent debate on the internet "Namaskar", October 1998. For Kiswahili, see Lodhi (2000).

dhows veered towards the African coast, where passengers from other parts of Arabia used to congregate. The web constituted by the routes of dhows was frequented by passengers who reinforced the social and cultural connections of the Indian Ocean by their movements. Thus, at Hafun, the first landfall at the Horn of Africa, Villiers' dhow took on passengers who had come from Muscat. Further down the coast, about 80 disembarked at Mogadishu, while 12 new passengers joined the dhow. There were 30 passengers for Mombasa and Zanzibar, and at the former port it took on 30 new passengers for Zanzibar, including Hadhramis going south on business, some Suris who Villiers suspected were involved in the hashish business, and Mombasans making an excursion to Zanzibar.[17] It was a rather mixed crowd on Villiers' dhow, but slaves were not amongst them.

The private merchants from Hadhramaut and Sur were on a trading venture much as their ancestors had been for centuries, those who Villiers had called "Sons of Sinbad". They were not interested in settling down on the Swahili coast (although some eventually did). For example, a certain Said from the Omani port of Sur used to go to East Africa with his father who had been a slave trader in the past. At the age of six he had travelled to Bagamoyo and then into the Congo. Another man, Majid, had been a captain and knew his way around the East African coast, the Rufiji river, Comoro islands and Madagascar, and eastwards up to the Gulf of Kachchh in western India. He spoke Swahili, Persian, Hindustani and several Indian dialects, Somali and Arabic, and impressed Villiers by his ability to curse in English. Mohammed was an English-speaking man from Sur who had a business in Mogadishu. He used to command one of the dhows belonging to his father that was then laid up (or lost). Now he had embarked on his own trading venture (Villiers 1940: 128–29, 140, 153).

Some passengers consisted of Hadhrami migrants who were going to Africa for the first time, while others returned from a short visit to Arabia. Some of them were early migrant workers

[17] Villiers 1940: 79, 128, 139, 141, 165, 168, 179, 195.

whose ambition was to make enough money by working hard for one to five years and then return home.[18] One passenger boarding at Mukalla, an Arab silversmith from Mogadishu, returned to his business after a brief visit to Arabia. In addition, there were 47 Bedouins, including a chief and his young son, who were going to the Swahili coast to seek their fortune. Another young man from the interior of Hadhramaut, near the edge of the Great Desert, sought to escape a famine that had caused many losses to his his tribe. Having heard the elders speak of opportunities in Africa he hoped to make a living there for three to four years before returning. In order to pay their fares, he and some of the other young men of the tribe had brought frankincense on their camels to Mukalla which they sold in the market (Villiers 1940: 84, 90, 103).

Hadhramis had been coming down to Mombasa and Zanzibar from time immemorial. Many who landed in Mombasa had little money in their belly belts. They sought work as porters, and they used to have a monopoly of stevedoring in the old dhow harbour, but they had begun to meet competition from local Africans. They were also water carriers, coffee sellers, night watchmen, petty hawkers and minor shopkeepers, which was an envied profession. As soon as Villiers landed in Lamu and Mombasa, he saw some of the passengers hawking through the streets, carrying small bundles of sarong, singlets, shawls and turbans. Others were already established as helpers in tiny shops, probably belonging to relatives. There was a considerable traffic of such shopkeepers between East Africa and South Arabia: One kinsman went home for a year or two, another came down to carry on the shop. Trans-local social networks assured that if a man was without money, he could go back on the credit of some tribesman, or one of their organisations (Villiers 1940: 58, 75, 78–79, 103, 178–83, 196, 211; Martin and Martin 1978: 48–50, 70).

Other cases show the intricate web of trade and settlement that encompassed the whole Indian Ocean from the interior of Hadhramaut to South-East Asia in one direction and inner

[18] Often such people eventually settled down more permanently in East Africa.

Africa in the other—and even beyond. Thus, a 65-year-old blind Yemeni Sayyid from the interior of Hadhramaut came on board at Mukalla to go to Africa to wind up the affairs of a brother who had died somewhere in the Congo. He himself had spent eight years on ocean steamers, had then worked as an automobile worker in Detroit where he had lived in the Polish quarter and picked up the language. Several other passengers travelling with Villiers were born in Indonesia or Malaysia, were half-Malay half-Hadhrami, they spoke Malay and Dutch, read newspapers written in Arabic and Dutch, and played an ancient gramophone with records from Cairo and Damascus (Villiers 1940: 56, 79–80, 167, 181).

Besides male passengers on board of the dhow, there were also a large number of boys, who travelled with other passengers but also on their own. A young boy of eight had come to Aden on a Suri dhow, he now worked for a Suri passenger who paid for his passage. In addition, he acted as the ship's servant to pay for his food. He was born somewhere on the Gulf of Oman and had been a beachcomber since he was three years old. He had already been to Zanzibar, and was now going to stay there because he thought it was better than Arabia. A blind beggar brought on two boys who he passed as his sons. He was supposed to feed them, but when he failed to do so, they chose another patron (Villiers 1940: 32–3, 82, 182).

At Zanzibar, Villiers' dhow took on three schoolteachers, the only passengers for the return journey. Villiers initially described them as Swahili who he said were more "Negroid" in appearance than any of the sailors. On closer acquaintance he found that in fact two of them were Baluchi brothers, progeny of an ivory trader and a woman from the Congo. The other was a distant relation of an Arab prince born in Zanzibar who was, according to Villiers, a quarter Negro. They all had relatives in Muscat. They had been boy scouts and were educated, speaking English well. To the chagrin of the captain they wore trousers and did not say their prayers regularly. They kept to themselves most of the time and spoke Kiswahili, apparently discussing politics, much as their modern compatriots. They wanted to join a British steamer in the Persian Gulf to see the world and then hire a car at Kuwait to take them to Mecca. But as soon as they approached Muscat, they changed to Arab gowns and began to say their prayers regularly in preparation for their adjustment to life in Arabia (Villiers 1940: 296–98; 1948: 415).

As pointed out before, sea life was predominantly the sphere of men into which women were allowed to intrude only grudgingly. But in Villiers' dhow, a few women passengers were present. The captain did not want women on his dhow because he felt they had to be sheltered and segregated and he found that "they often made trouble." The women were charged one-third more of the fare than men, and they had to pay in advance. The captain envied his fellow nakhoda who had only three women among his 150 passengers, while he had taken on 15 at Shihr. Unlike the men, the women had to travel most uncomfortably. They were stowed in the cabin that was more like a dungeon in which Villiers himself had refused to stay, and were shut up for the duration of the voyage lasting nearly three months. Only once did one of them come on deck to say her prayers with her husband. The husband was warned not to repeat it. A young girl of about 15, who was being taken to Zanzibar to be married, even died at Hafun and had to be brought out to be buried. The other women "mutinied" only once, when they were not allowed to land at Mogadishu. Three of them disappeared when the dhow stopped at the island of at Lamu. This brought trouble for the captain. In order to get clearance for departure, the dhow was forced to take on other female passengers for a free ride to Mombasa to substitute the missing ones. The latter were not as submissive as their Arab sisters and raised hell in the cabin down below. The captain merely clamped down the hatch, locked it, and paid no further attention (Villiers 1940: 58, 78–79, 88, 119–22, 150, 160).

The Longue Durée Dhow Culture

Since the coming of the steamship into the Indian Ocean in the nineteenth century, authors have been predicting the final demise of the dhow as the inevitable submission to modernity, and with it, presumably the disintegration of the dhow culture that had been engendered by it. Some would push it further back into the middle of the eighteenth century to the rise of the capitalism as the great temporal divide in world history. André Wink refers to the destruction of the "integrative network of Indian Ocean relations" with the imposition of British control over the Indian subcontinent in the eighteenth century, and Das Gupta refers to the "sundering of the organic unity of trade and shipping" (Bose 2002: 376). Chaudhuri says 1750 marked the end of a life cycle of human civilisation:

> If the Kwaiti (sic) booms and their Indian fellow-vessels continue to cross the Arabian Sea, they do so, it could be said, either as part of a backward economy or because their owners are not rational beings. Modern technology is intolerant of the living past going beyond, shall we say, the 1850s, let alone the 1750s. The sailing-ship. . .lived on for a century or more beyond the mid-eighteenth century. Its eventual disappearance can be traced to the invention of the steam-engine (Chaudhuri 1985: 221).

While these world historical changes no doubt had a major impact on the Indian Ocean and its littoral societies, Bose has questioned the dramatic transformation that is implied by such assertions. He points to the study by Rajat Kanta Ray who shows that the "bazaar nexus" of Indian and Chinese chain of trade and finance that stretched from Zanzibar to Singapore formed "a distinct international system that never lost its identity in the larger dominant world system of the West."[19] Bose argues that "pre-existing inter-regional networks were utilised, molded, reordered and rendered subservient by Western capital and the more powerful colonial states, but never torn apart until these came under severe strain during the 1930s" (Bose 2002: 372).

The dhow is a very relevant case in point. It has proved to be an icon of resistence that has refused to disappear altogether,

[19] The dogged survival of the *hawala* (promissory note) system of money transfers into the twenty-first century, as revealed by investigations since "Nine-Eleven", drives the point home.

surviving by adapting to changing conditions, giving a lie to the oft-repeated cliché that it is an anachronistic unchanging artefact of tradition like the rest of the "Orient". It adapted to the intrusion of the Europeans from the sixteenth century by adopting iron nails to tie its planks, in place of the former system of sewing them, to enable it to carry guns in confrontation with the armed Portuguese warships. Faced by the challenge of the steamship, which could sail regardless of the monsoons and with greater regularity and safety, and which thus robbed it of the more valuable cargo and passenger traffic, the dhow responded by concentrating on the bulkier commodities and less accessible ports and routes. As Prins and Martin show, the dhow became even bigger during the twentieth century to concentrate on mangrove poles and Mangalore tiles. According to Martin, by the early 1970s the average Arab dhow coming into Mombasa had increased to 150 tons, those from Iran to 155 tons, and those from India to 160 tons (Prins 1965–66: 5; E. B. Martin 1982: 107).

By the middle of the twentieth century, the dhow had to make another painful concession to the age of the machine, but again not without resistence. Inboard diesel engines began to be incorporated as a source of motive power, but while the dhow had to allow itself to be defrocked of its traditional lateen sail in certain sectors of the Indian Ocean, it still retained its own traditional form. Such motorised dhows began to appear in East African waters in any great numbers only in the late 1950s, and while they have now become generalised in the oil-rich countries, many Indian dhows use it only as an auxiliary source of power side by side with the sail. In 1980 only about a third of the Indian dhows registered at the Indian port of Veraval in Gujarat had an engine, and many of them continued to use the sail whenever they could (Martin and Martin 1978: 56; E. B. Martin 1982: 116). In coastal waters, such as the Swahili coast, the sail is still very much in evidence, transporting building materials and agricultural products, but also in the redistribution from Zanzibar of imported manufactured consumables such as televisions, refrigerators and garments to the mainland ports.

It was only from the 1950s that significant long-term changes began to leave a more devastating mark on long-distance dhow traffic in the western Indian Ocean. The most important single factor of change was the discovery of oil in the Persian Gulf which began to transform the economies of these states that had previously played such a central role in the dhow traffic. By the 1950s, dhow captains were facing a great difficulty making up their crew to sail these dhows when there were easier means of livelihood in the oil industry at their doorsteps. The last Kuwaiti long-distance trade dhow is said to have sailed in 1950s. The trend was to be followed in subsequent decades by other Gulf states and Oman. The shortfall in Arab dhow shipping was made up in the short run by an upswing in Iranian dhows during the 1970s. Although oil had also been discovered in Iran, but with a larger population and the poverty of its Persian Gulf littoral, the dhow remained an attractive proposition for the coastal Iranians. Indian dhows also appear to have partaken of this fleeting advantage. As trans-oceanic dhow trade became less profitable, they even participated in the local coastal trade along the Swahili coast during the 1970s, making numerous short-run sailings between East African ports for a couple of years before returning to India (Kamioka and Yajima 1979: appendix 1).

The discovery of oil, however, was only one of several factors that began to undermine the traditional dhow trade. In the Persian Gulf, cement and iron beams began to replace mangrove poles which had supported Arab roofs for hundreds of years and which had become the mainstay of the dhow trade in the twentieth century. While the oil wealth percolating down to the fishing and farming communities may have begun to sap the age-old trade in dates and dried fish, the newly independent states in East Africa—dominated largely by the educated elites from the interior with scant sympathy for the Swahili littoral—set about to drive more nails into the coffin of the dhow trade by imposing prohibitive customs duties. Before 1970 no duty was charged on dried fish which was the staple of the poor man's diet, but it was rapidly increased to 50 per cent by

1975, and dates had to pay a similar rate. In neither case could a case be made for protecting local industries or raising revenue to justify such punishing taxation. In 1970 only five dhows carried dates into Mombasa which has become a delicacy only during the Ramadan month of fasting, and a decreasing number brought dried fish. Another major bulk commodity on these dhows during the twentieth century, both Arab and Iranian, as well as Indian, were Mangalore tiles from southern India; but with the opening of a tile factory in Mombasa, dhow traffic also lost that item. Finally, immigration and navigational restrictions imposed by the colonial and post-colonial governments in East Africa deprived the dhows of their revenue from the previously highly lucrative passenger traffic.[20]

The death knell was sounded by the Zanzibar Revolution of 1964 when many people of mixed Arab origin were massacred, others were reportedly packed onto dhows then in the harbour and driven out to sea where some may have perished, and dhows were prohibited from entering Zanzibar harbour. Traumatic though the Revolution was for the society engendered by the dhow, the age-old dhow traffic had already left a rich social residue all around the rim of the Indian Ocean that has proved to be a resilient plant which was not suffocated by these political and economic changes. As Bose has stated, "the 'world' of the Indian Ocean and, for that matter, the Mediterranean have ingrained in them a much greater depth of economic and cultural meaning" (Bose 2002: 368). The return of people of Arab origin to Oman and the Persian Gulf, rather than sundering the age-old connection between the two sides of the rim of the Indian Ocean, has ironically revived and strengthened it. After several generations on the Swahili coast, these people had for all intents and purposes become Swahili. Most of them had long forgotten Arabic, and Kiswahili had become their mother tongue. During that long period of interaction

[20] By 1983 Kenya had limited the number of passengers on any dhow to five, and foreigners were prohibited altogether. By the mid 1970s, the number of foreign dhows entering Mombasa had declined to a mere 23 from a high of 321 a mere three decades earlier (Martin and Martin 1978: 51, 54, 56; E. B. Martin 1986: 47, 52).

they had enriched Kiswahili through Arabic loanwords, motifs and poetry in which some of them excelled to become major Swahili literary figures (Harries 1962). When they went back to Oman, they carried their new language which has become the unofficial second language in Oman, widely spoken from the international airport at Muscat to the farthest village in the interior. Over a few generations they may well revert to Arabic, but their Arabic is bound to be influenced by their Swahili experience.

Similar tendencies are discernible in other aspects of culture of the dhow such as in music and dress. The older influence of Arabic music in the Taarab of the Swahili coast has been studied in great depth, while the impact of Swahili and other African music cultures on that of the maritime peoples of Oman and Persian Gulf has begun to be explored (Topp 1994; Mallah 1994). The return of the people of Arab origin from eastern Africa to Oman has given a new impetus to artistic exchange between them. While several Taarab groups have been formed in Oman and Dubai, and one of the popular singers in Oman is a returnee, Omani marriage songs have become popular in Zanzibar, in some cases replacing the old Swahili ones. The same can be said about dress. Swahili *kangas* (rectangular colourful cotton wraps for women) are widely used in the households of the returnees in Oman, and their tastes and aspirations may begin to influence the design and the sayings printed on them. On the other hand, Arab dress has begun to influence the way people dress along the east African coast. Omani caps and Gulf designs of the long *kanzu* male dress have become commonplace in Zanzibar and other coastal cities, and the female black gown and scarf or veil has all but displaced the traditional Swahili *buibui* (black overall veil). All these are not merely aspects of a fossilised or unchanging dhow culture, but of the *longue durée* character of a maritime culture that gives new forms and meaning to changing relations between peoples brought together by the sea whose potential for social and cultural as well as economic interaction has not been exhausted.

3

*Sailors That Do Not Sail: Hinduism, Anthropology and Parochialism in the Indian Ocean**

Edward Simpson

Introduction

There has been a recent flurry of literature attempting to 're-imagine' the western Indian Ocean region as the 'cradle of globalisation' and as a zone of 'moving spaces'. Such work has drawn heavily on the theoretical contributions made by historians to the study of the Ocean, but by doing so much of the ethnographic detail of the region has been lost. This chapter is an attempt at evaluating recent debates in the light of patterns of trade and migration from the Kachchh district of Gujarat state, western India. It is suggested that by looking at connections of smaller units of population, families and castes, the picture is less frenetic. As Michael Pearson (2000) has recently suggested, the Ocean is not a region bound together by some nebulous notion of commonality or structure because people of the littoral identify strongly with their own countries as well

* I thank Helene Basu, Brian Didier, Christopher Fuller, Kai Kresse, Pierre Lachaier, Isabella Lepri, Lucia Michelutti, Mattison Mines and Jonathan Parry for reading previous versions of this paper. Time for research and writing was funded by the ESRC (TO26271189) and a Nuffield Foundation New Career Development Fellowship (NCF/00103/G). Fieldwork on which this paper is based was conducted in Mandvi, Kachchh, between September 1997 and March 1999. For a lengthier consideration of these themes see my monograph *Muslim Society and the Western Indian Ocean: The Seafarers of Kachchh* published with Routledge in 2006.

as being bound up in more general patterns of loyalty, such as belonging to the Muslim world. This chapter is an exploration of the construction of the local loyalties of a traditional Hindu Indian Ocean sailing caste. It also suggests that connections at a human level, although potentially infinite, are generally rather more limited and mundane than some of the recent literature suggests.

The goods the trans-Indian Ocean voyagers historically traded in, decorated their mansions with, and gave as gifts to potential allies may have had fantastic biographies but there were clear limits to human travel and cosmopolitanism. The networks that voyagers forged tended to be restricted, although often very geographically diverse, and for most part they were highly focused on their homeland. In light of this kind of observation, the assumption that any kind of movement over ocean or land automatically signifies cosmopolitanism or 'moving space' is misleading and, I suggest, in the light of ethnographic evidence, needs to be tempered. Therefore, this chapter describes how a caste of Hindu sailors, Kharvas, (who no longer sail but continue to be thought of as sailors) have constructed a caste identity in relation to the land, sea, history and others groups associated with the Ocean. In the past, they acted as crew on the mercantile fleet; today, many of them serve as manual labourers in Oman for the descendents of their own ancestors' patrons. This material shows them locked in individual and caste-based relationships that although clearly related to broader shifts in polity in the Indian Ocean are highly localised and also restrict the possibilities for their movement and activity in the region.

The central point I wish to make, however, is that Kharvas have invested the profits of their overseas forays in constructing a ritualised local identity that although replete with images and symbols of the Ocean, addresses very parochial concerns such as status as an attempt to give them a stake in local history. In other words, this is an attempt to look at the Ocean region through the units of value that are familiar to anthropologists such as kinship, caste, sentiment, hierarchy, social order and the relative values that people accord to spaces, social practices and to others rather than through colonial records, ledgers, travel accounts and images. By looking at the Kharvas' loyalties, migration patterns and the relative values they accord different kinds of space and experience, I hope to show that society has been formed, reformed and ordered by the movement of people in the broader Ocean region. Secondly, I wish to show that human movement in the Ocean fragments space and divides people. And finally, I wish to show that the values accorded to such spaces and the goods and movements within it are not equal in their value, prestige or in their capacities to be absorbed into local society.

The chapter is divided into three sections. The first briefly outlines the history of Kachchh in relation to the western Indian Ocean. The second describes how the Kharvas have created a particular kind of regional identity in relation to the Indian Ocean. The final section assesses existent theoretical perspectives on the Ocean given the material presented in the first two sections of the chapter.

Merchants, Sailors and the Indian Ocean

The most concise way of expressing the relationship between Kachchh and the western Indian Ocean is in the words of the late Manu Pandhi. In a volume dedicated to the historical traditions of Kachchh, he wrote that "our culture is wet with the sea" (1976–77). He was a Kachchhi who had a keen interest in the seafaring heritage of the lands he loved, and, like his eulogistic writing, Kachchhi society is replete with stories, phrases and songs derived from lives spent in the lap of the Ocean. Generous men have hearts as wide as the sea (*dariyadil*); sailors are described as oceanic progeny (*dariya chhoru*); the myths of the deities and saints entombed along the coast attest to the Ocean's power, mystery and hidden treasures. But there is more to Pandhi's analogy than meets the eye because water is associated with wealth and prosperity and, like the monsoon, with joy and fertility. The Ocean has brought riches to Kachchh from trade, compensating for the withering agricultural lands that, it is said, during the nineteenth century, drove Kachchhi people from the hinterlands to the coast and out to sea by ship.

Migration and shipping in the Indian Ocean over the previous two centuries dominates most local representations of the past found in books, magazines, temple iconography, and oral, caste and family history. Material so carefully compiled by the British colonial administrators schooled in Latin and Greek has also become integral to Kachchh traditions. Most books and newspaper articles written in Gujarati on the history of shipping start by cribbing a list of ancient sources (*Periplus Maris Erythraei*, Pliny and Ptolemy) that are said to attest to the glory of Kachchhi shipping. The most commonly cited sources are held, and have been so for at least a century, in the library of the Asiatic Society of Bombay. The source most often cited is a somewhat obscure and convoluted edition of *Periplus of the Erythrean Sea* (Vincent 1805). This work is commonly used to make such claims as: "According to Vincent (Periplus, I. 25, 35, 254) in the time of Agatharcides (BC 200) the ports of Arabia and Ceylon were entirely in the hands of the people of Gujarat" (*Gazetteer, Bombay Presidency* 1896, 1, 1: 492). More recently George Hourani's (1951) interpretation of William Vincent (1805) and Lawrence Hollingsworth's (1960) interpretation of Wilfred Schoff's *Periplus* (1912) have become popular. Hourani suggests that around 200 years ago merchants from 'Ariaca' conducted trade with the Somali coast. Hollingsworth claims that the 'Ariaca' of *Periplus* is the region around the Gulf of Cambay comprising Kachchh, Saurashtra and Gujarat. By combining these two sources it is possible to conclude that Kachchhi merchants were trading with East Africa some 200 years ago (see Sakarai 1980: 300–302, 330; 1981). While this kind of speculation is of a great deal of interest to many Kachchhi scholars, it is of dubious historical worth and actually proves very little.

A precarious relationship between the land and its people underlies the extremely high rates of commercial migration from the area that have characterised life since the turn of the nineteenth century. In the past, at some times of the year,

Kachchh was inaccessible—other than by boat—as the marshy plains to the east, north and west were inundated with monsoon waters. The semi-island territory formed between the Rann and the sea was for centuries the focus of contest between Saurashtra and Sindh as various ruling dynasties competed for mastery of the territory that sat between them. Migration from the western seaboard of India seems to have stretched back to the ancient times; historians are confident that Gujaratis were present in East Africa from the fourteenth century onwards (Pearson 1998b). However, in the Kachchh case, trade and its counterpart migration are most clearly defined and recorded during the modern colonial era, a period in which Kachchh has experienced drought, plague, earthquakes and political instability (Masselos 1996). This period can roughly be defined as stretching from the turn of the nineteenth century, when Europeans moved from sea to land in their colonial endeavours, to the middle part of the twentieth century and the independence of India from British rule. The town of Mandvi, on the southern shores of Kachchh, was a successful commercial port throughout this period. It was also home to many of the commercial castes to venture overseas, and its streets are littered with monuments to their success and generosity. Research on which this chapter is largely based was conducted in the town, with subsidiary research undertaken in Bombay and Saurashtra.

During the modern colonial era, the European interest in exotic goods gave way to the pursuit of Asian commodities for mass consumption in Europe (McPherson 1993: 198). Simultaneously, Kachchhi merchants made a similar transformation as they moved from a predominantly transient, although cyclical, seaborne trade to settle more permanently overseas. Traders, reliant on the monsoon winds, had to operate within relatively tight time constraints. This undoubtedly left them vulnerable to being charged higher prices for goods they purchased and similarly weakened their bargaining position on the items they were attempting to sell. This situation inevitably led to the settlement of brokers and the establishment of warehouses in the ports so traders could take advantage of fluctuating prices and avoid transacting commodities when prices were unfavourable. A clear pattern emerged in which merchants traded from their offices in ports; they employed a captain and crew, on whose loyalty they relied; sailors conveyed goods, and occasionally merchants, between ports. The simple division of labour was cemented through patron–client type relationships, tying individual sailors to a particular merchant and his ships. For Hindu merchants these sailors were in most cases Kharvas.

Of all the communities associated with the sea in north-western India, none is more (in)famous than the Hindu caste known as Kharva. Their name perhaps comes from the Sanskrit kh from *kharash* (salty) and *war* from *vat* (road or way). A gazetteer attributes the etymology to 'ksháraváhas' (salt carriers) from which 'Khar'rva' is derived (*Gazetteer, Bombay Presidency*, 1901, IX, I: 520). Colloquially, Kharvas are called *malam* (from the verb 'to know', in this case navigation) or more poetically *dariya chhoru* (sons of the sea). They form Mandvi's largest *samaj* (caste organisation), constituting as much as a twelfth of the town's population. They live on the southern edge of Mandvi in an area that previously would have been within the safety of the town walls but close to the port. Kharvas claim a mixed descent from the Rajput lines of *suriya* (sun), the related *ragu* (fire) segment, and *chandra* (moon). Their history and traditions are those of the sea, as are their names, deities and festivals; like sailors in many parts of the world, they are generally regarded as troublesome, dangerous and unruly.

Seafaring in the Indian Ocean is dictated largely by the monsoons which pass over the area with an inescapable rhythm. Annually, the cooler airs over the Ocean are sucked northwards towards the warming Asian landmass and then southwards from the Himalayas and the plains of northern India and out to sea. Harnessing the predictability of this pattern led to the development of trade routes and to the exchange of populations, ideas and social practices. These winds, for example, allowed the Kharvas to set sail by dhow from Mandvi in September for the ports of western India before heading to Madagascar or Zanzibar. When the southerly winds started to blow, the same dhow could head up the east coast of Africa and back to Mandvi. The winds follow coastlines, eddying at particular times of year into the gulfs that lie to the east, west and south of the Arabian Peninsula. As these ships traversed the waters of the Ocean they distributed goods and people in its ports, and many Kharvas settled in East Africa and the Gulf states, often retained by the merchant on whose ship they had crewed.

For Kachchhi merchants the conditions of trade became increasingly attractive throughout the nineteenth century. The English East India Company succeeded its Dutch equivalent and the predatory Portuguese slipped away. Although the Company openly encouraged indigenous trade, it was the suitability of indigenous credit networks for the new types of trade that really gave the impetus for the expansion of indigenous capital enterprise (Subramanian 1987). The volume of trade in the Ocean grew markedly as Europeans demanded raw materials and laid railway tracks and developed safe harbours to allow for the transportation of these materials. Kachchhi merchants, drawing on their knowledge of markets and pricing, derived from trading in agricultural surplus, moved to supply the British with raw materials, notably cotton, and into other niche markets. The vast majority of this trade was by sea, connecting with the caravan routes that came into Kachchh from the Thar Desert in the west to Palanpur, Ahmedabad and Ujjain in the east (Sampat 1935: 13).

The golden age of shipping came to a close with the partitioning of the Sultan of Zanzibar's territories in the 1880s. The wars and recessions of the twentieth century, before India's independence, further disrupted transport links and upset the terms of trade. The early decades of the twentieth century was a period of stagnation and community decline—at least in terms of the expansionist trade at which the Kachchhis had excelled in previous decades. The descendants of the great trading families lived from the wealth of their ancestors and from income from property bequeathed to them; they are described as having grown decadent and weak.

The enormous economic boom that followed the Second World War saw a parallel growth of tariff protection and the end to relatively unrestricted access to the ports of the Ocean region. Shipping declined and the ties of the overseas populations with their homeland began to weaken. Facing potential losses, many merchants sold or abandoned their fleets. During the 1960s and 1970s, political nationalism, xenophobia and the bureaucratisation of nationality and identity further restricted the movements of Kachchhi enterprise overseas, which was to some extent compensated for by the 'oil boom' of the early 1970s. The rapid expansion in both trade and the demand for labourers has brought renewed vigour to these communities. Many mercantile families had been resident in Muscat since the early nineteenth century. But recently, a new wave of migration has taken place towards the emirates of the Arabian peninsular. However, from Kachchh, there are parallel migrations that are easily confused with the present round of labour migration that are based on the old patterns of settlement. And, importantly, such migration is not only undertaken by Muslims given preferential treatment by their 'Arab brothers' because migration to Oman from Kachchh is primarily a Hindu phenomenon, and most prominent among the Bhatiyas, the main patrons of the Kharvas. The sustained Hindu presence in Oman and their intimate relationships with its rulers continues to be fruitful for young men who to this day leave Kachchh in droves, at least for a spell. A great many Kharvas continue to work in Oman for the merchant families for whom they crewed. Today, they specialise in manual and semi-skilled work (as drivers, cleaners, machine operators and so forth) predominantly in Muscat but in smaller towns throughout Oman as well. As with other migration patterns from Kachchh, the majority of Kharva men continue to return annually for the monsoon months to their homes in Mandvi.

Founded in or around 1581, Mandvi on the southern shores of Kachchh became the principal port for the area throughout the eighteenth and nineteenth centuries. The troublesome sand bar across the entrance to the port has always prevented the smooth passing of even the smallest vessel at low tide no matter how skilled the pilot. The general silting of the creek, as the subcontinent slowly obeys the principles of gravity and attrition, have made matters worse. Today, Mandvi has all but been abandoned as a commercial port. The only large ships that call there drop anchor a couple of kilometres out to sea to wait for tugs, towing dumb barges by the brace, to tranship low-value dry bulk goods to their holds. Such ships, having called at Kandla, Kachchh's modern container port, unflatteringly to Mandvi's heritage, load cargoes of nitrates or bentonite rather than making the passage home without ballast.

Mandvi remains a bustling town, prosperous, and very well served by buildings dedicated to the education, health and religious requirements of its population. The majority of these institutions started life as private trusts under the patronage of successful merchants. The town is also dotted with temples, shrines and mosques. The road that leads down to Mandvi's port is flanked with once-fine rest houses for pilgrims and migrants, each built by a mercantile group for the dedicated use of all its members or for the use of all but its members. The names on the plaques set aside and above the main entrances record the magnanimity of those donating money towards the building's construction. The list of philanthropic donors tells of times that have long past and of times when Mandvi was a gateway for migrants seeking fortunes overseas. These crumbling buildings now house the poor; their verandas host the conversations, chess games and reflections of the elderly, who look, melancholically, out to the seas they once risked their lives on. A solitary teashop is the only thriving business that remains in this part of the town, where mercantile houses, conducting trade throughout the Ocean and beyond, had once stood.

Over the previous two centuries, the human geography of the town developed around the social organisation of shipping. The language and traditions of shipping are to be seen in all areas of social life, and the caste iconography of the Hindu merchants and sailors is saturated with images of ships, reaffirming their seafaring past. Society is dominated by a pervasive material and social distinction between the personal qualities and attributes of *vepar* (merchants) and *mahjur* (labour) or *khalaasi* (sailor). These two social categories transcend all others such as religion and sect, and ethnicity and race (also see Varadarajan 1991: 2). It is traced out in the traditional urban geography of the town where there are clearly demarcated areas for the two classes. Broadly, the town is arranged around the central bazaars and an invisible line drawn from southeast to northwest. At the base of this line are areas traditionally inhabited by the Kharvas and others; at the far end of the line are the areas of mercantile houses, temples and social institutions of the Bhatiyas and others; while the middle areas are predominantly populated by townsfolk who do not traverse the Ocean. This is something of a simplification as pockets of other populations are scattered throughout the town and in a number of places the town walls have been demolished and residential areas have spilled outside their confines. However, it is broadly true that the traditional areas of merchants and sailors are located on opposite sides of the town, with merchants living furthest away from the port; it is also broadly true that this pattern encompasses the less pronounced divisions between Hindus and Muslims within both areas.

While both merchants and sailors are comprised of many endogamous units, often in competition with one another, there are striking differences in the social organisation between the two primary groups. The mercantile classes, such as the Bhatiyas, tend to cluster around guild-type organisations (*mahajan*) where their community and commercial interests coincide with religious interests (commonly represented by a private priesthood). Many labouring communities are not so sharply defined, often not having communal buildings, written community codes, laws and guilds acting in their interest. However, the Kharvas are something of an exception as they have a strong caste council and organisational structure. The overall result is a society broadly composed of mutually dependent, yet socially distinct, patrons and clients.

Structure, Myth and Ritual

The Kharva population in Mandvi is not an isolated one, and they are found in most of the ports of Saurashtra and Kachchh. Together, these settlements form the 'Bar Gam Samaj', an ideal society of twelve villages whose membership actually comprises sixteen settlements. This pan-peninsular organisation has its own legal code and semi-autonomous court, which has sat regularly since the 1860s. The *vanot* (president) and *mukadam* (assistant) head the *dayara* (a meeting, typically of Rajputs and allies) in Porbunder (Saurashtra); these positions are annually renewed on the day known as Nava Naroj, the ritual end of the monsoon. The mukadam administers justice and works to maintain relations between the geographically dispersed affiliate groups. The power of jurisdiction is derived from the *madhi* (seat or throne within the temple), which is typically the primary symbol of Kshatriya rule and power and, not as one might expect, the ruler's body or crown. Each Kharva settlement in the Bar Gam Samaj is headed by a *chovatiya* (leader) who is appointed by the local Kharva constituency. In Mandvi, the madhi is located in the Murli Manohar Mandir (a temple dedicated to a form of Krishna playing a beautiful flute). The whole organisation is clearly modelled on the typical structures of Rajput polity, with court power being sanctioned by a deity.

Many Kharvas claim that their ancestors migrated from Rajasthan to Saurashtra in the thirteenth century to defend the Shiva temple of Somnath against the Muslim Ala-ud-din Khilji (or his representatives). Like the now infamous Babri Masjid site in Ayodhya, Somnath is an important site in the landscape of religious conflict in India today. The Kharvas' claim to have come to Kachchh *via* Somnath is a politically and religiously loaded one. In 1992 the *rath yatra* (chariot pilgrimage) organised primarily by the BJP, set out from the Somnath temple to

Ayodhya. The choice of Somnath as a starting point for the yatra was no accident because the temple there had been rebuilt in 1950 as a symbol of Indian nationhood and Hindu dominance in western India. Prior to this, the temple had received considerable attention from successive Muslim rulers. Mohammed of Ghazni, one of the first 'Turkish' conquerors of western India, is reputed to have destroyed the temple's idol in 1026. The second struggle, characterised as a struggle between Hinduism and Islam, is said to have taken place at Somnath in 1297, when the 'Turkish' Sultan Ala-ud-din Khilji sent Afsal Khan to destroy the temple, which had been rebuilt after Mohammed's return to Ghazni. In 1701, the Mughal, Aurangazeb, sent Mohammed Azam, the Governor of Gujarat, to destroy the temple once again. Victorious, Azam constructed a mosque on its foundation (Krishnaswamy 1966: 81). The same idol, in the same place, had prompted three major battles over the course of eight hundred years. Each time the Muslims had been victorious and each time they had destroyed the image in the temple.

To many Hindus, Somnath is an elevated representation of their religious tradition and a striking reminder of Hindu–Muslim antipathy in India. Bhartiya Janata Party leader Lal Kishan Advani characterised the rebuilding of the Somnath temple as the first stage of a campaign to reinstate the ancient symbols of unity and amity in India—the liberation of Ram's birthplace in Ayodhya was to be the second. Naran, a retired Kharva sailor, told the story of Somnath in the following way:

> Somnath was the most beautiful and powerful temple in India. Hundreds of Brahmans performed rituals to the huge lingam. There was always singing and dancing. The temple had a vast wealth and was good to the people. Ala-ud-din Khilji came from the North to destroy it and to confiscate its riches. Our people were living in Rajasthan as kings and warriors. We were a noble and courageous race. When we heard that Khilji was coming to Somnath we left our lands to fight him. We journeyed down through Rajasthan and into Saurashtra and met with the kings there. They greeted us and gave us their best horses. Some people believed that Shiva had invited Khilji to Somnath to revenge him. Many thousands of us died in the

> battle to save the temple. In the end it was destroyed and the lingam was ruined. After the battle we were left weak and starving and fled to hide along the coast.

Although Kharvas also claim to have fought Mohammed of Ghazni at the temple, this is a typical description of the Kharvas defeat at the hands of Muslims and of their arrival in Saurashtra and Kachchh. Such origin myths are clearly political and interweave a national history of invasion with the plight of the Kharvas.

It has been suggested that village history in India is an expression of the history of the Indian civilisation (Redfield 1955: 14). Such a theory on the relationship between great and little traditions was a rather telling precursor for debates that were to take new turns in subsequent decades, in which the mythology of the Mahabharata and the Ramayana was transcribed, after a fashion, onto the political landscape. In Sheldon Pollock's view, the Ramayana text (later written down in a generally accepted form by Tulsi Das in the sixteenth and seventeenth centuries) offers unique imaginative instruments, whereby, on the one hand, a divine political order can be conceptualised, narrated, and historically grounded, and, on the other, a fully demonised 'other' can be categorised, counterposed and condemned (1993: 264). Attempting to explain how people come to believe what happened rather than to explain what really happened, Pollock demonstrates that the Ramayana text is frequently used as the basis for contemporary political action in India that aims to restore the glories of ancient Hindu rule and to demonise Muslims as foreign invaders. He carefully adds (1993: 292) that although these political notions are drawn from the general principles of the Ramayana, they are seldom more than tenuous representations of the 'object text'.

The twin themes of rulership and predatory invaders are evident in the narrative given above of the fall of Somnath and in the way in which the Kharvas have arranged their social and religious institutions in Mandvi. At the very centre of their settlement within the precincts of their marriage hall stands a temple dedicated to the royal deity Ram. At the two main entrances to their settlement are temples dedicated to the monkey-deity Hanuman. A prominent character in the fight against Ravana in the Ramayana, the fortunes of Hanuman are inextricably linked to those of Ram; in Mandvi, Hanuman is regarded as a deity with power over the winds, but his role as guardian to the entrances to the Kharva settlement reflects the idea that his enormous strength can destroy any advance of malevolent forces. Just outside one of these entrances, in a busy bazaar that leads down to the port, is a temple dedicated to Krishna (in the Vaishnava tradition the eighth incarnation of Vishnu), housing the Kharva court. Although the boundaries of the town associated with Kharvas are not explicitly walled or gated, the entrances to this area are narrow, clearly defined, easy to defend, and are for the most part inviolate for other groups in the town. The Krishna temple and court are outside this area, a condition that allows other castes to be called to the court without risking the pollution associated with the Kharvas' quarters while simultaneously keeping representatives of other castes out of the Kharva area. Towards the sea at the very southernmost part of their territory is the temple of Dariyalal, a newly reconstructed complex that houses a Sanskritised version of a traditional Sindhi deity (see below). Together, the temples of Ram, Krishna, Hanuman and Dariyalal and the associated institutions of kingship, justice, protection and 'samaj identity' mark out the boundaries of Kharva dominance on the southern edge of Mandvi.

The Kharvas' Dariyalal temple

Around two decades ago, the Kharva Samaj chose to build the Dariyalal temple on the site where in times past Kharvas and Muslim sailors had jointly celebrated Nava Naroj. In the compound, aside from the temple structure, are a small office block, a row of *paliyos* (hero stones) and a stone tortoise. The temple structure is small, square and domed; inside is an icon of the deity Dariyalal, sitting resplendent on a fish. He is brightly illuminated and surrounded by silver windmills; at his feet stands a series of statues of horses daubed with thick saffron-coloured paint. The dedication of this temple to Dariyalal is an expression of social aspiration. It replaces anterior representations of the 'syncretic' figure of Dariyapir, but it is also an appropriation of the mythology of the high-ranking Lohana Mahajan for whom Dariyalal is a central deity (*ishtdevta*). In Sindh, where he was also known as Jhule Lal (Markovits 2000: 285) and Uderalal, Dariyalal appears to have been associated with the waters of the Indus but has been transformed during his migration with the Lohanas from those lands. In Kachchh, *dariya* refers primarily to the sea and its deity is also referred to as *samudrastit* and *samudradev* (a deity of the ocean).

Dariyalal was a miraculous infant who transformed himself into an armed horseman and emerged from the Indus to rebuke a persecuting Muslim. The Sindh traditions (see Aitken 1907: 165–166) are remarkably similar to the myths of Dariyalal told by Mandvi's Lohanas, with the difference that the Indus has partially been transformed into the Ocean. Born to devotees of Varun (a water deity), the boy was blessed with the protection and generosity of the deity, and from an early age displayed miraculous powers. He took to hawking dhal to people congregating along the water's edge. While he was working, Varun would appear and take the child deep into the sea, always returning him to shore with twice the amount of dhal. The king of nearby Nagar Thatta was a voracious Muslim named Marakhshah. His court published an edict ordering the vassals to convert to Islam or face death. The terrified Hindus went down to the 'coast' to ask Varun to appear to Marakhshah to prove the legitimacy of the Hindu religion. Dariyalal appeared out of the waves before to the King's minister and asked him to cease his persecution. On hearing this, the King ordered the deity to be brought to him, but Dariyalal could not be found. Later Dariyalal resurfaced in the Indus river, from where he produced armed warriors from the water who so terrorised the King that he stopped his campaign of forced religious conversion.

A printed version of the myth (Maharaj and Dwivedi 1949: 88–105) contains an additional elaboration, which further emphasises key elements at work in the story. A merchant, a loyal devotee of Dariyalal, came to Bakhar (an island in the Indus) by ship with his family. When the King saw the merchant's daughter he wanted to take her as his wife but the merchant refused. Subsequent threats by the King so troubled the merchant's family that they fasted and prayed to Dariyalal for help. Dariyalal appeared in a dream to the merchant's daughter and said that he would protect them by sending an earthquake to destroy the kingdom. In the destruction that followed, the kingdom was left barren. The merchant and his family were unharmed and set sail to sea in order to pray and offer their thanks to Dariyalal.

In this story, the devotion of the merchant's family overcomes the temporal and corporeal power of the Muslim ruler. Of the myth of Dariyalal, however, it is important to stress the mythological representation of the struggle between Hindu and Muslim ritual and corporeal power, wrapped in the theme of forced conversion campaigns. The central foundation myth of the Lohana Mahajan—as with the origin myths of many of the lineages comprising the Bhatiya Mahajan—has roots in Hindu victories over proselytising Muslims. This is strangely at odds with the Kharva myth of origin, which describes their modern social form emerging from a defeat at the hands of Muslims at Somnath. Of the three Hindu mercantile origin myths, the Bhatiyas and Lohanas claim victory over Muslims, while the Kharva Samaj attributes its current lowly social position to defeat by Muslims. Rather than assuming that the merchants' victory and the sailors' defeat simply explains the hierarchical relationship between the two groups, I suggest that the sailors' mythology serves another purpose for them and the wider Hindu community, that is to place them in an antagonistic position vis-à-vis Muslims.

The myth of Dariyalal shows how oceanic power can be harnessed to generate wealth (trade goods such as dhal) and to overpower Muslims. However, the recurrence of such fragments not only attests to their social and historical salience in collective representations of the past. The structural forces inherent in the myth (land and sea, land holding and commerce, and Hindus and Muslims) are made contemporaneous both in their retelling and as metaphors that simultaneously reflect and create contemporary social division. Such myths may be archaic, and may or may not coincide with evidence from the archaeological record, but they are not primarily told as sequential narratives with a logical conclusion, rather they stand for a set of structural power relations that are salient in the present. Likewise, the appropriation of myths and deities also reflects and creates social division, in much the same ways as the Ramayana unifies local traditions and national political narratives.

The Dariyalal temple is the flagship of reinvented Kharva tradition, albeit largely appropriated from the Lohana Mahajan. Older Shaivite temples, such as the one dedicated to Ratnakar Sagar (the sea as a mine of jewels), are neglected and crumbling. The Dariyalal temple also serves as something of a museum for Kharva tradition and fame; while providing a series of rhetorical devices with which Kharvas can distance themselves from Muslims. On the internal walls of the temple are newspaper cuttings and other ephemera that detail the glorious history of Kharva seafaring. The horses standing before Dariyalal are said to have come miraculously from the sea, and are associated with the warriors that Dariyalal conjured from the waters to defeat the Muslim predator. Before this temple was constructed, many of the artefacts now contained within it had been lost and forgotten in the sand dunes. The horses and other images were uncovered and catalogued by an archaeologist from Bombay. The Samaj leaders arranged for the collection and incorporation of these artefacts in the construction of the new temple complex. At one level this appears to be an example of the 'invention of tradition', where forsaken images are couched in terms of a legitimate and established mythology. However, the traditions seen in and around the temple are clearly transformations of ancient themes, which have been given a renewed rigour through the construction of the temple.

The construction of the temple and the activities and myths that surround it reveal the atavism that is central to contemporary Kharva Samaj identity. The stories of the lives of illustrious ancestors parallel the narration of contemporary biographies. Typical biographic forms isolate traits in the lives of ancestors, such as courage, skill and deep knowledge of winds, tides and currents, in order to integrate them into the biographies of modern Kharvas. The figures commemorated and venerated by the hero stones were courageous and exceptional sailors. In their modern form, these hero stones commemorate the twenty, or so, Kharvas that lost their lives to Japanese submarines during the Second World War, and an array of personalities attributed with extreme knowledge and daring. The past is remembered and reinvigorated in other ways as well. Among the Kharvas there are model makers, amateur historians and linguists, journalists, short-story writers, biographers and artists who depict small boats in big seas. They all share a similar preoccupation with ships, shipping and the grandeur of Kharva ancestors, by cataloguing and painting the past in nostalgic colours. Their outpourings, which commonly construct causal relationships between themes derived from classical Hinduism and Kharva heritage and attributes, appear in local newspapers, galleries and on the internal walls of the temple.

In the Ramayana and its associated traditions, Vishnu has been incarnated in various forms in different ages where either *adharma* (anti-religion) was present or where *dharma* (religion, religious duty, law, custom, religion) was threatened. Vishnu is popularly held to have ten incarnations, which pass in a lineal sequence from lower forms of life to divinities that appear in the guise of men, a number of which have been incorporated into the traditions of the temple. The image of Dariyalal sits upon Matsya (a fish), the first incarnation of Vishnu, which saved the Vedas from being consumed by the *asuras* (demons). Vishnu's second (or third, depending on the tradition) *avatar* was Kurma (a tortoise). After the flood (which prompted Vishnu to appear as Matsya) the deities were weak and their power was lost in the ocean. To help them, Vishnu sprinkled the ocean with a variety of medicinal herbs, and advised them to churn the milky ocean for the elixir that would restore their strength. They attempted to use Mount Mandara to stir the waters but were not strong enough, and so they called on the help of demons. But even their united strength could not stop the mountain from sinking into the ocean bed. Vishnu came to their rescue in the form of a giant tortoise. He bore the weight of the mountain upon his hard-shelled back and stirred the ocean until the treasures arose from the depths. In the compound of the Dariyalal temple, nestling in the shade of a tree, is a stone tortoise. According to Kharva topographers, the cartographical outline of Kachchh resembles the shape of an upturned tortoise (*kachbo*). Rapar and Bhachau form the lowered head; Anjar, Mundra, Mandvi and Abdasa form the spine of the tortoise's shell; Nakhatrana and Lakhpat form the bottom of the shell; Bhuj and the Northern regions give the impression of a leg. The tortoise in the temple compound makes an explicit connection between the land of Kachchh and Vishnu as the defender of Hindus: the land of Kachchh itself being seen as a form of Vishnu, defender of the Hindu faith.

Another figure venerated in the temple is Kano Malam, a courageous and skilled sailor in the Kachchhi tradition. His knowledge of the Ocean is said to have been vast, but intuitive. While he was just off the African coast in the late fifteenth century he came across Vasco da Gama apparently lost and in need of direction. Kano showed the Portuguese explorer the way to Calicut. Contemporary versions of this story get rather muddled as to what the moral outcome of the tale should be. Should the narrator emphasise Kano's skill over that of the great European or should the narrator feel ashamed of Kano's naivety and innocence for having brought the Portuguese to India? Commonly, Kano is said to have lost his mind or, rather more creatively, is said to have realised his mistake and to have devoted his remaining years to tirelessly campaigning for the expulsion of foreign powers from Indian soil.

While these are undoubtedly modern twists on ancient stories, the collection of artefacts in the temple makes explicit the core values of the Kharva Samaj, emphasising the traditions of Vishnu and their heritage of seafaring. The moral weight of dead ancestors, their ethereal powers, and the ideal model of Kharva life they represent are embodied and venerated in the hero stones and in the ephemera contained within the temple. As putative descendents of Krishna and Ram, both incarnations of Vishnu and respectively of the Kshatriya lunar and solar descent lines, ancestral memory is given a deified ideal type as well as in the form of memorable seafaring ancestors. Ritually constructing themselves as warrior-sailors with traces of the deity in them on whose land they also tread, they have created a powerful charter through which they appear to be the legitimate defenders of the land against Muslim invaders.

Sailors That Don't Sail

Having described the Kharvas Samaj, its origins myths and new temple complex, the discussion moves to the question of Kharva livelihood. They are referred to as sailors. They refer to themselves as sailors. They build and worship in temples dedicated to the ritual cycles of the tides and moon. The internal social organisation of the Samaj reflects past degrees of seniority on ships. Old men are accorded status by the length and quality of their career at sea. Kharva social architecture, language and ritual are derived from the traditions of voyages and migrations, but the cores of such signs are hollow because the overwhelming majority of Kharvas no longer sail. Kharvas may not sail anymore, but they lead the lives of sailors. They do everything that their ancestors did, but without recourse to ships. In the midst of changing employment patterns and shifting social boundaries, Kharvas have reinvented and distilled the traditions of their ancestors. The fact that Kharvas continue to be known as sailors suggests that there is much more to being a sailor than going to sea on ships. Being a sailor means having a particular exogenous disposition towards the boundaries of India, living in certain parts of a town that developed as a port, following the ritual cycles of the sea and being enmeshed in client relationships with a mercantile caste. This explanation is offered, rather than the other possibility that the language of social ascription has not changed as rapidly as employment patterns.

In the past, Kharva men crewed Bhatiya ships, and Kharvanis (Kharva women) served in the houses of their kin's patrons. Such relationships have been in existence for generations and continue in the same form in the present. In some cases, Kharvas can trace a relationship to a particular Bhatiya lineage through seven named generations (of both client Kharvas and patron Bhatiyas) to the latter half of the nineteenth century and sometimes earlier. These genealogies also trace the success and failure of particular business enterprises in East Africa, sketch population movements throughout the Ocean, and identify men with particular ships that appeared at the nexus of patron-client relationships. Kharvas unify in speech (we, our) their own activities with those of their patrons. The success of particular Bhatiya patrons in Zanzibar or Oman, the strength of these relationships, and the material benefits (loans, houses, weddings and political representation) derived from them are a source of *abru* (reputation, honour) among Kharvas.

Kharvas do not intermarry with mahajan populations. There is no legitimate common substance shared between them. Commonality is derived from the sea and from the social and ritual organisation of shipping. Today, women continue to work as domestic servants in Mandvi, while men work as drivers, machine operators and labourers for Bhatiya firms in Oman, where the Bhatiyas have had long and fruitful relationships with the governors of that land. The logic of contemporary relationships originates from the ancestors who established reciprocal exchanges of service, protection and patronage. Kharva women are very poorly paid for their work. The benefit of domestic service does not lie in financial remuneration but in past and future rewards for her male kin. To break the relationship would be to dishonour the agreement and patronage shown by previous generations of Bhatiyas towards Kharva ancestors. Seasonal Kharva labour migration to Oman follows the traditional pattern of nine months at 'sea' and three months at home during the monsoon. As emblematic sailors,

Kharvas have remained enmeshed within samaj-mahajan relationships. They are working towards the unattainable goal of paying off the moral interest on the relations of reciprocity and social economy established by their ancestors. In summary, the Kharva Samaj, the largest single population in Mandvi, forms the constituency of the mercantile mahajans. Consequently, the economic and social position of the traders is supported by a large number of dependent Kharvas.

The term *laskhar* (lascar) means sailor, longshoreman, army servant or artilleryman and is also used to refer to Kharvas. The concomitance of these meanings points to the Kharva role within the political domain of the mahajans. Kharvas are the foot soldiers of the merchants, fighting their street battles and aiding in disputes when more than honed negotiating skills are required. This is not to say that Kharvas are the unquestioning recipients of mahajan orders because they also act autonomously in protecting their own interests. However, the general pattern of political and economic ties means that Kharvas are responsive to the demands and interests of their patrons. These days they are not called upon to protect and crew the merchant fleets, but their social position includes defending the generalised interests of Hindus from Muslim predation, a task for which, as has been shown, they are symbolically well equipped.

Many of the Kharvas are actively involved in local nationalist organisations and are well versed in the rhetoric of them. Thus, from a variety of religious, political and local traditions they have a developed sense of hostility towards Muslims, especially their ancient rivals the Bhadala. In the latter decades of the twentieth century the Kharva stopped sailing, although the decline had started long before then. In their eyes they lost their dharma and betrayed their ancestral heritage. To add insult to injury, Muslims—the cause of their original displacement, defeat and humiliation at Somnath—took over their role as sailors. In Mandvi, in the early 1980s, Kharvas could look over the river estuary and see the fine new houses of Muslim-Bhadala shipowners—who had capitalised on the creation of

Dubai as a free-trade port—rising above the water. They could see new elaborate minarets being erected and new ships being constructed along the water's edge. They would also see young Muslim men, well dressed and on new motorbikes, coming into the bazaars at night to taunt Hindu women. Kharvas heard stories, some true, some fictions, of smuggling and piracy being carried out by the Muslims, who were rumoured to be involved in the arms trade and other kinds of insurgency. The innovation and courage (roughly equating to smuggling and piracy) of Kachchhi sailors plays a central role in the aggrandisement of the Kharva seafaring tradition. However, when these stories were given an anti-Hindu tinge, the morality, nobility and legitimacy of smuggling changed and began to interfere with notions of political propriety.

While sitting with Kharva men on the river's edge and looking onto Salaya, I frequently heard the lament that the Muslims did not know how to 'plough the sea'. Kharvas resented the facts that Muslim ships were powered by engines and had sophisticated navigation equipment, and they dismissed Muslim shipbuilding as shoddy and as deskilled. It was not only the technology that Kharvas detested, they also disliked the methods and strategies the Muslims used in business. As 'crows among flamingos', Muslims were opportunistic, their profits derived solely from illegality. This flighty metaphor was one that an elderly wizened Kharva named Ramji would frequently draw upon to describe the new Muslim merchants and sailors. Looking out onto the estuary at certain times of the year, flamingos and crows could be seen feeding together. The metaphor relies on contrasting statures, colours, demeanours and feeding habits of the birds.

Ramji said of the Muslims: "Our trade in the past brought wealth and fame to our land, we did not harm the Kachchhi people. The Muslims are hurting Kachchh. They are terrorists, and their loyalties are not with Kachchh but with other Muslims. They are harming our land and our people with the things they do. They are not loyal and they are not *really* Indian." The suspicion that Muslims are not loyal to the Indian

State is informed by a number of sources. First, the facts of Muslim social hierarchy elevate and privilege foreign origins. Thus the stress or invention of Arab, Persian, or Turkish ancestry (rather than resting content with Indian origins) is seen as pointing to general Muslim antipathy towards India. Related to this, many Kharvas claim that Muslims, and Bhadalas in particular, do not accept the current Indian State as a legitimate political and geographical organisation (also Kakar 1996: 128). Instead, Muslims are seen as being loyal to the interests of Pakistan, and in times of crisis Muslims are united by their religion rather than by their ethnic, linguistic or regional origins. Empirically, these accusations are far from true, yet they retain particular and powerful currency among Kharvas.

Ramji's negative characterisation of 'modern' shipping is not simply the grumbling opinion of an old man who is unable, or unwilling, to accept and accommodate change. It is true that the technology, language and skills with which he matured have been transformed through innovation, but not beyond recognition. However, the resentment and frustration evident among many men similar to Ramji, old and young, is an expression of much more than nostalgia: it is an expression of Kharva failure, combined with bitter contempt for the men on the other side of the river that have become successful at shipping. This failure is in turn much more than the loss of individual or even samaj dharma, it is a betrayal of ancestors and everything that ancestors stand for. Ramji is a Kharva (a sailor who does not sail) whose traditional rivals, Muslims, sail very successfully and derive significant profits from their trade, but are viewed by Kharvas as barely human.

Kharvas do not talk about themselves as Hindus without a simultaneous awareness of the Muslim presence. Men, such as Ramji, refer to themselves as Hindus only when they talk of Muslims, otherwise conversations about others are conducted through the use of caste names. The image they commonly describe of the animalistic Bhadala is based on the perceived ferocity, rampant sexuality, immorality and dirtiness of Muslims. The accusation of 'dirtiness' relates to what in Kharva eyes are incestuous marriage practices. Cousin marriages, popular among the town's Muslims, are not only outlawed for Hindus, they are also thought to have dire consequences for the moral and social constitution of resulting offspring. The inner pollution of Muslims is compounded by their consumption of tabooed foods, such as meat, and excessive consumption of 'hot' foods, such as chillies and onions. The voracious sexual appetites of Muslims are further reflected in the size of their families. Kharvas allege, as is common in India, that Muslims produce large families as part of a generalised conspiracy to eventually outnumber the Hindu population. The rampant sexuality of Muslims is also seen as an immediate threat to Hindu women, who are seen as somewhat feckless and susceptible to the allure of Muslim wealth, which religious conversion through marriage would bring. Muslim men are attributed with rather different intentions towards Hindu women. They are seen to desire the pollution and depopulation of the Hindu community through religious conversion. The negative characterisation of Muslims by Kharvas centres on the Bhadalas and the particular view they have of them from across the river.

Social Theory and the Western Indian Ocean

If, as Arnold Toynbee (1981) suggested, Greek mariners were the first to name continents then there is some irony in the fact that the voyages of sailors are commonly used to display the arbitrariness of geographic classifications and to suggest ways in which space can be meaningfully redefined.

Fernand Braudel (1972) first suggested that the unity of a cultural and geographical region can be also be defined by the movements of people across the mass of water at its centre rather than by the lands around its periphery. His analysis of cultural unity and diversity in the Mediterranean region at the time of Philippe II shows, by using a triple analytical framework of space, time and structure, how the frontiers of physical units and human units are not coterminous. In his view, the Mediterranean region was a place of human activity defined by the journeys, exchanges, and the cultures of the merchants, sailors, traders and caravaneers that traversed its waters and lands. Kirti Chaudhuri (1985) adopted this hypothesis in *Trade and Civilisation in the Indian Ocean*. Focusing primarily on the technologies, sociology and mechanisms of long-distance trade, he suggests that the Ocean region includes the trans-Himalayan areas and the T'ien Shan as much as it does the waters of the Red Sea, the Persian Gulf and the Mozambique Channel. In his reading of Braudel (supported by mathematical set theory), the sea unites people and places through recognised systems of exchange; it also divides by distance, changing environmental conditions and cultural differences. In his view, the diversity evident in the whole is itself evidence of unity. Travel, movements of population, climate, waves of colonisation, mastery of sea travel and, at times, Islam, give unity in the Ocean. Diversity is to be seen in social systems and cultural traditions such as food, clothing, housing and, at times, Islam when its expansion created distinct zones of political tension.

But Chaudhuri perhaps places too much emphasis on the mechanisms of trade as the unifying feature of the region and not enough stress on social aspects of life in and around the Ocean. Echoing the world-systems approach of Wallerstein, the conclusion that diversity is evidence of unity is vague and, taken to its logical conclusion, suggests that everything is connected to everything else. While this may be empirically true, it is not a tenable theoretical position for a social scientist investigating particular phenomena or a particular region, who has, for a variety of pragmatic reasons, to draw artificial boundaries around his or her material. However, despite criticism aimed at the ways in which these historians glossed over the details of regional trade and polity (see for example Arasaratnam 1990), the paradigm of unity and diversity has remained a popular one for looking at the Indian Ocean.

Scholars specialising in regional studies are faced with the same problems as the macro-historians: where does maritime society stop and land society start? And, as it is nearly always concluded that land and sea form distinct types of sociality (see for example Braudel 1972: 187), what is the relationship between the two forms? 'Maritime culture', an idea elaborated by A. H. J. Prins (1965) in his monograph *Sailing from Lamu*, refers to a particular set of relationships given by trade, shipping and fishing between people and the sea that distinguish them from landlubbers. In his analysis, Lamu becomes a 'little world', formed from maritime rhythms and the movement of its people by ship. He asserted that such 'culture' is 'open' rather than 'closed' and is continuously influenced by the voyages and interactions of its members (1965: 57). This now seems a rather commonplace observation, but Prins took the idea a step further and argued of Lamu that: "It represents the local 'little civilisation' corresponding with the 'great civilisation' of Arabia and Persia" (Ibid.). Prins also saw Lamu as a 'little' culture in relation to the 'great' trading settlements of Mombasa and Zanzibar, which were "both so very much more influenced, by Western culture than Lamu itself" (Ibid.). Lamu is thus given a double cultural focus reflecting two 'great civilisations' that are mirrored in one glass.

Other historians have also sought, in various ways, to develop analytical perspectives on the Ocean: to define its boundaries and to identify other kinds of features that create regional unity and diversity. The time frames used in such studies are typically the pre-1500s, 1500–1800, and 1800 to the present (Arasaratnam 1990: 233). One approach has been to write macro-histories of particular eras (Das Gupta and Pearson 1987) or to write general histories of 'Muslims' (Risso 1995) or 'Portuguese' (Boxer 1969) and so on. A second trend, often using similar time frames, has been to study particular regions in depth such as Hadhramaut (Freitag and Clarence-Smith 1997) or particular places such as Surat (Subramanian 1998; Pearson 1976) and Lamu (Prins 1965). Similarly, the Mauritian historian, Auguste Toussaint (1966), was convinced that the best vantage point from which to understand the Indian Ocean was from the concentrated flows of people that passed through its islands. But for many years the panacea for historians has been the vision of the Ocean as a unified space or 'world'. More recently Kenneth McPherson (1993) has defined the Indian Ocean 'world' by its patterns of long-distance maritime trade, the boundaries of which were constantly shifting. By analysing 'cultural diffusion and interaction' (1995: 3) he is able to conclude, along with Chaudhuri, that the Ocean is not a homogenous cultural area and that any commonality between regions was determined by trade and the exchanges (material or otherwise) this entailed. As mentioned previously, Michael Pearson (2000) has recently suggested that the Ocean is not a region bound together by some nebulous notion of commonality or structure because people of the littoral identify strongly with their own countries as well as being bound up in more general patterns of loyalty, such as belonging to the Muslim world.

The starting point for anthropology in the Indian Ocean should perhaps be Pearson's conclusion. However, I want to take this argument a step further to suggest that travel and migration in the Indian Ocean can be as socially divisive as it is congealing. Here, I am not referring only to structural zones of geographical space but more importantly to divisions among a local population. By looking at Kharva loyalties and in the ways in which they have gone to considerable lengths to create a strong regional identity, it is apparent that the resources derived from lives spent in the lap of the Ocean and in foreign ports have been invested in rather more mundane activities such as status claims, the politics of religious differentiation, and colouring their displacement and origins with nationalistic sentiments. Over the previous two centuries, trade, commerce and, later, labour migration have formed and reformed hierarchical bonds between them and their patrons. In other words, their internationalism is premised on relationships formed on the streets of Mandvi.

The kinds of units of value of interest to anthropologists are not always accessible to the social historians who have been so influential in forming our ideas about what sociality in the Ocean region is like. The study of local caste identity, sentiment, hierarchy, social order and religious differentiation, rather colonial records and ledgers, tells a rather different story that goes some way towards debunking the myths of unity so central to the work of many historians.

Conclusion

Given that aspects of regional and political identity coincide in narratives of seafarers we could also ask what other aspects of Indian Ocean sociality have been simplified by overemphasising the unity paradigm. There are two further issues that are called into question by examining diversity over unity: the concept of diaspora and the role of caste in forming particular regional and spatial identities.

The economic historian Claude Markovits has convincingly argued that the notion of a unitary 'South Asian diaspora' has been conducive to a distorted view of the historical record (2000: 4). Likewise, Michael Pearson has noted that a bias in the historiography of what he calls 'Greater India' exaggerates the role of Indians in East Africa (1998b: 227–29; also Amiji 1983). Perhaps he is right, and this literature has emerged in India to emphasise or create a glorious and noble history of Indian seafaring to compensate for the humiliation of British colonialism (see for example Sakarai 1980, 1981). However, this does not explain the bias in Euro-American literature towards the 'Indians' in East Africa to the detriment of those in India or, until very recently, the surprising lack of attention paid by anthropologists to the human interaction between the two landfalls. Together, these factors have contributed to the feeble understanding among anthropologists of the complexity of migration from India and to a simplistic political view of Indians overseas that has had important implications for policy both in India and in the countries where they have settled.

The term 'diaspora', originally applied to Jews living permanently outside Palestine, is regularly used today to describe any group of people who live outside the confines of their homeland. Markovits questions the validity of the term in the South Asian context for three reasons. First, the majority of migrants settled temporarily overseas with the avowed intention of returning home. Secondly, studies of Indians overseas have misleadingly privileged religion as the basis of solidarity among migrants over their regional and local origins. Thirdly, differences in occupation and class among labourers, tertiary workers and commercial migrants are commonly overlooked (2000: 5–7). While the material in this chapter strongly supports these claims, in my view, Markovits underestimates the role of 'caste' (or at least caste-type aggregates of people) in determining patterns of migration. Keen to stress the importance of potential solidarities created at a local level, he suggests, on the basis of archive materials relating to Sindh, that ethnicity and religion were not crucial factors in the structures of migration. While this might well be the case for Sindh, given its particular historical conditions, the material presented here suggests that at times 'caste' (and its variants) is most important precisely at a local level. This is not simply because itself allows people to differentiate themselves from one another; it also provides the basis upon which other markers of identity such as ethnicity, religion, language and occupation can be embellished. This is particularly true of the migrant and mercantile 'castes' of Kachchh, which have historically been extremely adept at making communities for whom 'caste', 'religion' and 'ethnicity' are coterminous.

It is well known that migration to East Africa (and elsewhere) over the last two centuries has not created a unified Indian community overseas but at the same time the traditional patterns of caste and hierarchy have not been preserved in their original forms (Pocock 1957). More importantly, for our purposes, nor has it had an even effect on the population of Mandvi. In this chapter, I have attempted to indicate that migration among the Kharvas was first and foremost based on caste and inter-caste relationships with merchants, which were cemented by religion, community codes and organisation, and the restricted flow of information enhanced by a common language. The form of community leadership and structure held by any particular community also moulded the patterns of migration and commerce that emerged. Furthermore, the significance and influence of religious sites, tombs of saints, pilgrimage places, tutelage goddesses, marriage practices and so on influenced both the destination and duration of their sojourns overseas as well as the strength of the connections they maintained with Kachchh. In other words, trade and profits accrued from it were organised and distributed along caste lines. None of this is to deny the possibility of inter-caste cooperation but merely to assert that caste was and continues to be a tricky issue for the unity theorists.

The only way to make sense of the migrations and to account for the differences in destination and success and failure of enterprise is to look at each case individually. It is impossible to generalise about migration patterns and the consequences of movement in the Indian Ocean and any attempt to do so would be to necessarily ignore much of the data.

PART TWO

The Presence of the Ocean in Coastal Settings

A map of the Arabian Sea, including Pakistan and Sri Lanka

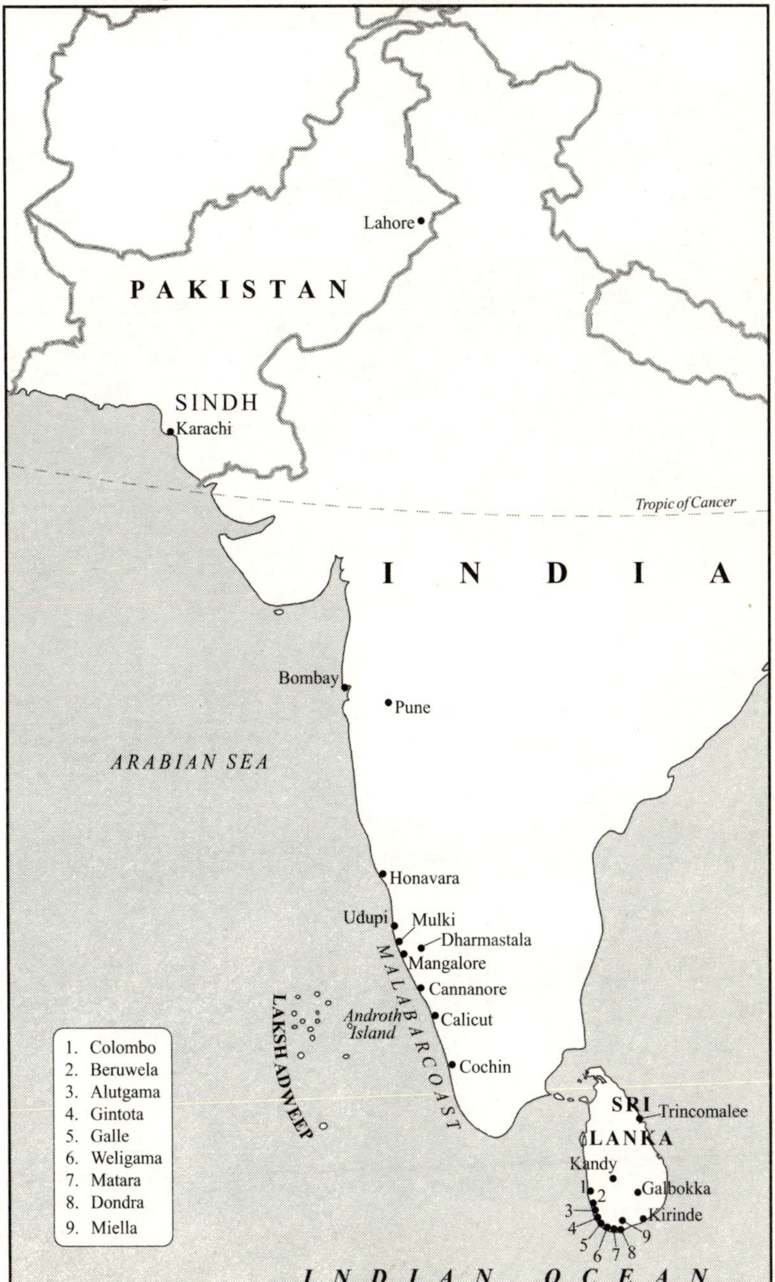

Map 5

4

Indian Ocean Trade and the Merchant Castes: India's West Coast, 1500–1800

Harald Tambs-Lyche

Introduction

Our knowledge of Indian Ocean trade in the early colonial period has increased vastly in recent years, as has our knowledge of Indian merchant communities. Here, I shall assess the influence of overseas trade on the latter's position, socially and politically, in different regions of India's west coast. I shall compare their situation in different locations along the coast, but a main point will be to see them as part of a single system of trade and finance, an 'economie monde' in Braudel's terms (1972; Borsa 1990).

Weber (1958) saw merchants largely as outsiders to the system—rather like Jews were once seen, in relation to traditional European society. For some fifty years after Weber's death, material on Indian merchant communities was scarce, but we now have the means to challenge his view. The situation of merchant communities shows considerable variation in the traditional Indian context, and the guiding hypothesis here is that it has been strongly influenced, in each region, by the relative importance of overseas links.

R. Grönhaug developed the concept of fields as a tool to extend interactionist anthropological analysis to larger-scale units (1974, 1978). Though social interaction forms networks that are, in principle, unbounded, he observes—like economists,

Marxists, and anthropologists concerned with complexity (Hannerz 1992)—that the effects of action do not necessarily coincide with interaction.[1] Such effects, then, constitute the specific causal relationships—'proper dynamics'—of each field. Though the attribution of a cause is necessarily subjective, the method consists of experimenting with possible causes to see what field they will define.[2] The field I investigate here concerns the social organisation of trade and finance in western India, and the effects of overseas trade on the position of merchants in different regions along the coast. A note on possible relations between trade and finance, between state and commerce, will make my hypotheses clear.

We know more than Weber did about the division of labour in commerce: bankers and traders, for example, were not always the same people. Traders might be bankers or moneylenders, but there might also be a division of labour between them, either as specialisation within a single community or as a relationship between different, specialised communities. In all cases, the relation between trade and finance is seen as symbiotic: but while trade depends on finance, there are other sectors, notably the state, which need and may underpin the financial sector. Thus state finance may leave some capital for investment in trade, traders may found their own financial network separate from the one based on land-revenue farming and state loans, or the financial sector may be strong enough to stand on its own feet, financing state and trade equally. The social consequences would be different in each case. Where

[1] We may be influenced by the actions of people we have not even heard about. The only way to obtain relative closure of networks is to specify particular kinds of interaction. This is how network theorists arrive at specialised networks, but they usually stop where manifest interaction ends.

[2] In principle, we could define, e.g. the price of pepper as a central "proper dynamics" of a field, in which we could then follow the causal effects of the fall in the pepper price as far as that logic would take us. In practice it might take us too far, since almost everything is somehow connected, so we would have to stop at a point where the effects of this specific cause are highly diluted. Such a "boundary" cannot be empirically established. But the process of forming a reasoned judgment of such effects may in itself prove a useful way of approaching, selecting and interpreting the data.

trade finance is just a spillover from banking for the state, we may expect the state's financiers to dominate trade: Brahmin communities in the Maratha country may be an example. In the south, on the Kanara and Kerala coasts, state finance and trade networks would seem to be separate, though some of the trading communities lent money to the state. In mainland Gujarat, the *shroffs* or bankers were strong enough to form a distinct financial sector, catering both to trade and state needs, but they were part of the larger, multi-caste merchant community which, through positions such as the Nagarshet in Ahmedabad (Gillion 1968), had real political influence.

This brings us to the importance of overseas links. Where they were weak, merchant communities would depend largely on finance derived from agrarian produce and revenue; as external trade grew, merchants would turn away from land and state to the market, becoming townsmen relatively independent of state bureaucracy, with the merchant republic as an ideal type—not fully realised in India. Coexistence of internal, land-based, and external trade may lead to an integrated business world where land revenue, political finance and external trade all contribute to commercial wealth; or to a separation of business communities, turned, respectively, towards inland concerns and towards the sea routes.

I shall view the various trading communities of western India according to a centre-periphery scale. I shall assume that the Gulf of Cambay was the effective centre of commercial networks in the region. Here, the Gujarati Banias dominated trade and finance.[3] There was indeed some shift in the relationship between Malabar and Gujarat, to the profit of the latter, in the

[3] There are problems in defining this category. While L. Subramanian (1985, 1987) sees the Hindu Banias of eighteenth-century Surat as a relatively integrated and well-defined group, Torri (1982, 1990) sees the term rather as a blanket category of "trader", at least as it was used by Europeans. My position is certainly influenced by present-day Gujarati usage, where a Bania is a member of a certain number of Hindu or Jain merchant communities. There is no doubt that the term can, under certain circumstances, be used to mean "merchant", but in general, Muslim merchant communities, and a number of Hindu ones (Shrimali Brahmins, Lohanas, etc.) are clearly excluded. In this paper, at any rate, I adopt the present Gujarati usage.

sixteenth or seventeenth century.[4] Again, Malabar may have been as central to trade as Gujarat, in the fourteenth century. According to Matthew, Calicut was "the most important centre of trade on the western coast of India during the fourteenth and fifteenth centuries". The rise and fall of Vijayanagar, the waning strength of the Jains in Karnataka, the Ming emperors' ban on overseas trade in 1433,[5] the shifts in balance of commerce between Gujarati and Arab merchants,[6] the coming of the Portuguese and the expansion of Gujarati trade networks when Gujarat became part of the Mughal empire (Moosvi 1992: 123), may all be factors here.[7] I deal, however, mainly with the situation from the sixteenth to the eighteenth century, when the predominance of Gujarat was clear.

I analyse, then, different communities' place in relation to the Banias of the Gulf of Cambay. Centrality, here, refers to trade networks, not physical space or political factors. Thus, Akbar's conquest in 1573 made Gujarat politically dependent on Delhi, but for the Banias it implied better access to northern India. As Pearson (1976) argued for Gujarati trade, the flag and the trade did not necessarily travel together. The Portuguese-controlled Indian Ocean trade networks were, of course, commercially dominated by Gujarati traders, as they came to terms with the Portuguese in the second half of the sixteenth century.

[4] Chaudhuri speaks of the Malabar ports as among the "casualties" of the changes in the circuit of trading emporia after 1600 (1985: 102).

[5] See e.g. Mathew (1997: 43–44). The last report of Chinese ships coming to Indian ports is from 1439.

[6] Specifically, the al-Karimi merchants of Cairo, who traded with Yemen and India and were well represented in Calicut, saw their trade destroyed by the state monopoly on the spice trade under the Mamluks in the fifteenth century (Mathew 1997: 44–45).

[7] Such changes need to be explained in a wider context, as Das Gupta did when he explained the decline of Surat, not by internal factors nor by European competition, but to the declining political situation and trading conditions in the three Muslim empires that formed the cornerstones of the city's trade networks: The Ottoman, Safavid and Mughal empires (Das Gupta 1994a: 8–9). The explanation implies, as he underlines, a collapse in the trade from Surat to South-East Asia between 1580 and 1620, making the port entirely dependent on its northern and western trade links.

The Division of Labour in Commerce: Surat and Gujarat

The main location of Indian merchant studies has been Surat, which was the chief port of the Mughal empire from the early seventeenth to the late eighteenth century (Das Gupta 1994a; Pearson 1976; Subramanian 1985, 1987; Torri 1982, 1990). It is probable that the conquest of Khandesh by the Mughals in 1601 contributed to the diversion of trade from the Cambay-Ahmedabad-Rajasthan route towards the south. By 1620, Surat was the dominant port in the area (Moosvi 1992: 125–27). Through the work done on Surat, we have a very reasonable idea of the positions of merchants in Gujarat. Though trade and finance was shared between many different communities, with a degree of specialisation among them, it is striking how they were all integrated into a common, market-oriented world—as the debate on the term 'Bania' shows quite clearly (Torri 1982, 1990; Subramanian 1985, 1987).

In this metropolitan trade centre, overseas trade was an important element and clearly contributed to both the wealth and the prestige of the merchant community as a whole. Land revenue was 'inconsiderable', so bankers mainly dealt with merchants, though under the British their most important creditor was the Company itself (Subramanian 1992: 156–59). The capital they lent was generated mainly from trade.

There were three distinct classes of commercial activity in the city (Das Gupta 1994a): the traders, the brokers and the bankers. The first were directly engaged in commerce, and were often shipowners. Generally they dealt either with the foreland or the hinterland of the port. Trade tended to be further subdivided according to sets of commodities and trade routes which made coherent networks possible. Brokers operated locally, though they had ties with the other groups, branching out in all directions. Bankers also operated locally, but in a context of long-range networks worked by the transfer of money through *hundis*.[8] A large-scale overseas trader, then,

[8] As Chaudhuri puts it: "For the merchants of Gujarat the Middle Eastern trade generated a larger volume of loanable capital than was possible elsewhere in India" (1985: 109).

needed a broker for access to the local market and a banker for credit and money transfers.

Singh and Rajshirke's study of Gujarati commercial records shows, in some detail, how Surat merchants were informed by mail of particular business opportunities elsewhere. Thus one trader was informed of scarcity of rice in Madras and the enormous profits made possible by the rising prices. Such information, however, flowed between those who were already doing business with each other—network links were essential. Partnerships were important in other ways: "The merchants entrusted goods to a trading partner who was financially not so sound as to be able to carry on overseas trade on his own. But what made him indispensable to his partner was his knowledge of the overseas markets and their commercial infrastructure" (Singh and Rajshirke 1992: 189–90).

I want to stress here the functional diversity of commerce, most clearly expressed in Surat where, we may assume, the commercial division of labour was developed to the fullest extent. This diversity was clearly related to a dense concentration of traders, who could benefit from the different kinds of expertise by collaborating in various ways. Thus risk was shared between the travelling partner, the financially stronger stationary partner, the broker who assembled or disposed of the commodities, and finally the banker. Such diversity would be hard to find elsewhere; Ahmedabad's traders were clearly less diverse than Surat's. At the village level, we may find a single trader who is his own broker and also does moneylending. My point here is that the diversity of the merchant community, in any single location, is a direct function of its centrality within the trade networks.[9]

For such diversity to develop, however, a certain degree of freedom for the merchant is needed, in relation notably to the state. In Gujarat, merchants played very much their own game as Pearson (1976) and Das Gupta (1994a) have shown, operating rather independently from the landowning and political

[9] "If the logistics of transport. . .determined where exactly a central-place should be located in the Indian Ocean, the growth and continued use of that place were dictated by the choice offered to merchants in a whole range of competitive products and services" (Chaudhuri 1985: 106).

interests. Here, merchants had high status: it has been common, in Gujarat, to place Vaishyas (in practice, the merchants) rather than Kshatriyas next to Brahmins among the four varnas. They were not only prestigious but also powerful. Though they might have been a 'state in the state', and their guilds and councils formed an alternative system of its own, they never formed the merchant republics that we know from the West. We may note that Ahmedabad's Nagarshet led a merchant community more united, politically, than Surat's diverse commercial class. While merchant power in Surat was a direct consequence of the importance of trade, such power, in Ahmedabad and possibly some other Gujarati cities,[10] resulted from the monopoly effect of a united commercial class (Gillion 1968).

Such power was certainly present under the Mughals and their successors, as several studies have shown (Pearson 1976). Ray shows that it was important in Cambay, too, even during the disturbed political conditions of the early eighteenth century. He also shows that the Marathas, often seen as 'plunderers', backed the merchant interests and supported free trade (Ray 1992). It seems, then, that the 'proper dynamics' of trade functioned relatively independent of political upheavals.

This relative liberty of trade may have been due to the sharp division, in Gujarat, between the landed interests and the merchants (Pearson 1976). Capital invested in trade largely came from commercial activities, among which overseas and long-distance trade was a dominant factor. Though some nobles took part in trade, they never came close to dominating it. And the capital generated for finance created a strong banking sector, whose services were equally available to traders, nobles or the state.

Periphery Close to the Centre: Saurashtra and Kachchh

As we leave the ports and cities of mainland Gujarat, this picture changes. Saurashtra was not really located on the main

[10] Bhavnagar, which became an important secondary port in the eighteenth century, also seems to have had a powerful merchant community led by its Nagarshet.

trade routes, but the trade of the Gulf of Cambay passed very close to its coast (Spodek 1976; Tambs-Lyche 1997). Here, the merchants may have been rivals of the Rajputs for status, but were definitely subject to their power. Here, too, most trading communities seem to have had their own networks, partly at least distinct from those of others, dividing the overseas, long-distance traders from the more regional or local networks.

In 1540, the Rajput prince Jam Raval founded a new port, Nawanagar, which rose to some eminence in the following centuries, known by its later name, Jamnagar. In the 1530s, the Portuguese had been making a major effort to curb Gujarat's trade by military means. Most of Gujarat's ports were sacked and burnt, including the main ports on the Gulf of Cambay and westwards to Mangrol, about halfway up the west coast of Saurashtra. It was hardly a coincidence that Jamnagar was founded just then, inside the Gulf of Kachchh and well north of the area of the Portuguese raids. In the following century, Jamnagar's trade expanded with the decline of Portuguese control of the seas between Saurashtra and the Persian Gulf, and really came into its own as Muscat and Oman broke away from Portuguese rule. From then onwards, the prosperity of the Bhatiya trading community was tied to the triangular trade between Oman, Jamnagar and East Africa. The Bhatiyas, then, clearly built their network in opposition to a Portuguese-controlled network, which it subsequently replaced.

We might think that, as the established Gujarati traders solved what they must have seen as the Portuguese problem, there would be no room for the Bhatiyas. But the peripheral location of Jamnagar—and Kachchh, where Bhatiyas also dominated overseas trade—was to become its strength. It seems that the Portuguese impact produced two distinct branches of the Gujarati trade networks: the main branch—including the Voras of Surat who traded on the Red Sea, for example—were able to re-establish their position by coming to terms with the Portuguese, while the Bhatiyas built theirs on the enemies of Portugal.

Thus, the Bhatiyas dominated the sea trade of Jamnagar, but as the town grew in the sixteenth and early seventeenth century they were soon joined by different Jain communities, whose networks were turned toward the umland and the hinterland of the port (Banks 1992). They were the main dealers in grain and other agricultural produce, and they, rather than the Bhatiyas, were involved in revenue farming and its associated activities. The pattern in Kachchh seems to have been similar.

The two types of business in Jamnagar were not entirely distinct, however, for as the Jains came to dominate the trade of the town's hinterland, they linked into the larger Gujarati-Marwari credit network. Thus the growth of the Bhatiya trade may have been a result of their position in relation to Portuguese and mainland Guarati networks, but at the same time they remained a branch of the larger system. This example, then, illustrates an effect we should expect from our centre-periphery hypothesis: conditions on the periphery produce particular trading communities which, however, link with the main network at certain defined points.

Specialisation in Jamnagar did not split the merchant community: overseas trade and state finance were still part of a single web of business transactions. In this small city, banking hardly seems to have become an independent sector of commercial activity. Typically, when modern banking came to Saurashtra, the rulers started state banks which had, for all practical purposes, a monopoly. Other monopolies were common in the Saurashtra states, such as salt. These monopolies point to a degree of state control in the periphery which was absent in the centre of the trading system. The best conditions for trade in Saurashtra were probably found in Bhavnagar, but resulted from conscious mercantilism on the part of its rulers rather than the dissociation of trade from politics that characterised Surat and the other ports of the Gujarat mainland.[11] Typically, the Bhavnagar ruler who Tod visited in 1821 had his own ships trading with Moçambique (1971: 263–64).[12]

[11] When Bhavnagar was founded in 1723, the ruler consciously built up its commerce through an alliance with Surat and, later, with the British.

[12] One of these ships traded in slaves, and had therefore been seized by the British.

Rajasthan

Rajasthan is important as an area of transit from Gujarat to northern India. Here, as in Saurashtra, there was opposition between rulers and landholders, on the one hand, and the merchants, on the other. Here, too, the dominance of landholders over merchants is clear. The structure of the commercial class was nevertheless somewhat different in Rajasthan (Timberg 1978). The transit caravan traders—the Banjaras—were not part of the urban trading community. Many were from the bardic caste (Charans) and based in the countryside, where many of them had land. Socially, they were closer to the landlords than to the urban merchants. Like the Jain Banias of Jamnagar, many Marwaris were tax-farmers and dealt in agricultural produce. They also acted as intermediaries, from their local base, in the long-distance trade network. But the Marwaris were also bankers, and gradually the long-distance transfer of money (through the *hundi* system) became one of their specialties.[13] As bankers, the Marwaris financed state, nobles and trade. Their political clout came mainly from the financial service they rendered to rulers; but in spite of the reciprocal dependence between rulers and merchants in Rajasthan, and in spite of the importance of some Marwaris as ministers or state administrators, they remained quite distinct from the nobles. In Rajasthan, there was no cross-caste assembly representing the commercial interests as a whole, nor was there a Nagarshet to head the community: it was the caste group (Marwaris and other Mahajan) which acted as a pressure group.

In the nineteenth century, the import of slaves seems to have been concentrated in Kachchh and some Saurashtra ports, no doubt because the British had difficulty in maintaining a close control of these ports. This trade went by Oman, where it was largely in the hands of Bhatiyas. Cutting the route into jurisdictionally separate stages no doubt helped spreading the risk, both financially and politically, of a trade officially banned by the British.

[13] Gillion says of the Marwaris: "The Jain Marwaris of Rajasthan come from an infertile country crossed by trade routes, and their business success in modern India derives more from this circumstance, and from the contraction of local opportunities in trade and the financing of princely wars, than from their religion" (1968: 22–23).

Rajasthan and the Saurashtra/Kachchh regions were peripheries to the Gujarat centre but closely linked to it. Yet in each of these peripheries, the situation of the merchant communities were different. Saurashtra and Kachchh profited from their peripheral location to develop distinct overseas links, but these were secondary to the Gulf of Cambay route, and the financial sector never became as strong as on the mainland. In general, the commercial class was in a weaker position. Rajasthan, on the other hand, profited from its intermediary position between two centres—Gujarat and the north Indian heartland—to develop a particularly strong banking sector. Even so, the strength of the commercial class as a whole, in Rajasthan, remained inferior to its position in mainland Gujarat.

Land, Capital and Commerce in the Maratha country

But a much clearer opposition emerges as we enter the Maratha country. It has sometimes been said that inland Maharashtra, like some other areas of India, lack a native trading caste: such statements ignore the commercial activities of Brahmins, whose role in trade and banking has, largely, been underestimated. Even in Gujarat, they form important commercial communities: the Shrimalis, for example, are heavily engaged in trade. In Poona, the Chitpavan Brahmins were preeminent in this field. But the Maratha country was an area where land revenue, trade in agricultural produce, and state finance relegated overseas trade to a very secondary position. In other words, the dominant merchant communities were tax-farmers and state bankers; they were not strongly engaged in external trade.

By the eighteenth century, Poona and Baroda had become important centres, not only politically but also financially (Subramanian 1992). Subramanian compares the political order of the Maratha confederacy with what she calls the 'Anglo-Nawabi' order of Bombay and Surat. She stresses the growing need for cash to fund military investments in the eighteenth century, a point corroborated by my work on

Saurashtra (1997).[14] This was a period when revenue farmers became prominent, both in Saurashtra and the Maratha country. The Peshwa's main source of income was, of course, land revenue, which was the basis of Poona's bankers.

Inland Maharashtra was far from the ports and the small number of towns were peripheral to trade. Commercial finance was in the hands of Gujaratis and Marwaris, and formed an extension of their credit networks: a large part of the remittances to Gujarat was handled by the Hari Bhakti firm of Baroda. But the main creditors of the Peshwa were Gopal Keshav and Keshav Bhat Karve, who were local Chitpavan Brahmins. Many of these Brahmin bankers were revenue farmers, and some even married into the Peshwa's family (Subramanian 1992: 162–63). They formed a secondary credit network based on Poona, which linked with Malwa, Rajasthan and northern India. "The Marathas", says Subramanian, "were not always succesful in mobilising large sums—the credit lines they used were under pressure from a general depletion in the volume of circulating specie in upper India. This was in contrast to the surplus revenues the English East India Company commanded" through linking into the main network of Gujarati, Marwari and Benares bankers.

Baroda was a special case. Here, "the bankers' overriding influence predated the formal organisation of the Baroda state.... Predatory bands of Maratha horse...were accompanied in their Gujarat campaigns by money lenders who satisfied the immediate needs of the troops and troop leaders. These camp financiers eventually assumed charge of the office of *potedar* and *bakshi*—military paymaster—a position they consolidated in due course in the Baroda state administration" (Subramanian 1992: 159–60). With the state in perpetual debt, the moneylenders benefited, which is why the Baroda state "was perhaps more a Bania raj than any other". The Hari Bhakti and Parekh family firms which dominated Baroda

[14] The eighteenth century brought considerable expansion in the military field, with generalisation of such technological advances as artillery, for example; and there was a concomitant expansion in bureaucracy. The century was known as the age of the great dewans (Tambs-Lyche 1997).

finance, says Subramanian, were originally bankers to merchants, but they rose to prominence as paymasters of the troops (Ibid: 172–74). The Parekhs were, of course, Banias, and so we may see the financial system of Baroda state as an instance of the commercial networks extending into the proper domain of the state. This, I take it, is the sense in which Subramanian describes Baroda as a 'Bania raj'.

Land revenue, then, could provide a local base for banking, but not to the extent of competing seriously with commercial capital, when the latter was present on the scale that we find in Surat. And it is probable that its localised nature worked against revenue farmers developing the techniques of long-distance banking associated with trade.

Goa: Landwards and Seawards Trade

In Goa, and in the rest of the Estado da India, trade was divided between two distinct sets of merchants. Overseas trade was largely controlled by the Gujaratis, while regional and inland trade seems to have been in the hands of the Gauda Saraswat Brahmins. The Gujaratis, especially, were also the main source of finance for the Estado's administration and for the Portuguese traders, which included both administrators and the *casado* settlers. On this basis, the locally settled Portuguese—often well beyond the control of the Estado—became an important trading community. Indeed, they did to some extent replace the indigenous traders in the course of the sixteenth century, as the Gauda Saraswat Brahmins left Goa due to religious persecution and better business opportunities elsewhere.[15] But they remained dependent on the established, Gujarati-controlled, financial links (Pearson 1981).

More than elsewhere perhaps, Goa seems to have exemplified a division of labour between foreland (overseas) traders, on the one hand, and those catering to the umland and hinterland, on the other. This corresponded to a social divide: Gujarati and Gauda Saraswat Brahmin traders may have col-

[15] This trend is very clear for Cochin, then under Portuguese control (Malekandathil 2001: 181).

laborated, but they did not mix. Yet the division of labour between the two trading communities was not absolute: both, for example, were involved in the trade through Diu to Mozambique in the late seventeenth and the eighteenth century[16] (Dias Antunes 1995). And, though very few of them are temple priests, we should not forget that the Gauda Saraswat Brahmins are Brahmins.

The Gauda Saraswat Brahmins were originally agriculturalists in Goa, though some were probably traders too, since we know that members of the caste were established as merchants on the Kanara and Malabar coasts centuries before the Portuguese came. Their rise to regional dominance in trade seems, however, to be intimately related to Goa's imports of rice from the Kanara coast, and several members of the community acted as intermediaries between the Portuguese and the Nayak rulers of Kanara in the seventeenth century.

Expanding in the Periphery: The Case of the Konkani Brahmins

On the Kanara coast, the Gauda Saraswat Brahmins are the most important commercial community. They are Konkani speakers and came, indeed, from Goa or the Konkan, but in several waves at different periods. We know they were taking over and restoring an important temple at Manjeshwar, in north Kerala, as early as the thirteenth century. About a century later, a group of five families settled in the port of Mulki, north of Mangalore. There was a major migration from Goa to the Kanara coast in the sixteenth century, and another in the eighteenth. The first was certainly related to two factors: the inquisition at Goa, with destruction of several of the caste's important temples, and the expanding export trade in rice, from the Kanara coast to Goa, where the Gauda Saraswat Brahmins seem to have controlled the network at both ends. There was also, from about 1520 to at least 1575, a continuing economic crisis at Goa, caused by the drain of money from

[16] Dias Antunes speaks of Banyans, i.e. Gujarati Banias, as well as of 'canarins', who must have been Gauda Saraswat Brahmins.

One of the lineage temples of the GSB—the Mangesh temple near Ponda in Goa.
Photograph by Harald Tambs-Lyche, 2005.

Portugal itself (Malekandathil 2001: 176–78); how much this affected the Gauda Saraswat Brahmins is uncertain. There are, in fact, other indications—mainly from inscriptions—that there was considerable draining of new lands for rice cultivation in south Kanara at a period roughly between the fifteenth and the seventeenth centuries, which corresponds quite well with the period of the Konkani diaspora (Vasantha Madhava 1991). The demand for rice in Goa must have provided ideal conditions for precisely the diaspora of the Konkani Brahmins. Indeed, the Gauda Saraswat Brahmins (GSB) still dominate the rice trade on the Kanara coast. That trade would have brought renewed migration to Malabar, too, for rice from south Kanara also went there.

In south Kanara, the locals—defined as the speakers of the Tulu language—view the Konkanis as immigrants, as they stand out from Tulu speakers not only in language, but also in religion and a whole set of other customs. Their position also reflects their earlier importance as moneylenders—not a popular role, of course, and a part of their past which the Gauda Saraswat Brahmins, today, prefer not to advertise. Yet, in spite of their local importance, these moneylenders did not build a banking system comparable to the Gujarat-Marwari network.

There are also numbers of Konkani-speaking Catholics, converted from the Gauda Saraswat Brahmins community, using Portuguese family names, and generally calling themselves Mangaloreans. They, too, have carved out a place for themselves in business, though not to the extent of the GSB. For example, in the temple town of Udupi, some sixty kilometers north of Mangalore, one Gauda Saraswat Brahmin trader, who had founded an organisation of traders, estimated that ninety per cent of the town's trade was in the hands of the GSB community.

Briefly, if we look for a counterpart to the northern 'merchant communities' in Mangalore and south Kanara, we have to turn to this community of apparent immigrants. Yet they are certainly integrated, in the sense that it is difficult to imagine the market economy, rural as well as urban, in the area without the Konkanis.

The Port of Mangalore and its Traders

Mangalore is one of the oldest ports in western India, mentioned in the *Periplus*, and apparently active ever since: still, the GSB settlement here seems to date only from the seventeenth century. It is probable that trade at Mangalore was until then controlled by other groups, among whom Muslims groups were prominent. Among them were the Malayali-speaking Mappilas, who are also prominent in northern Kerala, with Cannanore as an important centre. But there were also Konkani-speaking and Urdu-speaking Muslim groups: the former were and still are prominent in the port of Bhatkal, close to the boundary between north and south Kanara.

To the Arabs, Mangalore was, above all, a spice port, and many spice plantations inland are still owned by Jains, who probably controlled part of the spice trade once, at least from plantation to port. It is possible that they provided some of the overseas links too, but the indications we have of this date from the thirteenth century.[17] Later, these links seem to have been taken care of by Muslims, and there is a living tradition of Muslims supplanting Jains—or, in some cases, Jains converting to Islam—in the following centuries. Thus some of the Muslim merchant families at Bhatkal are supposed to have converted from Jainism, while several inland Jain families are supposed to have fled Bhatkal to escape conversion (Carrin, this volume). When Ibn Battuta visited Mangalore in the fifteenth century, he found a well-established Muslim community of merchants there, who, by his account, dominated the port's export trade, so that the king was said to depend on them rather than the other way round (Ibn Battuta 1990: 192–202). It is clear, then, that important changes have taken place in the relative position of trading communities of the Kanara coast, a situation quite different from the striking historical continuity of the Gujarat merchant castes.

In spite of Mangalore's role in trade, there were apparently no 'merchant princes' there—nobody like Virji Vora of Surat, Shantidas' family of Nagarsheths in Ahmedabad, or Gopaldas Sahu and Manohardas of Benares. There were, of course, local moneylenders, but like their counterparts in villages all over India, they charged the exorbitant interest rates typical of small-scale operations. Today, south Kanara has become a centre of banking, and two of India's largest banks have their headquarters here. These are the Bank of Canara and the Syndicate Bank. Both were started by Konkani Brahmins, and finance, like business in south Kanara, is to a great extent dominated by this community.

[17] Thus at the so-called 'thousand-pillar basti', a thirteenth-century Jain temple of Mudabidri, we find sculptured reliefs of African animals. Mudabidri is a small, predominantly Jain, town situated on the trade route between the plantation country and the port of Mangalore. It was a Jain chiefdom till the times of Haidar Ali and Tipu.

The Malabar coast

In Malabar, too, Brahmins were important in trade during the Dutch period. The GSB from Kanara were involved in the wholesale trade, mainly turned towards the sea, while the Pattars, or Tamil Brahmins, held a 'virtual monopoly' on the export of pepper across the Ghats (Vink 1995: 283–87). This division of labour is typical of the area: eastern and western links were clearly divided. With this division, we reach the limits of the west coast trading networks centred on Gujarat, for the Pattars must be seen as part of a different network, having its centre on the Coromandel coast.

The position of Muslim traders on this part of the coast was then certainly more important than it is now. But the situation Ibn Battuta describes at the ports of Malabar differed considerably from Mangalore, for in the former, merchants were clearly dependent on the ruler. This seems to have remained true of Calicut and the other Kerala ports when the Portuguese came: the Zamorin exercised far more control over trade than did the Mughal governors in Surat later on. In Cochin, merchant communities like the GSB had their own quarter in the city, and considerable autonomy—indeed they were included in the exterritorial rights exercised by the Dutch when they dominated Cochin's trade (Malekandathil 2001). Yet, all the 'foreigners', the Gauda Saraswat Brahmins included, had to deal with the ruler in order to carry on their tract.[18]

The Jews and Muslims were in the wholesale trade, like the Konkanis. Many St. Thomas Christians were certainly pepper farmers, while others were soldiers, craftsmen and merchants. It is less clear whether the pepper farmers were dealers too, but Vink is of the opinion that most of them sold "their crops in small quantities in the vicinity, in most cases the local *bazaar* or market" (1995: 286).

Certainly, the commercial community at Calicut was far from poor. Ibn Battuta had found its merchants able to buy a

[18] This may be one reason why van Leur (1955) accorded such importance to the state in his early analysis of Asian trade.

whole shipload single-handed (Chaudhuri 1985: 99). Vink stresses the intricate system of markets in Malabar (1995: 288–89), and the flourishing trade there in the seventeenth century. Yet as we have seen, the export trade was controlled by various communities of merchants, all immigrants to the area. At Ibn Battuta's time, they included the Chinese. He watched the arrival of envoys from the Chinese court; they had been shipwrecked and so lodged with their countrymen. Ma Huan, an interpreter with Cheng Ho's trading expedition in the early fifteenth century, describes their reception: "the king sent two trade officials to negotiate with the visiting merchants and fix the price of the valuable imports. The silk piece-goods were all inspected individually, and when general agreement was reached all the parties joined hands together and the Calicut broker read out the contract. The bargain was never repudiated and formed the basis for all subsequent calculation of financial transactions" (Chaudhuri, 1985: 99). This differs substantially from the procedure at Surat in the seventeenth and eighteenth century, where the foreign merchant simply had to find a broker and the authorities only intervened if no broker was found (Das Gupta 1994a). The state control of trade and markets was clearly more important in Calicut, and we may assume that it gave far less freedom of action to the merchants. Certainly, we hear of the Malabar rulers dealing with foreign merchants, but not with an organised, indigenous merchant community, like the one we find in Gujarat.

It is surprising, since the pepper trade is so old, that no 'native' trading caste should be involved in it, and Vink comments: "It is hardly surprising that none of these four groups originally came from Malabar since the native Malabar castes had only a limited radius of action" (1995: 284). This, however, is begging the question, for why should a seafaring people living on a rich coast with important exports—and a tradition both of shipbuilding and seafaring—refrain from trading in these exports beyond a 'limited radius'?

Indeed, large ships could be and were built both in Gujarat and on the Kanara-Malabar coast. Yet the Gujarati ships ranged all over the Indian Ocean, while Malabaris generally sailed their ships no further than Gujarat in the north, nor did they, as far as we know, take any major part in the southeastern trade to Acheh and Malacca. Vaidya (1945) states that the Malabari types of ships were mainly considered fit for coastal traffic, though they did sail to the Maldives. It is striking that his description fits rather exactly those of Tome Pires and Barbosa in the sixteenth century.[19] But while shipbuilding is often considered a conservative science, there is no reason why the Malabaris should not have developed or copied foreign craft, as so many other people have done. As a matter of fact, commercial techniques may prove harder to copy.

One point worth considering here is finance. In a business world dominated by the family firm, there must be limits to expansion by new investment, unless external finance is easily available. With expansion in pepper, it would seem more natural for the communities controlling the production of pepper to invest in its expansion, rather than to extend themselves into trade. This would leave the exporter's niche open for others, such as the Arabs, the Mappilas and the Konkanis.

Towards a Conclusion: Trade and Finance

I have noted the difference between the Gujarat and Malabar ports, between Surat and Calicut. The latter port did not develop the extensive division of labour in commerce that we find at Surat. Brokers certainly did exist, facilitating contact between the producers—of spices, for example—and the foreign buyers. But what about bankers? The Tamil Brahmins would seem to have had their own credit lines, centred east of the ghats. The Gujaratis had theirs in their homeland. Thus there seems to have been no indigenous banking comunity in Calicut, comparable to the Shroffs of Surat. Brokers, too, would seem to have played a lesser role: the Portuguese continuously had to deal directly with the Zamorin and other Kerala rulers. This was also what Ibn Battuta had found, here

[19] See Mathew (1997: 48). He also cites Hornell (1946).

and at Kanara ports such as Basrur and Bhatkal. There is no indication, in the literature, of an indigenous banking system comparable to that of the Gujarati-Marwari network, in the Malabar ports. It is in this sense that these ports form a periphery in the west coast commercial system. The same may be said of the Kanara coast; and in Goa, Gujaratis dominated finance. In the Maratha country, there was indigenous finance related to land revenue and the state, but it was the Gujarati firms who provided the links with the larger financial network.

The reasons for the different roles of Gujaratis and Malabaris in Indian Ocean trade should, I think, be explained by considerations proper to the field of trade and commerce, not by shady 'cultural propensities'. Capital for new and daring ventures requires an efficient credit network if the venture is to be a lasting one, and an efficient credit network is a large one, since ultimately the only way to assure against risk is to spread it. The credit network based on Gujarat and northern India became very considerable especially in Mughal times, as credit links spread across India. There was an important network, too, centring on the Chettiars and other commercial castes of the Coromandel coast. The first network came to dominate the west coast of India: the second the Bay of Bengal. It is hard to imagine comparable facilities within the confines of the Kanara-Malabar area. If it were otherwise, why should the Portuguese—and the English in their turn—have gone to the Gujaratis for finance? The point is not that the Malabar kingdoms were poor—far from it—but they were small, and their links with larger credit networks would seem to have passed precisely through those 'foreigners' who controlled their trade.

These considerations lead us back to the point from where we started. If Indian Ocean trade remained centred on the Gulf of Cambay during our period, this was not just because of its strategic location but equally because of Gujarat's role as a centre of finance. Yet this role was itself a product of the location, for Gujarat's position stemmed from its being on the crossroads of the links to the Middle East and Europe, to the north Indian heartland, to East Africa, to South India and to South-East Asia. The arrival of the Europeans, the direct sea link to Europe, and the importance of the pepper trade dislocated part of the trade: but it did not alter the dominant financial role of the Gujarati-Marwari banking network. This is why the Gujarati merchant community was different, socially and politically less tied to the state, than in other regions of India's west coast. Like the growth of that community in very early days, its central position in the Indian Ocean commercial world during our period was a function, not of local factors, but of the dynamics of trade in the whole region. But the effects of geographical centrality, in terms of internal division of labour in commerce and development of financial structure, outlasted that centrality itself to keep other regions, even when rich in commerce, peripheral to the Gujarat centre.

I conclude, then, that in order to understand the social organisation of any region of the Indian Ocean—and probably elsewhere—we shall need to understand its particular place and role in larger-scale networks. And this seems to be as true where our first impression is of locally determined forms as where the setting is obviously cosmopolitan. Along the shores of the sea, localism begs the question just as much as cosmopolitanism.

5

The Constitution of Islamic Community in Sri Lanka: Sufi Networks, Saints' Shrines and Ritual Practice

Llyn Smith

Introduction

Islam followed the Arab trade routes to Sri Lanka in the seventh century, and the history of those routes is reflected in current ideologies about the origins of the community and in its regenerative ritual practice. This paper examines the interplay of history, myth and ideology in the establishment and maintenance of a unitary Muslim identity from complex and competing ethnic and political identities (Arab, Indian, Moor, Malay) in a context of Buddhist, Hindu and Christian communities in an island ruled by European colonial powers. The foreign origins of the religion are also reflected in the structure of island mosques which are almost invariably attached to the shrine of a foreign saint. The distribution of shrines mirrors the historical pattern and relative importance of Muslim trade in the island with large southwest coastal settlements and extensive small-scale hinterland trade. In contrast to shrine practice in other cultures, Sri Lankan saints may be regarded as markers of an 'orthodox' Islam and their existence acts to sacralise mosque and island space. In this cultural context, shrines act to establish both orthodoxy and identity, and sign mosques as the basis of both religious practice and kin-based community. Saints' shrines, in essence, create sacred spaces upon which mosques may be built and in which Muslim communities may be created and sustained. Mosques are at the heart of a religious practice which reflects and protects community identity, through the celebration of an annual feast. More widely, regional Sufi networks extend from the island to south India and the Laccadives (Lakshadweep islands), reflecting the trade routes of the past, and current calendrical ritual practice orients the Indian Ocean Muslim community towards the Islamic heartlands.

Muslims here live in a world of Hindus and Buddhists who constantly assert, through frequent and public ritual practice, that the world is not an Islamic one; it is polytheistic and hierarchical not monotheistic and egalitarian. In the face of this tension, Muslims must continually establish their ideology as having real force in this particular world. Their Islam is 'imported" and must be constantly renewed. Thus their Islamic practice is arguably more reflexive in contrast to those followers of Islam closer to the Islamic heartlands, who may take their Islamic ideology for granted due to its totally embedded character. One cannot understand the horizons and depth of Muslim reality in Sri Lanka without a grasp of its Indian Ocean location.

Arab Traders and the Routes of Islam

The Sri Lankan Muslim community traces its origins to the arrival of Arab traders on the island in the pre-Islamic period. These traders married local Tamil women and established the first Moor communities on the southwest coast.[1] The Sri Lankan Muslim community is small and originally diverse, comprising around 8 per cent of the island's population. It is made up of Ceylon Moors (who trace their origins to the arrival of Arab traders), Indian or Coast Moors (who trace their origins to India), and the Malays (who were brought from Java and

[1] The Sri Lankan Muslim community speaks Tamil. New communities resulting from intermarriage between males of Middle Eastern extraction and local women are also found on India's western coast.

This paper is based on research carried out in the Matara district in the south of the island in 1984–86 with return visits in 1987 and 1997.

Sumatra by the British). The vast majority of Muslims in the island live in the eastern and north-central provinces and are impoverished farmers. Those who live on the island's southwest coast, though substantially fewer in number, have historically exercised far greater economic and political power through their engagement in trade and the increasing importance of trade to the island's rulers. In tracing the history of the Muslim community on the island and the Muslims' active role in the economy, it is necessary to focus continually upon the development of an indigenous trading/merchant class, and the role of a particular religious fraction within it.

The Indian Ocean was a lucrative and well-established mercantile arena that extended from the Red Sea and East Africa to Sumatra in the east and the China Sea in the north. It was their participation in this trade which first led 'Arab' traders to the ports of Sri Lanka.[2] The island was well known to the traders of the ancient world for its pearls, gems, elephants and ivory, and renowned for its cinnamon which supplied the Venetian and Middle Eastern spice markets. Known to the Romans as Taprobane and to the Arabs as Serendib, it has a prominent history in the trade of the Indian Ocean and the Arabian Sea. Both Romans and Arabs had discovered its resources in the first century AD; they were followed by Greeks, Persians, Sabeans (from Yemen) and Chinese. It was only the Arabs, however, who settled there and made it a permanent home (Mohan 1985: 2). Miller (1976: 40) has suggested that these settlements date from the first century.

The location of Arabia in a strategic position commanding the seaways of the Persian Gulf and the Red Sea made it a vital intermediary in the ancient trade between the major civilisations of east and west (Hourani 1951: 4–5). Its people were experienced seafarers and traders and had acted as maritime middlemen from the sixth century BC (Kiribamune 1986: 90). Similarly, Ceylon stood, fortuitously located, between Arabia and the route to the Malacca Straits, the South China Seas and

[2] At no time was this trade purely Arab, in terms of either shipping or traders (Kiribamune 1986: 89).

the major eastern ports of Sri Vijaya, Canton and Nanhai. Trade contacts appear to have been established between the Near East and Ceylon as early as the fourth century BC (Tibbetts 1956: 184). By the fifth century AD we have evidence of Ceylon's articulation into the China trade, through connections between Trincomalee on the east coast of Ceylon, and Tamluk, near the mouth of the Hooghly River in the Bay of Bengal, which was a crucial port in the China-Ceylon trade. By the ninth century AD the Arabs were using south Indian ports as an advanced base for their own China trade (Indrapala 1986: 117). Even after the discovery of the monsoons and the wind systems of the Indian Ocean which permitted travel across the Indian Ocean from East Africa, the Persian Gulf and the Red Sea to the Far East, it was still essential to break these journeys on the western coasts of Ceylon or India.[3]

Ceylon's trade with south India was long established and operated through the traditional ports of the northwest and across the narrow Palk Straits. These connections to the emporium ports formed the basis of the island's articulation into the trade of the Roman empire. It was during this period that Arab ships are first reported sailing to the Malabar coast in south India and Ceylon. The trade of Arabia was in decline between the fourth and sixth centuries, although the Arabs remained extensively involved as seafarers. After the rise of Islam in the seventh century and its rapid spread, a new dynamism was introduced to 'Muslim trade'.[4] A significant factor in this new dynamism, which peaked in the ninth century, was that the 'Muslim trader' had far greater freedom to travel, confident of the hospitality of fellow Muslims in any seaport from Europe to China (Kiribamune, 1986: 95). New Muslim trading communities were established to take advantage of hinterland trading routes and in littoral ports. This development also

[3] The word monsoon is taken from the Arabic *mawsim* meaning a 'fixed season' (Forbes 1981: 63).

[4] This term is a gloss covering the trading histories of a number of different peoples: Arabs, Yemenis, Persians from the Middle East, and East Africans. After the twelfth century it also included Muslim traders of Indian origin and later Indonesians (Kiribamune 1986: 89–93).

permitted an extension of the Arabs' traditional role as middlemen, and much local participation in ports of trade was eliminated. The expansion of Muslim trade in the Indian Ocean was checked by the rise of the Chola empire in south India in the tenth century, in particular its sea power. Prior to a Chola invasion of Ceylon, the island's external trade was entirely in the hands of the Muslims (C. R. De Silva 1986: 152) but K. M. De Silva argues that Sinhalese merchants controlled the internal trade (1981: 44). The latter point must take some qualification in my view and may not be taken as representative of the situation prevailing in the whole island at the time.[5] Certainly in the littoral areas of the southwest where Muslims were settled prior to the drift to the southwest of the Sinhalese kingdom (following the collapse of the eastern dry zone civilisations), there is little evidence of Sinhalese merchants controlling internal trade, although their participation is not in dispute. Island-wide, the Muslims are known for their ubiquitous settlement: "There is rarely a place without a crow or a muslim" is a common Sinhalese adage (Ali 1986, 148), and it clearly underlines their position as hinterland traders—the agent of transformation, of areca nut from every highland peasant's plot, into cloth. This exchange was the mainstay of small-scale Muslim trade, and the importance of the Muslims to the Sinhalese State as the converters of agricultural surplus should be noted. Their coastal settlements, particularly in the port towns of the southwest coast, also point to their importance as a trading community in pre-colonial times. During the period of colonial rule, Muslims sought always to pursue their trading interests, sometimes in opposition to the colonial powers and sometimes accommodating them.

[5] The scholarship on Muslims in Sri Lanka is slight and recent. Historians rely in large part for their information about the island's early history, on the Sinhalese chronicles of kingship; the *Rajavaliya*, the *Culavamsa* and the *Mahavamsa*. They are obviously of somewhat limited value in terms of information about groups outside the areas controlled by the Sinhalese kingdoms. Throughout the entire period under discussion here, the island was divided into a number of regional polities, ruled by Sinhalese and Tamil kings, and with constantly shifting boundaries (Kulasuriya 1976).

The Portuguese (1505–1658) sought to establish a trading monopoly throughout the Indian Ocean and to control the trade routes with the use of maritime power. Their particular interest was the spice trade (Malabar pepper and cinnamon from Ceylon), a trade controlled by the Arabs. Portuguese mercantile ambition was backed with an ecclesiastical mandate and they treated the Muslims as both religious adversaries and trading rivals. It was they who first applied the term "Moors" to all Muslims, irrespective of their ethnicity, and the first stirrings of a unifying local, "Muslim" identity in the island began with their arrival. The Muslims adopted the term and saw themselves as either Ceylon Moors (referring to the community established through the marriages of "Arab" men to indigenous women) or Coast Moors (Indian Muslims who had settled in Ceylon). The initial hostility towards the Moors eventually gave way to accommodation as the Portuguese were forced to rely upon Muslim trading networks internally and seafaring skills externally, in order to operate their interests. The Dutch (1658–1796) conquered all Portuguese settlements in the littoral and were determined to remove Muslims from any participation in the island's trade at all. Dutch policy was to leave only agriculture and navigation open to them as occupations, and they pursued explicit policies of social management (the creation of a local Burgher community as a result of Dutch marriage to locals) and repressive legislation to control Moorish settlement, banning them from some areas altogether. The upshot of their efforts was a significant increase in smuggling as Moors sought to avoid Dutch justice. Throughout the colonial period the Muslims provided a significant service to the Sinhalese king and the landlocked Kandyan kingdom in the central highlands. Both the Portuguese and the Dutch controlled the littoral but after the Kandyan war of 1815 the British gained control of the whole island. Prior to this, Muslims found a refuge in the kingdom and served as a means of access to outside trade and to diplomatic contact with the agents of foreign rulers. The British (1796–1949) removed all Dutch trading and social restrictions and were far more willing to support Muslim economic activity. They characterised Muslims engaged in trade as industrious and energetic in contrast to the largely agrarian Sinhalese and Tamil communities whose agricultural activities permitted them long periods of leisure. Muslim fortunes underwent a vigorous renewal in this period, and the economic gaps between rich and poor, which had begin to increase significantly under the Dutch, became even more marked. In the face of increasing nationalist Sinhalese and Tamil sentiment and increasing demands for self-determination, the British began devolving power along communal lines. This led to the necessity for Muslims to compete for power as a unified group. The British period may be characterised as one which saw the crystallisation of a polity increasingly defined in communal terms, a polity in which the Muslims remained a minority with a demographic distribution that confined them to consistent and acute minority status in most districts. During this period, multiple narratives of origin began to assume a more coherent form as the community came to participate in politics at the national level.

In the latter part of the nineteenth century, a Muslim revival followed those that had already taken place in the Sinhalese Buddhist and Tamil Hindu communities. All three were concerned with reasserting, after centuries of Christian dominance and through largely nationalist sentiments, an intention to participate in capitalist development. The Muslim revival was concerned with ethnicity and education but, importantly, with the religious meanings of Arab ethnicity. It marked the final articulation of an ideology of Arab descent. Prior to the revival, there had been recognition of two distinct traditions. One stated that the Muslims were the descendants of Arab traders and the other that they were the Tamils from Kayalpattanam in India. The revival involved the acceptance of one tradition and the firm rejection of the other. What was probably historical fact for a minority segment of the diverse Muslim population, became an ideology endorsed by the elite, and subsequently the history of the many.

The "ethnology debate" arose in 1888 when a prominent Tamil member of the Legislative Council delivered a paper entitled The Ethnology of the "Moors" of Ceylon, to the Royal

Asiatic Society in Colombo (Azeez 1957). Ponnambulam Ramanathan asserted that the ancestors of the Ceylon Moors were Tamils from south India who had embraced Islam and settled in the island in the fourteenth century. At this time the Muslims were not represented by a separate member, rather the Tamil member as representative of all Tamil-speaking inhabitants of the island represented them as well. A legislative restructuring was proposed which included a separate member for Muslims, and the fact that Ramanathan was the incumbent Tamil member at the time, made many suspect his motives. In Ramanathan's view, a few Arabs married into an Indian or Malabar community, adopted their language and some of their customs and merely changed their religion to Islam. For him this resulted in no significant alteration to the "material character" of the converting Malabar or East Coast Tamil matrilineal community. For the Moors, the patrilineal ideology of Islam leads them to understand that the children of Arab men who converted and married local women were of Arab descent and gave birth to a new racial/ethnic group—the Ceylon Moors. The general belief that Ceylon Moors are the descendents of Arab traders who converted and married local Tamil women makes a number of salient points. It clearly summarises the origins of the community, the manner of its arrival and the distinction between foreign men and local women. The Muslims on the east coast trace their presence to the arrival of Indian Muslims and there is a sense in which, although they are also Ceylon Moors, they are ideologically constituted as slightly less pure than those of the southwest who may claim that their Arab connections are more direct.[6]

Arabi Pasha, an Egyptian exiled in the island by the British became the charismatic focus of the Muslim revival. It was also at this time that a Muslim national elite emerged for the first time. Following Michael Roberts (1982), Samaraweera (1986) argues that prior to this, the fragmented Muslim community

[6] This situation is no doubt reinforced by the fact that east coast Muslims are matrilineal while those on the southwest coast are unambiguously patrilineal. All Muslim communities in the island however practise post-marital matrilocal residence.

had only local elites, in contrast to the other communities amongst whom national elites had already arisen. Arabi Pasha had chosen to come to Sri Lanka because of the widespread belief in the Middle East that Adam's Peak was the place where Adam had first set foot on earth.[7] It was Arabi Pasha's foreign origins, and the widespread perception that he was virtually on pilgrimage to the island that placed him in an encompassing position, regionally unconnected and nationally embraced. A further vital factor in his assumption of the leadership role (as symbol if not politically active figure) was the force generated in a sedimentation of the tradition of Arab origins, and as a consequence, the establishment of political and economic hegemony by the fraction of the community to whom these traditions most immediately applied. Thus, although the traders of the southwest coast already held a dominant economic position within the Muslim community viewed as a whole, the emergence during this period of a national elite among this group, in conjunction with a national revivalist movement which found much of its meaning in the final assertion of an Arab identity, determined that this fraction was placed in a position from which they could continue to legitimately dominate the community in both religious and economic terms. Alternatively, their continued economic dominance could be seen as religiously legitimated. Arabi Pasha may be seen as an "orthodox outsider". His success points to another factor active in community conceptions. That is, in order to maintain egalitarianism in the context of an hierarchical caste-based society it is crucial to avoid encompassment or subordination. The historical diversity in the Muslim community is still reflected in tensions in the social order and ongoing ideological friction. Tensions which are essentially those of class, are elaborated in a particular Islamic discourse, in which the governing ideas are those of social ranking based on Arabic purity, on the one hand, and the ideal of a unified egalitarian commu-

[7] The island had long been a site of pilgrimage for Muslims, the most famous being Ibn Battuta who visited in 1344 and travelled from Galle in the southwest to Colombo, inland via Adam's Peak.

nity, on the other. The existent social order is radically fragmented by great disparities in wealth and vastly different status positions arising in part from Arab or non-Arab origins. The contradictions born of this social reality which stands in stark contrast to an egalitarian ideal, generates a constant communal dynamic which seeks to resolve them.[8] The dynamic nonetheless contains the seeds of its own refutation. The idea of Arab traders as the basis of a pure Islam on the periphery itself reinforces the idea of rank which counteracts the egalitarian ideal.[9]

Saints and Shrines: The Roots of Orthodoxy

The location of saints' shrines on the island mirror the distribution of the Muslim community and their historical trading patterns, with heavy coastal settlement and extensive representation throughout the interior. There are over one thousand shrines throughout the island.[10] Saints' shrines are a common phenomenon throughout the Muslim world and equally common has been their classification by anthropologists as features of a "popular" as opposed to "orthodox" Islam

[8] It was suggested that given the above outlined 'ideology of decent' that Muslims on the East Coast would have to purify themselves through a new fundamentalism (Gunasinghe 1986: personal communication). The rapid growth of the guest worker economy in the Middle East during the 1980s resulted in significant wealth moving into the Eastern Province. The construction of many new mosques here at the time was also evident. Another result of Middle Eastern employment was that many Muslims (who otherwise would never have had the opportunity) were able to make the Hajj pilgrimage and acquire new status and the honorific, Hadjiar.

[9] I use the term peripheral deliberately notwithstanding Dale's criticism who argues "that apart from the size and vitality of the South Asian Muslim population, 'they' are weary of being classed as peripheral merely because they do not have Arab ancestors" (1986: 624). There is a constant tension that arises from the foreign men/ local women, religion/culture dichotomy that gives the community a reformist tenor.

[10] The 1975 list of mosques, shrines, places of religious worship and Muslim charitable trusts gives a total of 1219 mosques, shrines and takias. *Muslim Mosques and Charitable Trusts or Wakfs (Amendment) Act No 33 of 1982*. Supplement to Pt II of *Gazette of the Democratic Socialist Republic of Sri Lanka* of September 24, 1982. Colombo, Government Publications Bureau.

(Gellner 1972; Eickelman 1976, 1977; Currie 1992; Peters 1990; Von Grunebaum 1988). This position appears to be derived from a greater focus on shrine practice than shrine ideology. Shrine practice or saint "worship" has been viewed primarily as intercessionary activity in which Muslims seek boons from the entombed saint. The tomb itself in these cases is regarded as "a source of miraculous power" (Lawrence 1984: 121).[11] Neither shrine practice nor shrine ideology in Sri Lanka may be satisfactorily discussed within this intercessionary framework. In contrast to "folk/orthodox" distinctions, the shrines here are almost always located adjacent to a mosque, often under the same roof and in many cases the shrine has come first. The shrines thus stand at the heart of orthodox Islam on the island, and shrine practice continually engages an ideology which reasserts the position of the island as integral to an Arabic cosmology. Attendance at the shrine of an entombed saint is generated from an understanding of what a shrine is, rather than a concern with whom or what the saint is. This understanding is reflected in the beliefs and practices that surround death and burial in the community. When someone dies the ideal is that the body is washed and purified, wrapped in the kafan—burial cloth—and buried within twelve hours. Immediately the body is interred, the attending male community steps back from the grave site as it understood that an angel comes to interrogate the individual about their life on earth. If the person has led an exemplary life they are given a "window to heaven" and may see, if not participate in, its glories. This state of consciousness after death does not however imply any continuing relationship between the soul of the deceased and those remaining in the phenomenal world. Death in this cultural context has a marked finality about it.

[11] Currie (1992: 1) points out that "scholars have tended to use the word 'saint' to translate a plurality of Arabic, Persian and Urdu terms. By rendering wali, murshid, shaykh, darvis, sufi, pir or marabout as 'saint' the reader is led to believe that he is dealing with a single category. This obscures the considerable diversity which underlies these terms". Turner makes a similar point: "When Western anthropologists talk about Islamic saints, they use the term as a shorthand for a diversity of social roles" (Turner 1974: 61).

The death is regarded as a birth into the afterlife, excessive expressions of grief should be avoided and even the grave is designed to disappear.[12] The tombs of acknowledged saints then are rightly regarded as sacred spaces, places where the veil between heaven and earth has been withdrawn.

The myths which explain the origins of the saints entombed in the shrines fall into two categories which I have termed *stone boxes* and *miraculous revelations*. The first set of myths tell the stories of dead saints who travelled miraculously, in stone boxes on the seas, and were washed up on the shores of the island. The second set relate tales of Middle Eastern Muslims who had come to the island on pilgrimage to Adam's Peak and had died while meditating in the jungle. The location and existence of these saints, in unmarked graves, has been revealed by local miracles. Together, both sets of myths account for almost all of the coastal and interior shrines on the island. The vast majority of the stone box myths are located in the southwest coastal area, and all follow the same basic narrative.[13] It is believed that when this saint arrived at Kaparatota in the research area, another four floating tombs were also on the sea. This particular group of five was followed by a later group of seven.

The myth of Sheikh Inayathulla from Kaparatota near Weligama recounts that 350 years ago (around 1645) a stone box was seen floating on the sea near Weligama. The Sinhalese fisherfolk who were living in the area thought it must be debris from a ship wrecked at sea and rushed into the water to retrieve it. They tried a number of times to reach the box, but

[12] The two small wooden *mizan* (balance scales) at each end of the grave along with the mound of earth which covers the body are generally gone within a few years. (There are nonetheless some who do attend shrines to seek direct assistance and also a few local graves that have permanent gravestones on them.)

[13] The shrines are to found at Alutgama, Beruwela, Gintota, Galle Fort, Kaparatota, Dondra, Matara, Miella, Kirinde and Trincomalee. This list corresponds exactly to the list of sites commonly given as the original sites of Arabic settlement in the island. They are all coastal centres with a definite trading past, predominantly in the southwest. There is also a similar myth in the central highlands near Kandy where the saint arrived in a stone box travelling miraculously up the river (Rob Jones: personal communication p.c.).

each time they approached it the box moved further out to sea. By the following day, Muslims living in the town nearby had heard about it and came to the beach to see what the wonder was all about. To the astonishment of everybody present, the box came to the shore and the Muslims opened it. Inside they found a corpse fully wrapped in the Islamic kafan. With the corpse there was a *talappa* (turban), with the name Sheikh Inayathulla Vali Ullah,[14] a pair of sandals, a walking stick, a lamp and a *miswak* (a small toothbrush made from a frayed wooden twig). The Muslims carried the box from the beach up to higher ground and put it down. When they attempted to lift it again they were unable to pick it up. They went back to their homes and discussed the matter with other Muslims and all agreed that the body should be brought to the Muslim area (Galbokka/New Street) and buried. During their sleep they all dreamt that the saint was speaking to them and making it known that he wished to be buried on exactly the spot where the stone box now remained.

The land near the beach where the box stood, belonged to a Sinhalese man, and the Muslims approached him in the morning to tell him what had happened and to request some land from him. He refused their request and demanded that they remove the box immediately. The Muslims returned to the land and tried innumerable ways to remove the box, all of which proved unsuccessful. They informed the landowner that they would return in the morning with more men. That night Sheikh Inayathulla came to the Sinhalese landowner and beat him with a cane leaving marks all over his body. The landowner could not bear the pain and came running in the dead of night to the home of a moulavi, and told him what had happened, showing him the marks. He said he had no further objection to the corpse being buried on his land and donated two acres and some money towards the building of a small mosque.[15]

[14] Valli Ullah here reportedly means 'friend of Allah'. This is more often rendered Awliya, the term used to refer to all the saints. The Arabic word for saint is *wali* (pl *awliya)* literally 'friend' or 'patron' (Geijbels, 1978: 176).

[15] This version is adapted from one given to me by the Imam of the mosque and

Sheikh Inayathulla is believed to been a holy man who had lived in Iraq and who had spent his life preaching. His two disciples had buried him in the box according to his wishes and cast him into the sea. They then left Iraq and travelled in search of him. They found him in Kaparatota and became caretakers of his shrine until their deaths. The shrine contains a large oblong *ziyarram* (tomb) which stands directly above the actual grave of the saint. As is customary, the ziyarram is painted green and covered with a set of predominantly green cloths given as gifts. The tombs of the two disciples are also in the shrine on either side of Inayathulla's.

The details of the myth are reflected in current shrine practice. The saint's miswak was planted and has grown into a huge tree which stands beside the mosque. During the annual mosque feast, flags are hoisted on a rope which stretches between the tree and the mosque thus linking the two in this ritual celebration. The tree was for many generations a source of cures for asthma, burns etc and miraculously oozed blood when attacked by a Sinhalese person with a machete during the Sinhalese-Muslim riots of 1915.[16] This mosque is not located near a Muslim area of settlement but it does have an imam and is deliberately used for prayer by a group of young Muslim men from other areas. Its primary use, however, is as a venue for families who make pilgrimage and picnic and beach visits here, particularly when in need of finding a spouse for a daughter. They will often remain in the shrine overnight and return home in the morning.

There are a number of levels of interpretation to this myth. The first condenses around the miraculous journey of the dead saint to the shores of Sri Lanka. When entombed on the island, his tomb marks a sacred space. The second is the clear metaphoric reference to the arrival of Islam on the island, brought by Arab traders sailing from the Middle East and settling in

first appeared in (Smith 1997: 119–120). This mosque sits on a coastal headland adjacent to a Sinhalese fishing village and several miles from the nearest Muslim settlement.

[16] These riots were island-wide. One mosque in the local area (Koledande) and the shrine at a second (Station Road) were destroyed in these riots.

various coastal ports. This metaphor stresses the fundamentally pure nature of the Islam on the island, and further, the greater orthodoxy of the earliest sites of settlement. The myth also contains a clear ideological statement concerning the supremacy of the saint and his determination to be entombed on the headland. The "struggles" with a Sinhalese landlord are also a common feature of the saint's myths and refer to the situation of the first Muslims who were always in the position of having to acquire land, which they invariably did through the marriages they contracted with indigenous women.

The second type of shrine is that of the saints who initially revealed their presence through a miracle which occurs on the spot where they are buried. These myths also have a set of common features and outline a particular logic. These saints were men who came on pilgrimage to Adam's Peak and died while spending time meditating in the jungle. These shrines are all some distance from the coast and spread throughout the interior of the island. This myth is taken from the Dewatagaha mosque in Colombo. This is the most important shrine in Colombo and is routinely patronised by members of all social groups and all faiths. The myth elaborates both the original miracle which led to the discovery of the saint and his later identification by another foreign Muslim. Finally, it outlines the establishment of a feast in his name, to celebrate his "birthday". As with the shrines above, the sacred space once discovered is immediately cloaked in the surrounds of a new public mosque, thus rendering it the potential heart of a new Muslim community. While stone box myths stress the establishment of an Islamic presence on the island, these myths are distinct in that they stress the establishment of Islamic practice. Each miraculous revelation myth may be taken as an ideological statement which outlines both the movement of a pure and originary Islam from the Islamic heartlands to the island of Sri Lanka, and the establishment of its orthodox practices here, in a non-Islamic context. In short it is an ideology of the arrival of Islam and Islamic practice.

> The Dewatagaha myth recounts the tale of a Sinhalese woman who was an oilmonger and the sole wage earner in her family. She was

doing her daily rounds one day and tripped over the root of a *cadju* (cashew) tree and fell, smashing her clay pot to pieces. She cried bitterly because her family would have no food that day as her only source of income had been destroyed. Eventually she fell asleep exhausted. She awoke to hear a voice telling her not to despair, that everything would be alright. Again she heard the voice, and suddenly she saw "an old man in green garb (whose) holy mein was an inspiring sight". He told here that she had nothing to fear, and that he would give her oil, if only she would fetch him a pot. The woman ran to the house of a Muslim, Mamina Lebbe, in Maradana. He was one of her regular customers and she asked his mother to give her a new pot. When she returned to the jungle she found the old man leaning against a dawata tree. He told her to place the pot on the ground where the other one had broken. Then he pressed his foot on the ground and the oil bubbled up from beneath. The woman was able to scoop up the oil with leaves and refill her pot. The old man asked her to tell her Muslim customers the events and the spot where he appeared. She thanked him and invoked his blessings. The woman told the Muslims of this miracle and a party of them went to find the evidence in the jungle; the oil, the broken pot, the cadju tree and the dawata tree. The party then prayed and appointed Mamina Lebbe their leader and the trustee of the shrine.

In 1847 a saint came to Ceylon from the Maghreb and took up residence at the Maradana mosque. When he was informed of the miracle he went to the shrine with a number of other Muslims and they recited prayers together. The divine shrouded himself with his robe and knelt upon the ground, seeking communion with the buried saint. He said that the grave was that of a "most venerable saint. . .Seyed Usman Siddiq Ibn Abdurahman, from Arafat in Arabia, who came to this island on pilgrimage to Adam's Peak and after living in the vicinity for some time, died here". The divine having announced the name of the saint declared that henceforth each year there would be a ten day *mowlood* recital and distribution of ghee rice as *niyaath* to the people. He gave a sovereign to Mamina Lebbe to prepare ghee rice immediately and then he took a bamboo pole, and tearing off a piece of his white turban to make a flag, planted this flagpole in the ground at the head of the grave.[17]

The practice at this shrine also reflects the details of the original myth. An enormous oil lamp stands just outside the shrine and is kept burning continually, with gifts of oil.

[17] This version is adapted from Thawfeeq (n.d.: 109–111).

The two types of myths reflect the origins of Islam and the pattern of Muslim settlement. Traders settled in coastal ports, particularly on the southwest coast, and also were distributed sparsely throughout the interior where they handled much internal trade. When the myths are further placed in the context of the cosmological significance of Adam's Peak, revered by Muslims as the point of man's origin on earth, they have further ontological power. It was here that Adam first set foot outside of Paradise. The saints in the stone boxes in their miraculous return to the island are signing their closeness to the point of origin of man on earth, travelling through the waters of rebirth in their transcendent state. They further sacrify the primordial point of man on earth, by their entombed presence on the island. The other type of myth, the miraculous revelation, signs the arrival of orthodox Islamic practice on the island. In this case, it is the discovery of the burial places of saints who died during the performance of their religious practices—pilgrimage and meditation. In both sets of myths the veracity of the saint's holiness or their foreign origins is both critical and undisputed. Together, both sets of myths account for the shrines on the coast and in the interior, and stake out the entire island as a place where Muslims might practise their Islam. They also clearly reflect the two major patterns of Muslim trade in the island. Firstly, the coastal settlements and trading associated with the major trade routes on the seas. Second, the Muslims who traded in the interior, many of whom would have been concerned with petty trade but also the gem traders whose business would have led them to Adam's Peak in the heart of the gem district. The argument in the myths does much more than simply legitimate the presence of the Muslim community on the island, rather it creates them as a community located in a particular space in an Arabic/ Islamic cosmology. It deepens the links in the phenomenal world between the island and its already existent place in an Arabic cosmology. It states that there is a primordial and pre-ordained link between the island and Islam. Sri Lankan Muslims must construct their history in the context of other communities (Sinhalese and Tamil) whose own concerns with their history are profoundly ideological. The ideology of these myths explains the cosmological and historical attachments of Muslims and their practices to Sri Lanka.

Shrines are at the heart of orthodox Islam. Shrines are adjacent to mosques and mosques are seen as the heart of community. Differences in kinship organisation in the east coast and the southwest are reflected in different mosque organisation. All villages have a village mosque where prayers are offered individually, and each village celebrates its identity with an annual mosque feast. There are ten- or twelve-day feasts held at all of the mosques, during which a mowlood (story of a saint) is recited and donations of ghee rice are distributed from the mosque to all households in the village. On two final nights, the village and the wider community gather to celebrate and eat a huge feast that is cooked and consumed in the grounds of the mosque. Males eat in groups of six from a common bowl but women are expected to eat their feast at home. Jumma mosques, which are used both for individual and Friday communal prayers, may incorporate the identities of either one or two villages but those distinct identities are preserved in the feast structure. There is a constant tension between autonomy and subordination in this hierarchical cultural context.[18] Mosques are closely identified with males and the public, male Muslim community, while houses by contrast, which pass through the female line, are strongly identified with women. As most men must change their mosque when they marry and move to live with their wife, there is a sense in which women consistently split men away from the male Muslim community of their natal mosque. There is a subtle but

[18] There were a number of disputes in the research area which centred around different mosques and their relationship to their village community. The Galbokka and New St communities shared a jumma mosque and their distinct identities and rights were preserved in its organisation. Each community supplied an imam and they gave sermons on alternate Fridays. During the annual feast, each community was represented on a separate night during the last two nights of the ten-day event. In the cases of other mosques, some young men were challenging the fact that even though mosque trustees should be elected, in fact these positions were consistently held by the elite.

constant dichotomy between (Arab) men/religion and (Tamil) women/culture that shapes much individual understanding and practice.[19] In the research area, women generally observed purdah and their prayers were offered in the house, not the mosque. Mosques are nonetheless the point of articulation with the domestic sphere and women are not without clear relation to them. In a universally observed ritual in the research area, on the evening of Bara'at, two weeks before Ramadan, all women cook roti (breads) on domestic hearths and gift them to the mosques which redistributes them to the community. This evening marks the beginning of a part of the calendar concerned with the reconstitution and purification of the global Muslim community—*ummah,* which will culminate in the gathering at Mecca for the Hajj. This first night of Bara'at marks the occasion when each individual is given a clean slate for the next year and so is in a pure state. The local women on this occasion symbolically gift their fertility to the mosque as it is they who are the base of every Muslim household and the custodians of its regenerative hearth.

Regional Sufi Networks in the Western Indian Ocean

Many of the themes addressed above are highlighted in wider regional myths of conversion to Islam (in the Indian Ocean Laccadive/ Lakhshadweep and Maldive islands) that form part of the discourse in the research area. They are also evident in the sufi networks that still connect Sri Lanka's Muslims to the wider Indian Ocean region. The myth of the conversion of the Laccadives (Kutty 1972: 6–7) attributes it to Ubaidulla, a grandson of Abubakr, the first Caliph of Islam. He dreamed that the prophet sent him on a journey to propagate Islam and he set out from the Hijaz but was shipwrecked on Amini

[19] The local marriage ritual addresses the problem directly. The installation of the new bridegroom in his wife's household is only accomplished with significant ritual attention and is not complete until the marriage has been consummated and the *valima verundu* (bridegroom's feast) completed. On this occasion, the new groom acts as the new religious head of his wife's household as both families gather for a recital of a mowlood concerning the life of the Prophet and sharing a feast together (men and women separately).

Island in the Hindu Laccadives. He met the daughter of a high-caste Hindu family who embraced Islam and he married her. The marriage and conversion infuriated the islanders who attacked Ubaidulla but the couple was miraculously transported to Androth Island. They met a hostile reception but after a miraculous earthquake, the people converted to Islam. The myth recounts subsequent journeys to all of the inhabited islands in the group and in each case a miracle induces the population to convert. Ubaidulla is credited with establishing a jumma mosque on each island, and on Androth Island, where he is now regarded as a saint and entombed in the jumma mosque (Ellis 1924: 16), he created the khaziship of Androth. This myth attributes the arrival of Islam in the Laccadives to an originary journey of a doyen of Middle Eastern Islam and his saintly powers. In addition, it clearly outlines his establishment of religious spaces (mosques) and the sacred governing structure (the khaziship) of orthodox Islam.

The last Buddhist Raja of the Maldives is believed to have converted to Islam in 1153 AD and established the Maldivian Sultanate. In one myth, this conversion is ascribed "by Ibn Battuta...to a wandering Maghrebi skaykh and hafiz called Abu al-Barakat al-Barbari who through his piety was able to rid the islands of an evil, virgin-ravishing demon" (Forbes 1983: 47). This saint is enshrined in the Medu Ziyare (Central Shrine) in the capital, Male.

In each of these regional myths, the foreign Muslim saint, the "orthodox outsider" is a critical figure in the conversion of the population to Islam and in establishing a pure form of the religion in the islands. In the research area the "orthodox outsider" is once more a critical figure. I will initially examine the arrival of the Rifai (Rifai'iyyia) tariqa (sufi order) and the building of a new jumma mosque in the village of Kapuwatta. This established an ongoing link between a family of Muslim saints from Androth Island in the Laccadives and their Sri Lankan followers. Then I will briefly discuss the case of a Sri Lankan saint who serves as the "orthodox outsider" for a tariqa whose followers are predominantly located in Tamil Nadu in south India.

The Kapuwatta jumma mosque was established in 1886 in a village that had no mosque of its own. At the same time a branch of the Rifai tariqa was also established.[20] In this process, they effectively renegotiated their status in relation to the established orthodoxy located in Galbokka and also established a distinct village identity from nearby Koledande (Palathaddi mosque) where they had formerly attended jumma prayers. In the late nineteenth century there was an economic struggle going on between the local villages, at the same time as the economy of the island itself was transforming. In the research area, religious discourse and claims to orthodoxy formed one of the arenas in which this economic struggle took place. Historically, all the big traders were located in Galbokka in Weligama, and Kapuwatta had stood in a subordinate relation in economic and religious terms to other villages in the area. Economic dominance is interpreted, in part, as religiously legitimated, and in local practice, economic success is generally followed by increased religious observance. Through Kapuwatta's establishment of a separate and cohesive identity, condensed within their own jumma mosque, they were able to renegotiate their economic and religious relations. At the time, the wealthiest men in Kapuwatta were engaged in the copra trade and held large coconut estates while other villagers were engaged in petty trade, hawking coconut products or exchanging cloth for areca nut. The cloth traders would have had to deal with the larger Muslim traders in either Galle or Galbokka. Kapuwatta has no ancient history of Muslim settlement and while some informants state that "we have always been here", others say that "local Muslims came to Sri Lanka on the shoulders of the Salagama". The Salagama (Chalias) were a weaving caste from India and were turned to cinnamon

[20] At that time this was relatively new in the island. There have since been branches established in Matara, Godepitiya (Porwai), Colombo and Kandy. Most members of the village of Kapuwatta state that they are members of the Rifai tariqa and the majority of young men spend some time actively engaged in tariqa activities (Smith 1997: 164) In a survey conducted in the village of 857 Moors, 801 gave their tariqa affiliation as Rifai. This is a substantial 93.46 per cent (Ibid: 261).

peeling by both the Kandyan king and the colonial powers. Kapuwatta in Sinhala means "cotton fields" and it is located not far from the cinnamon gardens of Akuressa. There is no suggestion that cotton was grown here rather it refers to the fact that this was previously a village from which the Sinhalese acquired their cloth, being home to hawkers who traded cloth to the interior. A few other villagers express the view that some Indian Muslims called "Ambay" came here on business from Kayalpattanam in Tamil Nadu and then married local Sinhalese women. The name Marrikar was seen here in former times, which could also suggest an Indian Muslim community. The likeliest probability is that origins of this settlement were diverse.[21]

In the late nineteenth century, during the revivalist period, two significant events took place in this village. First, there was a successful attempt by members of the village to seek the spiritual patronage of a charismatic religious leader from Androth Island in Kerala. Second there was the establishment of a secular school with Tamil teachers. Both of these events reflect a clear interest in Muslim revivalist concerns.[22] In an era of increasing wealth in the village owing primarily to a coconut oil boom, leading men sought to renegotiate the relative social and political position of the village in relation to Galbokka. The arena in which this could take place was within the discourse on legitimate religious dominance. Kapuwatta sought the spiritual patronage of an outsider who could claim religious and ancestral orthodoxy, and who was a skilled Arabic speaker. Both factors made him a worthy adversary of the ulema in Weligama which prided itself on a particularly orthodox character, home to Arabic speakers always.[23] Through the

[21] A genealogy of this village revealed no family relationships beyond three and four generations, a pattern which certainly suggests relatively recent migration on the part of all inhabitants (Smith 1997: 263).

[22] The revival was noted to be a predominantly urban phenomenon, yet here is the evidence of its impact in a rural environment.

[23] The first Arabic Colleges in the island were established in Weligama (Irshard 1984: 51). Baari College, founded by a scholar from India celebrated its centenary in 1984. There are a number of colleges in the town and they train the

outsider's efforts a new village mosque was established here and his family have become inextricably linked with religious life and development within the village. The story of the building of the mosque reflects themes which appear consistently in the history of Islam in the south and west of the island and indicate the direction of religious consolidation. Two of these themes are the "drawing in" of religious orthodoxy from outside in order to purify local religious experience, and concomitantly a widespread understanding that signs "middle Eastern" dress and a facility with Arabic as clear evidence of religious knowledge. These themes are constant metaphors of the understanding of the original arrival of the religion with Arab traders.

> In the 1880s a group of Sri Lankan Muslims were attending a religious festival in Hyderabad and while there they were very impressed with the religious knowledge, and ability to speak and write Arabic, of a man they encountred. He was Seyed Mohammed Rifai Moulana Kolylad from Androth Island off the coast of Kerala. As a matter of fact he had such a stately figure and in his flowing robes looked every inch an aristocratic Arab and everyone thought him to be so (Nalla Koya Thangal, 1978).

They invited him to travel back to Sri Lanka. This he did and attended the Buhari Feast, the annual religious festival and feast at the Beruwela mosque.[24] It was here that he was seen by some men from Godepitiya and Kapuwatta who were equally impressed with his demeanour, and they invited him to come to Kapuwatta to visit and instruct them.[25] The Thangal duly

---

young Muslim men who after seven years of study will graduate with the degree of alim and be eligible to serve as imams in mosques. They take students from all over the island.

[24] Beruwela is commonly understood to be the first place of Muslim settlement on the island. Its originary status is reflected in an exclusive dimension to ritual practice here. When the mowlood is recited here on the occasion of the annual feast it is not, unlike everywhere else, broadcast on public speakers.

[25] In another version of the story, an informant stated that he had come to Godepitiya to the Porwai mosque "to see his relation buried in the tomb there". At this time a Kapuwatta man Noohu Lebbe, was visiting there and he called to the Seyyed (Rifai Moulana) saying "Come Thangal, to Kapuwatta because there are Muslims there, but they have no place to pray to Allah".

came to Kapuwatta and made a mosque from *cadjan* (coconut thatch). He returned a year later to build a small cement mosque. On this occasion, he brought with him his elder brother's son Seyyed Mohammed Faleel Fookoya Thangal, who was a sixteen-year-old student. Rifai Moulana charged the boy to rebuild the mosque and make it bigger as soon as he was able. After Rifai Moulana's death, Faleel Fookoya spent many years rebuilding the mosque.[26] He was assisted in his efforts by Rifai Moulana Yoosuf Koya Thangal, who later died in Galle, but was buried in the Kapuwatta mosque, where his tomb is now in the shrine. Faleel Fookoya is locally known as "rice moulana" or "ration moulana" because in order to build the mosque, he had each of the eighty families in the village keep a small "till". As the women cooked each meal they would take some measures of rice for each member of the household, and at the same time place a measure in the till. At the end of each week, this rice was taken to the mosque and from there sold to the wealthy people of the village and the money collected was set aside for the building of the mosque. This moulana is remembered for his single-mindedness, and during all the periods he spent in Kapuwatta over the years building the mosque, he refused to open any letters from home, saying that he did not want to be distracted from God's work. This also signs the originary nature of his undertaking.

From the time of the initial invitation to the moulana to come to Kapuwatta for the spiritual benefit of the Muslims living there, this Androth Island family has established a position of religious dominance in the community.[27] Seyyed Mohammed Rifai Moulana, as orthodox outsider, was initially responsible for constructing the first village jumma mosque which gave the village its primary symbol of distinct and independent religious identity, no longer encompassed by the Galbokka or Koledande jumma mosques.[28] The power and religious author-

[26] This was between 1913 and 1927.

[27] The Androth Island moulanas are also the spiritual leaders of Rifai groups in Colombo, Godepitiya, Matara and Singapore.

[28] In their move into Kapuwatta they disturbed the local religious hierarchy. There were a number of Moulana families living in the research area (especially in

ity of the moulana helped to confirm Kapuwatta's identity as an independent religious community with its own jumma mosque. The introduction of the Rifai tariqa along with its ecstatic practices and bodily mortification made it radically and irrevocably distinct.

The Androth Island Thangals visit the island periodically and spend time at the mosques in the areas where their followers are located. Nalla Koya Thangal was in regular attendance at the annual mosque feast and by remaining domiciled outside the island he retains his status as "orthodox outsider" with reference to the Kapuwatta community. Another saint in the Weligama area (Seyed Khaleel Awn Mowlana EI Hasaniyyul Hashimiy) also serves as a spiritual leader for a growing group of followers in Madras in south India and in Dubai in the Gulf. The movement was established by his grandfather, who was originally from Iraq, and migrated first to India and then to Sri Lanka. The Haqqiya tariqa which he founded caters primarily to a clientele of professional middle-class Muslims and doesn't have a large number of local followers. His grandfather is buried in a shrine in Sambai Pattinam mosque in Tamil Nadu and his father (Sayyid Yaseen Mowlana) is entombed in a shine at Thirumellaivasal in south India. The current moulana spends five or six weeks a year there, preaching and teaching to his followers. Many of them also make the trip

---

New Street in Weligama but also in the village of Wellipitiya) and they were highly regarded. Prior to this, however, there had been no moulanas in Kapuwatta. Cited locally as a fundamental obstacle to the spread of the Rifai, is the rivalry caused when other centres of religious/social power (resident moulanas) felt that their status was lowered by the arrival of a new and powerfully active moulana. The moulanas in New Street and Wellipitiya apparently organised some opposition but the power struggle was short-lived. A challenge was offered to Koya Thangal by way of an invitation to a religious discussion and debate. Not one to mince his words, he is reported to have declared to his protagonist "When you say anything Yes—I will say No. If you say anything No—I will say Yes!" With that all the assembled decided that he must be a highly educated man and they dispersed without further argument.

The opposition within Kapuwatta itself was slight but harshly dealt with. There are numerous stories of attempts to cross the Moulana all of which ended in disaster for the ill-wishers (from cats destroying party feasts to a stroke for one man who told the Moulana to shut up!).

to visit him in Weligama from time to time and he writes to them regularly. His position with respect to his followers (as was also true for his father) is that of orthodox outsider. He writes poetry and prose in Arabic and spent his own professional life as an Arabic school inspector. His father travelled frequently between India and Sri Lanka and maintained households in each country. As with all moulanas (members of the prophet's family), he is highly respected and understood to have high status. His religious services are sought by those who live in the immediate area, for healing purposes and prayers but he has more followers internationally than locally. His message, however, which is essentially that there are no tariqas; that "Heaven" and "Hell" are metaphors not reality—simply props whose reality is required by those who are not ready for full understanding, would not draw significant support in the local ideological context. He also maintains that there are no divisions recognized by God—that all people and religions are one. These arguments are more compelling to his followers in urban Madras and Dubai than in rural and semi-urban Weligama. His father had taken oaths in a number of tariqas (Jiffria, Naqshabandia, Qadiriya and Shasuliah but argued that Haqqiya (Haqqiyyatul Quadiria) was all tariqas bound together. He explained that first one followed shari'ah (law), then one may choose to follow a tariqa (path), but that then one must move to haqiqah (internal knowledge or essential truth). Although this spiritual leader has an international following and a growing web presence, he remains somewhat marginal in the local area.

The fact that he is both a 'saint' and 'local', in the context of my argument above, places him in an ambiguous category. There is a dynamic against status and towards egalitarianism, which renders him problematic as a local religious leader. He does not participate in local mosque activities or prayers and has held himself somewhat marginal to the local religious community since he had a difference of opinion with one of the imams in a local mosque. How this is interpreted by local Muslims I cannot say, but I suspect that the position of the community at large with respect to the saint is not the subject of much reflection or comment because at some fundamental level the logic of orthodoxy and 'outsiderness' is simply taken for granted.

In this Indian Ocean context it is clear that local Muslims consistently act through their religious ritual practice and ideological debates to establish their religion as rooted in the island's cosmologies and contested historical understandings. Claiming the purity of foreign religious and ethnic origins, and the preordained right to exist in man's first location outside of Paradise, means that they must continually recreate their community as egalitarian. The myths and ideologies, which they find themselves working with, are a constant source of internal contradictions which must be overcome. This effort is undoubtedly assisted by the fact that Islam itself, through its calendrical ritual practice, engages in constant communal renewal.

6

Dialectics of Autochthony and Foreignness in the Bhuta Cults of the Kanara Coast

Marine Carrin

Introduction

In North Kanara[1], as well as in South Kanara[2], we find representations of the indigenous character of the society as well as representations of the peripheral populations. This relation from the centre to the periphery changes from north to south and defines in each region a different kind of society. I shall look at this material in relation to Indian Ocean trade, and the guiding idea will be to look at the symbolic representation of the foreigner.

In North Kanara, the hilly forest is still associated with old kingdoms.[3] We find mainly Havik[4] Brahmins who cultivate

[1] North Kanara was part of Tipu Sultan's Mysore. After his defeat in 1799, the district became part of Madras Presidency, before being transferred to the Bombay Presidency in 1862.

[2] South Kanara (Dakshina Kannada) also known as Tulunadu, occupies the southern coastal strip of Karnataka and has held an important position in the history of south India since ancient times. The port of Mangalore is mentioned by Ptolemy, and the area was a centre of commerce under the Vijayanagara empire (Editorial Committee 1991:1)

[3] The Gangas followed the Kadambas. Around 540 AD, the Chalukyas took over, followed by the Kadambas of Banavasi. Then, the Hoysala controlled several regions in North Kanara until 1200. Around 1330, an Alupa princess controlled the north of the region from Barakuru in South Kanara.

[4] The areca nut gardens of the Havik Brahmins were generally situated in natural stands of evergreen forests in proximity to a watercourse. The Havik Brahmins

areca nuts, Vaishya merchants as well as agriculturists like the Halakki Vokkals.[5] Then there are craftsmen, low castes and untouchables as well as peripheral groups such as the Kudumbis (hunters)[6] or the Sidis who live in the forest. The latter are descendants of slaves that the Portuguese imported in the region from East Africa. The Halakki Vokkals (and Vakkals who are an inferior section of them) are considered as the autochthonous of the region. They still live in isolated villages and their women collect wild roots in the forests of Ankola. From a global point of view, the agriculturist castes sanskritise themselves and some of them are the devotees of Venkatarama and go on pilgrimage to Tirupati. The poorest among them do not call Brahmins for their rituals and worship *bhutas*, spirits associated with the mountain paths. These bhutas have no iconographic representations but their presence is signified by a stone or a *trisul* (trident), and the myths describe them as the *gana* (companions) of Shiva who came from the Ghats and, later, went down towards the sea (Carrin 2002: 312–17). I shall argue that these bhutas represent both autochthonous deities and figures of the foreigner. We must then look at the forest cults which show how the low castes relate to dominant castes like Brahmins or Jains,[7] who have arrived in the forest since the seventeenth century to establish plantations. We shall see that in North Kanara, the bhuta mediate between the dominant castes and their dependants, as well as between the autochthons and foreigners.

In North Kanara, most of the bhutas are associated with the forest, the Western Ghats landscape and the autochthonous

---

assured the greater part of the work but they also employed seasonal labour from outside the district or the surrounding areas. These labourers inluded low castes such as the Iddigas or Scheduled Tribes such as the Kudumbis who traditionally were hunters. During the colonial period, the latter were obliged to move to get employed in Havik areca gardens (Pouchepadass 1990).

5 The Vokkal include different subcastes and are seen as autochtonous.

6 Today, Kudumbis often work as labourers, but some have land.

7 Brahmins do not participate directly in the bhuta cult while Jains sometimes try to sponsor bhuta ceremonies in order to control their dependants. They do not participate directly in the sacrifices offered to these deities.

populations: the forest shrines are often marked by a stone which symbolises the boundary between two villages or two roads. The bhutas are always carnivorous and associated with destructive forces, like Hulidevaru the tiger. Yet, some other bhutas such as Yaksa bestow fertility on cattle and human beings. It is interesting to note that there are no Sidi bhutas, though the Sidis, who may be Hindu, Muslim or Christian, have kept an original pantheon where their ancestors are located on the East coast of Africa.[8] In other words, the foreign character of the Sidi ancestors relate only to the Sidis but other groups do not identify any bhuta[9] as Sidi even if they remain foreigners par excellence, black people who are excluded from the caste system. Yet, it is interesting to find Sidi shrines whose priestesses are possessed by the goddesses Ekse, Marekamba or even Yellamma on behalf of other castes during rituals of affliction.[10]

While some of the lower castes have their origin in neighbouring states, like the Lambani who carry wood between Maharashtra and Karnataka, the dominant Jains[11] of the Sagar region explain that their ancestors came to the forest escaping from Bhatkal where their Muslim trade partners wanted to oblige them to convert. Those who became Muslims[12] stayed on the coast while the refugees started a new life establishing areca nut plantations in the forest. The Jain patrons have often helped their dependants, the Kudumbis or the Ollerus who

[8] The cult of the hivaru, which takes place during Navaratri, is important for the Hindu Sidis who express their identity through myths relating to their coming to India.

[9] Some Sidi hivaru became bhutas but only Sidis refer to them during possession (Carrin 2002: 312).

[10] Sidi priestesses officiate in shrines dedicated to different forms of the Goddess. These priestesses wear a joto—matted hair—like female priestesses in Bengal (Carrin 1997a). Even so, their symbolic efficacy against affliction is attributed to their black skin.

[11] The emergence of Jain feudal chiefs in different places of costal Karnataka under Vijayanagar rule (1336–1650) marked a turning point in the history of land control in the region (Vasantha Madhava 1991: 49). A large number of Jains in Tulunadu were converts from the Bunt community.

[12] From the fourteenth century, the Muslim commercial associations known as hanjamana had often come into contact with the agrarian system of the costal region (Vasantha Madhava 1991: 52).

work for them, to establish shrines for local bhutas. These shrines are called *bhutasthanas*. In North Kanara, bhutas are inferior to goddesses and often considered as guardian deities *(ksetrapal)* of brahmanic gods or of the Tirthankaras of the Jain *basadi* (shrine). Usually these spirits appear to the members of the lower castes who work for the Jains or the Havik Brahmins as day-labour in the plantations. The Havik Brahmins, devotees of Shankaracharya, are vegetarians and do not worship local bhutas but are devotees of the goddesses or Amma. The Iddigas,[13] formerly toddy-tappers and devotees of the goddess Marikamba, are the main devotees of the bhutas whom they consider as autochthonous. Moreover, some male bhutas such as Biraru or Jattaka are associated with Shiva and their devotees address vows *(areke)* to them to get children. When these bhutas are located near villages, their bhutasthana is visited by a great number of castes. Among dominant castes or small landowners, we find Okkaligas[14] who worship both bhutas and goddesses and consider themselves as autocthonous. They live in villages but also form the urban elite in the region.

Myths associated with the bhutas tell us how they left the Western Ghats to descend towards the sea; travelling together along many roads these spirits used to possess villagers and ask for a shrine. Consequently many shrines were established along the bhutas' roads. The bhutas who travelled from the north stopped on the coast not far from Udupi, but their way was blocked. So, a giant bhuta, Bobbarya, put his legs on a pair of mountains and ordered his fellow bhutas to pass under his legs. Some of the bhutas protested but finally they accepted, and went to South Kanara.

South Kanara as a Region

South Kanara, lying between the coast of the Indian Ocean and the Western Ghats, is a region of lower hills where the culti-

[13] Many Iddiga farmers cultivate some acres of paddy and one or two acres of arecanut. Their economic condition is still precarious but as worshippers of the bhutas, they often officiate as priests in bhutasthanas.

[14] Agricultural castes fight each other to claim higher status in the caste hierarchy. The Okkaligas who possess an urban elite are superior to the Namdharis who are more rural.

vated and forested valleys, running east to west, are separated by dry ridges. Each village may be described as scattered homesteads of tenants cultivating rice or areca nuts, clustering around the manor of the chief. The village formed part or whole of the domain, which was itself part of the region. The chief of the region was the king, while the manor under him belonged to junior lines.

The Bunts and the Jains both claim to be descendants of the old kings[15] of South Kanara. Indeed, the cultural identity of the Tulu kings is problematic (Claus 1978). There are reasonable grounds to assert that by the tenth century, Jainism[16] must have made its way to South Kanara. While some Tulu historians, like Gururaja Bhatt (1975), holds there was a true kingdom having two capitals, one at Mangalore[17] or perhaps Ullal, the other at Barakuru[18] in the north, Kanara historians like Ramesh (1970) and Phalaksha (1989) are more cautious.

The port of Mangalore—located in South Kanara—has been for centuries a trading centre. The port itself, it would seem, has been dominated by the Muslim trading and seafaring community of the Mappilas for a very long time. This brings us to the importance of overseas links for the economy of the region which centred both on agricultural revenue and on commercial wealth. Arabian traders were certainly importing goods such as horses to Mangalore and buying spices (pepper, cardamom, and areca nuts) for export. Timber, another major export, used to be a Mappila monopoly but part of this trade has now been appropriated by Hindu Patidars from Gujarat. Chinese and Arabs were the chief foreign traders in the ports of Karnataka. But from the sixteenth century, the Portuguese tried to

[15] Most of the Tulu kingdoms were vassals of the Vijayanagar empire around 1500 (Saletore 1936; Sinopoli & Morrison 1995).

[16] The math of Mudabidri was founded between 1334 and 1429 (Bhatt 1975: 433).

[17] The Italian traveller Varthema who visited India in 1500 AD says he saw nearly sixty ships laden with rice, ready to sail, in the port of Mangalore. Ibn Battuta says the port of Mangalore sold enormous quantities of pepper and ginger (Bhatt 1975: 223).

[18] The governor had his court and his assembly at the capital—Barakuru, Mangalore or Honavara—and was assisted by a body of municipal councillors.

monopolise the trade of pepper, rice and other products of the region (Vasantha Madhava 1991:149).

In trying to analyse the mythic expressions of the foreigner, we face two series of questions. While some castes of foreign origin are peripheral and more or less ignored by the hierarchical order of regional caste society, some communities—like the Konkani from Goa, or the Muslims established on the coast—have a high status, since they are rich merchants and part of the urban elite, competing with the autochthonous castes. The Konkani, who control trade in South Kanara, are seen by the Tulu as immigrants who—in the sixteenth century—fled Goa to escape the Inquisition. The rice trade from Mangalore and other South Kanara ports to Goa was important, and the Gauda Saraswat Brahmins dominated local and regional trade to Goa.

Moreover, the Tulu, who consider themselves autochthonous, defend an image of the region where the idea of a Tulu kingdom composed of matrilineal castes implicitly excludes the Konkani.[19] This ethnic opposition is expressed linguistically, as the Konkani and Tulu languages are very different: Konkani is an Indo-Aryan language while Tulu is Dravidian. While the Konkani are patrilinear, the Tulu are matrilineal. The two populations have different temples and worship different gods. The Konkani are devotees of Venkatarama, a form of Vishnu, and concentrate their urban networks around his temples, while most Tulu live in villages—even if their dominant caste, the Bunt, has now entered the liberal professions and business. One may oppose, here, the banking activities of the Konkani to the hotels run by the Bunt. These differences in occupation and lifestyle are reflected in the ideological consciousness of both communities.

The Tulu always refer to their old kingdom or their ancient political units (*sime*) while the Konkani present themselves as merchants and have adopted a more westernised lifestyle. They prefer to claim modernity and mainstream Hinduism.

[19] We also find Christian Konkanis who settled as agriculturists along the coast from the end of the sixteenth century onwards.

Certainly, they do not pretend to rule anyone unlike the Bunt or the Jain. Yet, Konkani merchants have played a considerable role in developing commercial networks along the coast.

Today prominent descendants of Jain rulers and Tulu landowners who claim ancestry from chiefs, compete with each other by patronising splendid rituals dedicated to royal bhutas as guardians of the territory. Looking at the more recent political units, the anthropologist notes a structural difference between the Jain and Tulu chiefdoms. While Jains controlled small urban kingdoms where they built temples, palaces and monasteries, Bunt chiefdoms were centred on manors attached by feudal ties to the Tulu king in Barakuru, the old capital, or in Mangalore.

Udupi, north of Mangalore, is the centre of the Madhavacharya sect, a dualistic variant of Vaishnavism. Equally impregnated with a single religion are old Jain centres such as Karkal and Mudabidri. But it is the bhuta cult which gives to South Kanara its regional identity, though it reflects many different religious influences.

The Tulu-speaking castes of South Kanara comprise a system within which each caste occupies a place in a ranked occupational order. The castes who do not claim Tulu for their mother tongue are less integrated into this community of common ideology, partly centred around the matrilineal system. The Tulu speakers form a closely allied group while non-Hindus, Muslims or Christians are, to some extent, outsiders.

In the past, communication was difficult and villages were relatively isolated from each other. The village (*uru*) formed part of whole of the domain (*magane*) which was itself part of region (sime). The chief of the sime was an *arasu* king and a holder of the *gadi* 'throne' while the manors under him belonged to different *gutu* (junior lines). The Bunts were the king's warriors while the Billavas[20] were the Bunts' bowmen.

[20] The Billavas were un.ouchables some of whom converted to protestantism when the Basel Mission established themselves in South Canara. The Mission, influenced by the pietist movement, was founded in 1815 in Basel, and established itself in Mangalore by 1840. As a result of their turning Christians, the

The Bunt cultivators who were tenants of Jain chiefs became landlords and rose to political power when the Jains lost their lands by the end of the sixteenth century.

Previously, property in land was the means by which a family could acquire status. Land provided wealth which could be converted into authority; consequently, tutelary office under a manor was considered prestigious. Today it is still so, but involvement in business or other careers offer alternative positions to the elite. Very high dowries allow families to establish ties among the elite groups of the caste. The title *shetti* meaning 'headman' is the most common surname among Bunts (Claus 1971). They possess the characteristics of a dominant caste: high status, political and economic power (Mayer 1958: 22–23). The land reforms have not ended the responsablities of landlords towards their bhutas. From an ideological point of view, the bhuta cult enables the Bunt who possess wealth and prestige to control the political and moral order of the society as they have a very close link to the bhuta of their land who is also the village bhuta of their (previous) tenants. Even if this link is weakened by the land reforms, Bunts still occupy a dominant position. The Bunts who manage their rice fields and plantations of areca nut and spice would like to present themselves as the 'real' Tulu, autochthonous not just in ethnic terms but because they are figures of authority.

The road of the bhutas is marked by a series of rituals which recall how the bhutas fought each other. Each bhuta won his territory by fighting. Bhutas travel along mythical roads where

---

Billavas had to abandon their socio-ritual obligations and thereby lost their tenancies as well as the protection of their Bunt patrons. The missionaries took pains to learn local languages such as Tulu and Konkani in order to preach. They strongly objected to the performance of the bhuta cult as the rituals were associated with wild dancing, drumming, drinking, and blood sacrifice (Burnell 1894–1897). The Billavas acquired education through Christianity and improved their economic status. Later, they followed Guru Narayana, a religious figure from Kerala who came to Mangalore in 1912 to preach against caste. Joining this reform movement, some Christian Billavas returned to Hinduism, and the caste started to assert its identity more aggressively.

they encounter different kinds of autochthons as well as foreigners. Sometimes, they themselves incarnate the figures, either of foreigners, or of figures descended both from foreign and autochthonous stock. Bhutas symbolise the political boundaries of a territory, while worshipping the bhutas is the only way to get integrated into Tulu society. Yet the bhuta himself is sometimes seen as a foreigner. I shall illustrate this paradox by showing how bhutas serve to express, at the same time, metaphors of autochthony and land, and metaphors of foreigners and migrations.

The Bhuta Cult in Tulunadu as a Language of Autochthony

In Tulunadu, Konkani traders (Gauda Saraswat Brahmins) and Tulu castes produce different images of the society. While Konkani merchants value purity and non-violence, the Tulu castes value the notion of *shakti*, conceptualised here as the martial virtues of the chiefs, and the concept of royal justice. Under the patronage of small kingdoms, bhuta worship has developed as an organised system. The *rajandaivas* or royal bhutas who are celebrated during the *nema*, a prestigious annual ritual, are still associated with the coronation ceremony of the local kings in the coastal area (Brueckner 1995). During these rituals, the Bunts act as patrons of the rituals and ask the bhuta (through the medium) if he is satisfied with the state of his domain. It is also the patron (most often a Bunt) who presents the assembly's expectations to the bhuta before the oracular session which is the climax of the ceremony. The questions should express the concerns of an ideal ruler, who cares for the welfare of his subjects, while the answers of the bhuta should contain divine justice, beyond social considerations. Bunts enjoy playing their role as if they were still feudal chiefs. Paradoxically, the bhuta cult, which plays a major role in asserting Tulu regional identity, has suceeded in integrating peripheral groups in a common paradigm of Tulu identity. While the descendants of ancient Tulu chiefs try to control rural society, low castes like the Billavas (traditionally toddy tappers) who still work for the Bunts, try to assert their identity in other ways since they do not necessarily share the interests of their old lords.

In spite of the land reform of 1973, the dominant castes still retain some of their privileges. This situation may lead to conflict opposing low castes to the Jain and Bunt elites—who try to re-establish moral authority—while the Billava and the Moghavera fishermen struggle to improve their economic condition, without indulging in regionalist revendications. The Bunt would like to represent Tulu autochthony while Billavas or Gaudas (agriculturists) challenge Bunt dominance. These tensions are reflected in the epic of Koti and Chennaya, Billava twin brothers who fought injustice and became bhutas after their heroic death.[21]

The bhutas of South Kanara are capable of destruction by disease and death, or of blessing through fertility. Several bhutas are described in local stories as the army of Isvara, as forms of Brahmanic deities, or as spirits of singular men and women. More important than a bhuta's name is the place where his cult has been established. Bhutas of the same name may be associated with different castes and social groups. Thus Panjurli, the wild boar, may be attached to a Harijan family but may also be seen as a village bhuta.

Village stories relate to the founding of a bhuta cult, usually describing how the bhuta of a particular place followed the head of a lineage asking him to start a cult. Sometimes, the bhuta offers the villager a flower, which means that he wants an annual ceremony. Other bhutas followed men who wanted to leave the Tulu land, and foreigners who came to Tulunadu sometimes died a violent death to become bhutas. So foreigners excluded from Tulu society when alive may be included, after death, in the bhuta world.

The royal bhutas are said to have come from the mountains and made their way to the sea. They have a particular relation

[21] Koti and Chennaya are twin Billava brothers fighting for different Bunt chiefs, who exploit and humiliate them. They are seen as having died in defence of a just cause, and so have become the deified heroes worshipped by the Billavas. Today, their cult is linked to the assertion of Billava identity.

to territory, and we may see the lord of the manor as the trustee of the bhuta's auhority over his land. In Tulunadu, Brahmin priests incorporated the bhutas into a localised hierarchical structure, dedicating shrines to them in the temples of higher brahmanical deities. Similarly, Digambara[22] Jains worship bhutas as subsidiary to the Tirthankaras and to goddesses like Padmavati. The bhutas are treated as guardians of the higher gods and are thus ritually inferior to them. They are seen as controlling minor bhutas who are often caste-specific.

But the Bunts or their traditional dependants, the Billavas, do not see the bhutas' powers as dependent on higher gods, nor are they in any sense impure. The cult of a royal bhuta requires the efforts of the village landlords who contribute to the expenses of the ceremony. Major village disputes are settled during religious ceremonies. The Jains and Bunts perform the ceremonies separately, involving different feudal alliances.

Bhuta Associated with the Forest

But bhutas are also frightening figures, associated with forest wilderness or with the dangers of the sea. In Tulunadu, some bhutas are associated with the forest. Thus, different forms of Panjurli, the wild boar, are worshipped and correspond to different forms of the wild pig. One version of the epic (*paddana*), tells of change and development of this spirit. He was born from two wild pigs, who were brother and sister but wanted to become husband and wife. Subramanya blessed them and soon four children were born to them. One went to Shiva and Parvati kept it as a pet. But as Panjurli started to destroy the garden, Shiva killed it, then brought it back to life at Parvati's request. Shiva then transformed it into a spirit and sent it to earth as the protector of truth. Panjurli was allowed to receive offerings and to safeguard people's interests. There are different forms of Panjurli in Tulunadu: in one story he appears to men, declaring that he will settle in their place if they will wor-

[22] The expression digambara "clad in wind" alludes to the naked digambara ascetics.

ship him. In another version, an uncle and his niece visit the local chief to worship a god. The latter orders the carpenters to cut trees in the forest so as to build a shrine to the bhuta. In these stories, the foundation of a Panjurli shrine describes the degradations imposed on the forest by men cultivating the land. These epics emphasise the dimension of autochthony and stress the relationships of Billavas to the Bunt landlords.

Koti and Chennaya are two Billava brothers who serve a local chief, fighting injustice. After a heroic death they are worshipped as martial gods. Their mother who is a Brahmin was abandoned by her family in the forest, since she menstruated before getting married. She is adopted by Billavas and grants them miraculous powers: they become medicine-men. The story of Koti and Chennaya shows us how the identity of the region is conceptualised around the image of the forest and its transformation into a feudal chiefdom. Even the Jains who were once the kings are sometimes perceived, today, as foreigners since they are less integrated with Tulu castes than the other Tulu-speaking communities.

Koti and Chennaya symbolise the region as a territory that men have cleared for cultivation. Later, the region has grown a particular political order characterised by Jain kings and Bunt warriors who became the devotees of royal bhutas. But the bhutas also represent a moral order, which fits the political order since the justice of the bhutas concerns everybody, including the non-Tulus who must integrate in this ideal order. Even today, when a non-Tulu, such as a Konkani, buys land in South Kanara, he soon discovers he must offer a cult to the bhutas attached to the land. If he does not, they will appear, torment him and ask him to perform an annual ceremony or *bhuta kola*.

Bobbarya, a Bhuta Associated with the Sea

The story of Bobbarya, the sailor bhuta, helps to understand how north and south, forest and coast area, autochthons and foreigners are integrated in an ideal order defined by the figures of the bhutas. Some stories claim that Bobbarya came from Goa. Bobbarya is known as the god of the sea and worshipped mostly by the members of the fishermen communities (Karve and Moghavera). He is the soul of a young man born of a Muslim father and a Jain mother. This unusual union is explained in the legend itself: A Jain girl was in distress, as all her bridegrooms were killed by a serpent coming out of her nose at midnight. Murava Byari, a Muslim youth, goes to Mecca and prays to God Allah, and comes to her and offers himself as a bridegroom. After having prepared a replica of rice powder paste, he keeps it close to the bride. A cobra emerges from her nose at midnight. Murava Byari kills it and marries her. Their son Bappa goes on a shipping expedition with his followers. In one version of the story, the ship is wrecked by a cyclone sent by the goddess Ganga, while in another the ship is wrecked in a maritime battle. Murava's son Bappa alone survives and he is transformed into a spirit. This spirit takes rest at Mulur, near Kapu. A toddy-tapper came that way and was blessed by Bobbarya. But he was not supposed to disclose the secret to his wife. He became very happy when he got maximum yield that year. But next day, he found only blood in his toddy pot. And when he went to a pond to clean his knife he was immersed in the water of the tank. The villagers dedicated a shrine to the spirit.

In this version Bobbarya, the sailor, blesses a Billava with good crops, which we may see as a way to adjust the sailor figure to the language of autochthony. In the story where Bobbarya is defeated in a maritime battle, he cuts many forest trees, of different species, to build his big ship. So Bobbarya acts in a way which denies the integrity of the forest and appears as a very different figure from other bhutas—such as Kallurti who protects the trees of the forest and punishes the villagers who cut the trees. But Bobbarya is defeated by a foreign ship which is made of stone. All the merchants who sail with him die and some of them become minor bhutas.

Here there are similarities with the Chinna bhuta who, according to another myth, were Chinese sailors who died in shipwreck and became bhutas after their death. Their bodies were found near Benakudru and their statues are in the shrine of Mekkekatu[23] where there are more than a hundred wooden figures of bhutas, among them Bobbarya and the Chinese bhutas.

Is Bobbarya so different from the other bhutas? Some myths show his superiority and tell us that he opened his legs wide in order to allow all the bhutas to pass through and descend from the Ghats to the sea.

In Tulu villages, Bobbarya is worshipped in the form of a pillar covered with a platform of stone to serve as an altar. Sometimes, a pyramidal stone is placed on the top of the pillar. A wooden mace *(daanya)* represents Bobbarya's weapon. On the front of the Bobbarya shrine in Yermal he is shown seated on an elephant, while his companion Banta Bobbarya has a horse.[24] The Moghavera consider Bobbarya as their bhuta and the main deity of their village. In Yermal, there was a dispute over the shrine of Bobbarya some twenty years ago as the village split into two hamlets Bada and Tenka Yermal. The villagers of both hamlets wanted theirs to be the main shrine, with Bada Yermal finally succeeding.

Bobbarya's bhuta kola is celebrated by the Moghavera fishermen in different villages of the coastal region. The possessed medium wears a special crown while dancing. A dish of rice and coconut is prepared by villagers who give it the shape of a mace. The impersonator circumambulates the temple with his mace. At the end of the ritual, the procession goes to the seashore with the impersonator to obtain the blessings of Bobbarya for a good catch of fish.

As Bobbarya's father was Muslim and his mother Jain, he exemplifes all the oppositions we find in Tulunadu today. But he transcends them: Muslims as well as Hindus attend his kola.

[23] In Mekkekatu, we also find different representations of Nandi as a bull with five heads, a bull with two heads, a turbulent bull, all connected with Shiva.

[24] The term banta means either a warrior, a soldier, a hero or a servant. Bante is often a mute companion to the bhuta and this character is impersonated by a less prestigious medium.

Bobbarya's Story

There was a girl Durgu Shetty. While her husband was sleeping, a black snake emerged from her right nostril and killed her husband. She had already been married forty times. At last, her seven brothers received a proposal from a Muslim to marry their sister. His name was Madhava Bayri and the seven brothers gave their sister to him. The Muslim took her to his house. Where she slept in the night, there was a banana tree. The Muslim put a white cloth near her, to fake his own shape, then went some little distance to spy on her. In the middle of the night, a white snake, Bulu Santamane, came out of her right nostril. The Muslim killed the snake. Then, a black snake, Kala Santamane, emerged from the girl's left nostril, and the Muslim killed him too. The next day, the Muslim went to see the brothers and told them he had killed the snakes. But the brothers were still reluctant to give him their sister. Madhava Bayri then took Durgu to the masjid and changed her name to Bibi Fatima. She got pregnant with a child, Bobbarya. He grew very quickly and reached the age of six in no time. Then he built a big boat from one big tree in the forest and went to sea. Before using his boat, he made a sacrifice: cutting his finger, he offered his own blood to the sea, paying allegiance to its goddess Jala Devi. Then, he took the boat to the sea and sailed with some other bhutas who followed him. But soon he lost control of the boat. Then, he went to Mulur and Kapu and his boat sank at Mulur.

At that time, Pangadera Baydya, a Billava, had climbed a coconut palm to drink. He had his *tawere* (knife) with him. On the road, there was a lotus pond. He saw a man near the pond, and then he saw an aswatha tree. Then, the man he saw told him: "do not tell anybody you have seen me, go and do your work". Pangare Baydya had one *shendi*, tender coconut, but soon there were plenty of them. Meanwhile, his wife wondered why her husband did not come back. She went to the lotus pond, and found her husband's *topi* floating on the water among the lotus. Pangagra Baydye is dead, said the villagers, but his *atma* (soul) has returned and she has been able to tell it to the village people. But, who was this foreigner who had appeared near the lotus pond? Then, the people from Mulur and Kapu began to understand, and built a bhutasthana at Mulur to Bobbarya. From Mulur, Bobbarya went to Yermal and stayed at first in the temple of Janardhan.[25] Janardhan then said to him: "Near me, in my temple, there is no room, go near the ocean, go near the ocean, there are Moghavera fishermen, they will make puja".

In this story, the identity of the merchants is not revealed. Who were Bobbarya's companions, and to which community did they belong? We know only they were stranded on the coast and became bhutas after their death. We understand, also, that the goddess of the sea did not protect Bobbarya who had offered her the blood of his finger.

The Darshan of Bobbarya

In Bada Yermal, I attended a *darshan* (divine vision)[26] ceremony in honour of Bobbarya. I stress here some essential sequences, to show how Bobbarya travels from his shrine to the sea and back to the village. He is impersonated by a *darshan patri* (possessed priest) who belongs to the washerman caste, Madhivala. The fishermen at Yermal stress that formerly the bhuta was impersonated by a Moghavera, who died; then they had a Billava patri who became exhausted; so they called the present patri, whose bulky appearance evokes the gigantic Bobbarya. The ceremony begins around six o'clock when the village dignitaries (*gurukar*), who organise the ritual, assemble in front of the Bobbarya shrine, its entrance richly decorated with flowers.

Bobbarya is not a rajandaiva but he is called *raja* and wears an umbrella. The village elders and dignitaries fine the fishermen who do not attend the ceremony. The patri prays inside

[25] The most popular Vaishnavite deities are Krishna, Janardhana, Anantapadmanabha, Vishnumurti and Narasimha.

[26] When Brahmins speak of *darsana,* (Skr.) the term refers to the vision that the devotee gets from the divinity in the temple during the ritual (*puja*). In Tulu, darsana also means a shivering caused by the possession of a spirit or bhuta (Carrin 1997b; 1999: 415).

the shrine, and when he emerges the music plays loudly, and he is possessed while the statues of Bobbarya and his companion Banta are placed on a palanquin decked with flowers. Then, the trustees question the patri about a recent violent death in the village: "Why did my uncle commit suicide," asks a young man. "Because he suffered a financial disaster." "Why he did not tell me?" Then the medium says: "Even fellow villagers had become foreigners to him; he used to fish in deep sea and then, he got attracted, and he drowned." In this example, the tragic story of a fisherman suddenly evokes the tragic death[27] of Bobbarya and his companions. Will this suicide also become a bhuta?

Without answering this implicit question, the bhuta thanks the villagers for organising the ceremony, then leaves the shrine, walking proudly, balancing his bulky body clad in pink silk. His right arm carries the mace and his wrists show his golden bangles. The musicians precede him and some devotees carry the flags of the bhuta, while two or three Madhivalas carry the palanquin with the two statues. Then starts a long procession towards the sea, which is followed by a rickshaw carrying a heap of tender coconuts to be sacrificed along the road, as the bhuta stops to answer his devotees' questions. They want to know whether they will get a good catch, whether they will be able to sell it, or, if they are not fishermen, whether they will get success in their work. Wherever the occupants of a house have lit a candle on a chair to attract the bhuta's attention, Bobbarya and the procession will stop. Some devotees' faces are anxious, as they question the patri about the ghosts of some recent death or about an illness.

A fisherman friend who walks along with me tells me how Bobbarya may take away the soul of the dead. Bobbarya is restless, not just because of his own violent death, but also since he caused the death of his companions, who came with him trading in the Indian Ocean. "But," adds my companion, "because he was restless, Bobberya can help us to find peace."

[27] The idea of a tragic death is central to the deification of men who become bhutas, though all bhutas do not have a human origin (Blackburn 1985).

The whole ceremony aims at allowing Bobbarya to return to the sea with the fishermen and other villagers such as Bunts, Billavas and even Muslims. When the procession reaches the seashore, the patri breaks a great number of tender coconuts, throwing them towards the sea; he then enters the sea himself while his companions light torches in the night. Then, the bhuta addresses the goddess of the sea, Jala Devi—whom some villagers also call Ganga Devi these days—and he declares: "I came from the sea, and I return to the sea. Give us your protection, protect those who go to distant lands!" This formula alludes to the travellers of the myth, as well as to present-day fishermen who stay at sea, fishing for a week.

Returning, the procession stops at another shrine, where the main gurukar ceremonially thanks a particular Brahmin, whose father gave the land to build another Bobbarya shrine. The Brahmin has become Bobbarya's devotee, and he gives his permission for another rite. On the way back to the main shrine, Bobbarya, violently possessed, meets Babu,[28] a bhuta of the dry land who is associated with the Billava and other untouchables and is the champion of the downtrodden people. The fishermen worship Bobbarya for the last time that evening, and consult the patri about the future of the community. In these last sequences, Bobbarya becomes a village deity, who transcends differences of faith as well as hierarchical position.

We find a number of villages where Bobbarya is supposed to stop and rest on his way from the island of Bennekudru—near the old capital of Barakuru—to the forest. He goes inland after visiting Hiriadka where he sits on his wooden throne, blessing the villagers. Bobbarya is the only bhuta who goes back and forth between the sea and the forest, returning to cut wood for another ship. The incessant movements of Bobbarya may be understood as describing the merchant's way of life, in contrast to that of the farmer.

But like many bhutas he is also a tragic figure, as he died violently. In the village of Kalumadi (not far from Hiriadka), I was

[28] Kordabbu or Babu is a bhuta worshipped by untouchables caste such as the Meera and Mansa. Babu was pushed into a well by a landlord; he has become a bhuta after his death.

told that several men have committed suicide by throwing themselves from the top of the rock that was once lifted from its base by Bobbarya. In these cases, the bhuta keeps the souls of the suicides, and their families, fearing the revenge of these *preta* (ghosts),[29] consult astrologers and patri to appease them and worship them as new bhutas.

Near the rock of Bobbarya, the medium of his bhutasthana got possessed by a pair of siblings, Abbage and Darage, famous in the region, who also died violently. These bhutas are the grandchildren of Siri, a queen who, after losing her chiefdom, knew great suffering (Carrin, forthcoming). Abbage and Darage quarreled when playing *cenne*, and one sister killed the other with the *cenne* board.[30] The story of these twins exemplifies the tragic destiny of a household where sisters quarrel, endangering the stability of the matrilineal order.

Near the stones dedicated to Abbage and Darage, women get possessed and sometimes commit suicide. As for the men who committed suicide at Bobbarya's place, I was told that Abbage and Darage were possessing the patri, telling him they will retrieve the souls the patri was looking for. Thus Bobbarya is keeping captive the souls of those who die violently near his abode, like the merchants who died along with him and were retained on the coast where they became bhutas. It is not clear why the twins try to get back these souls, but we know they are associated with individual distress[31] which is perceived in Tulunadu as a form of marginality. In a way, the foreigner, the desperate who commit suicide, or the sisters of the matrilineal

[29] As in other parts of India, ghosts are feared. In order to pacify the wrath of the pretas, Tulu villagers perform exorcisms where a patri possessed by a violent bhuta such as Guliga tries to free the devotees's mind from the frightening image of the preta. Exorcisms also take place in haunted houses.

[30] The holes of the cenne board represent granaries and it is taboo for sisters, or for husband and wife, to play as winning implies depriving the other player of his subsistence (Claus 1986).

[31] In the Siri epic, the twin sisters die because they play the cenne game but also since their parents have forgotten to fulfill a promise they had made to Bermeru. Their tragic death results from a divine curse. The story of Abbage and Darage show the sufferings of women in matrilineal society. The female bhutas possess women every year during a therapeutic cult.

household who kill each other, represent the dangers that threaten the stability of the Tulu ideal order.

Bobbarya's identity, born from a Jain mother and a Muslim father, evokes traditions of conversion from Jainism to Islam, found in several places along the coast. Thus in Honavara, further up the coast in North Kanara, I was told that due to the pressure of Muslim merchants some Jain families were obliged to convert to Islam in the eighteenth century, to secure their commercial ties with their Arabian partners. It is well known that some Muslim families in Bhatkal port were Jains formerly, and their old houses can still be seen. But some Jains refused conversion and fled towards the northern forest, towards Sagar, where they established plantations of cardamom, pepper and areca nuts. Today these families tell a myth explaining how they came from Honavara, saying they followed a white cow who showed them an invisible forest reaching from the sea to Sagar. They arrived at Kollamaguru, where they settled. They say they saw Parasunatha himself and decided to build a Jain basadi in the forest.

Curiously, this story has a parallel version in Puttige, a village subsidiary to one of the Madhvacharya maths[32] near Udupi, where we find Bobbarya represented inside the premises of the local math in the form of pillar. In this case the bhuta is associated with Panjurli, the boar, which is considered slightly inferior to Bobbarya, and who symbolises the territory.[33] Bobbarya has tamed Panjurli, say the people of that

[32] There are eight mathas founded by Madhava in Udupi in the thirteenth century. Each of these maths has another math in the countryside where a bhuta acts as a guardian spirit (ksetrapal) to the Brahminic deities.

[33] Tulunadu as a region might be symbolised by two animals: the boar and the fish. The boar descending from the wilderness and the fish which rises from the marine depths are fused. In the epic of Kuppe Panjurli, one Ballal (king) summons a magician as he had heard enough of Panjurli, the boar, during the year. Then he orders the bhuta to refrain from afflicting his family and says: "Don't emerge during our time. Be fish to water and boar to the forest." In another epic, Koti and Chennaya, the twin brothers, fish a boar-faced fish in a pond, and the woman who prepares the curry starts vomiting. The boar-fish animal threatens the Tulu world, where fish and boar should be kept separate. Damodar Rao (1996: 165) stresses that the odd figure of the boar-fish is associated with a ferocious bhuta, Kalanja, who is the only active spirit during the critical month

locality. The bronze mask of Panjurli is represented inside the math of Puttige, and a nema (annual possession ceremony) is celebrated during the last week of May, the time of the year, preceeding the monsoon, during which Bobbarya is supposed to sail. During the same period, Panjurli helps the villagers to prepare the rice fields for transplantation. Here, finally, we see the complementarity of coastal and inland elements.

In this last example, Bobbarya ceases his incessant moving. It is also the only time of the year where he can be at peace with himself, sailing just before the monsoon which provokes typhoons on the coast. It is noteworthy that it is a legend and a ritual attached to the Madhvacharya math of Puttige which conciliate the opposites, the foreignness and strangeness of Bobbarya, the restless giant, and Panjurli, the boar associated with agriculture, who represents righteousness and justice, opposed in the epic to the cruelty of the landlords. The story of Bobbarya as told in Puttige ends by telling how he sits on a wooden throne behind the math. Then, in front of him an invisible forest stretches to the Ghats. As Panjurli is said to have come down from the Ghats to Puttige, Bobbarya is supposed to return here to fetch trees to build new ships. The dominant role of the Madhavas, in the religion of this region, seems precisely to be based on integration of, and mediation between, opposites in the local religious set-up: thus they also integrate the Konkani merchants, most of whom are Madhavas, with the Tulu-speaking, autochthonous populations. The Swami of the Puttige math, in fact, sits on a wooden throne, like Bobbarya.

The main shrine of Bobbarya at Bennekudru, near Barakuru, is of special significance to the Moghavera fishermen. Here, we also find the missing link with Abbage and Darage, for it is told that long ago the siblings, after their quarrel, became bhutas and moved to Bennekudru. With them came Trisula and Masti, bhutas identified with the penance performed in

---

of Aati (July). The author underlines how the boar-fish paradigm is projected into inauspicious time, the month of Asti, to suggest that movement is inauspicious during that month. It is a time where fishermen should not fish.

The procession of Bobbarya come to the beach to propatiate Jala Devi, the goddess of the sea.
Photograph by Harald Tambs-Lyche, 2003.

these shrines once a year when the devotees walk on fire (*gende seva*) in order to get children. Abbage and Darage are the main deities here, but at the entrance is an image of Bobbarya, along with his wooden pillar. Close to this shrine is another small shrine dedicated to Venkatarama (the god usually associated with the Konkani merchants), where higher-caste devotees perform puja. At some distance from the sibling shrines, we find a *sedimara*, a wooden post which served as a pivot for the hook swinging ceremony in the old days. We may suppose that, for the Moghavera, hook swinging was a way to get the protection of Bobbarya before sailing. Today, women are still walking on fire to secure offspring.

At last, the souls of the turbulent sisters may rest in peace near Bobbarya whose figure represents an attempt to conciliate the opposite cultures of Muslim and Jain, the violence of the sea and the roaming life of the merchants with the values of purity, non-violence and justice of the Jains who formerly tried to be 'ideal kings' in the region. If some stories tell us how the Jain were not so virtuous, accepting Islam in order to continue their trade, others have them sheltering in the forest so as to be faithful to their gods. In other shrines near Bennekudru, like Barakuru, the ancient port and seat of administration of Tulu and Jain chiefs, legends tell us how the chiefdoms had developed trade contacts with distant countries. A local legend connects the place with China. The Mudukeri Panjurli shrine which belongs to the Billavas has five wooden figures representing Chinikara daivas—Chinese bhutas. A horde of them were roaming in the vicinity and on a particular occasion made fun of Panjurli, the boar. Panjurli got enraged and retaliated by causing five of the Chinese to remain forever in his shrine.

As we have seen, the Madhvacharya math of Puttige shelters images both of Panjurli and Bobbarya, and hosts a ceremony which aims at conciliating these opposite figures, offering an interesting metapor of integrating the foreign and the autochthonous.

Today the Tulu lower castes try to assert their identity and the cult of the royal bhutas does not answer their needs. The Siri cult, with the possession of the turbulent sisters, is slowly declining as fewer women get possessed every year. Bobbarya is still worhipped by the fishermen in the region of Bennekudru but the Moghavera—who have become richer nowadays as they possess freezing plants and purse-seine boats—now prefer to worship the goddess Mariamma, trying to monopolise the temples dedicated to her in South Kanara. Strikingly, the Billavas who represent the autochthons in the region are the rivals of the Moghavera fishermen for the monopoly of the goddess' temples. This rivalry which opposes the champions of autochthony to the Moghavera also expresses itself in the Mariamma[34] temples in Mangalore city. In other words, the old conflict which opposed agriculturists and fishermen has moved to the urban sphere as the elites of both castes try with different strategies to impose themselves as in order to challenge both the political power of Bunts and Jains, and the intellectual and commercial influence of the Konkanis and Muslims.

[34] The annual cult of Mariamma is celebrated in great pomp in temples such as Urva in Mangalore. This annual ceremony stresses the violent nature of the goddess who however receives vegetarian offerings inside the temple, while her guardians bhutas receive animal sacrifices outside the temple.

Till recently, the bhuta cult was a way to integrate the marginalised groups into the mainstream of Tulu society: any newcomer buying land had to worship the bhuta attached to it, so as to survive the malevolence of the bhuta. One may think that the bhuta cult was, for the Tulu castes, an efficient way to integrate foreigners—Jains or Konkanis, Muslim or Chinese.

Today the Jain community tries to resist Tulu assimilation by promoting the cult of bhutas such as Annapa Panjurli, which is a sankritised form of Panjurli venerated in the very important temple of Manjunatha in Dharmastala. This attempt to sanskritise Panjurli recalls the arrangements of the Puttige math forged under Madhava influence, to present a more peaceful figure of Bobbarya. Nevertheless, at the lower-caste level, Bobbarya is still a tormented figure attracting those feeling the urge to die in merging with the sea. Somehow, the suicide souls who roam the coast reminds us of the companions of Bobbarya who became bhutas after their death.

The paradox is that the Bunts have become so central in the renewal of the bhuta cult that they have succeeded in marginalising other dominant communities, even the Jains who were the previous rulers. The only Jains who compete with Bunts are the landlords who can still act as patrons[35] and offer a nema to their territorial bhuta. Aristocratic Jains who have not been able to adjust to the land reform are upset by the 'nouveau riche' behavior of Bunts who like to display their wealth.

Bobbarya represents a tormented figure because he mediates between foreignness and autochthony, reconciliated in his cult, at the cost of life and peace, as integration is often obtained after death. Bobbarya's place of death at Molur is still a symbol of his vulnerability, as the giant bhuta is tamed by the sea, which incarnates the dreams of fishermen and traders who finished by dying on its shores. The mediation operated by Madhava ideology contrasts with the bhuta cult, as the Madhavacharyas promote the order and values of urban life, attempting to mute the cry of Bobbarya the sailor which echoes the anger of the Arabian Sea.

[35] A few of the descendants from Jain aristocratic lineages try to go through the installation ritual to keep their traditional right of patronage.

7

*Transformations of Trans-oceanic Relationships: The Gulf Migration and the Nayars of South India**

Elizabeth L. H. Chettur

Introduction

Kerala, a small state on the southwestern tip of the Indian peninsula, supplied spices to the merchants of the lucrative Indian Ocean from the days of the Egyptian empire through European expansion. Today, one of Kerala's major exports is human labour to the Gulf.[1] While there is no direct link between the Arab spice trade and the contemporary migration of workers from Kerala to the Arab world, there is a similarity: both commercial enterprises brought wealth into Kerala. However, wealth remained concentrated among a privileged few throughout the spice trade, whereas, today, labourers from diverse caste and religious communities from Kerala earn money in the Gulf. In fact, the labour force is dominated by males from

* The material in this chapter draws on fourteen months (2000 and 2001) of ethnographic fieldwork which I undertook among an urban Nayar community in central Kerala and a rural one in the southern Malabar region. As I promised my informants, I have completely changed all names and personal details.

[1] The labour migration to the region of the Middle East is called the "Gulf migration" in Kerala, and people joke that Dubai is the capital of Kerala. It would be more accurate, however, to call it a "Middle East migration," because Keralites migrate to many Middle Eastern countries in addition to the Gulf states. About 40 per cent of labour migrants go to Saudi Arabia alone (Zachariah, Mathew and Rajan 1999). In referring to the "Gulf migration" throughout the chapter, I am following the lead of my informants.

low-caste and Muslim communities. Gulf migrants remit or bring home relatively large amounts of cash to purchase consumer goods that communicate and display wealth and/or prestige. As migrants return home with money in their pockets, shops, goods and the consumer market has had to keep pace. The desire for goods associated with wealth and prestige is palpable in towns and villages. Shops, shopping centers and restaurants now crowd town centres. A combination of Gulf-earned money, an explosion of consumption in Kerala, and the recent commodification of land and houses resulted in a unique opportunity for Keralites to purchase goods that were once inalienable possessions[2] signifying the prestige of high-caste communities. As the labour migration escalated, so did the market in Kerala for housing and land, two of the most important symbolic indicators of the prestige of high-caste lineages. Nayars, the high-caste community highlighted in this chapter, respond to new consumption patterns through specific stylistic considerations in their consumer decisions, and they devalue the display of wealth through consumption. They maintain a disciplined attitude toward life which is supported by Hindu philosophy. In this way, Nayars insulate their status and preserve the prestige inherent in their caste identity.

While this chapter does not depict a direct interaction between two or more geographic localities in the Indian Ocean region, it does demonstrate the effect on Kerala of centuries of interaction with Indian Ocean merchants, and, now, short-term migration to the Gulf. It is, essentially, a story of the effect of global movements on local lives and shifting conceptions of social hierarchy. Katy Gardner (1995) brought to the fore the importance of analytically valuing home communities amidst so much emphasis on the emergence of transnational ones, since the movement of people changes the social relations of new communities as well as the one left behind.

[2] I was inspired to use the concept of 'inalienable possessions' by Annette B. Weiner's theoretical and ethnographic study of Oceania societies in which she emphasises the power relations (in reference to gender) inherent in a strategy of exchange that she calls "keeping-while-giving" (Weiner 1992).

Introducing the Nair Family

In this chapter, I trace the story of a high-caste Hindu family in its struggle to preserve and insulate their high-caste status[3] amidst the recent explosion of consumerism. By concentrating on a particular family,[4] I aim to bring to the fore the power of the details of daily life, and the sense of social hierarchy as a subjective experience socially expressed in recognisable social patterns.[5] As Unni Wikan argues, one of the most useful ways to assess the cultural constraints that shape social patterns is "to steep oneself in detailed and particular cases" (1990: 18).

The Nayars are a small, extended family that belongs to the Nayar caste community. When I met them, they were living in an old apartment building in the middle of a large urban centre in the central region of Kerala. To simplify, I have given them the family name, Nair, a common family name in the Nayar caste community. Their story illuminates a time in Kerala of intense social change at the turn of the twenty-first century. It is at this time that the Gulf migration, although it had reached its peak before the first Gulf War and was on the decline, was still a major source of income for more than half of Kerala families. Govindan Nair is a bank manager. He brought his family to live in the Gulf for thirteen years. Upon their return from

[3] Throughout the chapter, I use the term "status" in the Weberian sense of a social formation based on social honour, prestige, and accumulated approvals and disapprovals, and the underlying social exclusivity. Caste communities are hereditary status groups. Contrastingly, social classes are marked by the stratification of social groups in terms of socio-economics and the relative ease of upward social mobility. The concept of upward mobility in terms of socio-economic status is quite new in Kerala. A different method of social mobility, sanskritisation, has long been an option whereby low-caste communities emulate the lifestyle of upper castes and change the name and origin myth of their community to raise the ranking in the caste hierarchy of their particular community. Today, low-caste communities appeal to the possibility of upward mobility by purchasing prestige goods, such as houses and land, and goods that display monetary wealth in an eye-catching way, such as flashy electronics, brightly coloured clothes, and heavy jewellry.

[4] I use the story of a single family as a lens with which to focus common experiences among families of this community.

[5] It has been well established that one's conception of social hierarchy depends upon one's position in the caste structure (Mencher 1974).

the Gulf, the Nairs purchased an apartment in a building in which nearly all the apartments were owned by Nayar families.

The Nairs left Kerala in 1978 for the Gulf. When they returned in 1991, Kerala had visibly changed. Govindan's mother, Kachi Amma, was the oldest member of the Nair family. The changes in Kerala caused much hand-wringing for Kachi Amma. She fondly remembered her childhood days when her social world rarely reached beyond the beautiful wooden veranda of her family household, and others behaved with respect for her family. She frequently bemoaned the greed and ostentatiousness of new-monied families. Kachi Amma had a passion for discussing the dissolution of the great matrilineages and the division of their property, especially their houses. She wrung her hands in dismay over losing her own lineage house. Her constant struggle to hold on to the Kerala she knew as a child, and to preserve the social status that, she felt, was her birthright, was very frustrating for her. She and other Nayar families around her were acutely aware of the transformation of hierarchical social relations.

Kerala's Geography and History

The social life for which Kachi Amma yearned was that which was shaped by a deeply stratified hereditary caste organisation which had emerged during the Arab spice trade (Jeffrey 1993). Kerala is a small, coastal state stretching about 360 miles (approx. 579 kms) from the southern tip of India to the state of Karnataka in the north. Its shape is defined by the Arabian Sea and the Western Ghats, a mountain range separating it from its eastern neighbour, Tamil Nadu. The northern part of the state of Kerala is covered with tropical rainforest, which is protected by various wildlife sanctuaries and parks. Kerala is a rather long and narrow state, reaching one hundred kilometers at its greatest width. The mountain range that forms the eastern border between Kerala and Tamil Nadu is extremely rugged and steep, and it effectively isolated the lush coastal plain from the dry hinterland, except for a few passable gaps. Kerala's west coast is open to the Arabian Sea, across which the annual monsoon winds blow.[6] The monsoon of the Indian Ocean shortened a thirty-month overland journey to a three-month oceanic trip. Consequently, Kerala became a key trading entrepôt; moreover, it was a convenient meeting point between Chinese and Arab merchants.[7]

Kerala gained its notoriety as a supplier of pepper to the Roman markets; the desire for Kerala pepper nearly drained the Roman coffers (Disney 1978). The enduring relationship between Kerala and the Arab world grew in importance with the decline of the Roman Empire.[8] Arab merchant activity in Kerala's rich seaports spanned more than a thousand years—until the arrival of European ships in the Indian Ocean. Both the Roman and Arabian empires dealt in trade with Malabar for the attainment of luxury goods (primarily exotic spices), and goods that would benefit the wealthy members of those societies. Similarly, in Kerala, the income from this trade was limited to elite landowning lineages and politically powerful lineages that also owned land.

The southwest coast of India was not unified or politically significant until the Kollam era, or the Second Chera empire, from 825 to 1102 AD.[9] At this time, three small kingdoms were

[6] The Indian Ocean monsoon between Africa and India has been instrumental in the emergence and continuation of trade in this part of the world. The monsoon (derived from the Arabic term *mausam*) refers to a special pattern of wind, not a storm, as is so often thought by Western scholars. Kerala experiences two monsoons: 'winter' and 'summer'. The 'winter' monsoon blows northeast from the direction of India diagonally across the Arabian Sea towards the east coast of Africa during the months of October to April. The 'summer' monsoon blows roughly in the opposite direction, southwest, from eastern Africa towards India during the months of June to September. This criss-cross pattern of winds makes the Indian Ocean a relatively easy ocean to navigate, and it has thus given strength to the relationships among the peoples of the Indian Ocean.

[7] See Das Gupta (1967), Chaudhuri (1985) and Disney (1978) for a comprehensive history of Kerala and the Indian Ocean world.

[8] The Arabs, however, had been trading partners with the west coast of India throughout the Roman times. The Romans relied upon the Arabs as middlemen because of their intimate knowledge of the people, language skills, and their ability to interact with the merchants and kings of India.

[9] According to local custom, the final Chera king, Cheraman Perumal, left Kerala for Arabia in the ninth century and converted to Islam following an unusual dream. In the dream, the moon split into two; half remained in the heavens and

emerging: Calicut in the north; Travancore in the south; and the central kingdom of Cochin sandwiched between the two.[10] Between the eleventh and the sixteenth centuries, the Calicut kingdom in northern Kerala, also known as Malabar, became the port of trade preferred by the Arabs. In the Zamorin's ports, Arab merchants maintained control of the trade, while the Zamorin controlled the ports and earned his income from customs duty. The Zamorin's military strength came from his military forces, which consisted of young males from the Nayar community. The Nayars were matrilineal (*marumakkattayam*) and their unusual marriage system effectively allowed young Nayar soldiers freedom of movement, because conjugal ties and fatherhood duties were extremely loose (Gough 1961). The growth of trade and the friendly alliance between the Zamorin and the Arab traders was further solidified by the Zamorin's unusually high level of integrity; his honesty is mentioned by a number of Arab traders.

Between the tenth century and the arrival of the Portuguese at the end of the fifteenth century, Arabs maintained control of the spice trade.[11] In the fifteenth century, the Portuguese

---

half fell to the ground. The moon reunited afterwards and set. Some time after Cheraman Perumal had this dream, a group of Muslim pilgrims told Cheraman Perumal that the Prophet Mohammad converted people by the miracle of the moon. When he left Kerala, Cheraman Perumal sent word back to Kerala that it was to be divided into three smaller kingdoms: the northern kingdom of Calicut was left in the ruling hands of the Zamorin; the central kingdom of Cochin was left to be ruled by Cheraman Perumal's descendants; and the very southern part of the west coast became the kingdom of Travancore. He also instructed the people of Kerala to establish mosques and propagate the "fourth Veda". The "fourth Veda" is a term used by Mappilas to refer to the followers of the Koran and the religion of Islam (Miller 1992 [1976]: 48).

[10] Kerala can still be roughly divided into the three areas that historically comprised the three kingdoms, because the organisation of their castes and their customs differed (Schneider and Gough 1961).

[11] During the Arab spice trade, the ultimate destination of Kerala's spices was Europe, and the Italian city-states emerged as important trading partners with Arabia. Prior to the arrival of the Portuguese, trade was structured in such a way that goods were sold and re-sold en route to Europe in a 'relay trade' in which the Sultan of Egypt received five per cent ad valorem from both sides of each transaction. Spices from Kerala arrived with Arab traders in Cairo via the Red Sea, and, in the fifteenth century, Venetians were the only Europeans allowed to

invested heavily in the attempt to discover an all-sea route to India. With this investment came the hope that one day they would control the spice trade and the world economy, which they did, for about a century.[12] Between the fifteenth and the seventeenth centuries, with the arrival of the Portuguese in Calicut, and political forces in Europe and the Mediterranean[13], the spice trade went through a transitional period.[14] The arrival of Vasco da Gama's fleet in 1498 marked the final days of significance for Kerala's ports in the Indian Ocean world, though Kerala remained an exporter of Indian goods throughout the British Empire.

Fifteen years following the arrival of the Portuguese, the Zamorin had fully acquiesced his power, and the Muslim community living in the Calicut kingdom began a long economic decline. More than half of the Arab community fled back to the Middle East. Of those who stayed, the Portuguese forced many

---

trade in Cairo. The Arabs maintained a monopoly of the spice trade between Kerala and Cairo, and the Venetians maintained a monopoly of the spice trade between Cairo and the rest of Europe.

[12] Braudel points out that, although the Portuguese captured the pepper trade via the new route around the African continent, the Venetians, and the Mediterraneans in general, were able to subsequently recapture the market. This is partially attributed to the movement of prices after the 1540s, the shorter and less risky journey from the Red Sea to Malabar, and, Braudel claims, it may have been due to the fact that the aroma of the spices diminished on the long voyage around the cape of Africa (Braudel 1995 [1949; 1966]: 545).

[13] The expansion of the Ottoman empire directly threatened the entrepôts of the Mediterranean where the Italian merchants received their spices (Braudel 1995 [1949; 1966]).

[14] In Malabar, the transitional period was marked by political crisis. As mentioned previously, three kingdoms had emerged along the southwest coast of India: Calicut, Travancore and Cochin. By the thirteenth century, Calicut was the dominant port of trade and the Zamorin was one of the wealthiest rulers on the west coast of India. However, the smaller rajas of Cochin, strongly resented the power and control that the Zamorin had gained through the spice trade as a result of liberal economic policies. There was a long and troublesome rivalry between the Zamorin and the Raja of Cochin, and when the Portuguese arrived in 1498, they took advantage of this old enmity. By the beginning of the sixteenth century, following a number of violent struggles between the Arab traders of Calicut and the Portuguese, the Portuguese established a positive trading relationship with the Raja of Cochin. In the end, the Portuguese chose the port of Cochin as its settlement and brought it onto the world stage.

to convert to Roman Catholicism. The unfortunate result of the period of Portuguese dominance for the Muslim community was economic decline, a more uncertain relationship with the Hindus, and a new militancy (Miller 1992 [1976]).

The Spice Trade and Kerala's Social Hierarchy

For most of its commercial history, middlemen in Kerala exchanged spices primarily for gold, which almost exclusively remained in the possession of kings (*rajas*), resident Arab merchants, and the landowning elite. Agricultural labourers were paid in kind, and only the high-caste communities benefited from trade. During the days of British-ruled India, a cash economy was introduced in which cash transactions very slowly replaced those based on birth or ritual status. In fact, the cash economy was so slow to infiltrate that villagers still remember the days when all transactions were based on paddy, or rice. Arab merchants established communities along the coast and inland along the major waterways that form a complex network of transport throughout the lowlands. Arab merchants dealt with middlemen who bought and sold agricultural goods from high-caste landowners. Kerala's village economy was self-sufficient; and it did not encounter the market economy until the nineteenth century.[15] The redistributive economy of villages was organised in such a way that agricultural produce was distributed in return for land rights, rights to cultivate, or subsistence needs through the links of the hierarchically organised caste communities.

Young males of the Nayar community formed a strong military protecting the kingdom in which they resided.[16] Nayars

[15] In fact, through the 1960s, villagers still used paddy as the main currency in transactions.

[16] The Nayar community lived in matrilineal joint families, in which women had relations (*sambandham*) with other Nayar men (or Nambudiri men, if their caste status was high enough), but they both resided in their natal households. There were two performances that may be interpreted as marriage. The first ritual is known as the tali-tying ceremony, *talikettukalyanam*, which was performed before puberty when a Nayar male suitable for marriage would tie the *tali* (a leaf-

lived in houses called *taravads*,[17] a word that refers both to the house and the lineage that owns it. Networks of reciprocity, obligation, deference, worship, and labour bound landlords, tenants and cultivators. Nayar taravads were the primary tenants of the village land, and they subsequently subleased land to tenant cultivators. A community of service castes lived on the taravad land and belonged to it. These included communities such as the Vaniyars (oil pressers), Vannans (washermen) and agricultural labourers.

Kerala was an important entrepôt in the spice trade throughout the last millennium, and at the height of the spice trade, rajas, merchants, and a few high-caste lineages became wealthy with Arab money. Until the beginning of the twentieth century, the agricultural economy of Kerala shaped, and was shaped by, the caste organisation. One's caste status was tightly linked to one's social status, and monetary wealth never reached the agricultural labourers and serving communities, who were paid for their services in kind and in keeping with their position in the caste hierarchy.

Moreover, the stratification of caste communities in Kerala was more rigid, elaborate and strict than it was in other parts of South Asia, and a rich symbolic language tightly constrained social interaction among the communities. For example, the untouchability of lower castes was refined to unapproachabil-

---

shaped ornament on a string) around the girl's neck. The second type of marriage was the *sambandham* relationship. It was a sexual relationship initiated by a proposal made by friends or parents of either the man or the woman. The relationship lasted for as short or long as was mutually agreed upon. For a more detailed discussion of the Nayar marriage rituals, see Moore 1988.

[17] The Nayar taravad, interpreted by Gough (1961) as a matrilineage, is more accurately described as a house-and-land unit (Moore 1986). A taravad name is used both to refer to an individual's lineage identity and the house in which the lineage resides, and these are impartible. House and land units were inalienable property, and, as such, signified caste status. Houses also spatially organised castes: "serving houses would be settled as tenants on the land of one of the houses they served, which would in turn be settled on the land of one to whom they owed allegiance, on up to the level of the rulers of kingdoms" (Moore 1986: 533). The Nayar taravad was also a property group; it was an economically independent unit headed by the eldest male member of the family.

ity in which the mere sight of a low caste individual was enough to pollute a high caste.[18]

The Legacy of the Spice Trade and Its Effect on the Gulf Migration

The Gulf migration and the Arab spice trade are not connected in a direct sense, but, indirectly, the spice trade influenced both the scale and the migratory pattern. Four hundred years after the end of the Arab spice trade, Arab money still fuels the Kerala economy, but, today, labourers earn and control their own income and the state treasury is bankrupt.

One of the legacies of Kerala's ancient and lucrative relationship with Indian Ocean traders is its rich religious diversity. There are three vibrant religious communities in Kerala that originated as merchant communities: Muslim, Syrian Christian and Jewish. Today, the Syrian Christian community owns a significant proportion of the land in some parts of the state, and they operate lucrative agricultural enterprises. Nayars refer to them as an aristocracy. Muslims, who are concentrated in the northern region of Kerala, are typically agriculturalists.[19] Today, Muslims and Hindus interact on a daily basis, and children often go to school together. They do not intermarry, though, and their social spheres rarely intertwine, especially

[18] In 1940, Howard Somervell, a Christian missionary, wrote that when he arrived in 1924, he witnessed "a Brahmin walking along a public road, with a Nair some 20 yards ahead of him armed with a stick, warning all outcastes off the road, so that they could run away their regulated 30 yards from the roadside before the Brahmin came along". He never saw this happen again. The anthropologist, Adrian C. Mayer, wrote that when he visited Kerala in 1950, he was advised against visiting a Nambudiri house because the purification bath the residents would have to take after his departure would cause too much trouble. An eighty-year-old informant quietly admitted to me that he remembered the feeling of shame as a young boy, as he dived behind a bush when he heard the bell, rung by his attendant, signalling that a Brahmin was walking toward him along a village path.

[19] In October of 1994, Kerala was the first and only state to include its entire Muslim population in the OBC (Other Backward Community) category. This bureaucratic maneuver was relatively easy since the Mappila community, the Muslims of the northern part of the state, was already categorised as OBC, and the state government simply redefined Mappila to include all Kerala Muslims.

after they leave school. In villages, both Hindus and Muslims are quite adamant that, although they have heard of violence between Hindus and Muslims in north India, they have very peaceable relations in Kerala. Actually, there have been, and still are, outbreaks of violence between the Hindus and Muslims in northern Kerala. Skirmishes between the two communities usually have to do with political elections. The majority of Hindus and Muslims feel strongly that although these skirmishes occur, it is only on the very northern part of the state, and that Kerala in general is unique in its religious tolerance. One Hindu family in the village was keen to introduce me to their Muslim friends, although I discovered that their friendship was little more than an acquaintance; they spoke when their paths happened to cross, but they could not recall a time when they socialised together.

The long relationship between Arab traders and the political and social elite of Kerala probably influenced the initial migration pattern of Keralites[20] to the Middle East, although a direct connection is difficult to establish. About half of the Indian population in the Middle East is from Kerala, despite the fact that Kerala is only about three per cent of India's total population. This perhaps bears testimony to the historical relationship between Kerala and the Arabs. According to one study, "the concentration of Gulf migrants in Kerala may be linked to its prior experience in migration and the close ties the coastal pockets of the region have always had with the Arab countries" (Isaac 1993: 77). Another study also argues that the old trading relationship shaped the initial migration pattern, and "Gulf pockets" formed in regions that experienced particularly high migration rates (Kurien 2002). Keralites informed me that they feel welcomed by the Arabs because they are aware that the Keralites once welcomed Arab merchants during the

[20] In this chapter, I refer to the people of Kerala as 'Keralites' instead of 'Malayalis,' which is more common and refers to the language of this region, Malayalam. In using 'Keralite,' I am following the lead of the state government. While this reflects an orientation toward national identity within the Indian context, it also serves to include the large diaspora that has spread to many parts of the world, and may have lost the language.

spice trade. I spoke with many Kerala Muslims who longed to visit the Arab world, and this was a clear factor, beyond financial considerations, underlying their desire to work in the Gulf. A few Muslims spoke of knowing Keralite *Arabis*, Muslims who are descended directly from Arab traders, but they spoke of them with such awe that I am not sure whether they were mythical or not.

The Gulf Migration

The Gulf migration has touched nearly all Keralites, even if it is just by the mere possibility of it. A state-funded study of the economic impact of migration on Kerala's economy, carried out by three economists who are themselves Keralites, argues that the migration is changing every facet of social life in Kerala, including economic, social, demographic, political and even religious (Zachariah, Mathew, and Rajan 1999). Gulf migrants of all skill levels spend long hours on the job and little money (or time) on entertainment. They periodically send money home, prompting Kerala's reputation for being "a money-order economy."

In the 1970s, Kerala's labour migration to the Middle East increased sharply, and it continued to increase slowly until 2000 when it began to decline, for various reasons. In the early decades of migration, visas were issued quite liberally, but since the peak of migration in the 1970s, bureaucratic procedures have become increasingly complex and restraining.

There are two clear patterns of migration to the Gulf; one is a longer-term migration of white-collar, professional, or skilled labourers; and the other is a short-term migration of unskilled or semiskilled labourers. Professional or skilled labour migrants are generally from Nayar and Christian communities, while unskilled migrants tend to be low-caste Hindus and Muslims. Companies in the Gulf hire doctors, nurses and bankers, but Kerala artisans, especially carpenters, are particularly sought after for the mastery of their skill. These workers earn a tax-free salary, receive free housing, and they are given an extra stipend for family expenses. The company also pays for the whole family to return to Kerala to visit each year. This type of migration lasts from about fifteen to twenty years. Unskilled labourers follow a different pattern of migration. They spend less time in the Gulf, usually between three and nine years. Migrants generally try to negotiate for three- or four-year contracts. The majority of unskilled labourers work in the construction business; there are advertisements in the daily newspaper for construction jobs in the Gulf. Many are hired as household servants through contacts, who are as likely to be friends as family. There are also cases in which an unskilled labourer is hired by a friend or family member already in the Gulf who already owns, or at least manages, his own company.[21] In many cases, unskilled labour migrants earn more money during a four-year work contract in the Gulf than their fathers earned in a lifetime in Kerala.

There are other reasons Keralites migrate to the Gulf, in addition to the lure of tax-free foreign currency. First, is the high unemployment rate in Kerala. There are few jobs because large industries do not want to be located in a state with very strong labour unions, and the agricultural sector is unprofitable.[22] The Gulf is also attractive because of its relative proximity to Kerala and the labour contracts are relatively short (travel to and from the Gulf is easy and much cheaper than travel to England or the U.S.). This allows Keralites to return to their homeland and their families more often, and to feel that they are only temporarily residing outside their homeland. Kerala Hindus rarely migrate to the Gulf for more than ten years, and it is more commonly two sets of four-year terms of employment. Gulf migrants talk of intense longing for their

[21] All companies in the Gulf must be owned by an *arabi*, a arab citizen of the country in which the company is located. However, most informants told me that this was only for legal purposes and that the *arabi* was often not involved in the company at all and might not even be known to the employees.

[22] The state government hopes that the tourist and technology sectors will provide more jobs and money for the state in the near future. To this end, a fancy new technology park was recently built near Thiruvananthapuram, the state capital. Many new large national hotel chains have built hotels and resorts, and smaller, privately owned safari-like resorts have sprung up over the past ten years.

homeland, the "bad living" in the Gulf, and the strong desire to raise children in Kerala so that they can be educated with Kerala values—this especially refers to placing importance on family. One informant told me that the most important reason that Gulf jobs are so popular is that they do not require a long commitment. Otherwise, men would prefer to suffer poverty in Kerala than uproot their families to a foreign country. Many Keralites want to raise their families in Kerala because they believe family is more important there than anywhere else in the world.

Muslims have advantages over Hindus in procuring Gulf jobs: a wider network of family already working there; the partiality of Arab business owners to sponsoring a Muslim rather than a Hindu; an easier time obtaining a visa; and the opportunity to get a visa at any time for a Muslim pilgrimage. Pilgrimage visas, however, entail the moral compulsion to pay for one's trip with honestly earned money, not money obtained under dubious circumstances. It was evident, however, that some Muslims ignored this compulsion.

Most Hindus that I interviewed felt that living in the Gulf was not agreeable, but I was not able to elicit a clear explanation for this. Some women did not like the restriction of movement for women in an Islamic country. The common sentiment among Hindus was that one should minimise the amount of time spent in the Gulf while maximising the amount of money saved. Consequently, migrants spent very little money on entertainment or enjoyment. Many Hindus maintain private shrines in their own houses in the Gulf (which, of course, they do in any case, if they are able to financially), but a few houses maintain public shrines, which they allow any Hindu to visit. In this context, informants often added that most Hindus had little contact with Arabs because Hindus preferred to maintain a community amongst themselves.

Although there is great variation, the typical migrant is an unskilled or semi-skilled male Muslim. Unskilled jobs in the Gulf are especially lucrative, in comparison to wages in Kerala, or any other Indian state, and this partly because money earned in the Gulf is tax-free and enters Kerala at a very favourable exchange rate.

New Gulf Money, Caste Prestige and Consumption

The separation of caste hierarchy from symbols of prestige is largely a consequence of commodification; and the money to purchase commodities may be earned by migrating to the Gulf.[23] As the wealth of the Arab countries trickled into Kerala, consumption grew. In 1998, the total annual remittances, both in cash and in kind, received on a state level were about 11 per cent of the state domestic product (Zachariah, Mathew and Rajan 1999).

Until recently, Kerala's caste organisation was deeply stratified and rigid. The social world of Kerala's elders was steeped in proscriptive rules for inter-caste interaction. Caste identity largely restricted one's wealth, prestige and occupation.[24] Social hierarchy in Kerala was once indistinct from its caste hierarchy. Today, social rules governing the interaction between high- and low-caste communities are more subtle and dramatically less elaborate than they were just fifty years ago. At the beginning of the twentieth century, the symbolic concept of distance pollution severely restricted the interpersonal interaction between members of economically interdependent caste communities.

Today, a tense relationship appears to be emerging between high-caste and newly wealthy low-caste communities. Any consumer can purchase prestige goods that traditionally were

[23] It should be noted that other factors were necessary in the unbundling of the intimate relationship between social hierarchy, caste status and prestige. These include: British bureaucratic procedures; Gandhian reform movements; indigenous lower-caste movements; the struggle to form a modern state bureaucracy; and most recently, communist land reform measures.

[24] The elaborateness of caste rules is best captured by the symbolic mechanism of distance pollution, which dictated that polluting castes had to maintain a distance of sixty-four feet from non-polluting castes. Distance pollution is no longer relevant, especially in Kerala's cities and towns, but the elders remember it. For more on the topic of distance pollution and inter-caste interaction, see Mayer (1952), Gough (1961), Mencher (1965) and Fuller (1976).

inherited, such as houses, land, jewellery, and clothing. However, for Nayars, social prestige is inherited; possessing particular prestige goods cannot confer status. Instead, prestige is most powerfully expressed in social behaviour that betrays values of modesty, simplicity, and understated living style. Low-caste communities do not fully share these values, and this, for Nayars, restricts their upward mobility.

Land Ownership and Nayar Prestige

Low-caste communities of Kerala emulate Nayar lifestyle to gain social prestige.[25] Individuals from low-caste communities do not desire to *become* Nayars, only to acquire their associated prestige. The technique of emulating Nayars includes symbolic expression, but methods rarely extend as far as values like simplicity, modesty or discipline in style and character. Low-caste communities now have access to symbolic prestige markers that are commodities, such as clothing, personal adornment (especially jewellry). Thus, accent, bodily comportment, and specific values are less attainable and less desirable. The most significant commodities signifying prestige are houses and land.

During British colonial rule, the traditional pattern of land ownership began to disintegrate and the value of private property gained favour. One of the most powerful disruptions to the traditional social hierarchy of Kerala was the emergence of socialist conceptions of land ownership. From the late 1930s through the 1970s, a series of land reform acts legislated the redistribution of land to low-caste tenants and labourers. This also solidified the shift in the concept of land as an inalienable possession of high-caste communities to the idea of land as an ordinary commodity. As the female head of an old matrilineal Nayar taravad described it:

> When the land reforms bill came into effect in Kerala..., the taravad lost all the paddy fields and gradually started feeling the

[25] Osella and Osella (2000) provide a comprehensive study of this process among the Ezhava (or Izhava) community of the south-central region of Kerala.

> pinch of money.... The house needs repairs and with soaring prices and wages, maintenance of the house and farm is getting difficult....I...would like to keep up this old and beautiful house for posterity.

Land and houses are the most sought-after and expensive commodities in Kerala (despite the unprofitable nature of agricultural land). This is not surprising since land and houses only recently shifted from their traditional designation as inalienable possessions of high-caste lineages to commodities. Land reform measures disengaged caste status from the pattern of landownership.[26] An economic analysis of a village in central Kerala found that: "the land basis for caste inequality and caste exploitation has been entirely eliminated by the land reform" (Franke 1992: 112). Similarly, the commodification of the house turned "what was once a centre of a nexus of hierarchical social relations [into] a piece of property—partible, objectified, alienable" (Moore 1986: 538).

Despite the separation of caste status and house ownership, the house remains the most powerful symbol of prestige. As soon as agricultural labourers gained full rights to the land on which they lived, and the Gulf migration gave many the opportunity to earn money, the number of small, tiled houses increased dramatically.[27] A housing construction boom and skyrocketing land prices coincided with the onset of the Gulf migration. Between 1971 and 1981, the number of houses in Kerala increased by about 15 per cent (Gopikuttan 1990), and the value of land in rural areas increased by 600 per cent (even

[26] Traditionally, housing style, in addition to ownership, indicated one's caste status. High-caste lineages lived in wooden structures of two or more stories with tiled roofs. Low-caste families generally lived in small wooden or mud huts on the land to which they belonged. Nayar taravads were almost always surrounded by lush garden land (*parambu*), whereas the huts of the low-caste communities had no surrounding land at all. The parambu still indicates prestige. In describing one's house, Keralites qualify the description by adding whether the house has an attached garden or not. Some Nayar family names use 'parambu' as a suffix denoting status.

[27] Report of the Survey on Socio-Economic Conditions of Agricultural and other Rural Labourers in Kerala, 1983–84. Department of Economics and Statistics, Government of Kerala, 1985.

though it is unprofitable) during the very same decade that the Gulf migration grew to its peak (Isaac 1993: 84). Newly constructed mansions line the roads throughout Kerala, in both rural and urban areas. It seems there is not a town or village left untouched by this trend. New houses are often washed in a pink colour, which gives them greater contrast with the deep green of the surrounding coconut palms and paddy fields. Today, villages and towns display a unique mixture of Gulf-style mansions, small clay-brick structures of two or three rooms, small traditional wooden houses, and large abandoned wooden taravads that loom like ghosts behind the coconut groves and overgrown banana trees.

Empty Vessels Make More Noise: The Nair Family

Although they are consumers and participate fully in Kerala's market economy, many Nayars devalue the consumption of prestige goods characteristic of low-caste communities. Nayars feel that money is something that anyone can make, but the prestige of high-caste lineages is innate and inalienable. It cannot be purchased. Gulf money has penetrated Kerala and inspired an active consumerism. Newly built houses are commonplace, and fancy Gulf-style shops crowd city and town centres. In the days before commodification and large-scale consumption, one's position in the caste hierarchy was immediately visible in the symbolic language of clothing, speech, housing and personal adornment. Most of these symbols are now commodities.[28] In the new context of monetary wealth and the commodification of traditional inalienable high-caste possessions, high-caste families have had to find new ways to insulate their status and preserve the social prestige attached to their lineage and caste identity. I heard many stories of low-caste males "striking it rich" in the Gulf and building great mansions in their natal villages for their extended families.

[28] Speech, clearly, is a symbolic communication of prestige that betrays one's origins in terms of caste community and locality. For instance, an educated medical doctor is quickly identifiable as a low-caste Ezhava by his accent.

Nayars argue that while low-caste families can become wealthy, they can never "become Nayar." They explained the ostentatious pink mansions of Gulf migrants as evidence that "empty vessels make more noise" (*niranja kudam thulumbilla*). When a vessel is of full of something, it makes very little noise when it is tapped. For Nayars, displaying wealth is just noise. Nayars are full vessels; they need not display prestige since they are full of it already.

To insulate their high-caste status, Nayars use a combination of different techniques, depending on their financial resources. One way is to communicate modernity and westernisation in clothing, interior décor and housing style. These consumption patterns are markedly different from the choices made by individuals from low-caste communities. "Nayars have always been more aware of western style" (which is equated with modernity), according to one informant, because "our caste status gave us more privileges during British times, so we became more modern than the lower castes. The lower castes are more concerned about throwing their money around, but Nayars are more progressive and modern." The important quality of Nayar consumption patterns is that the goods they buy are usually understated, simple and modest in style. In contrast, low-caste tastes are generally less simple and meant to attract attention rather than deflect it. Not all Nayars have the financial resources to purchase consumer goods that reflect a modern or western lifestyle. Nayars who do not have the cash tend to preserve their prestige from low-caste monied families through an appeal to Hindu values, which also explains, defines, and supports their high-caste status. In most cases, however, Nayars combined both style and values.

Even after thirteen years of living and working in the Gulf, the Nair family lived a modest lifestyle when I met them in Kerala. There was little outward sign that Govindan's job as a bank manager was lucrative. In fact, his salary was quite significant: he earned the equivalent of 60,000 rupees (US$ 1,327) in the Gulf, on which he did not have to pay any tax, and his living expenses were reimbursed. In Kerala, Govindan's pre-tax salary was 20,000 rupees (US$ 442) with no paid expenses.

The Nairs kept their consumption to a minimum. They purchased just enough to live a comfortable life (a small apartment, a dining table, a small couch, a small television, an electric mixer (*mixie*) and a household servant). Their clothes were similarly modest.

Leela felt that families who live extravagant lifestyles veer away from what the cosmos has ordered for them. Displaying wealth is simply stepping off life's natural path. For instance, a "good Hindu" maintains such traditions as the style, placement, and design of a house that astrology dictated, and does not build modern concrete structures that do not adhere to Hindu house proportions (*taccasastram*). From their own perspective, the Nairs maintain their high status by reasoning that the lifestyle of the newly wealthy was not the path of a "good Hindu."

One of the more important ways that Nayars seek to maintain an auspicious lifestyle is through astrology.[29] As Govindan's wife, Leela, described it, astrology plays an important role in a fatalistic approach to life, and lack of entrepreneurialism, that is characteristic of the Nayar community. Human life on earth is preordained, or determined, by cosmic processes. Leela explained important events in life with reference to fate, astrology and auspiciousness, but she tempered this with reason. Her husband's career was the consequence of a particular star alignment as well as his hard work, for example. When negative events occurred, like her sons not doing well on their school exams, she explained it as bad luck, or a bad alignment of the stars, because they had worked hard.

The old apartment building in which the Nair family now lives in central Kerala was one of the first to be built in the city,

[29] Astrology in Kerala is based on Vedic teachings, and it informs the most important decisions in an individual's life as well as many of the smaller and less significant ones. Astrology is a method of understanding the life course of people and events within the natural structural relations of the universe and has been influenced by the great work of Indian mathematicians, some important ones from Kerala, who worked on such topics as: the mean motions of the heavenly bodies; the true motions of the heavenly bodies; miscellaneous mathematical rules; the systems of coordinates, direction, place and time; and eclipses of the sun and the moon.

foreshadowing the trend in which large old taravads are sold to urban developers.[30] The apartment building is well known because it was one of the first of its kind to be built in the city in the 1970s, and it was thus associated with modernity. It was built on the site of a high-caste Nayar taravad, and all the residents of the building are Nayars with the exception of two Nambudiri Brahmin[31], families and a couple of families from

[30] These old wooden house are fully dismantled and sold piece by piece. The wood, usually teak, used to build the old taravads, has become very expensive and is sold to various consumers, including wealthy Keralites wishing to build a new house in the 'old style', or large hotels who use pieces of old houses to recreate the feel of Old Kerala. The furniture inside the old houses was also crafted from teak or rosewood. The roof tiles of old houses can be sold for huge profits. After the building is dismantled and sold, the developer builds a block-style complex of apartments on the house site. The owner of the original taravad is given an apartment or two, but the family usually purchases enough apartments so that the joint family can all live under the same roof. It should be noted that this is a general trend throughout urban south India.

[31] Throughout Kerala, Nambudiri Brahmins are the highest Hindu caste, and in the past, they ranked ritually "above and outside the political system of the kingdoms" (Gough 1961: 306). Although ritual rank was considered to be above, or to transcend, the political system, the Nambudiris maintained control of the whole political system because even the political authority of Nayar kings had to be ceremoniously and ritually sanctioned by them. It has been argued that Nayar kings were simply servants of the Nambudiris (Gladstone 1984: 21). Furthermore, the Nambudiris were ritually sanctioned landlords who leased land to Nayars in return for military and other services. Nayar tenants managed the further subleasing of the land. Mythically, the Nambudiris created the land tenure arrangement as a way of maintaining their hereditary right to land originally bestowed upon them through the temple system of the Vedic culture. Nambudiris explained their inheritance of the land to the Parasurama legend, which provides a general introduction to the origin myth Keralites still cite when explaining the Nambudiri-Nayar relationship:

> The story tells of Parasurama, an incarnation of Vishnu, who killed all the Kshatriyas or warriors in India. To expiate his hideous sin, he made over the country to holy men. However, finding that now he himself had nowhere to live, he appealed to the holy men for a piece of land. They replied that he might have all the land within a single throw of his axe, whereupon he threw his axe from Kanyakumari [southernmost tip of India] to Gokarnam, and the sea receded from the foot of the Western Ghats to form the narrow strip of land that is now Kerala. To populate the new place, Parasurama imported a special race of Brahmins, the Nambudiris, to whom he gave control of all the land. Beneath them, they established a caste of warriors and retainers, the Nayars. Though Sudras, the lowest of the four ranks of classical Hinduism, Nayars were far too exalted to perform the unpleasant tasks of agriculturalists and artisans, so beneath them in turn were established a number of subservi-

north India. The Nairs live in a small two-bedroom apartment, about twelve hundred square feet. Kachi Amma lives in a smaller apartment on the floor above. Govindan explained, "in a modern context, times have changed, but we live in an apartment building that is well known." Although they had Gulf money, the Nairs lived frugally and tried not to draw attention to themselves in any way.

The Nair family's lifestyle was predictable and uncomplicated. They followed a very disciplined daily routine, with no excesses and precious few deviations. Every morning, Leela had a bath and performed her own *puja*, or ritual to honour the gods. The family—Govindan, Leela and his mother—had breakfast and Govindan left for the office. Leela recited mantras and then read the newspaper. She spent her morning supervising the cleaning and cooking in the household. The afternoon was a time of rest, and then she (not her servants) served tea to her family at four o'clock. Between tea and dinner, Leela again supervised the preparation for the evening meal. On a couple of days each week, she would go to the local vegetable stand at five o'clock for fresh vegetables and fruit. After darkness had set in, Nayar women rarely left their homes, unless accompanied by a father, husband or son. Men, however, were free to move about. Days, in both the city and the village, were framed by visits to the temple, meals, and the afternoon and night time rest. The only days that were different were Sundays or *bandhs* (all-day strikes affecting all commercial and government businesses), when Govindan stayed home from work and the servants did not come. The predictability of daily life in the Nair household reflects the family members' belief that consistency and routine in work (and non-attachment to that work) is essential to maintain status in this life and the next. Leela referred me to Swami Vivekenanda[32] "to really understand

ent, polluting castes. Nayars were taught to revere their Nambudiri superiors (Jeffrey 1993: 24).

[32] Swami Vivekananda is a popular Hindu spiritual leader for many Nayars because his philosophy appealed to educated and high-caste Hindus. He was one of the first Hindu leaders to travel to the United States to share the philosophy of Hinduism. He is therefore associated with modern, western values.

why we are so disciplined." Swami Vivekenanda explained that "birth and position in life and in society largely determine the mental and moral attitude of individuals towards the various activities of life" (Vivekenanda 1978: 206).

When the Nair family returned to Kerala after living in the Gulf for 13 years, Kerala was visibly changed by Gulf money.

> When I came back to Kerala in 1995 after my father died, my mother was living in our taravad alone. The servants were still there, but my brother and sister had moved out of Kerala for job reasons. My wife's taravad was much smaller and most of her family still lived in it, so we didn't have to worry about her family. We decided to buy two apartments—one for us and one for my mother. She was getting old. We are able to get all the things here that we had there because there are so many shops selling gadgets from the Gulf. But my mother hasn't been happy since she left the taravad. She is bored here and I think she misses her servants. We bought her a TV and she loves the Malayalam programmes. She takes all her meals with us, but what is there for her to do here? My sons are grown now and have moved out. They come to visit, but not all the time. There is nothing for my sons to do here because of the whole labour problem, you know. Now the lower castes have so much power in the labour unions and they make money in the Gulf and build ostentatious houses. This is not the way it used to be. (Govindan Nair)

For Nayars, like the Nair family highlighted here, relative economic wealth is nearly (but not entirely) irrelevant to social status. Nayars interpret conspicuous consumption as evidence that one is not following the path of a "good Hindu," and this reflects a low status in this lifetime and predicts a low one in the next. Indian social hierarchy has always been a complex mixture of economic, political and caste hierarchies, but, as Milner (1994: 58) points out, social mobility has been severely limited by rules of ascription and inalienability. One of the most important sources for the restriction of mobility is the centrality of ritual status in Indian society. In Kerala, the unprecedented access to Gulf jobs and money over the past few decades has challenged its social hierarchy, and the preservation of ritual status has become even more important for the high-caste communities.

The Dream of Social Mobility

Through short- and long-term jobs in the Gulf, Keralites can earn significant amounts of money, which they bring home to Kerala. In general, members of low-caste communities use this money to purchase the prestige goods that were once the inalienable symbols of high-caste prestige. In response to this new context of consumption and new dreams of social mobility, Nayars devalue consumption and insulate their status group by appealing to values not fully shared by the low-caste community, such as simplicity, modesty and other Hindu values. In a revision of Thorstein Veblen's work on the class structure of the United States in *The Theory of the Leisure Class*, Steiner and Weiss argue that social mobility is not a simple process of emulation and that "the nouveau succeeds by his exhibitionism in gaining the regard of the masses, but the adoption of the canon of restraint by the old elite forces him in turn to recognize its superiority. By seeming to value little what is of such cardinal importance to the newly rich, the old elite successfully undercuts the props from the prestige system of the nouveau" (1951: 264). To comprehend the emergence of social mobility and the shifting social conceptions of hierarchical organisation in Kerala, it is important to retain an understanding of how prestige is insulated as well as appropriated.

The increasing importance of class—a social hierarchy that is organised, at least in part, in terms of relative economic wealth and characterised by social mobility—is undeniable in India; the sheer size of India's middle class lends it a visibility that is difficult to ignore. Class is certainly not a new concept in India, but its significance in relation to caste hierarchy and everyday social life has increased dramatically. As caste organisation in India is well researched (and contested) by social theorists, perhaps similar research needs to be done on the competing values underpinning class and caste in India to fruitfully discuss the relationship between these models of hierarchical organisation in India.[33]

[33] Substantial work has been done in this direction recently (See Fuller 1997, Osella and Osella 2000, Mines and Lamb 2002, Dickey 2000, Chakravarti 2001, Sharma 1994).

The organisation of social hierarchy in Kerala is contested now, probably more than it was in the recent past, but the principle of hierarchical relations remains strong, as Osella and Osella (2000) have argued. The struggle to insulate, define, and challenge social conceptions of status groups and social prestige is a crucial part of social relations and daily interactions. Commodification and new patterns of consumption have not weakened the value of prestige and social distinction. The explosion of consumerism in Kerala has begun to introduce new ways of conceptualising and communicating prestige, and new relations among social groups. The most significant new quality of hierarchy in Kerala is social mobility, and it is this quality that compels Nayars to insulate their hereditary status. Kerala's historical relationship with the Arab world influenced the size and pattern of the contemporary Gulf migration, in which money earned there is used to purchase traditional symbols of prestige that were once considered inalienable possessions of high-caste lineages.

PART THREE

African and Arab Presences in India

Map including the Swahili Coast, the Arabian peninsula and southwest Asia

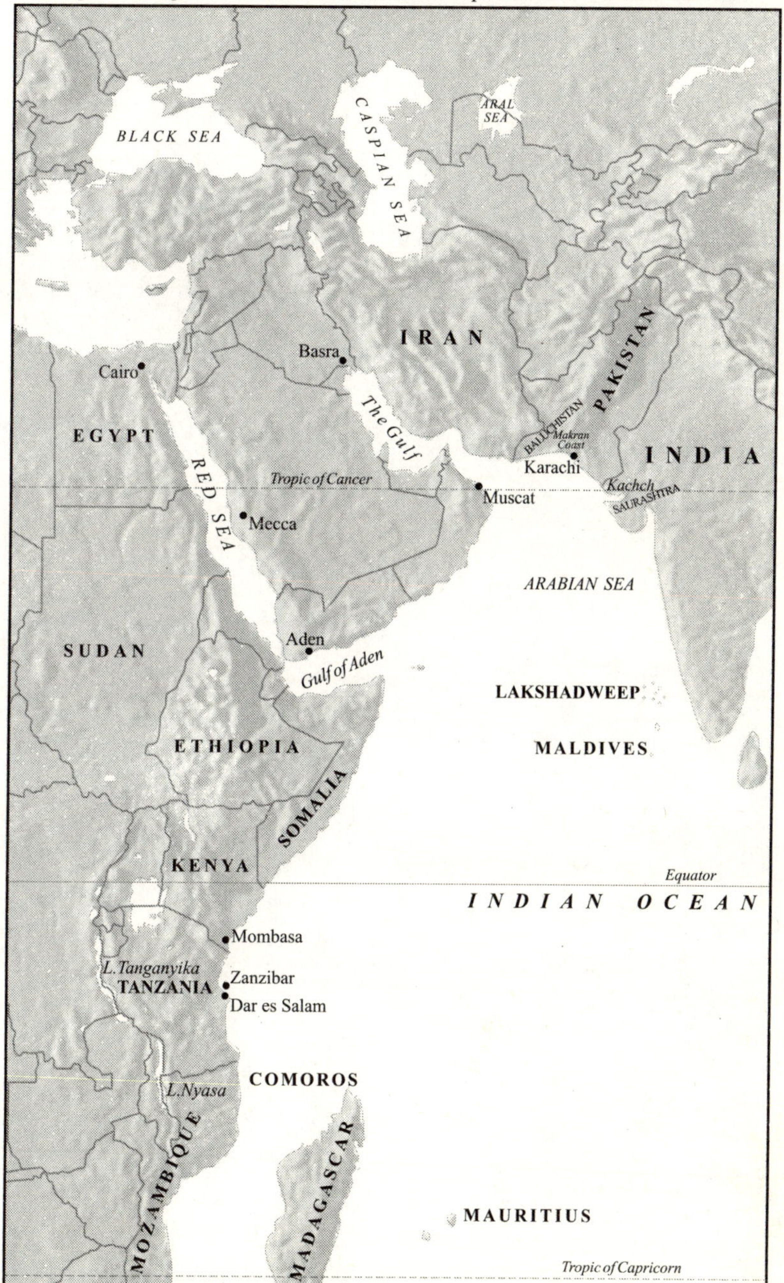

Map 6

8

A Gendered Indian Ocean Site: Mai Mishra, African Spirit Possession and Sidi Women in Gujarat

Helene Basu

> I wept bitterly, but it was of no avail. The coast people took me to their hut, and there I met four boys and two girls. The coast people put food before me. I would not eat but screamed and cried. At sunset we started our journey and travelled by night, for the moon was shining....In wiNamwanga the Arab became so ill that he could not travel, and we stayed there....When the Arab was somewhat better we set out once more and reached the village....There the coast people said to one of the girls who was about my age, 'You are to stay here with our relations until we come back and fetch you.' But we found ivory in the hut and exclaimed, 'Where did that come from? That was not here before! You have sold our sister for ivory!' (Wright 1993: 26ff.)

Slaves and ivory were the most important items exported from central East Africa to the Middle East and western India in the nineteenth century (cf. Alpers 1975; Sheriff 1987). How women experienced both the reality and the threat of capture is conveyed in the moving life stories recorded by Elise Kootz-Ketschmer at the turn of the twentieth century (Wright 1993). The passage quoted above is taken from the story of a woman who was born in the region between Lake Nyasa and Lake Tanganyika sometime in the middle of the nineteenth century. When she was about seven years old, her village was raided by a hostile neighbouring people, who took her and her sister captive. She herself managed to escape her African master a few years later. But her story, like the memories of other women, speak of a ubiquitous fear of falling into the hands of coastal slave traders, Arab or Swahili, which considerably increased the chance of being sold to distant places such as Zanzibar or even further across the Indian Ocean. This risk did not diminish with British attempts to take control of the sea by making the slave trade illegal in the first half of the nineteenth century. On the contrary, even after the success of the anti-slavery campaign itself, the Indian Ocean slave trade continued to grow (Alpers 1975: 209; Beachey 1976). Although the available statistics do not differentiate between male and female slaves, a report by Captain Sullivan, a British officer recalling his experiences of 'chasing dhows' for slaves in the 1870s, is instructive in this regard. The captain of a dhow carrying slaves, Sullivan told his readers, was fully aware of the prohibitions imposed on the trade by the British and thus sought to conceal Africans—many of whom were women—who were destined to be sold in the ports along his route. This might be done in the following way:

> When. . .the number. . .reaches to a hundred or more. . .twenty or thirty, perhaps, are told to represent part of the crew; the half-dozen Arabs, who are generally on board and concerned in the matter, dress up some of the women slaves, each representing one as his wife, and sometimes he is fortunate enough to have two; the remainder of the Negroes, or as many as possible, are dressed up in Arab costumes, turbans, &c., and called passengers, and they too sometimes have their wives sitting by them, if the women are too plentiful to pass off in any other way. (Sullivan 2003)

So far, historians of the Indian Ocean have taken very little notice of women slaves and the relevance of gender when investigating movements of people that resulted in 'littoral cosmopolitanisms'. It has been taken for granted that the sea was a male seascape (e.g. Sheriff, this volume). On land, by contrast, the institution of slave concubinage in Muslim societies is a well-known fact, and Islamic legal texts abound with detailed descriptions about the status of slave wives and their children (Brunschvig 1971; Levy 1965). Thus, most African women who were enslaved were probably destined for markets in the Arabian peninsula. Some, however, were secretly shipped further east by Gujarati and Arab merchants, until the late nineteenth century, being landed in Bombay or, when enforcement of the British policy of abolishing the slave trade made immigration difficult, in one of the many smaller ports in Kachchh and Saurashtra on the coast of Gujarat. In Bombay the arrival of new Africans (also called *kaffrees* by the local press) was advertised in the local vernacular press (Srinivasan 2001). In Gujarat, some of these women ultimately ended up in the service of Rajput and Muslim royal courts on the Saurashtra and Kachchh peninsulas.[1] Others remained with the Kharvas, the Gujarati sailing caste dealt with by Simpson (this volume). Like their male counterparts, African women were referred to as 'Sidi'. Most Sidi women became maidservants in the female quarters of royal, shipowning or merchant households. In Rajput and Kharva castes it was quite common for Sidi maids to be given as part of the dowry of a bride, which accompanied her to the husband's house after marriage. At the royal courts, at least, Sidi women (and men) were 'owned' by the household of their masters to the extent that they could not always decide their own marriages. In the late 1980s I was still able to meet women who had been born into royal service in Kachchh and married off by their masters to Sidi men employed at the same court as palace guards.

However, not all Africans landing in Gujarat came as slaves, and not all were given in marriage by their masters. Men in particular were often sailors who had come in dhows from Zanzibar and had to spend some time in a Gujarati port waiting for the monsoon winds to turn and thus allow their ships to start the return journey (cf. Sheriff, this volume; Ewald 2000). Some of them remained in Gujarat in the nineteenth or early twentieth centuries (Basu 1995). In the nineteenth century in southern Gujarat, the tomb of an 'Abyssinian' holy man called Bava Gor, known to Muslim historians in Gujarat at least since the sixteenth century (Lokhandwalla 1970),

[1] This paper is based on ethnographic research carried out from 1987 to 1989 and in 2004 in Zanzibar and Gujarat.

became the sacred centre (*dargah*) of a Sidi fakir brotherhood. Although the dargah (shrine) is usually only referred to by the name Bava Gor, its core in fact consists of three saints, all described as Sufis, namely Bava Gor, whose original name according to Sidis was 'Sidi Mubarak Nobi', his younger brother Bava Habash, and their sister Mai Mishra. My ethnographic research has shown that many of those sailors and seamen who remained in Gujarat were drawn to this shrine and that Sidis were already settled there. Situated in the former Rajput kingdom of Rajpipla, where Sidi men served at court as stable boys or coachmen and women as maidservants, newcomers from Africa were integrated into the Sidi group by marriage with 'local' Sidi women. Today, Sidis form a Muslim *jamat* (kinship association or caste) of about 20,000, whose households are spread all over Gujarat (cf. also Misra 1964). Today, the importance attributed to endogamy in the social organisation of Hindu as well as Muslim castes is shared, at least theoretically, by many Sidis in Gujarat. Since their bodily features set them apart from the rest of the population, the ideal of endogamy has assumed in Sidi thinking a concrete and visible form: a truly 'endogamous' marriage is one between a man and a woman who both have 'frizzy hair'. Thus, Sidi collective identity is established by reference not to pedigree, as is the custom in other Gujarati castes, but to bodily signs, most importantly frizzy hair and black skin. Not all those who belong to Sidi's community, however, 'look' Sidi. In the past (and occasionally in the present too), Sidi men married women with 'straight hair'. The reverse also happened occasionally, with a Sidi woman marrying a man from another community. Whether it was a man or a woman who was marrying in, in both cases the non-Sidi partners were assimilated by Sidis already present in Gujarat. This was facilitated by an overlap of relationships between the fakir brotherhood and the kinship group (for details, cf. Basu 2000). On a conceptual level, the merging of ties of fakirs with ties of marriage is expressed in terms of a sacralised exclusivity of the Sidi body: frizzy hair and black skin signify kinship bonds between Sidis born in

Gujarat and the three saints who came from Africa in the past. Consequently, and contrary to Gujarati standards of beauty that devalue dark skin and associate frizzy hair with 'crookedness',[2] Sidis regard these features as the seat of *karamat* (magical powers) inherited from the 'ancestor saints'. As will become clearer below, this has a bearing on practices related to the veneration of Mai Mishra and her saintly brothers. While the African female saint stands for a ritual domain dominated by Sidi women practitioners (*fakirani*), frizzy hair determines privileged access to specific activities in the context venerating Mai Mishra.

At present, Sidi women hardly remember the painful experiences of rupture and displacement that their great-grandmothers went through in east Africa before becoming domestic servants in Gujarat. On the contrary, the collective memory of the Sidi jamat has transformed the forced journey of their predecessors into a voluntary mission by ancestral spirits to rid the people of Gujarat of evil spirits. A key role in this mission is attributed to Mai Mishra, the female African saint, the sister of male African Sufi saints. These African saints are classified as the highest level of a class of Sidi ancestor saints. The multiple symbolic identifications of Sidi saints as African, Sufi and ancestral spirits indicate their ambiguous position at the margin of Sufism in Gujarat. But what appears marginal from the point of view of South Asian Islam may well turn out to be a major Indian Ocean theme when looked at from the perspective of the sea. More specifically, the gendered relationship between Sufism and African religions of spirit possession is a theme that shapes ritual practices in many parts of east and north Africa, wherever Islam has been absorbed into African cultural settings. A further noticeable Indian Ocean connection derives from the embeddedness of the relationship between Sufism and African religions of possession in the history of the enslavement of Africans. While I have dealt with the journey of this relationship in terms of a fusion of practices like drumming and praying elsewhere (Basu 2004b), in this

[2] A dishonest person in Gujarat used to be called 'as crooked as a Sidi's hair'.

paper I want to explore another Indian Ocean theme: gendered ritual practices as expressed in the transformations of female ritual agency connected to the figure of Mai Mishra.

Mai Mishra is seen as the leading woman to have guided African women to Gujarat. She represents several ideals at once: an exemplary sister aiding her brother to obey a command of the Prophet; a good Muslim woman keeping *purdah*; one with healing powers who heals female infertility; one who is stronger than evil spirits and expels them from the bodies of the afflicted; one who takes possession of those she loves, removing their sufferings and bestowing knowledge upon them; one who speaks through their mouths; and finally the ancestress of all Sidis. However, Mai Mishra not only stands for the presence of women from Africa in Gujarat: her worship also integrates Sidis with a wide circle of people from other communities of various denominations (Hindu, Muslim, Jain, Parsi; for the latter, see Shroff, this volume) in the context of the veneration of Sufi shrines.

The present chapter contains six sections. The first deals with the narrative of the journeys of Mai Mishra and her two brothers from Africa to Gujarat. In this context, it is instructive to reflect on the names of the three major Sidi ancestor saints. Each name points to a region in northeast Africa: 'Mishra' is the Arabic for Egypt, 'Habash' for Ethiopia, and Nobi/Nubi (the original name of Bava Gor) for the Nile region in Sudan. These regions used to be important suppliers of slaves long before the slave trade extended further south along the Swahili coast in the eighteenth and nineteenth centuries.[3] Another term used by Sidis, *goma*, points to the performative dimensions of African possession practices encapsulated by the Bantu word for drum, *ngoma*. Ngoma is associated with the Swahili coast and Zanzibar, the last hub of the slave trade until the late nineteenth century. In Sidi parlance, *goma* is used interchangeably with *damal* for drumming, singing and

[3] Abir writes of the slave trade in the fourteenth century: "[Ethiopian] slave girls were renowned for their beauty and sexual temperament, and [Ethiopian males] for their belligerent character" (1985: 102).

dancing performances that form the core of the ritual practices related to Mai Mishra and her brother saints.[4] Following these mnemonic traces, in the second section I shall deal briefly with African religions of possession in the older and newer regions of the slave trade, that is, with *zar* possession in Sudan and *ngoma ya masheitani* in Zanzibar. These provide the comparative background for the analysis of the symbolic construction of the assembly of Sidi ancestor saints and the position of Mai Mishra in it in the third section. In the fourth, fifth and sixth sections of the paper, I consider the embeddedness of the female African saint in South Asian Sufism and Muslim values of gender, as well as dealing with ritual practices performed by Sidi women.

Mai Mishra: Sister and Conqueror of Evil Spirits

Sidi narratives depict the migrations of Mai Mishra and her two brothers to Gujarat as a one-way journey. Leaving Africa one after the other, never to return, and eventually to be buried in Gujarat, Mai Mishra and her brothers Bava Gor and Bava Habash take precedence over all the many Sidi saints who are venerated in different places in Gujarat. These three saints are buried in a shrine on a hill in the south of the state. This dargah provides the sacred focus for Sidis and serves at the same time as a regional pilgrimage centre. The dargah is named after the elder brother, Bava Gor, and consists of a series of the tombs of Sidi saints scattered over several hills. The tomb of Mai Mishra is located in a separate shrine behind the building sheltering the tomb of Bava Gor. A salient feature of Sidi ritual practices consists in the elaboration of complementary domains of male and female ritual spaces and agencies. Thus, the

[4] *Goma* and *damal* indicate the merging of an African code with the code of Indo-Muslim Sufism. Goma derives from ngoma, a complex term originating in the Bantu language family which has a wide range of related meanings, such as drum, song, performance, healing association, spirit possession and ritual (Janzen 1992). Damal, on the other hand, derives from the Hindi-Urdu word *dam*, 'breath', and is closely associated with the Shah Madari Sufi brotherhood of north India.

tombs of male saints are served by Sidi men, those for Mai Mishra by Sidi women. Assuming a role comparable to that of a priest, Sidi women mediate the powers of Mai Mishra to both female and male supplicants. Whoever approaches Mai Mishra's shrine may hear the story of how and why the female saint and her brothers came from Africa. In the early days of my fieldwork, I heard the story from Saiba. She was then more than seventy years old and spent a lot of time near the tomb of Mai Mishra, helping her daughter carry out the rituals at the shrine. One day I joined a group of shrine visitors from a nearby urban centre, who had come to the dargah for the first time. They had gathered around Saiba and were asking her about Mai Mishra. Saiba told them the following story:

> Our ancestors are from Africa. Bava Gor is our pir [saint]. His home was in Habash [Ethiopia], but he became a military leader and stayed in Mecca. His name then was Sidi Mubarak Nobi. One day, he received a command from our Prophet in his dream. Our Prophet told him to call many Sidi soldiers and to defeat a demoness (*rakshas*) who was troubling the people of Gujarat. Her seat was right here. Sidi Mubarak Nobi summoned many soldiers. All of them were Sidis—like us, black and with curly hair. Then they marched for a long time. They passed through Baghdad, where Sidi Mubarak Nobi became a disciple [*murid*] of Ahmad Kabir Rifa'i.[5] The pir gave him his new name, Bava Gor. Then Bava Gor and the Sidi soldiers continued their journey until they met the demoness. She was very fierce, and the people were sad and full of fear. But when Bava Gor met her, he realised that he could not fight her physically because she was a woman. So he suggested instead having a competition by playing *choras* [a local game played with stones]. They agreed that if she won she could kill him, but were he to win he would kill her. But because Makhandevi was a demoness she cheated and the game did not come to an end. Meanwhile the brother of Bava Gor, Bava Habash, was still in Africa. He began to worry about his brother and followed him in a dhow across the sea. Seeing his brother being cheated, Bava Habash became very angry. But Bava Gor continued to play with the demoness. After her two brothers had gone, Mai Mishra wondered what had happened to them. She called on all her sisters and women friends to accompany

[5] Ahmad Kabir Rafi'i was the founder of the Rifa'i Sufi order in Baghdad in the thirteenth century.

> her in searching for her brothers. They crossed the sea in a dhow, whose captain was called Pir Kisti [from Gujarati *kishti*, ship]. His tomb is here too. When Mai Mishra saw her brother being cheated by the demonness, she became furious. She grabbed the demonness's hair and pushed her with such force into the earth that she never emerged from the ground again. However, she still does her evil work from under the ground. She sends all these *bhuts* [malevolent spirits] which trouble people. It is her evil work. Since then people come for help to our Mai Mishra.

This story is told in many variations, but the basic plot is always the same. It is notable that slavery does not figure in the story at all. The eldest ancestor was sent on a mission by the Prophet Mohammed for the good of the people. On his journey overland, he became the spiritual disciple of a well-known Sufi saint. But neither he nor his younger brother, who came by sea, could overpower the demonness. As men, they were restrained by Islamic rules of modesty that prohibit direct physical contact between men and women. It was Mai Mishra, the sister, who solved her brothers' dilemma by ultimately defeating the demonness. However, although the mission was successful it remained incomplete, since evil spirits continue to afflict innocent people. Mai Mishra's and her brother's historical mission therefore extends into the present: they still defeat spirits by healing cases of affliction through evil spirit possession. And, as a corollary, it is the task of living Sidi women in the present to help her (and the other ancestors) continue to accomplish their task of defeating evil spirits in perpetuity.

What is interesting here is that Sidi narratives of migration knit together several thematic strands of Muslim history in Gujarat. Bava Gor, the military leader who came overland, is a metonym of the history of Muslim conquest, state-building and African slaves serving in the military; in another version he is a trader exporting precious stones (*akik*) across the ocean to Africa (Basu 2003). Similarly Bava Habash metonymically refers to the maritime history of Sidis, while Mai Mishra recalls the fact that crossing the sea was not confined to men. Whether soldier, trader or sister, spiritual Sidi ancestors are also Sufi saints. The different strands of the story do not culminate in narratives of military conquest, successful trade or the conversion of the local people to Islam. Rather, these issues are transformed into the idiom of spirit possession. The battle is between good and evil spiritual forces, embodied by holy ancestors and evil spirits. In this way, the stories of the immigration of African ancestors provide the context for fusing fragments of African religions of possession with a Sufi idiom. In other words, concepts and performances outlining the veneration of Sidi saints display a remarkable synthesis of female-centred practices of African possession with male-centred South Asian versions of Sufism.

African Religions of Possession: Zar and Ngoma

Explanations of possession are as varied and many as the phenomenon itself (cf. Boddy 1994). In its most general sense, possession refers to an individual being temporarily changed into an 'other', so that he or she is temporarily governed by a spirit, that is, a non-human agent. In many religious systems, the spirits of ancestors, deities, the dead, aliens or demons are represented as powers that humans temporarily feel 'captured' by or to which they make their bodies available as a 'host'. A spirit that has taken possession of someone manifests itself through embodiment in trance, in which condition it makes the possessed person move and behave in a way that is alien to that person's everyday existence. Of relevance to the present context is the emphasis on possession as a culturally constructed idiom of communication—a language—in which people articulate social, religious and cultural experiences (Lewis 1971, 1986; Crapanzano and Garrison 1977). More recent studies conceptualise possession as forms of cultural knowledge and ways of knowing and healing (Boddy 1989; Lambek 1993). From this perspective, two important corollaries must be noted: a) possession as a means of dealing with alterity; and b) possession as a means of working and reworking through historical changes. Often, the repertoire of spirit images that is deployed in possession rituals makes reference to the historical experiences of change, to processes of ethnic heterogeneity, migration, colonial confrontations and social crises (Kramer 1987; Behrend and Luig 1999; Janzen 1992; K. Larsen 1998). Thus, possession rituals provide an important framework for the performance of collective social memories.

An important aspect of the anthropological discussion of possession, especially of African possession rituals, is its relationship to gender. On the level of the actors, it has been noted that in the majority of cases, women are the prime agents of possession. While this has been taken as a sign of the marginality of such cults, feminist studies have shown that possession may provide a means of empowerment for women, a vehicle to subvert and challenge gender categories that privilege men (Boddy 1989; Boehringer-Thaerigen 1996). On the cosmological level, many African spirit pantheons are gendered. Behrend and Luig write: "In forming hierarchies, they often replicate the inequalities between women and men. However, spirits of various pantheons often establish their masculinity or femininity as fluid rather than fixed, offering gender as a continuum of qualities found in both females and males" (1999: xvii). It is this relationship between gender and possession that is particularly relevant for understanding the Sidis' veneration of Mai Mishra in Gujarat. In order to situate it against the background of African possession rituals for comparative purposes, I shall briefly discuss two east African contexts: *zar* and *ngoma*.

In Ethiopia and Sudan, spirit possession rituals are known as *zar* (Boddy 1989; Boehringer-Thaeringen 1996). In Sudan, zar rituals are widely disseminated among the Arab-Nubian population of the Nile valley society.[6] This multi-ethnic society is shaped by complementary dualisms, such as inside/outside,

[6] The word *zar* is derived from Arabic *zahar,* 'he visits'. The term also denotes several other concepts: 1) categories of spirits; 2) illnesses that these spirits may cause; and 3) the rituals that are performed to expel them (Boddy 1989: 133). The zar cult is also practised in other societies of northeast Africa that have been shaped by Islam, in Ethiopia, Egypt, southern Algeria, Somalia and the Arabian peninsula (cf. Boehringer-Thaeringen 1996: 96). It also extends to Iran (Mirzai 2002b).

male/female and sacred/profane, which, among other things, are visibly manifested in the spatial division of male and female living spaces (public space/house). Zar practices go back to the nineteenth century, a period of colonial expansion and unrest occasioned through warfare and waves of intensive campaigns of Islamisation. At the present time, zar centres exist in the towns as well as rural settlements of Sudan, where they function as ritual complements to Islamic Sufi brotherhoods such as the Quadiria and Khatimiya (Boehringer-Thaeringen 1996: 69; Boddy 1989: 163).

Zar possession is practised mainly by women. Moreover, zar spirits always come from distant parts and are believed to have been brought to Sudan by women.[7] The pantheon of zar spirits is gendered and ideally consists of seven 'stocks' or 99 alien spirits, including their daughters and grandmothers, who represent ethnic, religious or alien forms (Boehringer-Thaerigen 1996: 76). These embrace, for example, the following sociocentric categories: dervishes; Sufi masters and founders of orders in thirteenth-century Sudan, such as Abdul Qader Gilani, the founder of the Quadiria brotherhood; Habashi, the male and female spirits of Ethiopians; warlike and aggressive Arabs; rich Europeans;[8] pashas, murderous conquerors and officials of the Ottoman (i.e. Turkish) empire; gypsies and street-traders; West African pilgrims on their way to Mecca; and *zuruk*, black slaves from the south of the country. However, the pantheon of zar spirits is not fixed but may include new spirits of all sorts. Moreover, formerly marginal spirits may gain in popularity, while others become gradually forgotten. Thus, one important aspect of the zar spirit pantheon is

[7] For example, in Sudan there are Ethiopian spirits that are not part of the zar phenomenon in Ethiopia itself (Kramer 1987: 113). In Sudan, according to the indigenous tradition, the zar cult was introduced by a woman called Fatima, the wife of a Turkish ruler (cf. Boehringer-Thaerigen 1996: 67).

[8] The spirits of Europeans may take, for example, the form of an archaeologist wearing khaki shorts and a bush shirt as well as socks, shoes and glasses, or of an Englishman, recognisable because he demands that a mattress be fetched for him and is a chain-smoker of Benson and Hedges cigarettes (Boehringer-Thaerigen 1996, 69ff.).

that it serves as a performative archive of historical experiences in Sudan right up to the present day.

In zar contexts, the spirit is identified with the causes of the disorder experienced by an afflicted person. Instead of exorcising the spirit, however, the cure consists of transforming the spirit into a benevolent and supportive agent, with whom the patient enters into a life-long relationship. The cure involves initiation into a zar ritual community. Healing is achieved through rituals focused upon possession dances. The possessed women embody their spirits by means of costumes and modes of behaviour appropriate to that particular zar.[9] During possession, dancing women who, in their day-to-day lives, behave in a shamefaced and submissive manner in accordance with the rules of the gender hierarchy, now show themselves to be what they are not by smoking, demanding blood, wanting to fight, drinking alcohol, or acting aggressively or immodestly (Boddy 1989: 131).

South of Ethiopia and along the Swahili coast, one meets a wide variety of spirit possession practices that have been classified together under the term ngoma ('drum') (Janzen 1992).[10] Here, distinct classes of spirit, most prominently Arab or other Muslim royal spirits and African slave spirits are to be encountered (Giles 1999: 156). In her study of Zanzibari spirit possession, Larsen found four classes of spirit. As in zar contexts, all spirits have their origin outside Zanzibar. Their divisions correspond to social categories defined in terms of ethnic and/or religious affiliation (see Table 1). These constituted Zanzibari society in the past and continue to represent major

[9] For example, while dervishes wear white clothing, women possessed by Ethiopians wear red; some drink coffee, others alcohol. In staging possession, women change themselves into 'others of their own culture', which they represent mimetically.

[10] In his ethnographic survey of cults of affliction spanning central, southern and East Africa and corresponding to Nguni-, Bantu- and Swahili-speaking regions, Janzen (1992) identifies a cluster of core features that are shared across a wide range of local settings. These are contained in the multivocal term *ngoma* (derived from Bantu *goma*), which has several related meanings: first, 'drum'; secondly, music, singing and dancing accompanied by drums in ritual performances; and thirdly, performers organised in ritual associations or 'ngoma cells' directed at the healing of possession.

social divisions in the present. Again, as in zar contexts, the aim of ritual healing is not to exorcise spirits, but to transform the relationship between host and spirit from one of suffering to one of support. Of special interest here are three classes. The first is *masheitani ya ruhani*, which in Zanzibar denotes Muslim spirits from Arabia (K. Larsen 1998: 133), including the spirit of Abdul Quader Gilani. They represent different degrees of Islamic knowledge imparted to those who host them. As Larsen points out, a relationship with a knowledgeable *masheitani ya ruhani* can turn a person into an acknowledged medical practitioner who works with the Koran, whereby his social status may simultaneously be enhanced (ibid.: 134). The second class of spirits, *masheitani ya ruhumba*, consists of non-Islamic spirits of Swahili and Bantu slave origin. They also impart knowledge of healing, but also sorcery. The third class is called *masheitani ya habshia*, or spirits linked to Ethiopia. These spirits' foremost characteristic is the elaboration of imagining and remembering the Zanzibari society of the past, which was divided into a class of high-ranking queens and kings and low-ranking slaves. Thus, Larsen concludes: "These spirits represent a society consisting of a small Arab dynasty and a great majority of slaves and, like this dynasty, the spirits remain distant to most Zanzibari women and men" (ibid.: 136–7). As in zar contexts, spirit identities are visualised in possession rituals through different types of dress, food, smells, sound and other aesthetic qualities. Zanzibari spirit classes form the focus of ritual networks that are often organised around female leaders of rituals (*fundi*). Moreover, like zar ritual associations in Sudan, those in Zanzibar also complement male Sufi brotherhoods by carving out a ritual sphere of influence dominated by women. In Zanzibar, the female fundis of one or several spirit classes command great authority and influence.

The Classification of Sidi Ancestor Saints

If one compares the classification of spirits in Zanzibar with the classification of Sidi ancestor saints (see Table 2), similarities and differences are revealed. In Gujarat, Sidi ancestor saints are not divided into classes but form a single category which is internally differentiated with reference to kinship and gender. The status of male saints differs according to the principle of seniority (elder/younger brother) and is opposed to the status of the sister. In addition to these three saints, the assembly of Sidi ancestor saints includes other named figures who are classified as 'ritual brothers and sisters'. There are ideally eleven 'brother saints' and seven 'sister saints' who are related to the former through the Sufi master-disciple relationship (*piri-muridi*). Sidi saints share with zar and masheitani spirits the fact that their origin lies beyond the place where they are venerated. All three came from Africa, but their distinctiveness is further marked by different places of origin (elder brother/Mecca; younger brother/Ethiopia; sister/Egypt). While the highest status in the assembly of Sidi saints is accorded to the eldest brother, who is explicitly associated with Islam through the reference to Mecca, the Prophet and Sufi sainthood, the status of the sister is associated with spirits. In this construction we thus find a fusion of kinship, gender and religious hierarchies (elder/younger brother, male/female saints, Sufi saints/spirits). Hierarchical differences are further revealed by the routes that Sidi saints took while journeying to India: whereas the elder brother brought Sufism and Islam by travelling over land, the sister brought ritual powers over spirits by crossing the ocean in a dhow. Thus, the hierarchical relationship between Islam and African spirit possession that is found in many Indian Ocean societies (Lambek 1993; Parkin 2000) surfaces in Gujarat in a gender idiom and in memories of the modalities of journeying. However, in the context of Sidi ritual practices, gender and religious hierarchies are reversed: the female is stronger than the male, and African-derived practices are more powerful than Islamic ones.

Some of the attributes qualifying the distinct characteristics of the ancestor spirits partly overlap with those found in Zanzibar. Thus, each ancestor spirit is connected with a specific type of instrument: the elder brother with the standing drum

Table 1: Spirit Classes in Zanzibar

Category	*Local origin*	*Language*	*Name*	*Status*	*Colours*	*Function/ Knowledge*	*Rituals/Music*	*Food*
Masheitani ya ruhani	Arabia, Mecca, Muscat, Jiddah	Arabic	e.g. Jinni Sheikh Suleman	Arabic civilisation	white: purity red: power green: mosque	Qu'ran	recitation of the Qu'ran praises for Allah and the Prophet in Swahili	e.g.. honey, *halwa*, dates, rosewater, boiled *eggs* *sharbat*, coffee served on plate with white cloth
Masheitani ya ruhumba	Swahili Pemba	Bantu	e.g. Muzi wa Sanda	non-Islamic, not 'civilised'	black: impure: clothing of slaves	healing and sorcery	stick drumming	raw eggs; same as above, but in 'uncivi-lised style', i.e. without plate and cloth
Masheitani ya habshia	Ethiopia	*kihabash*	kings and queens with personal names slaves without names	sophisticated kings and queens: unsophisti-cated slaves	red	*zar*	*drums*	popcorn, *halwa*, coffee, ginger tea

Source: Based on K. Larsen (1998) and fieldwork by Basu in 2004.

Table 2: Classification of Sidi ancestors saints

Name	*Origin*	*Route*	*Temperament*	*Status*	*Representation*	*Function*	*Rituals/ Instruments*	*Food/Colours*
Bava Gor/ Sidi Mubarak Nobi	Ethiopia, Mecca	by land, via Baghdad	cool	elder brother	soldier of the Prophet	power over spirits	*mugarman*, footed drum	sweet milk: white
						healing negative possession	*jikar* (Arabic *dhikr*)	sweet dish from wheat and ghee red: power green: Islam red cornelians (*bava gori*)
Bava Habash	Ethiopia	by sea	hot	younger brother		male virility	*musindo*, kettle drum	ginger tea:
						healing negative possession		black
Mai Mishra	Ethiopia/ Egypt	by sea	hot-cool	sister	moral woman: veiled (*purdah*)	healing of negative possession	rattles *jhikar* (songs)	sweet dish made from white rice and black lentils

(*mugarman*), the younger brother with the kettle drum (*mu-sindo*), and the sister with rattles which are called 'Mai Mishra'. In contrast to the Zanzibari classification, however, no distinction is made between civilised and uncivilised ancestor spirits, nor between royals and slaves. Instead, in Gujarat the colours black and white are associated with different types of temperament conceptualised in terms of 'hot' and 'cold', and again with gender. The elder brother, Bava Gor, has a cool temperament, that is, he is benevolent and lenient like a mother and therefore consumes white and sweet milk. By contrast the younger brother, Bava Habash, has a hot temperament and can become angry and dangerous: he therefore consumes hot, black ginger tea. Both types of drink are referred to as *kavo* (black and white), the Arabic for coffee. The sister, by contrast, is neither hot nor cool but both: she can act in a cool and benevolent manner like her elder brother, or become hot and angry like her younger brother. Her food is a dish made of white rice, black lentils and sugar (*Mai Mishra ni khichadi*). Finally, unlike Zanzibari ritual healing associations, where possession by ethnically defined spirits is not confined to people of the same ethnic category, in the Sidi context, types of possession are differently evaluated. Thus, being possessed by 'indigenous' malevolent spirits who cause individual crises and illness may happen to anybody; but the embodiment of a Sidi saint is mostly (though not exclusively) confined to Sidi women and men. Moreover, in Gujarat at least, cross-gender possession does not take place (but cf. Basu 2002 for Sidi in Sindh): while Mai Mishra (or one of her sisters) embodies herself in women, Bava Gor, Bava Habash and other brother saints embody themselves in Sidi men.

Sidi ancestor saints embody themselves in their 'descendants' on specific ritual occasions, most notably during annual '*urs* rituals, which celebrate the anniversary of a saint's death. But Mai Mishra may also embody herself during certain rituals performed by female practitioners on behalf of followers, as will be seen in the next section.

Mai Mishra in the Field of Sufism in Gujarat: the Values of Purdah

The most widespread pattern of Sufi shrines in Gujarat is focused upon a single male saint—ideally a Sayyid—whose religious teachings, heroic deeds and spiritual pedigree (*silsila*) are commemorated in oral and/or written hagiographies and enacted in shrine rituals. Although the central saint's tomb may be surrounded by a host of minor tombs attributed to disciples, followers and relatives, including females, most studies of Sufi practices do not have much to say on the latter. Demonstrations of ritual respect towards the tombs of a pir's female relatives serve to enhance the symbolic prestige of the paramount male figure. In accordance with this, the ritual management of a shrine is normally a privilege of men. In particular, women who belong to Sayyid families, in whom the charisma of a Sufi saint is inherited in the male line, are rarely seen in the precincts of a shrine. Adhering to the norms of purdah, they may contribute to the working of a shrine by cooking and other services, though these are always performed out of the public eye (cf. P. Jeffery 1979). However, those who visit Sufi sanctuaries and become the followers (*murid*) of a pir are not exclusively male but include women as well. In contrast to the mosque, which in Gujarat is an exclusively male space for praying, Sufi shrines are frequented by large number of pious Muslim women. Cast in the idiom of Muslim norms of modesty and gender segregation, the spatial arrangements reflect the gender hierarchy by barring women from entering the most sacred parts of a shrine, especially the tomb of the central saint. At some shrines a wall separates the area of the tomb that is forbidden to women, while elsewhere they are only kept from coming too close to the most sacred spot by a low fence.

In contrast to this widespread pattern of Sufi shrines in Gujarat, Sidi dargahs are characterised by a consistent balance of gendered saints, spaces and ritual practitioners. This does not imply normative gender equality, but rather than stressing the subordinate position of women by protecting male spheres from contact with femininity, the Sidi ritual pattern emphasises complementary relationships between male and female powers, afflictions and domains of action. Thus, rules governing the behaviour of male supplicants at the tomb of Mai Mishra in southern Gujarat mirror those valid for female supplicants at a male saint's tomb. Consequently, male followers are not allowed to step behind the iron grills separating her grave from the courtyard open to the public, nor may men kiss or touch the tomb as they would in case of a male saint. Moreover, Mai Mishra's tomb is managed exclusively by female ritual practitioners.[11] Female ritual practitioners are called fakirani. They perform daily ritual services at the tomb and special services for the follwers of Sidi saints. The female domain of rituals is explained by reference to Muslim norms of gender segregation epitomised by the veil or purdah. Men are not allowed to approach Mai Mishra's tomb too closely because she is 'in purdah'. In Gujarat, the African female saint (spirit?) from across the sea has been transformed into an icon of exemplary Muslim womanhood, in that she mediates a model of and for Muslim norms of femininity to lower-class and often poorer sections of the Sunni Muslim community of the region.

Purdah, or spatial segregation, rules of modesty and the concealment of women, is of major concern in respect of validating claims to high status among Gujarati Muslims (cf. also Jacobson 1976: 7ff; P. Jeffery 1979). Historically, the veiling of women had not been a universal practice of Indian Muslim women, but was most important for high-status women of Sayyid families and those who emulated the latter's values. Most Muslim women who come to Sidi shrines are clearly not confined to a life 'behind the veil', that is, to the inside of the house. Few women use the black *burqa* (a coat with a veil covering the head and face) when they leave the house.[12] Still,

[11] At other Sidi shrines for female saints, this exclusivity is not observed in the same way. Although Sidi saints are generally referred to in a common idiom, shrine practices may differ in regions within and beyond Gujarat, for example in Sindh (cf. Basu 2000).

[12] In recent decades, in many parts of the Islamic world the veiling of women has received a tremendous boost and come-back, even in social circles where it had become unpopular. Anthropological studies have shown the wide range and

wearing the burqa has become more popular in recent years. In the context of the veneration of Mai Mishra, however, purdah is a multivocal symbol of holy female status, non-ordinary powers (karamat) and the idealisation of female domesticity.

Mai Mishra does not only keep to the values of purdah, she is also an eternal bride. Symbols of marriage are of general significance in the field of popular Sufism. The principle ritual event at a Sufi shrine consists of celebrating the anniversary of the Pir's death or 'urs, meaning 'marriage' in Arabic. In South Asian Sufism, the death of a holy man is conceptualised as the final union with the divine, which is metaphorically expressed as 'marriage with God'. In relation to God the beloved, a male saint, is likened to a bride or female lover. In elite and literary-minded Sufi circles, the eroticisation of the relationship between a male spiritual personage and a male God has been of great symbolic relevance and inspired many traditions of poetry (Schimmel 1975). In this context, by contrast, marriage symbolism and Mai Mishra's status as a bride assume a rather practical meaning: at her 'urs the bond with a non-Sidi local saint is ritually recreated, just as an engagement ceremony creates an exchange relationship between families.

The saint who is regarded as the bridegroom of Mai Mishra is called Sultanji Bava. His tomb lies in a village about twenty kilometres from the Sidi shrine. The dargah of Sultanji Bava is managed by fakirs of the non-Sayyid.[13] Mai Mishra is said to have been engaged to Sultanji Bava but to have died before the marriage could be consummated. The engagement ceremony (*sagai*) of Mai Mishra and Sultanji Bava is staged during their respective 'urs celebrations. It consists of mutual visits by rit-

---

diversity of meanings that may be attributed by women to old and new forms of their concealment. Under the impact of modernisation and transnational migration, veiling may give expression to the assertion of cultural identity or resistance to hegemonic domination, or may be interpreted as providing personal protection for women against aggressive male assaults (cf. Watson 1994).

[13] The dargah is managed by fakirs of the Sufi brotherhood of Shah Madaris. The main shrine of Shah Madar is located in north India, but the brotherhood has many shrines and a popular following in Gujarat as well. Madaris are also known as Malang fakirs.

ual women practitioners of both shrines exchanging the same type of gifts that are given during a Muslim engagement ceremony.[14] Thus, at the time of the 'urs of Sultanji Bava, a group of Sidi women goes to his dargah carrying flowers, a new *chadar* (decorative cloth for the tomb), a ring and several kilograms of sugar.[15] At the time of the 'urs for Mai Mishra, people from Sultanji Bava's dargah reciprocate with a visit and gifts. Women bring gifts for Mai Mishra, such as flowers, a new chadar for Mai Mishra, items of female adornment (*kajal*, *mehendi*, bangles, rosewater, perfume) and, again, a large sack of sugar. The sugar is used to make *sharbat* (lemonade), which is distributed to all Mai Mishra's 'guests', that is, to all the visitors thronging her shrine during this most sacred occasion of the year. Thus, the enactment of the engagement ceremony of Mai Mishra links the Sidi saints to the wider network of Sufi saints through ritual exchanges modelled upon affinal relationships.

Mai Mishra and Possession by Malevolent Spirits

Symbols of purdah and marriage not only define Mai Mishra, the 'African woman saint', in terms of Muslim gender norms and domestic roles, but also have a bearing on her superhuman powers, especially those relating to curing possession illnesses and female barrenness, which are often closely linked. The most common types of spirit to afflict people who seek a cure at the Sidi dargah are Hindu spirits called *bhut* and Muslim *jinnat*. While the former are spirits of the dead, the latter are derived from the Qu'ran. Spirits are thought to reside in the hair of the possessed. Both types of spirit are classified with the demonness vanquished by Mai Mishra, so that the plot created by the narrative is enacted at the shrine each time someone possessed by a malevolent spirit seeks relief.

[14] These consist of a new headscarf (*odhni*), jewellery and sugar for a girl, and a ring, a loin cloth (*lungi*) and sugar for a boy. The distribution of sharbat, sweet lemonade, concludes the ceremony.

[15] In this social milieu, sugar is a luxury item.

Malevolent spirits are considered impure beings who feel attracted to bodily processes such as urinating or sexual intercourse. Women are especially endangered on their wedding night, because the state of sexual expectation attracts spirits. Spirits of the dead are envious, destructive, and 'eat up' a woman from the inside, thus causing female barrenness. The majority of patients who seek a cure at the Sidi dargah are women, although men may also be afflicted. In women, symptoms of possession are manifested typically by behaviour that violates standards of female modesty and norms governing women's roles. Thus, an afflicted woman may be barren or neglect her new-born child, display defiant or insulting behaviour towards superiors such as their husband or mother-in-law, or worse, indulge in licentious sexual behavior (cf. also Pfleiderer 1981). Usually women suspected of being possessed are brought by relatives to the shrine. The cure, however, does not consist of elaborate healing rituals like those described in African contexts. Exorcism is mainly effected by bringing the patient into contact with the tomb of Mai Mishra,[16] though a successful cure requires the active participation of relatives as well.

Sidi ritual practitioners mostly mediate the entrance and exit points of the process in which Mai Mishra is thought to fight against the influence that a malevolent spirit is exerting over the mind and body of an afflicted person. The patient is more or less left to herself near the tomb of the saint while enacting the embodiment of her spirit. At the beginning, the patient opens out her hair (which women normally carefully groom into a tight knot) and begins to hyperventilate until she enters into a trance called *hajri* (presence). In the state of hajri the spirit reveals itself by such actions as screaming obscenities, attempting to defile the sacred space by spitting on the tomb or vomiting, or simply verbally abusing close relatives.

[16] Other Sidi saints also have power over spirits. Which tomb a patient selects depends on the *hukm* (order) received by the saint in a dream. Often, patients choose between all three of them. The final ritual, however, is always performed at the Mai Mishra dargah.

The patient may spend hours near the tomb of Mai Mishra while the latter is struggling with the spirit. This involves bargaining with the spirit: on behalf of the patient's relatives, a female Sidi ritual practitioner asks the spirit what it needs to leave the body of its host. Occasionally, the caretaker may intervene by making fun of the spirit and laughing at its threats, or even beat the back of the patient with a wooden stick. In most cases, the patient is brought to the shrine regularly for at least six to eight weeks, and sometimes for several months. It is thought that this repeated contact with the spirits of Mai Mishra and other Sidi saints ultimately weakens the spirit's resistance. When the spirit indicates that it is about to give up, the patient is given water and rose petals to swallow that are charged with the power (karamat) of Mai Mishra. Mai Mishra has defeated the spirit when its demands have been established and a promise made by the relatives to fulfill them. Finally, the ritual practitioner leads the patient to a tree next to the shrine of Mai Mishra, whose trunk is covered with a host of large nails. The Sidi practitioner then nails a tip of the patient's hair into the trunk, an action that permanently banishes this particular spirit.

'Service' and 'Play': Being in Contact with Mai Mishra

Sidi women practitioners refer to the ritual activities they perform on behalf of the supplicants of Mai Mishra as *khidmat* (service) or *khel* (play). Mediating vows is a major task of Sidi women, in which service (e.g. cooking) and play associated with ritual singing, drumming and dancing (damal) are conceptually merged. Making vows (*mannat*) is the primary way for women followers to relate to Mai Mishra through the intercession of Sidi female ritual specialists (fakirani). In this way, individual Sidi fakirani may assume central positions as ritual leaders who are able to attract their own followings.

A fakirani organises, among other things, the practicalities of their followers making vows. While vows may be made for a variety of reasons, one important motive is to give a promise to the saint if she cures a relative from being possessed by a malevolent spirit. If the desired ends have been met, that is, when the relative has been cured, the promise is fulfilled by giving gifts to Mai Mishra and by feasting her female 'descendants', who mediate contact and communication between non-Sidi supplicants and the female Sidi saint. Gifts and feasting consist in sponsoring the cooking of Mai Mishra's favourite dish and a women's performance of damal.

The ritual performed on behalf of a woman follower in fulfilment of a vow is referred to by the name of the saint's favourite food, Mai Mishra ni khichadi, a luxurious sweet dish made from lentils and rice cooked in milk, sugar and ghee. This dish must be consumed by 'seven Sidi sisters', who are seen as replicating the 'seven holy sisters' of Mai Mishra. Eating takes place behind closed doors, that is, 'in purdah'. Afterwards, the leftovers are distributed to other Sidi women and men and to shrine visitors. The ritual itself consists of several phases. To give an example, I shall describe a Mai Mishra ni khichadi which I observed during my fieldwork in 1988:

> A woman from a Muslim trading community (Memon) had arranged a Mai Mishra ni khichadi after her newly married daughter had been cured of a possession illness. To begin with, she donated several sacks of sugar to Mai Mishra, the amount of which corresponded to her body weight. A portion of this was used to prepare the dish, for which she had brought in addition several kilograms of rice and lentils and several litres of milk and ghee. While three women began the cooking process, four more Sidi women were called to attend the ritual meal. The efficacy of the ritual meal depended, I was told, on keeping to the proper 'protocol'. It was of utmost importance, I was told, that only women considered 'true Sidi', that is, those born with frizzy hair, were entitled to eat the khichadi in seclusion. Women with straight hair or wives who had been assimilated into the Sidi community after their marriage with a Sidi man could not become one of the 'seven Sidi sisters'. When the dish was ready, the seven Sidi women all retreated to a small room adjoining the shrine. Settling around a large plate, they jointly and ceremonially consumed the khichadi. When they were satisfied, the door was opened and the leftovers were distributed to the waiting crowd, many of them children.
>
> The seven women then moved outside, where they were joined by other Sidi women. All of them settled in front of the tomb of Mai

Mishra in order to play damal. Two women began beating kettle-drums (musindo).[17] The other women joined them with rattles, the instrument of Mai Mishra, or simply by clapping their hands. An elderly woman led the singing of *jhikar* (Sidi ritual songs), while the other Sidi women and girls sang the chorus and the woman on whose behalf the ritual was performed placed five-rupee notes on the kettledrums from time to time. The songs were addressed to Mai Mishra, such as the following:

Come playing, o Mai!
On the hill of Mai Mishra we will have fun
frizzy hair
o, hair, frizzy hair
when we all are at Mai Mishra's *chok* (place)
eating khichadi, we all have fun
frizzy hair,
o, hair, frizzy hair
when we are all there, up at Bava Gor
playing damal, we will have fun
frizzy hair,
o, hair, frizzy hair
when we are all at Bava Habash's *chok*
o, hair, frizzy hair
come playing, o Mai!

During this song invoking the saints, one of the seven women who ate from the khichadi dish in seclusion suddenly began to tremble, her body shaking. Mai Mishra had arrived, embodying herself in the woman experiencing *hal* (possession by a saint).[18] The drumming became faster, and the woman got up and began to move her body in accordance with the rhythm, flinging her arms above her head and stamping her feet. Soon afterwards she was joined by three or four other women, all of them now embodying the presence of Mai Mishra and her sisters among the living. Women not experiencing hal got up and covered the face of the dancers with the end of their headscarfs. Several women from the crowd which had gathered around the damal group approached an embodied holy sister, telling her about their own problems and listening to her advice. The whole performance lasted for about an hour and concluded the cure of the possession illness of the daughter of the patron of the ritual.

[17] In Zanzibar, a drum called *mzindo* is used in rituals for masheitani ya habshia.

[18] In other Sufi contexts, *hal* refers to a state of ecstatic love for a saint. In the Sidi context, hal is used for describing a positive form of possession as opposed to possession by malevolent spirits.

While the ritual in its totality may be analysed in terms of its syncretic character, its combination of elements from several popular Indian religious traditions, here I would like to draw attention to its hidden structural relationship with African rituals focused upon specific types or classes of spirit (as discussed above). In this case, however, it is not control of a spirit but closeness to the female saint Mai Mishra that is at issue, whereby ritual groups consisting of a female ritual leader and her adepts are born. Former patients and their relatives usually maintain lifelong ritual relationships with Mai Mishra and other Sidi saints and their spiritual representatives (Sidi fakirani and fakirs) after a cure. This implies regular visits to the shrine, attendance of all its major rituals and continued financial assistance to 'their' respective fakirani (or fakir). This structure is anchored in damal performances that clearly reveal family resemblances with their African counterparts (for details, see Basu 2004b). But significant transformations on the cosmological and practical levels also have to be taken into account. First of all, in the Sidi ritual context, spirits and saints are clearly distinguished. Instead of transforming the relationship of a patient and her spirit from a negative (disturbing) to a positive (supportive) one, a successful cure results in the place of the spirit being taken by Mai Mishra (or any other Sidi saint). Secondly, there is no such distinction between Sufi brotherhoods and possession groups in terms of a gender division of their respective actors as encountered in Sudan or on Zanzibar. Sidi practices in Gujarat merge Sufi sainthood and positively evaluated manifestations of possession derived from African traditions.

Conclusion

By concentrating on women and sacred images of femininity in relation to their historical, structural or symbolic links to Africa, I have attempted to draw attention to a much neglected dimension of Indian Ocean studies. This dimension is embodied by female slaves, ritual practices travelling with women and the agency exercised by African women in creating the much celebrated cultural diversity of Indian Ocean littoral societies. Through the lens of the Sidi saint Mai Mishra, a glimpse is caught of what this may mean in Gujarat, a land which became home to countless Indian Ocean traders, Sufis, and African sailors and slaves, while Gujarati merchants had been setting out on journeys to Africa for centuries. Historical research on the dispersal of women slaves in the Indian Ocean region is still conspicuous by its absence,[19] but Sidi memories and embodied practices tell their own stories.

Beginning with the fate of African women in being enslaved and displaced in the late nineteenth century, I have explored some of the ways in which their descendants have symbolically transformed and healed the trauma that their great-grandmothers experienced. Sidis have created an image of a powerful African holy woman who crossed the ocean not as a victim, but as a rescuer of all those who were troubled by cruel powers, of which the demonness is a symbol. While history reappears in symbols and cosmological constructs, in the present it is transformed into female ritual agency. Ritual performances speak of the significance of African women in the process of forging a Sidi jamat (kinship association) and in rooting the collective Sidi self-image in a synthesis of African memory and Islamic Sufism.

In bringing about this synthesis, the figure of Mai Mishra as a multivocal symbol is of crucial importance. First of all, she introduces female agency into male-dominated South Asian Sufism through 'African cultural retentions' that can be traced back to African religions of possession like zar and ngoma.[20] Paradoxically, male dominance is subverted by symbolic representations of Mai Mishra in terms of Muslim gender norms

[19] A noticeable exception is the work of Indrani Chatterjee (1999), though she focuses on slavery in Bengal during the colonial period and does not consider Indian Ocean connections.

[20] The concept of 'African retentions' was coined by Herskovits in relation to the African Americas (1966). While in the 1940s the emphasis was on the identification of African 'culture traits' in the 'New World', more recent approaches stress 'retentions' in terms of 'critical practice' (Apter 1991). 'Retention' is used here in the latter sense.

(purdah). At the same time, she accommodates a gendered Sidi jamat within the Muslim community that forms part of the heterogeneous society in Gujarat. Thus, a striking resemblance to the strategies used by historically displaced Africans elsewhere in the world becomes evident: Sidis share with Africans in the Americas a history of accommodation and resistance embedded and articulated in syncretic rituals of possession (for the former, see Apter 1991). In the cultural context of Gujarat, however, accommodation and resistance are cast in a different idiom. The image of the female saint Mai Mishra as an 'eternal bride' embodies an aspect of women's existence in India that is crucial for the reproduction of hierarchically ranked collectivities: patrilineages are linked and ranked through the marital exchange of women. Thus affinity, a major South Asian value, provides a symbolic template for the accommodation of 'strangers' into Gujarati society. Sidi resistance to the ascription of low status (association with slavery, service and black skin) in a society shaped by values of hierarchy is articulated through a series of symbolic reversals and ritualisations: female victims of slavery are turned into powerful agents controlling the forces of evil (spirits), black skin and frizzy hair signify spiritual power, and service is transformed into healing. In doing this, African women have played a major role in giving Gujarat an Indian Ocean face that is marked by cultural diversity and religious pluralism.

9

Spiritual Journeys: Parsis and Sidi Saints

Beheroze Shroff

> Trade between Iran and the western coast of India flourished from very early times and from the 6th century AD the Iranians had begun to take a leading part in the trade of the east.... The Sasanians had been an important maritime power in the Indian Ocean during the 5th and 6th centuries. The Hindu rajas were therefore not unfamiliar with Iranians before the advent of the large scale migration...the migration of Parsis to the west coast of India was not so much a flight, as a readjustment of commercial patterns brought about by the activities of the Arab merchants who began to challenge the Iranian supremacy (Kamerkar & Dhunjisha 2002: 24, 26).

Introduction

On Thursdays, *jumme raat*, there is always a big crowd here. Today, Monday, it is quiet. The setting sun slants behind this memorial shrine or *chilla* of Bava Gor, the ancestral saint of the Afro-Indian Sidi community. This Bava Gor chilla, in Bombay, was built with major financial support of a Parsi devotee, Dinshaji Kerawalla in 1947. At that time, the caretaker (*mujavar*) and the spirit medium of Bava Gor at this memorial shrine was Sheikh Makbul whom devotees respectfully gave the title of Bava. Makbul Bava dominated this space and managed it with a combination of charisma and command that sprang from many years of training and discipline in the profession of being a spirit medium. From my childhood, I have known this space as a place of worship, that is as significant to me as the Fire Temple, the Parsi place of worship, in India.

Only five other people are here today, among them is my mother and Savak, another devotee from my mother's generation. After the muezzin's call for the evening prayer or *magrib azzan* there is always a fixed ritual that devotees follow at this Bava Gor chilla. In single file, the men go around the chilla, offering the incense, *loban*, and light the lamp, *batti*. My mother and other devotees have brought flower garlands and flower shawls (*chadar*) which all of us place on the memorial tomb of Bava Gor and on the actual tomb of Makbul Bava, which was added behind the Bava Gor memorial tomb. After Makbul Bava passed away in 1983, his family sought special permission from the Bombay municipality to place his body next to the memorial tomb of Bava Gor whom Makbul Bava served for many years.

In Makbul Bava's time, as the spirit medium of Bava Gor, he held regular *baithak* sessions, at first, on Sundays and later on Thursdays. The *baithak*, so called by Makbul Bava, involves the spirit medium holding a seance session. The spirit medium prays in order to invoke the presence of the saint, and then possessed by the saint, the medium falls onto the ground, held firmly by two *makandars* or interpreters. The spirit of the saint then speaks through the medium to enable devotees to consult individually about their problems. At the present time, these sessions are held once a month, on the day of the new moon, *chandraat*, or on some special occasion, or at the request of a devotee. The present medium of Bava Gor, Yasin who holds down a regular nine-to-five job finds it difficult to hold baithak sessions every week. There are many such changes since the time of Makbul Bava. Not only have mediums and the practice of mediumship changed, but devotees too have grown up from toddlers, like my brother who came here as a baby and now brings his wife and teenage children to this Parsi chilla. The space of the chilla too has changed, from open land outside the compound to a congested locality of shops, a vegetable market, small bungalows and other poorer makeshift homes.

Many questions come up for me about my parents' connection to the Sidi saint Bava Gor, a connection which has been passed down from one generation to another. When he first came in contact with Bava Gor around 1956, did my father realise that he as a Parsi, an Indian of Persian descent, was making contact with yet another minority, Sidis, who are Indians of African descent? Did he ask himself questions about Sidis? Did he realise that despite stark economic disparities between him and the Sidi community, Sidis were an important spiritual resource for him and other Parsis? Did he acknowledge the extent to which the worship of an 'African' Sidi saint filled a lacuna in his life and brought fulfillment to his needs and desires? Some of my questions led me to long interviews with my mother and Savak, a Parsi devotee from my mother's generation, both of whom I interviewed extensively from 2002 to 2004 in order to construct a narrative of the Parsi connection to Bava Gor.

A look at the trajectory of Parsi immigration to India reveals a history of considerable assimilation and economic prosperity in the country of adoption, a history quite different from that of Sidis. The coming of Parsis as refugees to India, in roughly the seventh century[1] is celebrated through a cherished mythology of the Parsi arrival, recorded in a sixteenth-century document called the *Kisseh-i-Sanjan*.

> According to this, the Iranian Zoroastrians were met with consideration, and were able to establish some sort of communication in spite of the barrier of language. Here again, it is possible that there might have been persons knowing Iranian traders on the coast and vice versa. A legend current in Parsi folk songs (*garbas*) is that the king Jadav Rana (Jadi) was persuaded to permit the refugees to stay in his kingdom when the leader of the group convinced the king of their good intentions by putting two grains of sugar into a bowl of boiling milk, thus indicating the "sweetness" that would be added to the kingdom by the presence of the refugees.
> (Kamerkar and Dhunjisha 2002: 27)

[1] There is some dispute about the exact date. For more information see Karaka (1977), Nanavutty (1977), Kulke (1974), Luhrmann (1996), Palsetia (2001).

While the Parsi community revels in a grand and illustrious past and its contributions to Indian society, the Sidis' contributions to India are all but forgotten and have to be ferreted out from the pages of dusty history books. However, scholars of Africans in India, like Joseph Harris, Helene Basu, Shanti Sadiq Ali, Edward Alpers and others have foregrounded the illustrious African Indian history of Sidi rulers and leaders who were called Habshi at the time. Basu (2001: 262–63) has also delineated the ways in which the contemporary Sidis in Gujarat, through their association with Bava Gor and his sister Mai Mishra, continue to maintain inventive connections with the past and construct a distinctive identity in the present:

> the historical context of African slaves in India shows that those Habshi who were part of the Muslim nobility did not constitute a separate ethnic or social unit that survived the disintegration of the Muslim systems of power. Rather noble Habshi (or Sidi) merged with the Muslim elite of former rulers. At the lower level of society, by contrast, African slaves transplanted to Gujarat formed a community that defined itself by reference to an African origin and a common religious cult. Contemporary Sidi do not forge any genealogical links with the aristocratic Habshi or Sidi of the past. Rather, the cult of black ancestor-saints [Bava Gor, Mai Mishra] provides the conceptual frame for the present 'Sidi *jamat*'. . . as a means for maintaining their identity, which is in this case tied to an African past commemorated in rituals dedicated to African ancestor-saints.

Parsis have an older historical connection to Sidis (Basu 1993: 292–93), going back to the 1840s, when many freed Sidi slaves, in Bombay and Surat, were employed by Parsis (among other communities) as domestic servants. However, the later spiritual connection of the Bombay Parsis with the Sidis, of which my parents were a part, came through Makbul Bava, about a hundred years later, in the 1940s. As the spirit medium of Bava Gor, Makbul Bava established a stronger connection with Sidis and through them to Bava Gor, by taking the Bombay Parsi devotees, at least once or twice a year, to Gujarat, to the shrine of this Sidi saint.

In baithak sessions, Makbul Bava referred to himself as a 'fakir', while the devotee who approached him to consult Bava

Gor was called *nadaan* or "innocent one". It is important to note that Makbul Bava brought his own variations into the Sidi practice of being a fakir and to the practice of the spiritual arts of healing, which he inherited from Sidis and their ancestral saint Bava Gor. The former's interpretation of what it means to be a fakir is described in considerable detail by Basu (1993: 290):

> Fakirs are not subject to celibacy vows but live in households. They differ from other people by the specialised work they perform in relation to the upkeep of shrines and the organization of the cult of Bava Gor.... Many Sidi fakirs (men and women),...are known as *mastfaquir* or "mad fakirs". The term *mast* as used by them refers to a positively evaluated form of madness which arises from a close relationship to one of the saints believed to guide the actions of his/her adept. [The ritual] headman, the *gadi varas*...is a *mastfakir,* a madman...a person with a hot mind whose behaviour is unpredictable and not assessable by norms.... The role of Sidi fakirs is defined in opposition to the religious discipline of Sayyid *pirs* at the top of the hierarchy and reflects principles governing relations between superior and subordinate in the political sphere as well as in the worship of Sufi saints.

Subsequently, Basu (1993: 290, 293) also traces how the Sidis acquired the role of entertainers in royal courts, evolved into a complex and elaborate identity construct of the fakir, invented by Sidis to create a meaningful social structure and community that would give them the status and dignity that the dominant culture denied them:

> at noble courts, aside from their work as domestic servants [and] from court jesters, Sidis became ritual clowns endowed with charismatic gifts. Their role as religious specialists and fakirs is based on their bond to the shrine of Bava Gor.... Sidi's [*sic*] assimilation into Gujarati society [thus] turned them from homeless slaves of no status into the marginal role of fakirs. Slaves without caste affiliation, ancestry, or family were integrated into a caste of black people by the mediation of fakirs. Fictive kinship ties provided such single individuals with a social identity necessary for establishing marital relations.

The Sidi community's self-representation as spiritual healers can be traced to roots in traditional healing arts in Africa.

John Janzen's extensive study of central, eastern and South African healing institutions called *ngoma*, (also called 'cult of affliction') provides many connections to ritual healing practised by Sidis:

> Ngoma provides the fabric of personal transformation; it helps sort through personal and societal experience with prevalent metaphors and other types of knowledge... Ngoma brings together the disparate elements of an individual's life threads and weaves them into a meaningful fabric. It does this, particularly, through devices of mutual "call and response" sharing of experience, of self-presentation, of articulation of common affliction, and of consensus over the nature of the problem and the course of action to take.... In another sense the text of self-presentation is never completed, for as long as the ngoma participant lives, there will be moments and times of self renewal, in the context of others (Janzen 1992: 109).

In different regions of central and south Africa, Janzen examines variations in the healing rituals and practices. Some of the healing techniques of ngoma include divination by bone throwing, spirit possession or trance—sometimes accompanied by music and drumming. In each case, Janzen points out how the practice accommodates itself to the socio-economic situation and the needs of the particular communities to reinvent themselves through healing. According to Janzen (1992: 36), ngoma groups sprang up where dislocated or divided communities in need of healing existed. The case of south Africa, for example is described thus:

> The societies that had newly formed as states were engaged in battle and defeated; their proud citizens were reduced to servants of the Afrikaaners on their own lands. This was followed late in the nineteenth century, by the discovery of gold and diamonds and the emergence of the major labor migration pattern that engulfed the entire mines and farms of the white man to make a living. The story of ngoma in Southern Africa also needs to be situated in the context of a divided society, of broken homes, of labour camps and mines, and in the twentieth century, of the urban settlements and townships.

It is important to note here that in the context of India, displaced or migrant Africans who made their way to the shrine of

Bava Gor in Gujarat also felt a need to come together and re-create community and social organisation, which in many ways resembles the function of the institutions of ngoma that Janzen has studied. Basu's analysis (2001: 267–68) of the Sidi kinship association (*jamat*) and initiation into the Sidi brotherhood of fakirs, bears some resemblance to Janzen's study of the ngoma communities and initiation practices:

> The term *jamat* thus refers simultaneously to the Sidi 'caste' as well as to a brotherhood of fakirs. Initiation into the Sidi fakir-brotherhood, which calls itself after the name of Bava Gor, is embedded in the special relationship between a spiritual seeker in the position of a child (*balako*) and a spiritual "master-fakir" in the position of parent and teacher (*murshid*). Initiation provided the means for integrating strangers into the Sidi fold. This occurred, as older Sidi still vividly remembered, when an African—whether formerly ensalved or "freed" from a slaveship—found his or her way to the *dargah* [shrine] of Bava Gor where he/she met other Sidi. Individual Africans were integrated into local Sidi groups through the creation of ritual kinship bonds between them. The stages of initiation mark the developing bond of mutual protection and support between a person learning the ritual craft of a fakir and his teacher-parent.

The teacher-student relationship that Sidi initiation involved can be compared to Janzen's (1992: 109) example of "doing ngoma":

> In both content and structure, this ngoma performance reveals that here, in the consciously formulated exchange of song-dance, and in the movement of the individual from sufferer-novice to accomplished, singing, self-projecting healer, lies the heart of the institution. I believe it is a classic—that is, ancient and formative—institution in Central and Southern Africa.

Some of the healing practices in Africa under the institution of ngoma involve spirit possession, dream interpretation, songs, dances and drumming rituals. Elements of these are part of the healing rituals practised by Sidis through the ceremonial ritual and dance that they call *goma*. Basu (1993: 292) explains the historical context of *goma*:

> The word *goma* is derived from the Swahili word for dance, *ngoma*, which in the East African cultural context is applied to a wide vari-

> ety of different dances. Sidi servants used to perform goma dances with drums, rattles and shells on different occasions (births, weddings) at noble courts. . . . Today, goma dancing is considered to be a gift which the Sidi have received from the saints defining essential activities of Sidi fakirs. This is manifested especially at the saint's day (*urs*) of Bava Gor when large numbers of Sidi are collectively possessed by the saints. In this context, the dance is called *masti goma* or *masti dammal*.

Commenting on changes in the practice of ngoma on the Swahili coast, Janzen (1992: 20–21) writes:

> One of the foremost common charateristics of the cults of affliction of Kinshasa and Dar es Salaam is that they are rituals imported by immigrants from all regions of the nation. In Tanzania these cults of affliction from the coast and the interior are differentiated around particular themes and issues; they are also ethnically diversified. In the urban setting, their practitioners continue the particular emphasis of the classic rite. But they are also sensitive to the changing expectations upon healers in the urban setting and many shift their emphasis to new issues.

Janzen's observations on changes in the practices of ngoma has some relationship to Makbul Bava and his work. Makbul Bava brought a different dimension to the healing practices of the ngoma. One could say that he transformed the Sidi practices of healing, and added different elements to it, never losing sight of the vital connection of his practice to Bava Gor and the rituals venerating Bava Gor and his sister Mai Mishra. In this respect, Makbul Bava invited Sidis to perform the sacred goma dance, also called *damal*, at the Parsi Bava Gor memorial shrine in Bombay. Sidis came specially to perform the goma/damal on the annual veneration day of Bava Gor's sister Mai Mishra, at the ceremony called *ghat*. First the physical presence of Sidis metonymically signifies the presence of Bava Gor and Mai Mishra at the Parsi memorial shrine. Secondly, since the goma is a sacred dance "gifted" to Sidis, only they could perform the dance in order to invoke the presence of the ancestral Sidi saints. Parsis could participate and join in, but they could not initiate the dance, because as the Parsi devotee Savak points out, "the Sidis have ownership of the dance as a sacred part of their healing and possession rituals" (Shroff interviews 2004). Sidis begin goma with an elaborate prayer, offer incense, garland their instruments, especially the tall footed drum, the *mugarman*, after which they start the goma/damal dance, gradually building up the momentum towards collective possession.

Just as the Sidis in India reinvented the practices of ngoma from fragmented memories of Africa, Makbul Bava as spirit medium of Sidi saint Bava Gor reinvented ritual practices focused upon Bava Gor, bringing in variations, perhaps with the changed circumstances. Most importantly Makbul Bava was not a Sidi but a Sunni Muslim, secondly, his spiritual training combined different spheres of influence which informed his practice as a fakir, and thirdly, he confronted a more middle-class group of supplicants in the urbanised and highly commercialised setting of Bombay. From interviews with my mother and with Savak, I learned that Makbul Bava's training as a fakir started when he was a young boy of about eleven years. Savak pointed out that from this young age, Makbul Bava was groomed to be the medium for Bava Gor, under the rigorous tutelage of a spiritual mentor, a Sufi master called Gul Hazarashah. The latter was the sole in-charge or gadi varas at the shrine of Mira Datar in Bombay. According to Savak, there were many pupils in training under Gul Hazarashah, but Makbul Bava was the most outstanding and was selected for the mediumship of Bava Gor.

Makbul Bava was so focussed on his spiritual training, that he was not interested in his family, land or property, which was in Harsul village, Nashik district. However, when he was about twenty years old, he was persuaded by relatives to return to Harsul, his ancestral village, to get married. He got married into a wealthy family of the Patels of his village. Within three years, his wife passed away. Unable to deal with the grief, Makbul Bava came back to the only work he knew well, spiritual work, at the shrine of Mira Datar. Since his family was well off, he was able to leave his two small daughters in the care of the women relatives of his extended family.

This period was the early 1930s in Bombay. However, in the absence of his mentor Gul Hazarashah, who had passed away, the shrine of Mira Datar was a changed place, with different people claiming the space. Makbul Bava left Mira Datar and stayed for a brief time at the shrine of Pedrushah near the Crawford Market area of Bombay. It was at this shrine of Pedrushah that Savak's father Dinsaji Kalianiwalla, owner of a small business, crossed paths with Makbul Bava. Although at that time, he was a small boy, Savak remembers Makbul Bava whom his father invited into his shop and eventually into his home. Savak recalls that his father, Dinsaji himself, was experiencing spirit possession and didn't know whom he was channelling, or how to handle the experience. Finally, Makbul Bava helped to reveal whose medium Dinsaji was. Thereafter, Dinsaji Kalianiwalla became Makbul Bava's first Parsi patron and initiate who was eager to learn more about spiritual practice, and he in turn brought other Parsis to seek help from Bava Gor through Makbul Bava.

During this period, the 1930s, the commercial, harbour city of Bombay (Kamerkar and Dhunjisha 2002: 169–72) was witnessing tremendous changes and development. Additionally, Gandhi's calls for independence from the British had already made inroads into the city. Uncertainty and change hung around businesses and family relationships. It is worth noting that at this time, a Muslim entrepreneur by the name of Ibrahim Seth met Makbul Bava and established him as his spiritual teacher and guide. Perhaps, it was becoming increasingly apparent to Muslims, even middle-class businessmen like Ibrahim Seth, and to the Parsis like Dinsaji that their position in India was vulnerable, to say the least. However, it was Ibrahim Seth who had the resources to rent a room furnished with the basic amenities for Makbul Bava, in the densely Muslim populated area of Byculla, in Bombay. Ibrahim Seth helped set up Makbul Bava with a private space to conduct the rituals of offering incense and lighting the lamp, (loban, batti) after which prayers are said and a seance session or baithak follows.

Ibrahim Seth introduced his entire family and other Muslims to Makbul Bava, and according to Savak (Shroff interviews 2002), Gujarati and Marwari businessmen also came to meet Makbul Bava. The flow of Parsi devotees also continued to grow. In fact, it was at Ibrahim Seth's place in Byculla that my father was first introduced to Makbul Bava by a Parsi colleague, an architect. As Makbul Bava helped people to deal with their problems, the number of Bava Gor devotees grew and the small room in Byculla was not enough to hold the gathering.

Makbul Bava decided to relocate to a new space in order to help even more people. He put together the money from some family sources, and some wealthy Parsi businessmen like Dinshaji Kerawalla, Ibrahim Seth's son Kassambhai, and some other Parsis pitched in with Makbul Bava to purchase some land in north Bombay, in order to set up a bigger space for Makbul Bava. At that time, north Bombay had much open land and it was here amidst fruit orchards that a memorial shrine or chilla to Bava Gor was constructed. It was a makeshift structure that was built around 1944. Here Makbul Bava established himself as mujavar and spirit medium of Bava Gor and started regular, weekly baithak sessions, single-handedly making himself available for healing work, for any kind of problem, ailment, affliction. This makeshift structure collapsed in 1946, after which a new one was rebuilt largely with the generosity of Dinshaji Kerawalla, in 1947.

According to my mother and Savak, in one of the baithak sessions, Bava Gor, speaking through Makbul Bava revealed his identity as descended from slaves or *ghulam khandaan*. He also revealed that his original tomb was in Gujarat and that the devotees should go there and locate it. In 1950, a group of devotees went with Makbul Bava to locate the dargah of Bava Gor in Gujarat. From this time onwards, Makbul Bava took devotees on several trips to the original shrine of Bava Gor in Gujarat. Almost fifty devotees would go on these trips. My mother and Savak remember these trips as tremendously fulfilling.

It was Makbul Bava's objective that in Gujarat, Parsis interact with Sidis and regard them with respect and veneration. In turn, Sidis respected Makbul Bava as a spirit medium of Bava

Gor. In Gujarat, at the shrine of Bava Gor, Parsis performed all of the regular rituals of prayers, offering incense and the lighting of the lamp, with Sidis in charge of the rituals, starting with the beating of the drum, which heralded the call for evening prayer, the magrib azzan. Often, at the request of the Parsis, Sidis also performed the goma/damal dance, as a highlight of the visit of the devotees. The goma dance energised Makbul Bava who possessed by Bava Gor's spirit would hold a baithak session and express great joy, through many blessings to the devotees and to whoever approached him. My mother comments that important healing work would be done through such baithak sessions at Bava Gor's original shrine. Once contact was made with Sidis of Gujarat, the connection was maintained by Makbul Bava who made it a point, every year, to invite Badshah Sidi from Gujarat with his group, to perform *qawali* or devotional songs at the Parsi chilla in Bombay, especially at the annual veneration ceremony of Bava Gor called the *'urs*. For the goma/damal dance, however, local Sidis other Bava Gor memorial shrines were invited to perform.

Makbul Bava initiated three Parsi men as mediums who also took baithak sessions and helped the devotees with problems. Rustamji was a medium for Usmanshah and gave out many remedies for health. As a child who suffered many years of respiratory tract infections, I was given many remedies from Usmanshah. Ratansha was the medium for Sher Shah who offered advice on a variety of matters. Both Usmansha and Sher Shah were supposed to be men in Bava Gor's retinue. Finally, Makbul Bava initiated Savak as the medium for Gul Hazarashah who was Makbul Bava's own spiritual mentor. Rustamji and Ratansha have passed away, so Usmansha and Sher Shah do not interact with the Parsi devotees, any more. However, Savak, as the spirit medium of Gul Hazarashah, still takes baithak sessions at the Parsi chilla. Since the mid 1990s, a young woman, Binaifer has been given the mediumship of Mai Mishra. At present, the group of devotees who come to the Bava Gor chilla numbers approximately 300, and it includes some Hindu families as well as members and friends of

Makbul Bava's family, some Christians; the majority, about 250, are Parsis.

Regular, weekly attendance has decreased at the Parsi chilla as travel in Bombay has become difficult, and also since the current medium Yasin does not hold weekly baithak sessions, except on the day of the new moon, chandraat. His grandfather, Makbul Bava on the other hand, could give all his attention to the running of the Bava Gor chilla. He was present every day for the evening prayer and the chilla rituals of incense and the lighting of the lamp (loban-batti). If he could not be present, he put someone in charge, because the evening rituals have to be undertaken everyday to welcome the spirits of Bava Gor, Mai Mishra and the rest of Bava Gor's family and retinue called *parivar.* At present, with the heavy constraints on his time, as a paid employee, Yasin often finds it difficult to be present for the evening prayers, especially in the season when the sunset is early, around 5 p.m. Yasin and the devotees have devised a system of rotating responsibility by which individual devotees take turns to be present at the sunset for the evening call to prayer. Every day, one devotee must take his turn to supervise and manage the evening rituals of offering incense and the lighting of the lamp at the Bava Gor memorial shrine.

The experience of my parents as devotees of Bava Gor indicates how a relationship of trust developed between the spirit medium and the supplicants who called themselves followers or *savalis* of Bava Gor. In the 1950s, my father, a civil engineer, made the decision of leaving a difficult job situation in order to work independently. This turned out to be a daunting task for him as a young man with very little money in a flourishing construction industry. My mother (Shroff interviews 2002) revealed that my father went through tremendous stress and suffered a nervous breakdown. He was desperately looking for emotional healing and a Parsi colleague who had become a Bava Gor devotee introduced him to Makbul Bava.

The healing strategies used by Makbul Bava were many and varied. My father was first requested to bring with him a bottle of rose water. Makbul Bava said some prayers, *kalmas*, and gave the bottle back with instructions on how to drink the contents. My mother recalls (Shroff interviews 2002) that my father "calmed down completely and the healing prayers enabled him to function without stress."

However, the rose water bottle was only one element of the healing process and initiation into the group of Bava Gor devotees. Makbul Bava asked my father to attend the baithak sessions at the chilla regularly, every Thursday, and sometimes my father was called along with other savalis to attend "all-night prayer sessions". My mother explained this relationship of devotees to Bava Gor through the spirit medium. She told me that often people approach Bava Gor through the spirit medium with personal problems seeking quick solutions. But for the spirit medium, the seeker of solutions had to first become a participant within a community, like an initiate. One could not seek solutions and disappear, though there were many who did that—disappear after their work was done. For the spirit medium, the seeker of help, the supplicant begins a lifelong process of healing himself or herself and continues the process of healing others. In this regard, my father and the other savalis who attended nightly prayer sessions, were gifted some kalmas that they could themselves use as healing prayers for their family or friends. Makbul Bava also created in the Bava Gor devotees a sense of an extended family. The devotee would develop an ongoing relationship with the spirit medium and eventually bring in members of their entire family into the circle of believers who would collectively honour the saints. There was always a sense of celebration and festivity created in the rituals honouring Bava Gor, so the whole family could participate. My mother explained that people did not always have to come to Bava Gor memorial shrine with a specific problem. They could come for the infinite blessings from participating or witnessing Sidi goma/damal dance or in listening to the devotional songs, qawalis, sung by Badshah Sidi to invoke the presence of Bava Gor and Mai Mishra.

My mother who is now considered one of the older devotees at the Parsi chilla, formed an intense relationship with Bava

Gor, but started the relationship rather uneasily. My father, a devotee of Bava Gor from the mid 1950s, was the one who introduced my mother into the community of Bava Gor devotees. It was not an easy relationship, at the beginning. As a young woman, my mother could not easily grasp the terms of the relationship with Bava Gor through his medium Makbul Bava.

My mother's experience as a devotee indicates some of the variations, like the use of dreams that Makbul Bava brought to his work as a spirit medium. In the interview, my mother described that at first, it was just my father who attended the chilla regularly, while she was indifferent and did not participate much except on the day of chandraat, an auspicious day when the spirit medium had more power and energy. My mother describes that things began to change for her when she had a dream. My mother recalls that in her dream, she was standing in front of her own dressing-table, with Makbul Bava standing behind her. Makbul Bava spread some powder onto the table and asked my mother to move her hand on the powder while he said some prayers. Opposite them, in the mirror, there appeared a *sadhu*, a holy man, complete with the beads, bearded, and he was a black man. This man addressed my mother and told her, "Your work will be done." She asked him to give his blessings before he left. She remembers the man saying: "All the blessings in the world are yours."

My parents were advised by senior devotees to relate the dream to Makbul Bava during baithak. At the following new moon, chandraat baithak, when Makbul Bava asked my mother why she had come to see him, she described her dream. He responded by repeating: "Your work will be done." The interesting part here is that my mother did not know what this "work" was until she realised that my grandmother and father were both eager for a male child after three daughters. My mother says she did not have enough "trust" and so she would stay away from the chilla. However, Makbul Bava asked her to attend another chandraat baithak. Like the other devotees, my mother approached Makbul Bava with a garland of flowers in the baithak session. Makbul Bava speaking as Bava Gor refused the garland saying: "Don't feel bad, but the day you do my work and have faith in me, I will accept your flowers." My mother says that she realised that if such a high soul spoke to her, she had to have faith, but there was still some uncertainty within her.

In the meantime, my mother had a second dream. This time in the dream, Makbul Bava addressed another devotee, Savak, and told him, "If you don't have faith, why do you come here?" This dream was interpreted for my parents by an older devotee as Makbul Bava's indirect way of communicating his message to my mother.

The interaction between Makbul Bava as the spirit medium of Bava Gor and my mother, clearly shows a variation of the manner of initiation into the cult of Bava Gor. My mother belonged to the group of devotees from the 1950s and from this group, Makbul Bava demanded stronger commitment in his role of teacher-parent. This entailed regular visits to the chilla often on Monday and Thursday. My father often went on both days and he, along with other men, was often asked to stay overnight, in order to learn more, or as my father put it, 'to advance spiritually.'

My mother told me that when she was pregnant, she took a garland of flowers again to Makbul Bava and this time he accepted the flowers, blessed my mother, said some prayers, and told her to place the garland of flowers under her pillow, until the day of her delivery. My mother said: "So I must have had the faith in me now to accept, though I thought, that even suppose something goes wrong and if it's a girl, it's quite alright, whatever it is I accept." By the time my brother was born in 1961, Makbul Bava had become a member of our family. He used to have lunch with my family every week, either Monday or Thursday and accompany my father to his work sites on those days. That same evening, my father would accompany Makbul Bava to the Bava Gor chilla for the evening prayers.

Makbul Bava's healing work added a different dimension to the work done by Sidis. For my parents and other devotees,

Makbul Bava and Bava Gor were one and the same person. The healing work whether it was emotional or medical came through a spiritual space. The devotees who came to consult Bava Gor through Makbul Bava were middle class and poor. Although the memorial shrine drew many Parsis, there were many Hindus, Muslims and Christians as well. On the day of the Bava Gor 'urs, several people from the neighborhood came to participate. Religious and ethnic boundaries between different communities were not as clearly defined in Makbul Bava's time as they have become today.

When Makbul Bava, the first spirit medium of Bava Gor, passed away in 1984, his grandson Yasin, the present medium, was the named and already-initiated inheritor of the role of caretaker-mujavar and spirit medium, gadi varas, of Bava Gor. Yasin was too young and inexperienced to take on the task of spirit medium. Consequently, Yasin's father, Makbul Bava's son-in-law Sheikh Hussein, temporarily took up the responsibilities of running the memorial shrine for the devotees. However, the shadow of Makbul Bava's charismatic personality hung over Sheikh Hussein and today it continues to haunt even Yasin, as both these spirit mediums are continually compared to Makbul Bava. For the devotees, Makbul Bava's tenure as spirit medium continues to be seen as a golden and glorious period.

For Parsis then, even though the Sidi saints Bava Gor and Mai Mishra are a vital presence in their lives, it is a presence mediated through the work of Makbul Bava, and contact with Sidis comes mostly through the visits to Gujarat, to the Bava Gor shrine or when Sidis come to the Parsi chilla to perform the goma dance. Savak commented that "Sidis have a natural power and healing gift and that is why Makbul Bava as medium of a Sidi saint created extensive contact with Sidis, even taking Parsis to local shrines in Bombay that are managed and run by Sidis." Additionally, Savak also pointed that there are Parsi Bava Gor devotees in Gujarat whose contact with Bava Gor is directly through Sidis. Some of those Gujarat Parsis enabled Makbul Bava and his Bombay Parsi group to travel to Bava Gor village.

Makbul Bava regularly invited qawali singer Badshah Sidi from Bava Gor village to sing at the Bombay Parsi chilla. Badshah Sidi himself interacted with Parsis and talked to them. His devotional songs were immensely popular and often devotees requested him to sing their favourite qawalis that were Badshah's own compositions. Badshah Sidi also commanded a voice and presence that made him a natural leader and spokesperson of his people. My parents and other devotees almost always stopped at his house in Bava Gor village as we made our way to the Bava Gor shrine. Badshah and his wife Hassina welcomed everybody and extended their warmth and hospitality.

In conclusion, I circle back to the questions I posed in the opening section of this essay and admit that my questions are not the same as those of my parents who approached Bava Gor primarily through Makbul Bava, so much so that Makbul Bava merged into Bava Gor and perhaps blurred the markers of race and ethnicity. In interviews my mother makes statements about Bava Gor that clearly demonstrate how the figure of Makbul Bava is superimposed onto Bava Gor. For example, in response to my question "What does Bava Gor mean to you?", my mother said, "He means a father figure to me...I think he loved me and I loved him." To me, her response indicates her close relationship to Makbul Bava who, as a spirit medium in the baithak sessions, spoke to my mother as Bava Gor.

For me as a scholar and film maker, questions of race, class, gender and ethnicity are part of my teaching and documentary film-making practice. Therefore my questions about Sidis and my relationship to them (Shroff: 2004) have taken shape accordingly. However, there could be other explanations offered: that perhaps as a privileged minority the Parsis have not been racially stigmatised in India and therefore have been able to ignore the hierarchical dimension of race in their relations with Sidis even as they have acknowledged Sidis as racially different. Again, when I questioned my mother about how she regarded Sidis, she said, "[They are] different people, gentle people...but I didn't show so much interest in them at that time, I just accepted them that they are Sidis. . .I didn't even know that Bava [Gor] was a Sidi, after a long time I came to know about it."

While my parents acknowledge Sidis as a significant spiritual resource and acknowledge the economic disparities between the two communities, there is no real questioning of their own privileged status in India. That is glibly passed off as resulting from self-motivation and industry, much of which is true; but then so is the fact that Parsis had a head start in India despite their status as refugees who came to India with very little. It is important to note, however, that the contemporary Parsi community in post-Independence India has been marginalised and has moved away from the once glorious, entrepreneurial community that built the commerce and trade of a city such as Bombay (Kulke 1974; Nanavutty 1977; Luhrmann 1996; Palsetia 2001; Kamerkar and Dhunjisha 2002). Not only have the Parsis diminished in numbers, but so has some of their glory, memorialised though it is in street names and the many charitable, educational and medical institutions that Parsis have set up in Bombay. From a largely upper-middle-class community, many Parsis have slipped into lower middle class status and perhaps some have been pushed into the designation of poor—a fact that is rather difficult for Parsis to accept. So while my parents and other Parsi devotees would acknowledge that the worship of Sidi saint Bava Gor filled a lacuna in their life, their perspective of Sidis is mainly to see them as a conduit into a spiritual life, albeit an extremely meaningful part of their spiritual life. However, this becomes a fixed frame of reference that denies issues of race and class and essentialises Sidis in generalised terms that "naturalise" the spiritual gifts and healing abilities of Sidis. Additionally, this perspective also disavows the historical framework of analysis in which Parsis were, as Kamerkar and Dhunjisha (2002: 22–25) point out, part of the flourishing Indian Ocean world trade and commerce nexus, while Sidis were mainly part of the flow of goods and services in this prosperous political economy.

Nonetheless, I need to emphasise that the Parsi-Sidi connection continues to be very strong and extremely meaningful, even to Parsis in the diaspora. Although some of the children of the devotees have migrated to North America or elsewhere, on their visits to India, they make the journey to the Parsi chilla and to the original shrine of Sidi saint Bava Gor, and now bring their American-born children into the cult of Bava Gor.

10

*On the Presence of African Musical Culture in Coastal Baluchistan**

Sabir Badalkhan

Introduction

The Makran coast in Baluchistan had played an important role in the maritime trade among the peoples of South Asia, the Middle East, Central Asia and the African continent (Badalkhan 2002b). It was involved in all types of trade including the slave trade from Africa to South Asia. The slave trade was once the most lucrative trade of the region (Wink 1999, 1: 32), and the Arabs, who occupied the northeastern and northern parts of Africa, were staunch dealers in this human trade. In this trade, the Omani Arabs, such as the Azdi tribe, who were also settled on coastal Makran as early as the third century AD (cf. Badalkhan 2002b: 218, fn. 29; Siddiqi 1991: 19), "emerged as the most important slave dealers" (Wink 1999, 1: 30). Makran was a transitory zone for slaves destined for different South Asian markets. During their forced sojourns through

* This is the revised version of a paper presented at the Conference on Cultural Exchange and Transformation in the Indian Ocean World, held at UCLA, April 5–6, 2002. My thanks go to Prof. Lorraine H. Sakata, UCLA, and Prof. Brian Spooner, University of Pennsylvania, for making my participation possible. I am also grateful to Prof. Margaret A. Mills, the Ohio State University, Columbus, for all the help extended to me. Special thanks go to Mahmad Azim Baluch of Shahrak (then posted at Ormada and Pasni), Ikhlaq Ahmad in Pasni, and Dr Aziz Shambey in Gwadar. Sincere thanks are also due to all of my informants on whose information this paper is based. I am also thankful to Prof. Adriano V. Rossi, Unior, Naples, for having read an earlier draft of this paper and for making valuable comments.

Baluchistan, thousands of slaves were possibly sold in the local market. According to Swidler, around 30 per cent of a total population of one million or so in Makran are descendants of slaves brought from East Africa (Swidler 1996: 172–73).[1] It should be noted that neither these Baluch call themselves African or Afro-Baluch nor are they called as such by others in Baluchistan. The black population is completely absorbed in the Baluch ethno-linguistic group. For the sake of analysis, and being aware of the delicacy of using a term which might displease certain social groups, I shall use 'Baluch of African origin' in this paper to distinguish them from other tribal Baluch. Baluch of African origin are generally known as *gulam* (slave), *naukar* (servant, slave), *dada* (black), or *shidi* (black). Dada is more often used in Sindh but less so in Baluchistan, except in some towns on the Makran coast. The term 'shidi' is mostly used in Karachi. *Balochi Ganj*, a Baluchi-English dictionary in preparation, gives the meaning of the terms 'shidi' and 'dada' as "negro, person of African descent". Both carry pejorative connotations. Sometimes they are also called by the general term of *syah* 'black'. Moreover, the non-Baluch population in Karachi use the term 'Makrani' for the Baluch of black skin as they originally migrated from the coast and settled in Karachi during the late nineteenth and the first half of the twentieth century. This was a time when Karachi was in the process of being developed to a metropolitan city and needed manpower in large numbers. There are also other social groups of possible African origin, such as the *darzadag*[2] and the *nakib* with strong "signs of African blood in the short curly hair and thick lips" (*Baluchistan District Gazetteer, Makran*, 1986: 111; Field 1959: 64; Pastner and Pastner 1972: 129).

Along with these Africans, slaves or not, came their culture, music and religious beliefs—many of which are still preserved in rites such as in the music therapy for evil spirit possessions

[1] Probably not all Baluch of African descent were brought as slaves or were war captives as is commonly believed. Some of them came as seafarers.

[2] The name *darzadag* means 'of alien origin' and suggests that they came from outside, supporting the common belief that they are of African origin. Spooner believes that they "are serfs" (1964: 60).

or in dance sessions, such as *damal*. These aim at purification in which men and women of all ages participate. Music is of great importance for people of African descent in Baluchistan (as elsewhere in South Asia, cf. Catlin-Jairazbhoy 2002; Mirzai 2002a; Mirzai 2002b; Basu, Schwerin, Minda this volume). As the role of music has been recognised universally as one of the most effective tools of liberating oneself from the daily hardships of a discriminated and less advantageous life and to express rage and sufferings in a most natural way, the Baluch of African origin have retained their musical heritage with a great degree of authentication.[3] While dancing and singing activities carry a low profile among high-class Baluch Muslims, the musical tradition of Baluch of African origin were closely related with maritime activities. In the following I shall discuss some of the characteristics of the music and dancing traditions of the Baluch of African origin.[4]

Maritime contacts of the Makran Baluch with the eastern and northeastern coasts of Africa lasted until the first half of the twentieth century. A large part of Baluch were engaged in seafaring. Most of the seamen I interviewed had visited many of the major coastal towns in this vast sphere of the Indian Ocean. Besides working on ships owned by local proprietors, Baluch seamen were also employed in the neighbouring countries, and in the early nineteenth century Grant found a large number of Baluch "employed by Arabs in their dhows and ships of Muscat, and they are reckoned very faithful" (Grant 1839: 340). In recent years, seafaring has declined, although it still continues to some extent. Sailors sometimes spent up to six months in Africa before returning back to Baluchistan. As their journeys were dependent on the monsoons, they often halted along the African coast for several months. When I interviewed Nurjan-i Gamani, a seaman in his 70s, he told me that he had started working on *sapari boji*s (long journeying

[3] Catlin-Jairazbhoy observed a similar situation among the Afro-Indians. She states that to dissolve the "burdens of discrimination, Sidi culture relies greatly on the devices of humor, playfulness, satire, and fun, with music and dance playing a major role in the embodiment of these attitudes" (2002: 4).

[4] I collected data in the 1990s in southwestern Baluchistan and in Karachi.

trading/transportation sail) at the age of eight and had continued until losing his eye-sight a few years back. He recalled:

> In Africa all people are Shidi and their language is Swahili. We have learnt the language[5] and their songs there in Africa, in Zanzibar and other African port cities. When we reached there our return was blocked because there were no favourable winds.[6] We would spend three months there, or even more, depending upon the arrival of seasonal winds. From here (Makran) we went to Africa in winter. When we reached we pulled our ships out of the sea and kept them standing on woods. We went around during the day time and slept in our ships during the night. When summer winds began to blow, the king of the country raised his flag. It was the signal that foreign sailors were allowed to put on their sails and leave for other destinations. Sailors coming from all over the world would be gathered there during this period. We loaded goods in our ships and left for our countries or for other destinations to the Arab countries or to India.

Another old sailor recalled that there were always drumming and dancing sessions on the shores or in towns when their ships were stationed in an African coastal town, and sailors from all over the Indian Ocean region joined them in music-making and dancing.

Musical Genres: Amba *and* laywa

The musical traditions of the coast are more diverse than the music of interior Baluchistan. Here we find two most famous genres, *amba* and *laywa,* which are not found in other parts of Baluchistan. Both of these seem to be of African origin. Both are performed only on the coast. Amba and laywa both are

[5] He spoke Swahili fluently with a young black man who had been brought from Zanzibar as a young boy and had settled there in Ormada. Nurjan also told me that he speaks some Arabic, which he had learnt during his frequent visits to the Arabian Gulf as a seaman.

[6] He and other sailors, who had spent all their active lives in sapari bojis, said that even if they wanted to depart, the king of the country would not allow them to pull their anchors off until the arrival of the favourable season when the king of the place would raise a white flag signalling that foreign sailors could pull their anchors off and put on sails.

Sidi musicians playing at the astana of Hazrat Bava Gor, Karachi. Photograph by Sabir Badalkhan, October 2, 2005.

group dances accompanied by drums of different sizes and chorus songs. The former includes work songs meant to incite collective work as well as prayers and praises to God, the Prophet Muhammad, Muslim saints, and so on, while the latter is a festive singing-and-dancing style and its subject matters vary from soft love themes to rude and, often, hard sexual themes and so on. Because of the use of obscene language in the laywa songs, women usually avoid these performances but there are always some, especially elderly women, among the audience, though always from among the black population.

The common belief among the black population of the coast is that both amba and laywa had originated from coastal Makran and then migrated to the African coast. The reverse seems true, though. According to Anderson Bakewell, a knowledgeable British ethnomusicologist of African, Arab and Indian musical traditions (and with whom I first made recordings of these performances in 1991), this music is found in the whole of the Indian Ocean world from India to the Persian Gulf countries, and on the East African coasts. As regards the origin of the term amba, it is hard to propose any etymology but we find a song genre in Swahili where *wimbo* is "song in general, and more specifically, a song of 12 syllables in the line" (cf. Knappert 1982: 23, 30). Laywa, on the other hand, is also found in Arab countries and it is attested to being basically an African song genre (cf. Graebner 2002: 11, fn. 26; Al-Khan et al. 1989). The description of *lewa* by Christensen, as it is performed in Oman, very much corresponds to the performance of laywa in Makran. He writes:

> *Lewa* groups, consisting of men who are descendants of slaves, perform for profit.... Several drums, including African-type drums called *musundu* [cf. Baluchi *mugulmani*]; conch trumpets (*jim*) [cf. Baluchi conch shell *gurr*], and metal trays of canisters [cf. Baluchi *tal*, a steel plate] used to beat the time line.... Altogether twenty to forty people...make up the group.... Dancers and singers revolve while circling around the instrumentalists. The song texts, in poorly understood Swahili and Arabic, abound with references to East Africa and seafaring. (2002: 678–79)

Christensen further notes that "*lewa* carries strong African connotations that are neither Arab nor Muslim" (Ibid: 679).[7] However, the only difference between a lewa performed in Oman to that performed by Baluch of African descent is that in the former, "performances frequently lead to a trance" (Ibid.), while in the latter no trance is involved as it is simply a festive and merry-making dance.

[7] The term laiwa "has been given different interpretations although various sources agree on its Swahili origin" (Al-Khan et al. 1989: 4). Some believe that "the word signifies a 'dance-circle' and that it also refers to a type of African marine vessel which has a circular foredeck. The name was given to that particular dance whose choreographies assumed a circular form" (Ibid: 4–5).

The presence of African musical tradition is also attested in the case of *malid, gwat* and *damal*. The first, malid is basically a votive ritual but is also organised as a healing ceremony to ward off evil spirits after entering in a state of trance with the help of music and singing (cf. Badalkhan 2000a: 779–80). The second, gwat, is a healing ceremony where the patient is treated with the help of music and singing, leading her/him to a state of trance (for *gwati* see Ryahi 1977; Sultana 1996; Badalkhan 2000a: 779–80, 2002a; During 1989: 37ff.; During 2002). This latter seems to be a Baluchi variant of the African zar phenomenon, though zar is predominantly performed by women (cf. During 1989: 47–53; Sengers 2003: 89, cf. Basu, this volume). Gwat is performed both by and for men and women. In both cases when the healer enters in a state of trance s/he sometimes speaks in Swahili or in a mixed language of Swahili, Urdu and Baluchi, etc. The third, *damal,* is basically a sacred ritual dance organised at saints' shrines (*astana*) or at sanctuaries (*tikana*)—also in other places in modern times—where, with the help of music and singing, spirit-possessed persons enter into a state of trance and are thus cured. It was originally performed by Baluch of African origin but now Baluch of all backgrounds, and of both sexes and of all ages, except for very young kids, take part in damal rituals. The difference between gwati and damal sessions is that the former are mostly organised for curing individual patients while the latter are collective trance sessions where tens of women and men (women are almost always in the majority) enter into trance and are cured by the *sheik(h)* (male master) or by the *sheik(h)ani* (female master) in sequence. Damal rituals of the Baluch of African descent seem to be similar to the *ngoma/goma* rituals of the Africans which are also found among the Afro-Indians (for details see Basu 2002: 12; 2000). There are several shrines in the Baluch-majority areas of Karachi where damal sessions are held almost every Thursday night except for the month of Ramadan and the first ten days of the month of Muharram, which is observed by Shiites as a period of mourning for Imam Hussain, the grandson of Prophet Muhammad.

Sailing, Fishing and Music Making

The Baluch love for music and singing can be seen in the following episode which a former sailor in Ormada narrated in 1993. Mazar, who was in his 70s when I met him, gave the following account:

> I tell you, once I was at the Karachi port when a beautiful ship of Syrians came. I was then working on a ship owned by the Ismailis. We were loading fruit in our ship. Arabs then traded dates. When the Syrian ship came, they anchored their ship to the berth and started beating drums and singing amba in Arabic. Tell you, Arabs do not have any proper amba, all their amba is to shout loudly and yell. I don't know Arabic but heard their drums beating: *dibbuk u tibbuk, ti ti u ti ti, dibbuk u tibbuk, ti ti u ti ti*. . . I was young then and could not control myself, so I started to dance. When I started dancing, men from all sides gathered around me and labourers started handling sacks with shouts and yells. Some men held me up and put me on the sack of a labourer who was carrying it off the ship. I was on top of the sack and dancing there to the rhythm of drums and singing amba. Each time I was taken to the ship on shoulders and then brought back on sacks and then again taken to the ship on shoulders. This continued for as long as the ship was being unloaded. Once the ship was unloaded, the Arabs gave me two *kosara* [sacks of dates] and asked me to join them as their dancer but I told them that I was not a professional dancer and was taken up by *ishk* [excessive passion] of music and had not been able to control myself.

He added with a great nostalgic tone that when he remembers those days, his heart desires that he take off his shirt, take off his trousers and dance naked in public so that the people realise how beautiful were the days of his youth. When he was going to marry, he took his team of dancers and their drums on a ship and went to the open sea. There they danced to their heart's content before coming back to the town where they organised dancing and drumming sessions which continued for days until the conclusion of the wedding festivities.

In amba performances, the following instruments are used: one or more footed drum (*mugulmani*), two or more big double-headed drums (with the generic name of *duhl* but the bigger one is called *rahmani* and the smaller one is called *kyasar*), two or more small double-headed drums (called *timbuk*), one conch shell (*gurr*), and sometimes one or more steel plates (*tal*) played with sticks. Amba songs are sung in groups by fishermen when they pull or spread their nets in the sea, or pull or push their boats into the sea or out of the sea during the start or end of the fishing/seafaring seasons. It was also performed on board when sails were used for trade and transport and for pulling or releasing anchors.

Until the mid twentieth century, a lot of trade was carried out from the Makran coast to the Perso-Arabian Gulf ports as far as Basra where dates were loaded and transported to India or to Africa. These ships frequently visited all major coastal towns on the east African coast as far as Kilwa (Kalwa of the Baluch seamen), Mtwara (Matwara of the Baluch seamen), Pangani (Pingani of the Baluch seamen), Mombasa, Somalia, Dar es Salaam, etc., and all major coastal towns along the Indian subcontinent up to Sri Lanka and beyond. Perso-Arabian Gulf ports were like their second homes of the Baluch seamen and they frequently visited Muscat, Aden, Basra and other major towns on the coast. Similarly, they often defined Zanzibar as their 'play land' (*laybja*), explaining to me that the way one visits a playground very often as it is the nearest place in a village, with the same frequency they would visit Zanzibar.[8] The crew of a ship depended upon its size but most ships had from twelve to twenty-five members. It needed a joint and harmonious force to fold or spread the sails or to do other heavy work on board as well as on the shore. Baluch seamen recall that four drums would be taken on board the ship during the journey. The person holding a drum would take his seat in the front of the boat, beat the drum and lead the singing of amba songs to provide synchronisation to the movements of the working body. Adra records from the Arabian Peninsula, which has much in common with the Baluch seafaring tradition, that "large merchant ships, which had more space and afforded

[8] Women in Makran still sing in their wedding songs: *salonka zangbari zabad mushtag* ("the bridegroom has rubbed *zabad* [the name of a sweet smelling substance] from Zanzibar").

more leisure time, would sometimes take along a professional singer and master of ceremonies (*nahan*) who would organize nightly music and dancing events" (Adra 2002: 708). Ruth Stone also records that lewa was danced at Sohar by sailors on the decks of *booms*, the large ship that sailed to Africa (cited in Alpers 1997: 70).

When ships returned from their long journeys, their sails would be seen from a long distance so people of the town would gather at the shore to receive them. The crew would anchor their ship in open waters, as there were no harbours anywhere in coastal Makran, and sit on small boats (*battel*) and go to the shore. From the shore, other fishermen and relatives of the crew would also sit on battels and go to greet them on their way to the sea in order to bring them with pomp and amidst celebrations. The crew members would start singing amba, to the accompaniment of their drum(s), from their battels while those going to greet them would respond with similar songs. On the shore, the whole town's folk—of both sexes and of all ages—gathered to receive the crew. Drums were beaten and men of all ages joined in singing amba and danced until the crew, and those who had gone to greet them, reached the shore and joined them.

Seamen received a similar kind of welcome on their arrival at African coasts. With the sight of the land the seamen would raise a flag of white colour which meant that the ship was coming with peaceful intentions. As soon as the local population of a coastal town saw such a ship approaching, people of all ages, from all walks of life and from both sexes gathered at the shore and welcomed the approaching ship. A Makran sailor recalled that local seamen and fishermen from passing boats would often greet them singing ambas in their own languages and they (the Baluch) would respond them by singing ambas in Baluchi: "This was their way of welcoming us", the sailor said.

Amba songs begin with the call of *(h)eylambey*, which is calling men to work ("get ready").[9] The group leader, as in other

[9] I am grateful to Prof. Abdulaziz Lodhi for the translation of the word *(H)eylambey*. In Swahili *halambe* means "let us go forward, move ahead", etc.

dances and collective songs, is called *sarogan* (the leader), and the chorus is called *jawabi* (respondent, chorus), which is also the working body when sung in the working context. The guide/leader of the working team starts singing the first line and the workmen reply singing the second line, or the refrain, with the rhythm of drums and the movements required for performing the work. Usually, drums accompany the working body providing rhythm to their songs and their work. But amba may also be sung without the accompaniment of drums. Being basically a work song it has sometimes very short lines and sometimes even single-worded formulas which are repeated again and again, like *hey, yi, ji, ji Alla* ("O, yes, praise be to you, praise be to God"), or *tarma bidey dema* ("put the *tarm*[10] in front" [of the boat being pushed into or pulled out of the sea]) and the jawabi respond in chorus, *heywalla* ("yes, with the name of God"), etc. In addition, there are longer amba songs and famous amba singers, called ambai, who have their bands and are invited for special occasions.

In laywa performances, the same musical instruments are used as in amba. Until recently, laywa was organised during festive occasions, such as, for example, marriages. Special laywa teams are invited with their drums, joined by tens, and sometimes even by hundreds, of men of all ages. At present, however, laywa performances are undergoing significant changes related to the influence of so-called cultural events organised by the government or for the benefit of modern mass media.[11] Nowadays laywa performers colour their faces and decorate their heads with plumes or tie bird feathers around their arms. This type of body decoration is only used in officially sponsored performances that are advertised as 'Black dancers from Makran'. This has raised considerable criticism,

[10] Tarm is the block of wood put under the ship when pulled or pushed on the shore so that it does not touch the ground.

[11] In recent years, laywa dances are also organised on occasions such as on the 14th of August when the Government of Pakistan celebrates the day of Pakistan's coming into existence in 1947. I observed laywa dancing sessions on the midnight of 14 August 2003, at the Mombasa Street near the famous Sheedi Village Road in Lyari, Karachi.

as people feel that an 'African culture' is fabricated that bears little resemblance to the lively tradition that had evolved at the Makran coast in response to Indian Ocean links.

Final Remarks

Makran has served as a gateway for different immigrants as well as a meeting point of Indian Ocean sailors and traders for centuries. As I have tried to show in this paper, the musical culture of coastal Baluchistan is deeply embedded in the maritime culture of the Indian Ocean region. Until today, one finds music and songs of African, Indian or Arabic origin in all coastal towns of Baluchistan. People of different cultural backgrounds have lived and worked side by side for centuries, adopting the language of the Baluch but maintaining their cultural characteristics. Amba and laywa are expressions of the cultural diversity allowed to flourish in Baluchistan. As the seafaring tradition of Makran is coming to an end, however, the popularity of amba songs will probably decline in the future.

11

Daff *Music of Yemeni-Habshi in Hyderabad*

Helene Basu, Kerrin von Schwerin, Ababu Minda*

Introduction

In the study of Sidis in India, music has become a major focus through which it is sought to establish cultural links to Africa. In Hyderabad, one of three well-known sites of the African presence in India (besides Karnataka and Gujarat), people of African origin also make music. But they reject being called Sidi because in their view the term is loaded with pejorative connotations. Rather, they prefer to call themselves 'Habshi'.[1] The most common self-denomination, however, is 'Chaush', a term devoid of ethnic reference, but which includes Habshi as well as people defining themselves as 'Yemenis', that is Arabs. Correspondingly, what is popularly referred to as the 'African' or 'Black' music of Yemeni-Habshi is in fact shaped by a blending of Arab (Yemeni) and African-derived styles of music epitomised by the term *daff.* In Arabia, as in certain Indian Sufi contexts, daff is the term for a tambourine; in Gujarat, for example, the daff tambourine is used by members of the Rifai

* This chapter is the result of joint efforts by all three authors. We have all acquired some experience or knowledge of Yemeni/Habshi in Hyderabad. Von Schwerin studied the history of Yemeni/Habshi related to the court of the Nawab of Hyderabad. Basu did research on Yemeni-Habshi performance styles in Hyderabad in 2001. Minda collected data on Yemeni/Habshi constructions of identity and social change in 2002 (cf. Minda 2004).

[1] See the Introduction for a more detailed discussion of these names.

brotherhood in performances of *zhikr* (recollections and recitations of the names of God). In Hyderabad, daff is the name of a small circular drum played with one stick. In addition to referring to the drum, in Hyderabad, daff also denotes a particular style of musical performance involving other instruments (e.g. double membrane drums, brass vessels) and dancing that are regularly performed by men of the Yemeni-Habshi communities. The remarkable correspondence displayed by the fusion of ethnic categories (Arab/African) and musical traditions derived from Arabia (Yemen) and possibly East Africa (or, to be more precise, Zanzibar and the Swahili coast), we argue, effectively highlights the distinctiveness of Indian Ocean themes that continue to shape pluralistic regional societies in India. In order to demonstrate this, in the first part of the paper, the history of Yemeni/Habshi in Hyderabad is explored. We then briefly describe what is meant by daff music and situate this performance style in the context of Chaush constructions of identity.

The City of Hyderabad

Hyderabad in the Deccan was a city of unique charm, due to its geographical location and its specific character as the capital and seat of a cultured Qutb Shahi court. Planned and constructed at the end of the sixteenth century, it housed a population of diverse origin, language and culture that served the needs and tastes of the ruling class. These Shiite Muslims, a military and administrative nobility of Irani origin, created a liberal culture whose Dakhni language and literature stood for the visible integration of various ethnic elements. When the Thuggy Amir Ali approached the city, he was amazed:

> Before me, on the gentle rise of the valley and beyond where I supposed the river to be, lay the city, its white terraced houses gleaming brightly in the sunshine.... The Char Minar and Mecca Masjid rose proudly from the masses of buildings by which they were surrounded, and here and there a white dome with its brightly gilded spire marked the tomb of some favourite or holy saint, while smaller mosques, I might say to the hundreds, were known by their

A map of Hyderabad

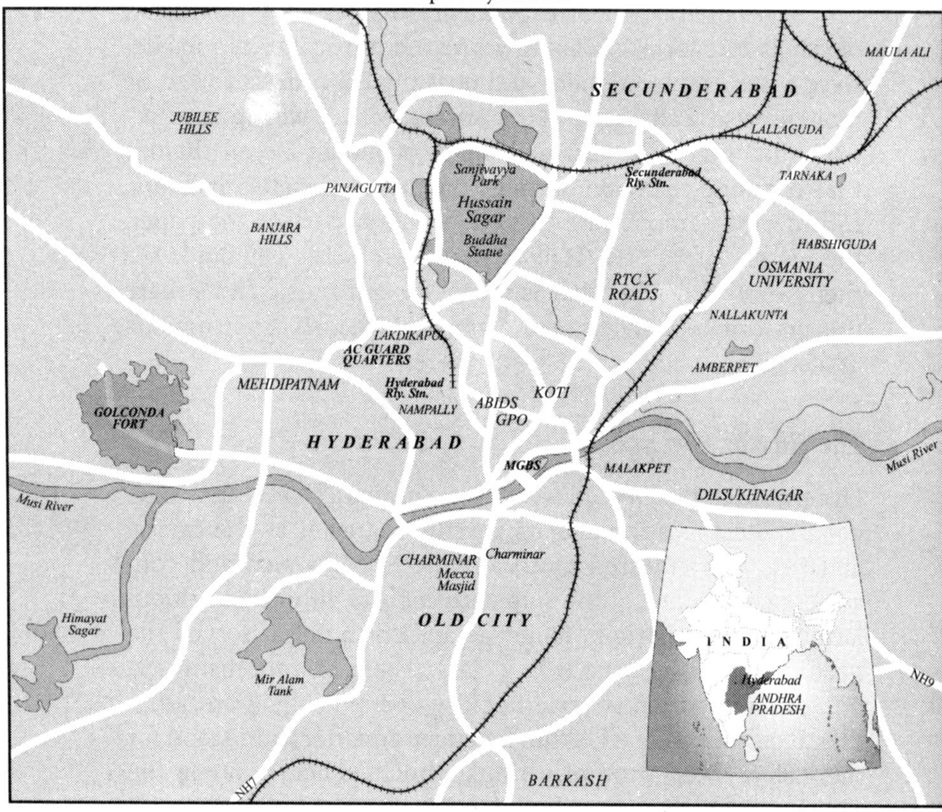

Map 7

> slender minarets.... The city seemed to me of immense extent, but I thought from the number of trees, that it was composed principally of gardens and enclosures, and was much surprised afterwards when I entered it, to find its streets filled with houses, and the whole so thickly populated. (Taylor 2002: 124)

The Deccan sultans had succeeded in building a beautiful city, "the pearl of the Deccan".

In the course of the nineteenth century, the population of Hyderabad increased steadily. Due to the presence of British troops, a twin city developed around the cantonment, called Secunderabad. The old walled city, Andarana, housed a population of about 50,000 people, mainly Muslims.

Religion and population in Hyderabad/Secunderabad, 1881 census

	Hyderabad	*Secunderabad*
Hindus	45,543 (36.8%)	144,972 (62.7%)
Muslims	78,007 (63.1%)	70,826 (30.6%)
Other	125 (0.1%)	15,489 (6.7%)
Total	123,675	231,287

Fourteen per cent of Hyderabad's population was born outside India. Among the eight languages spoken in the city, Urdu (Dakhni) and Telugu were prominent, followed by Arabic, Marwadi and Marathi (Census of India 1881).

The various ethnic and religious communities were concentrated in specific *mohallas*, for instance the Shiite (Irani) population lived north of Char Minar, which is where all their mosques are located and where a lively Moharram tradition is still cultivated. Most of the palaces of the Nizam and Paigah families were within reach of the centre of Hyderabad.

After Independence, Hyderabad city and its population were affected by the collapse of the Nizam's rule and the introduction of a parliamentary system. Hyderabad became the capital of the newly formed state of Andhra Pradesh, with a Hindu-majority population (89 per cent). In the process of a new distribution of power between the coastal Andhra and Telugu Deccan Hindus, the Muslim population was marginalised politically and economically. Traditional architecture, palaces and housing quarters were neglected or torn down and replaced by modern constructions. The Hyderabad city of today shares the fate of other Indian cities, with uncontrolled growth and traffic jams.

Historical Background: Arabs and Africans

The influx of African slaves into the Indian Deccan states was first recorded in the fourteenth century, when Habshis began to play a prominent role in the administration and army of the Bahmani kingdom and its successor states, the Deccan Sultanates (Khalidi 1993; S. Ali 1996). Communities of African and Arab descendants in Andhra Pradesh and particularly Hyderabad city can be traced back to the eighteenth and nineteenth centuries, when the slave trade was revived by local brokers. Slaves served as domestics and were recruited to serve as soldiers in the native armies of local rajas and the ruler of Hyderabad State, the Nizam.

Up until the late seventeenth century, the Shiite Qutb Shah dynasty of the Deccan Sultanate of Golconda ruled over a Hindu population and founded the regal city of Hyderabad. In 1687, its territory was conquered by the Mughal ruler Aurangzeb. The governor of Hyderabad State, the Sunni Qamar-ud-Din, Chin Qilich Khan, was the leading representative of the Turani party in Delhi and the founder of the dynasty of the Nizams of Hyderabad (1712–1948). Although nominally subject to the Mughal emperor, he began to act as an independent power as part of a general struggle for supremacy in the Deccan (1724). The armies employed in the ensuing conflicts between local powers and the British East India Company were ethnically diverse and contained, among others, Arab soldiers and *jamadars* (military officers). In the course of these conflicts, the large territory of Hyderabad State was repeatedly reduced due to its inability to defend itself without the help of the British. By 1800, the British stationed a so-called Subsidiary Force (infantry and cavalry) in Hyderabad "to protect the Nizam", that is, to maintain order in his territory. These troops were under the command of British officers and were paid with the rent surplus of the "Ceded Districts".

The Nizam continued to maintain his own 'native army' (Nazm-i-Jamiat) which consisted of various soldiers and ethnic groups (cf. also Leonard 1978). His army had no central authority, but was commanded by *jagirdar*s (landed aristocrats), Arab jamadars and members of the city's noble families (Paigah). Since the heavy expenses for the maintenance of this army undermined the state's finances, the British kept pressing the Nizam to reform the administrative system. The soldiers were chronically underpaid and thus presented a constant source of potential trouble and revolt in the city. It was not unusual for armed soldiers of different ethnic backgrounds and loyalties to clash in street fights. The government fell hostage to its own army and its vested interests. The British, alarmed by the chaotic conditions of the Nizam's native army, demanded a reduction in the numbers of foreign troops.

Many of the Arab soldiers had been settled in the Deccan for generations. Foreign soldiers from beyond the Indian Ocean were usually subsumed under the term 'Arab', because the trade in African slaves and soldiers was conducted via the Arabian peninsula and the Hadhramaut coast. In British reports, Africans are usually not listed separately or under the terms 'Sidi' or 'Habshi'. The recruitment of Arabs and African slaves was renewed in the decades between 1820 and 1840 (Temple 1868: 17). In 1841, an Arab merchant reported that Hyderabadi agents in Muscat were buying African slaves. In 1842, the British Resident in Hyderabad observed that a heavy traffic in slaves was being conducted in the city by Arabs, "some of whom were mercenary soldiers" (Khalidi 1993: 11). One slave dealer, however, was a Habshi married to a Hyderabadi woman. These slaves were then bought and employed by families as domestic servants, a number of them entering military service, being shipped from the Hadhramaut coast via Bombay. In 1862 a new law required special entry permits from the British Resident in Hyderabad, but these were practically ignored. When, towards the end of the century, checks were established in Bombay, immigrants entered at Karachi and other harbours along the western coast.

Many came from Mukalla on the Hadhramaut coast, situated midway between Aden and Muscat. This port had strong trade relations with the state of Hyderabad. Merchants, including Gujaratis, staying in Mukalla had connections with Arab traders from Mukalla who had settled in Hyderabad. Mukalla also had a considerable African population of dock workers and seamen. Many African seamen sailed to the western Indian coast on Arab *dhows* (S. Ali 1996: 193; cf. Badalkhan, this volume). In 1869, a British official reported that men disguised as women were posing as the wives and daughters of Arab dealers in order to evade Bombay customs regulations (Harris 1971: 101–2). Sometimes, Arabs from Hyderabad returned from a pilgrimage to Mecca with one or two Africans posing as members of the family.

The majority of the 800 Arabs counted in the cantonment of Hyderabad in the middle of the nineteenth century, by contrast, were born in the Deccan and had migrated to Hyderabad from neighbouring territories. They were thoroughly integrated into the local power structure and could not possibly be shipped back to the Hadhramaut coast. They used their arms to collect revenue in the districts and to protect a lucrative business as moneylenders (*saukars*). Since the Nizam could not pay them, they were compensated with the right to collect the revenue of entire districts. In about 1845, the British Resident described the Arabs as "sober, steady men, for the most part earning good pay, [lending] their savings, at what we should call usurous interest, to borrowers of every rank and class, through the medium of their jamadars or superior officers, who undertook to collect and administer the fund and to give each man his due." Sometines "a landed estate or a district was occupied by force, and the jamadar in possession collected the rent or the revenue for the benefit of his band" (Fraser 1885: 239). The Arab jamadars maintained their own court of law and a jail. It can be assumed that Hyderabadi Arabs were also involved in the slave trade with the Arab coast.

Temple reports the presence of almost 6,000 Arabs (out of a total of 24,000 soldiers) in the infantry of the Nizam's native army for the year 1868. This number does not include all those Arab or African troops in the service of the Nizam's feudal lords, jagirdars, or Hindu *rajas*, called *samasthans*. These were Hindu families with a history going back some three hundred years and with strong local roots.[2]

In 1860, the Nizam's minister, Salar Jung, began to reform parts of the irregular troops of the Nizam's army. The intention was to centralise its command, discipline its men and become independent of the British-administered contingent. In 1872, a mounted 'African Guard', was listed among the reformed cavalry. Apparently this African Guard had been part of the late Raja of Wanaparthy's army. In the 1850, the Raja of Wanaparthy had bought a number of slaves in Bombay. "These served as the praetorian guard in his principality. In 1863, the raja was asked to 'loan' his African Cavalry Guard (the 'AC Guards') also known as the African bodyguards" (Khalidi 1993: 12). This was commonly called 'Risala-i Hubbush', which then became a permanent part of the irregular army. By 1895, the African Cavalry Guards numbered 305 mounted troopers. Membership became hereditary. The African Guards were given free quarters in a new cantonment at Masab Tank. They were generally watched with suspicion and even fear. Although Habshis came from many different parts of eastern Africa, they were bound together by a common fate and a common faith, most of them being Sunni Muslims. As soldiers in the Nizam's army, they perceived their economic position as being privileged and secure.

When the British Resident discovered arms factories in the old city of Hyderabad, the British clamped down on the 'reform'. The jamadars were generally opposed to the reform because they were beginning to lose their clients and power as a result. When Salar Jung died in 1883, all reforms came to a halt. The British government in Calcutta lost interest in the condition of the native army after the Nizam contributed 800 mounted troops under native command to the Imperial Ser-

[2] The three most important samasthans were Wanaparthy, Jatpole (Mahbubnagar district) and Gadwal.

vice Corps (1892).[3] Consequently, it maintained its original character as the 'colourful', ethnically diverse and unruly collection of soldiers described by Singh. The irregular army "was composed of many races, has no distinct uniform, and men, therefore, wear their national dress and carry old fashioned arms. In feature and costume they differ so widely that to see three or four of them is to witness a picturesque spectacle not easily forgotten" (Singh 1923: 130).

The advent of India's independence and of a parliamentary system was perceived as a threat to Muslim (minority) rule in Hyderabad. The Nizam decided to remain outside the Indian Union. The expected end of the Nizam's rule, however, led to the polarisation of the two religious communities. Muslims organised in the Razakar movement pressured the Hindu population. When, in 1948, the Indian Army moved into the state of Hyderabad, it met with little resistance. In September of that year Hyderabad State merged with the Indian Union. The Nizam's feudal government was dissolved, and innumerable Muslims, rich and poor alike, including Arab and African (Habshi) soldiers, lost their patron. According to Khalidi, many Arabs and Habshis were deported to Aden or left for Pakistan. By 1950, the Nizam's army had been disbanded by the new government.

The Muslim minority (11 per cent) was ill prepared for the dramatic change in the political system, both the ruling elite—parts of which subsequently migrated to Pakistan—and their dependants. One such ethnic community was the Habshi of Hyderabad. The Habshi and Yemeni ex-soldiery generally had no wealth and had no other profession. They were often illiterate, and their pensions were insufficient to sustain a large family. Many were forced into unskilled low-salary jobs, some working as *khanazad* (house boys). The greater part of the Habshi community stayed on in the area of the former quar-

[3] Calcutta informed the Secretary of State for India in London that the native troops could not be disbanded because of its many important local functions, but also because it posed no threat to the British power, due to its lack of discipline and ineffective arms.

ters of the 'Risala-i-Hubbush', which by that time had come to be known as 'Sidi Risala' and to be regarded as 'a neighbourhood of slums' in the city of Hyderabad.

The Contested Identities of the Yemeni-Habshi

At present, the old quarter of the AC Guard is still home to a large number of Chaush households, the total number of which was estimated by community leaders in 2001 as roughly 8,000. Another important area of residence for the Chaush is Barkash, at the other end of the city. The name 'Chaush' originally refers to the position of Arab and Habshi soldiers in the military organisation. As we have seen, the two ethnic categories were not only lumped together by the colonial administration, they also shared a common background established by Indian Ocean maritime connections between the Hadhramaut coast and Zanzibar (cf. Sheriff, this volume). Today the name Chaush is used by both Yemeni and Habshi people. On the most basic level, the difference between the Yemeni and Habshi is conceptualised in terms of patrilineages with different apical ancestors. Thus whereas Yemeni refer to various lineage ancestors of the Hadhramaut coast and Somalia, Habshi trace their pedigree to Hazrat Bilal, the Abyssinian companion of the Prophet and first caller to prayer in Mecca.[4] On another level, there is a status distinction associated with the spatial claims of 'original' Yemeni or 'African' origins. This distinction is further manifested in the contrast between the two main areas of residence: Habshi tend to live in the AC Guard quarters, Yemeni in Barkash. Moreover, Yemeni informants in Barkash stress status distinctions by reference to hypergamous marriage rules. A Yemeni man would marry a Habshi woman, it is said, but would not give his sister to a Habshi man.[5] Habshi in the so-called 'AC Guard quarter' or 'Sidi

[4] The same idea of descent from Hazrat Bilal is articulated by the Sidis in Gujarat and Sheedi in Sindh (cf. Basu 1998, 2000).

[5] Given that Yemeni and Habshi were both all-male Indian Ocean populations who married local women in Hyderabad, the struggle over Yemeni and Habshi origins is an exclusively male discourse.

Risala', by contrast, tend to downplay status distinctions by claiming that their forefathers had first come, in the very distant past, from Africa to Yemen, from where they had moved on to Hyderabad together with Yemenis. Other Habshi, however, still remember a predecessor having come from Zanzibar, as in the following recollections of a very old man:

> My father was from Zanzibar. He found work on a British ship when he was young and not yet married. One day, their ship arrived in Bombay. My father and some of his friends decided to stay in Bombay rather than go back home because they found life much better here than in Zanzibar. At that time, Mahboob Ali Khan, the ninth Nizam (1869–1911), went to Bombay with one of his Hindu officials, who was a Raja. In Bombay the Nizam came across some of the Africans. He then sent his officers to bring some Africans to be his bodyguards. At first twelve Africans were brought from Bombay. Later three hundred more followed, of whom my father was one.

Still, most Chaush today prefer to identify with Yemen instead of Africa as their place of origin and as a social marker in their present environment in Hyderabad. While outsiders, Indians and others, continually and increasingly confront them with their presumed 'African-ness', Chaush respond with intensified protestations of denial. In their view 'Africa' is associated with the stigma of slavery, from which they are striving to rid themselves.

Situated at the lower level of the urban economy, Chaush derive their livelihood mostly from activities such as shopkeeping, providing a variety of services (e.g. as barbers, cooks, taxi drivers etc.) and crafts (e.g. plumbing, electrical work etc.). The better-off are employed in government services. In addition, some Chaush also derive an income as musicians performing daff. A considerable number of young men, moreover, are migrating to Middle Eastern countries in search of work. The influence exercised by migrant labourers upon those who remain in Hyderabad is noticeable in reinforced identifications with Yemen, on the one hand, and a growing trend towards the purification of Islamic practices, on the other. The latter has a specific bearing on the practice of daff music, which used to be (and to some extent still is) an important source of income for the poorer sections of the Chaush people. Thus, there is considerable debate going on among Chaush whether performing daff music is in accordance with Islamic law or not, and many in the community frown on those who continue to do so.

Criticisms of daff performances are mainly made by Islamic reformers whose aim is the purification of Muslim practices. Young Muslim men in Hyderabad display a noticeable fervour in living up to the moral standards believed to have been laid down in the Qur'an. In their view, daff performances are driven by sensuality and incite actions that are perceived as immoral and thus belong to the realm of the demonic. A situation was witnessed in which a daff group had been invited by members of a Muslim family to perform during a wedding feast. When the group arrived at the marriage hall, the bridegroom, as a pious Muslim, strongly objected to the idea of watching a daff performance at his own wedding. In spite of his relatives' disappointment, the bridegroom refused to proceed with the wedding rituals until the daff party was sent away.

Daff Music: Performing 'Arabness'

In the past, Chaush musicians used to be summoned to the palace of the Nizam to perform daff music for festivals, royal coronations and other official state events.[6] Today, Chaush perform daff during the annual saint's day celebrations at Sufi shrines, for example at the *dargah* (shrine) of the Yemeni saint Habib Idrus in the centre of the city. Moreover, daff has not only become a popular entertainment performed for money and on demand from wealthy customers at weddings, but also at hotels for Indian and foreign tourists and during cultural festivals organised by the government, or, recently, certain other cultural organisations. To meet these demands, in the quarter of AC Guards several organised daff groups have been

[6] Similar customs were observed at the court of the Sultanates of Yemen in the past. Soldiers formed musical bands that used to play at state events (Abdulbaki 1999).

formed with names like 'Chota Abbu Marfa Party' or 'Arabi Daff Party'. The leaders of these groups own their instruments, train five to fifteen musicians and manage performance contracts.

The instruments most commonly used in these performances are 1) The daff, a circular drum held in the left hand and played with a stick in the right; 2) The *marfa*, a larger two-membrane drum slung around the waist; 3) brass water vessels used as an instrument, again played with wooden sticks; 4) sometimes a *tamburah*, a stringed instrument, and a *musmala*, a kind of a flute. During a daff party performance, about five to six daff, three to four marfa, one or two brass vessels, and, if at all, one tamburah and one flute are played. Except possibly for the daff, the other instruments are employed in Indian music as well, or are of Indian origin. The drum that Chaush call a marfa is the same as the Indian *dhol* (two-membrane kettle drum). The daff resembles the *al-marfa'a* drum used in Yemeni folk dances. Moreover, all of these instruments are well-known and employed in Yemeni music, as a description by Abdulbaki shows:[7]

> The...drum, called in Tihama [a region of Yemen] Al-Marfa'a is hollow on the inside [and] covered on top with a piece of cow's skin tightly fastened down. The group usually performs their dance with the notes of the flute and the beats of the drums. The group begin this dance in a row...and later they move around themselves in circular motions. Suddenly, the tempo of the dancers turns into fast bodily motions as the dancers will go down and move up in a quick and stunning successive motions. (Abdulbaki 1999)

The double-membrane drum that Chaush in Hyderabad call a marfa, on the other hand, resembles also a drum called *mzindo* in Zanzibar, which is used in *ngoma ya habshia* performances (cf. Basu, this volume).[8] As in Yemen but unlike in

[7] Conversely, Yemeni music is apparently characterised considerable musical influence from India (Bakewell 1995). The tamburah is used and *ghazal* is the name of sung love poetry practiced by Yemeni fishermen (Ibid.).

[8] *Ngoma ya habshia* refers simultaneously to a type of drum and to possession rituals that deal with spirits originating in Ethiopia. The same type of drum is used in Sidi goma and damal performances in Gujarat.

Zanzibar or Gujarat, drumming and dancing are exclusively male activities. Women take no part in daff performances. And although the names of the daff parties tend to privilege Arab references, daff is performed by men of both Yemeni and Habshi sections. There is, however, considerable competition between existing daff parties for contracts and artistic recognition.

During a performance, the players wear brightly coloured *lungis* (loin cloths) covered by a loose white shirt. To begin with, the musicians (usually about twelve) line up in two rows facing each other. One row carries daff, while the other carries marfa drums and brass vessels. Gradually, the musicians move into a circle while beating their instruments, a form very much resembling the Yemeni performance described in the above quotation. Proficient dancers, singly or in pairs, carry sticks in their raised hands and move their bodies up and down to the rhythm of the drums while turning on their own axis. Daff music builds on a repertoire of several rhythms. Daff performances are only rarely accompanied by singing, but they feature cries such as "Ya Abu Bakr, Ya Hazrat Abu Salah, Hazrat Kayamba Rehmatulallah". According to informants, these are Arabic invocations of Hasaniu-l-Hussaini Dastagir referring to Abdul Quader Gilani by one of the many names used by Indian Muslims for the founder of the Quadiria brotherhood, who died in Baghdad in 1166. These invocations, the Chaush explained, were uttered when the flag of the saint was raised over his tomb in Baghdad at the time of his death.

All this seems to underline the fact that daff music stresses Arabic rather than African links by means of performance. Ironically, however, and contrary to the strategies of creating images of identity deployed by Chaush themselves, the popularity of daff music spread by the media hinges on stereotypes of 'Africanness'. For example, *The Hyderabad Chronicle* wrote on 14 February 2001: "Wearing traditional headgear [consisting of peacock feathers], long *kurta* and *lunghi,* the band is a treat to listen to and watch. From routine wedding parties to the five star hotels, Abbu Bhai's [daff] band is in demand, as it is a rarity. And why not, as they say, 'Black is Beautiful'. The proof of which can be found in AC Guards". Once the state government of Andhra Pradesh hosted an African-American diplomat in a luxury hotel. To pay respect to his ancestry, Hyderabad government officers sponsored a performance by 'African Indians'. They did their best to meet expectations of their appearing 'African' by decorating their heads with peacock feathers. However, the African-American diplomat was apparently appalled and soon requested that the performance be stopped.

Yet traces of African musical traditions are not completely absent in Hyderabad. Allen Roberts, a specialist in African anthropology who visited Hyderabad in the late 1990s with a team of students and colleagues, reported the following incident:

> We had read that Chaush still perform. . .music and dance in what are described as 'African' ways. . . . When I asked about this, my questions were. . .met with initial denial, but then a white-haired gentleman, probably in his 50s or so, stepped forward and said that he did indeed remember a song and accompanying dance that he had learned from his grandfather. He informed us that he did not know what the words mean, but that he would be happy to sing the song and perform the dance for us. . . . The man sang his song and did a little dance. . . . Barbara Thompson an anthropology graduate student studying spirit possession in Tanzania [and a member of the team]—much to our surprise, and that of our Indian hosts, then sang the refrain to the same song. . . . As she then explained [in Tanzania] it was sung in Shambaa [a Bantu language spoken in north-eastern Tanzania], and is a song still commonly used in the first moments of possession rituals, performed to effect healing. (Quoted in Alpers 2003: 34–5)

Perhaps the song heard by Roberts and his team is the one that Minda transcribed in 2002.[9] Again, nobody could be found who knew the meanings of the words. However, what this incident indicates is that daff music has its origins in multiple

[9] *kulala yem toto*
kulala way
shekrem tembo (or *shembo)*
toto kulala way
olala yemgo shakram shembo (or *tembo*)
alilaya gom lambiyasa musalmara
yaburaka abusala oleya oleba simba
yahabole wahambole simbo tamtam tole
yabaya bamsalanga

sources, most noticeably Arab and African. Depending on the context of the performance, daff music may be defined as either Yemeni or Habshi.

Conclusion

As we hope to have shown, the history of Chaush in Hyderabad has become embodied in their music. Contestations of both African origins and music-making reflect on one level the struggle of Chaush to come to terms with being labelled 'former African slaves' (*ghulam*), while on another level Islamic identity and status are being negotiated. The privileging of 'Arabness' may be understood in two contexts: 1) in relation to the actual life-world in which Chaush are situated in contemporary Hyderabad; and 2) as a reflection of Indian Ocean realities that have been implemented in Hyderabad through relationships of power in the colonial period. Thus, trans-ocean trade and seafaring connections did not end in the port towns of the coast but extended far inland into the subcontinent. In addition to providing transport facilities for Muslim pilgrims from Hyderabad on their way to Mecca, they also channelled the spread of common patterns of court culture established by Muslim rulers in which soldiers and bodyguards from places across the ocean were regularly employed. Thus, while the Sultan of Zanzibar maintained a bodyguard of Baluchis, the Nizam of Hyderabad had Arab and Habshi soldiers, as did many other rulers in India, Hindu as well as Muslim. A regular feature of court culture and state rituals is the employment of music to mark specific events. The forming of bands from the military, like the Yemeni-Habshi bodyguards, may have received further encouragement from colonial patterns of military music bands. In any case, the daff music of Chaush seems closely related to their history at the court of the Nizam. But at another level the specific relationship that Chaush emphasise between Arabs and Africans points to realities across the Indian ocean, to the coasts of the Swahili and southern Arabia, which were shaped in major ways by Arab and African interactions and fusions of cultural styles.

Glossary

abru	reputation, honour (Kachchhi)
adharma	anti-religion
amba	musical style (Baluchistan)
areke	vow (Kannada)
astana	saints' shrines (Baluchistan)
asura	demon
atma	soul
avatar	divine incarnation
baghalas	Arab. sailing ship (100–300 tons)
baithak	spirit mediumship séances held by Parsis
bakshi	military paymaster
balako	child; initiant through a Sidi fakir (Gujarat
bandh:	all-day strike
basadi	Jain temple
batti	lamp
bazar	market
bebes	ladies (Swahili)
beden	fishing boat (Oman)
bhut	Hindu spirits
bhuta kola	ceremony performed for a spirit (Karnataka)
bhuta	deity, spirits associated with the mountain paths (Karnataka)
bhutasthana	shrine of a spirit (Karnataka)
bint	girls, daughter (Arabic)
bismillah	In the name of Allah
buibui	black women's garment (Swahili)
bum, boom	Kuwaiti sailing ship
cadjan	coconut thatch (Sinhalese)
cadju	cashew (Sinhalese)
casado	a settler of Portuguese or mixed Portuguese-Indian *descent (Goa)*
cenne mane	Tulu game (Karnataka)
chadar	cloths or flower carpet gifted to a Sufi saint's tomb
chandra	moon
chandraat	new moon

chilla	memorial shrine of Sidi-Sufi saints
choras	a board game played with stones
chovatiya	leader
daanya	wooden mace
dada	black (Baluchistan)
daff	tambourine, drum (Hyderabad)
damal	Sidi ritual music
dargah	Sufi shrine, tomb of a saint
dariya	sea
dariya chhoru	sons of the sea (Kachchhi)
darsana	vision of a divinity
darshan patri	possessed priest
darzadag	stranger (Baluchi)
dast	hand, unit of measurement from the tip of the stretched middle finger to the elbow
dhangi	Indian sailing ship
dayara	meeting
dharma	religion
dhol	double membrane drum (big)
dholak	double membrane drum (small)
dhow	the Arab sailing ship
fundi	ritual specialist (Swahili)
gadi varas	ritual head of a (Sidi-)Sufi shrine
gana	companion
gende seva	fire walking
ghanja	Arab sailing ship
ghat	ritual performed by Parsis for Mai Mishra
ghee	clarified butter
ghulam	slave
gurab	ship
gurr	conch shell (Baluchi)
gurukar	village dignitary (Kannada)
gutu	matrilineal line
gwat	healing ceremony
hadithi	stories (Swahili)
hajri	presence; state of possession
hal	trance, ecstacy, positive form of possession (Gujarat)
hawala	promissory note system of money transfers
ishk	love
ishtdevta	personal deity
jagirdar	landed aristocrat
jamadar	military officer

jamat	Muslim kinship association (caste)
jawabi	chorus (Baluchi)
jinnat	Muslim spirit
jhikar	remembering the names of God (from Ar. dhikr)
goma	ritual music, drum, possession
jim	conch trumpets
jinnat	Muslim spirits
jumme raat	Thursday
kachbo	tortoise (Kachchhi)
kaffree	African
kangas	Swahili women's dress
kanzu	Swahili male dress
kavo	coffee (Ar.)
khadim	servant
khalaasi	sailor
khel	play
khichadi	rice-lentil dish
khidmat	service
kosara	sack of dates
ksetrapal	Hindu guardian deity
ksharavahas	salt carriers
laskhar	sailor, longshoreman, soldier
laywa	Baluchi musical genre
lewa	Omani musical genre
loban	incense
madhi	seat within a temple
magane	domain
magrib azzan	evening prayer call
mahajan	merchant guild
majlis	sitting room in an Arab house
makandar	interpreter
malid	votive ritual
mamluk	slave
mannat	vow
marfa	drum
masheitani	spirit (Swahili)
math	Hindu monastery
ma'tuq	emancipated
miswak	toothbrush made from a twig
mizan	balance scales
mowlood	birthday celebrations for the Prophet Mohammad
msondo	Swahili drum

muadhin	caller to prayers from a mosque
mugarman	standing footed drum
mujavar	ritual servant of a shrine
mujra	dancing-girl performances
mukadam	assistant
murid	disciple of a Sufi master
murshid	fakir teacher
musindo	kettle drum
mzee	honorific title (Swahili)
nadaan	devotee, "innocent one"
nagarchi	drummer
nagarshet	head of a merchant guild
nahan	professional singer
na'ib, naqib	ruler of a Hadhrami port town
nakhoda	captain
naukar	servant, slave
nema	annual possession ceremony
ngoma	ritual drum, possession healing
paddana	Tulu epic
paliyo	memorial stone
pardesi	foreigner
patri	possession priest
pir	Sufi master, saint
piri–muridi	master-disciple relationship
preta	ghost
puja	Hindu worship
purdah	veil; female modesty; female segregation
qawali	Sufi devotional music
ragu	fire
rajandaiva	royal spirit
rakshas	demon
ramato	flag (Baluchi)
rath yatra	chariot pilgrimage
sadhu	holy man
samaj	caste organisation
sambuk	Arab ship
sapari boji	Baluchi sailing ship
sarogan	group leader (dance/song)
sarong	loin cloth of Indonesian origin
saukar	moneylender
savali	supplicant
sedimara	wooden post

shakti	power of the Goddess
shari'ah	Islamic law
shendi	tender coconut
shetti	headman
shidi	black
sime	ancient political unit (Karnataka)
suriya	sun
syah	black
tal	steel plate
talappa	turban
tariqa	Sufi path/order
tarm	block of wood put under the ship when pulled or pushed on the shore
tawere	knife
taravad	house and matrileal household of Nayars
timbuk	small double-headed drums
trisul	trident
ummah	global Muslim community
'urs	annual death celebration of a Sufi saint (Ar. marriage)
uru	village
valima verundu	bridegroom's feast
vanot	president
vepar	merchant
walad	sailor
wali	saint (Arabic)
zabad	a sweet smelling substance
zar	wind; spirits
ziyarram	tomb
zuruk	black slave

References

Abdulbaki, Saleh. 1999. Folkloric dance of Tihama. Yemen Times: http://www.yementimes.com/99/iss27/culture.htm

Abir, Mordechai. 1985. The Ethiopian slave trade and its relation to the Islamic world. In *Slaves and Slavery in Muslim Africa*, vol. 2, ed. J. R. Willis, 123–35. London: Frank Cass.

Abu-Lughod, Janet L. 1989. *Before European Hegemony: The World System,* A.D. 1250–1350. Oxford: Oxford University Press.

Adra, Najwa. 2002. Dance in the Arabian Peninsula. In Danielson et al. 2002, 703–12.

Ahuja, Ravi. 2002. Subaltern networks under British imperialism: Exploring the case of South Asian maritime labour (c. 1890–1947). Paper presented to the International Conference on Cultural Exchange and Transformation in the Indian Ocean World, University of California, Los Angeles.

Aitken, E. H. 1907. *Gazetteer of the Province of Sind*. Karachi: The "Mercantile" Steam Press.

Ali, Ameer. 1986. Politics of survival: Past strategies and present predicament of the Muslim community in Sri Lanka. *Journal Institute of Muslim Minority Affairs* 10 (10): 147–70.

Ali, S. S. 1996. *African Dispersal in the Deccan. From Medieval to Modern Times*. Delhi: Orient Longman.

Al-Khan, W. A., F. Suyyagh et al. 1989. *Laiwa Music of the Gulf.* Vol. 3. Doha, Qatar: The Arab Gulf States Folklore Centre.

Allen, James de Vere. 1980. A proposal for Indian Ocean studies. In *Historical Relations Across the Indian Ocean: Report and Papers of the Meeting of Experts Organized by UNESCO at Port Louis, Mauritius, from 15 to 19 July 1974*, 137–52. Paris: UNESCO.

Alpers, Edward A. 1975. *Ivory and Slaves in East Central Africa*. Berkeley: University of California Press.

———. 1997. The African diaspora in the northwestern Indian Ocean: Reconsideration of an old problem, new directions for research. *Comparative Studies of South Asia, Africa and the Middle East*, 17 (2): 61–81.

———. 2002. Imagining the Indian Ocean world. Opening address to the International Conference on Cultural Exchange and Transformation in the Indian Ocean World, University of California, Los Angeles. [www.accd.edu/sac/history/keller/IndianO/Alpers_IOWorld.pdf]

———. 2003. The African diaspora in the Indian Ocean: A comparative perspective. In Jayasuriya and Pankhurst 2003, 19–52.

Amiji, H. M. 1983. The Asiatic bias in the historiography of the East African coast. *Journal of African Studies* 10: 66–72.

Amin, Shahid. 1995. *Event, Metaphor, Memory: Chauri Chaura, 1922–1992.* Delhi: Oxford University Press.

Anderson, Benedict. 1983. *Imagined Communities: Reflections on the Origins and Spread of Nationalism.* London: Verso.

Appadurai, A. 1996. *Modernity at Large: Cultural Dimensions of Globalization.* Minneapolis: University of Minnesota Press.

———. ed. 2000a. *Globalization.* Special issue of *Public Culture.* Durham: Duke University Press.

———. 2000b. Grassroots globalization and the research imagination. In Appadurai 2000a 1–20.

Apter, Andrew. 1991. Herskovit's heritage: Rethinking syncretism in the African diaspora. *Diaspora* 1 (3): 235–60.

Arasaratnam, S. 1990. Recent trends in the historiography of the Indian Ocean, 1500 to 1800. *Journal of World History* 1–2: 225–48.

Arp, Susmita. 2000. *Kalapani: Zum Streit über die Zulässigkeit von Seereisen im kolonialzeitlichen Indien.* Stuttgart: Franz Steiner Verlag.

Azeez, I. L. M. Abdul. 1957. *A Criticism of Mr Ramanathan's "Ethnology of the "Moors" of Ceylon".* Originally published under the auspices of the Moor's Union, Colombo in 1907. The Moor's Islamic Cultural Home Incorporated, Colombo 9.

Badalkhan, Sabir. 2000a. Balochistan. In *The Garland Encyclopaedia of World Music.* Vol. 5, *South Asia: The Indian Subcontinent,* ed. Arnold, 773–84. New York, London: The Garland Publishing Inc.

———. 2002a. The Baloch spirit healing ritual of Gwat and its relations to the north African Ritual of zar. Talk given at the Department of World Arts and Cultures, University of California, Los Angeles.

———. 2002b. Coastal Makran as corridor to the Indian Ocean World. *Eurasian Studies* 1 (2): 237–62.

Bakewell, A. D. 1995. Traditional music in Yemen. http://www.al-bab.com/bys/articles/bakewell95.htm

Baluchistan District Gazetteer, Makran. 1986 [1907] Quetta: Gosha-e Adab. Bombay: Bombay Educational Press.

Banga, I., ed. 1992. *Ports and Their Hinterlands in India,* 1700–1950. Delhi: Manohar.

Banks, M. 1992. *Organizing Jainism in India and England.* Oxford: Clarendon.

Barendse, R. J. 1999. On the Arabian Seas in the eighteenth century. Paper presented to the workshop on Western India and the Indian Ocean, Heidelberg.

———. 2002. *The Arabian Seas: The Indian Ocean World of the Seventeenth Century*. Armonk, NY: M. E. Sharpe.

Basu, Helene. 1993. The Sidi and the cult of Bava Gor in Gujarat. *Journal of Indian Anthropological Society* 28: 289–300.

———. 1995. *Habshi-Sklaven, Sidi-Fakire. Muslimische Heilgenverehrung im westlichen Indien*. Berlin: Das Arabische Buch.

———. 1998. Hierarchy and emotion: Love, joy, and sorrow in a cult of black saints in Gujarat, India. In *Modernity, Locality and the Performance of Emotion in Sufi Cults*, ed. P. Werbner and H. Basu, 117–39. London: Routledge

———. 2000. Theatre of memory: Ritual kinship performances of the African diaspora in Pakistan. In *Culture, Creation and Procreation in South Asia*, ed. A. Rao and M. Boeck, 243–70. Oxford: Berghahn.

———. 2001. Africans in India: Past and present. *Internationales Asienforum/International Quarterly for Asian Studies* 32: 253–74.

———. 2002. Indian Sidi–African diasporas: A query. Paper presented to the International Conference on Cultural Exchange and Transformation in the Indian Ocean World, University of California-Los Angeles.

———. 2003. Slave, soldier, trader, fakir: Fragments of African histories in Gujarat. In Jayasuriya and Pankhurst 2003, 223–50.

———. 2004b. Drumming and Praying: Sidi at the junction of spirit possession and Islam. Proceedings of the workshop on Struggling with History, ed. E. Simpson and K. Kresse. St. Andrews, Scotland.

Beachey, R. W. 1976. *The Slave Trade of Eastern Africa*. London: Rex Collins.

Behrend, Heike, and Ute Luig, eds. 1999. *Spirit Possession: Modernity and Power in Africa*. Oxford: James Currey.

Bertz, Ned. 1998. Indian immigration in East Africa before the Second World War: Railways and racialism in the historiography of the migration of traders, indentured laborers, and dukawallahs. M.A. Essay, University of Iowa.

Bhatt, G. 1975. *Studies in Tuluva History and Culture*. Manipal: Published by the author.

Blackburn, S. H. 1985. Death and deification: Folk-cults in Hinduism. *History of Religions* 24, (3): 255–74.

Boddy, Janice. 1989. *Wombs and Alien Spirits: Women, Men, and the Zar Cult in Northern Sudan*. Madison: University of Wisconsin Press.

———. 1994. Spirit possession revisited: Beyond instrumentality. *Annual Review of Anthropology*, 407–34.

Boehringer-Thaerigen, Gabriele 1996. *Besessene Frauen: Der zar-Kult von Omdurman*. Wuppertau: Trickster im Hammer Verlag.

Borsa, G. 1990a. Recent trends in Indian Ocean historiography. In Borsa 1990b, 3–14.

Borsa, G., ed. 1990b. *Trade and Politics in the Indian Ocean*. Delhi: Manohar.

Bose, Sugata. 2002. Space and time on the Indian Ocean rim: Theory and history. In Fawaz and Bayly 2002, 365–86.

Boxer, C. R. 1969. *The Portuguese Seaborne Empire, 1415–1825*. London: Hutchinson.

Braudel, F. 1995 [1949; 1996]. *The Mediterranean and the Mediterranean World in the Age of Philip II*. Trans. Siân Reynolds. 2 vols. Berkeley, CA: University of California Press.

Brennan, James R. 1999. Indian nationalism in an African context: The case of Tanzania. Paper presented at the Western India and the Indian Ocean workshop, Heidelberg, Germany.

———. 2002. Nation, race and urbanization in Dar es Salaam, Tanzania, 1916–1976. Ph.D. Diss., Northwestern University.

Broeze, Frank, ed. 1989. *Brides of the Sea: Port Cities of Asia from the 11th to the 20th Centuries*. Sydney: New South Wales.

Brubaker, Rogers, and Frederick Cooper. 2000. Beyond 'Identity.' *Theory and Society* 29: 1–47.

Brueckner, H. 1995. *Fuerstliche Feste. Texte und Rituale der Tulu-Volksreligion an der Westkueste Suedendiens*, Neuindische Studien 12. Wiesbaden: Harrassowitz.

Brunschvig, R. 1971. Abd. *Encyclopedia of Islam*, 24–40. Leiden: Brill.

Burnell, A. C. 1894–97. The Devil Worship of the Tuluvas from the Papers of the late A.C. Burnell, ed. by MaJ. R. C. Temple. *Indian Antiquary*, 23–26 (vol. 23, 1894: 1–24; 29–49; 85–99; 183–93; vol. 24, 1895: 113–21; 141–53; 211–15; 242–44; 267–72; vol. 25, 1896: 61–72; 216–27; 237–42; 272–77; 295–310; 328–42; vol. 26, 1897: 47–53; 60–69).

Campbell, Gwyn. 2004. Indian Ocean Africa: A new paradigm for the study of the economic impact of Islam in East Africa. Paper presented to the workshop on Struggling with History, University of St. Andrews, Scotland.

Carrin, M. 1997a. *Enfants de la Déesse, Dévotion et Prêtrise Féminines au Bengale*. Paris: CNRS Editions et Editions de la Maison des Sciences de l'Homme.

———. 1997b. Le spectacle des *bhuta*, observations sur les rapports du théâtre et du rituel.

Purusartha 20: 247–268.

———. 2002. La Forêt désenchantée: Relations de pouvoir et culte des bhuta au Nord et au Sud du Karnataka. In *L'homme et la forêt en inde du Sud, Modes de gestion et symbolisme dans les Ghâts occidentaux*, ed. Pouchepadass and Puyravaud, 292–339. Pondichéry-Karthala: Institut Français.

Casson, L. 1989. *The Periplus Maris Erythraeai*. Princeton: Princeton University Press.

Catlin-Jairazbhoy, Amy. 2002. To tour or to be toured: Sidi African-Indian at home and abroad. Paper presented to the International Conference on Cultural Exchange and Transformation in the Indian Ocean World, University of California-Los Angeles.

Catlin-Jairazbhoy, Amy, and Edward A. Alpers, eds. 2004. *Sidis and Scholars: Essays on African Indians*. New Delhi: Rainbow Publishers.

Census of India. 1881. *Hyderabad, Vol. I, Statement I and IX*. Bombay: Government Publications.

Chakrabarty, Dipesh. 1992. Postcoloniality and the artifice of history: Who speaks for 'Indian' pasts? *Representations* 37: 1–26.

Chakravarti, Anand. 2001. *Social Power and Everyday Class Relations: Agrarian Transformation in North Bihar*. New Delhi: Sage Publications India, Pvt. Ltd.

Chandra, Moti. 1993. *The World of the Courtesan*. Delhi: Vikas Publishing House.

Chatterjee, Indrani. 1999. *Gender, Slavery and Law in Colonial India*. Delhi: Oxford University Press.

Chatterjee, Partha. 1993. *The Nation and its Fragments: Colonial and Postcolonial Histories*. Princeton, NJ: Princeton University Press.

Chaudhuri, K. N. 1985. *Trade and Civilisation in the Indian Ocean: An Economic History from the Rise of Islam to 1750*. Cambridge: Cambridge University Press.

Christensen, Dieter. 2002. Musical life in Sohar, Oman. In Danielson et al. 2002, 671–83.

Claus, P. J. 1971 Kinship organization of the Bant-Nadava Complex. UMI Dissertation Services, Ann Arbor, Michigan.

———. 1978. Oral traditions, royal cults and materials for a reconsideration of the caste system in South India, *Journal of Indian Folkloristics* 20: 1–25.

———. 1986. Playing *cenne*: The meanings of a folk game. In *Another Harmony: New essays on the folklore of India*. ed. Stuart Blackburn and A. K. Ramanujan, 265–93. Berkeley: University of California Press

Clifford, James. 1997. *Routes: Travel and Translation in the Late Twentieth Century*. Cambridge, MA: Harvard University Press.

Crapanzano, Vincent, and Vivian Garrison, eds. 1977. *Case Studies in Spirit Possession*. New York: John Wiley & Sons.

Currie, P. M.1992. *The Shrine and Cult of Mu'in al-din Chishti of Ajmer*. Delhi: Oxford University Press.

Dale, Stephen F. 1980. *Islamic Society on the South Asian Frontier*. Oxford: Clarendon Press.

———. 1986. Review of *Islam in Asia*. Vol. 1, *South Asia*, ed. Yohamen Friedman. *Journal of Asian Studies* 45(3): 624–25.

Danielson, V., S. Marcus, and D. Reynolds, eds. *The Garland Encyclopedia of World Music*. Vol. 6: *The Middle East*. New York, London: Routledge.

Das Gupta, Ashin. 1967. *Malabar in Asian Trade, 1740–1800*. Cambridge: Cambridge University Press.

———. 1994a. *Indian Merchants and the Decline of Surat*. Delhi: Manohar. [Originally published from Wiesbaden, 1979].

———. 1994b. *Merchants of Maritime India, 1500–1800*. Hampshire, UK: Variorum.

Das Gupta, Ashin, and M. N. Pearson, eds. 1987. *India and the Indian Ocean, 1500–1800*. Calcutta: Oxford University Press.

De Silva, C. R. 1986. Muslim traders in the Indian Ocean in the sixteenth century and the Portuguese impact. In Shukri, 1986, 147–65.

De Silva, K. M. 1981. *A History of Sri Lanka*. Delhi: Oxford University Press.

Deutsch, Jan-Georg, and B. Reinwald, eds. 2002. *Space on the Move: Transformations of the Indian Ocean Seascape in the Nineteenth and Twentieth Century*. Berlin: Klaus Schwarz Verlag.

Dharker, Anil. 2002. Bar bar *dekho*. In *Bombay Times* Anniversary Special, *The Times of India*, 22 October.

Dias Antunes, L. F. 1995. The trade activities of the *Banyans* in Mozambique: Private Indian dynamics in the Portuguese state economy, In Mathew 1995, 301–32.

Dickey, S. 2000. Permeable homes: Domestic service, household space, and the vulnerability of class boundaries in urban India. *American Ethnologist* 27 (2): 462–89.

Disney, A. R. 1978. *Twilight of the Pepper Empire: Portugese Trade in Southwest India in the Early Seventeenth Century*. Cambridge, MA: Harvard University Press.

During, Jean. 1989. *Musique et mystique dans les traditions de l'Iran*, Paris: Institut Français de Recherches en Iran-Peeters.

———. 2002. Music, trance, and therapy in Baluchistan, *Garland Encyclopedia of World Music*. Vol. 6, *The Middle East*, ed. V. Danielson, S. Marcus, and D. Reynolds, 881–90. New York and London: Routledge.

Editorial Committee, Mangalore University. 1991. *Perspectives on Dakshina Kanara and Kodagu*. Mangalore: Mangalore University.

Eickelman, Dale. 1976. *Moroccan Islam: Tradition and Society in a Pilgrimage Centre*. Austin: University of Texas Press.

———. 1977. Ideological change and regional cults: Maraboutism and ties of "closeness" in western Morocco. In *Regional Cults*, ed. R. P. Werbner, 3–28. London: Academic Press.

Ellis, R. H. 1924. *A Short Account of the Laccadive Islands and Minicoy*. Madras: The Government Press.

Ewald, Janet. 2000. Crossers of the sea: Slaves, freedmen, and other migrants in the northwestern Indian Ocean, c. 1750–1914. *American Historical Review* 105 (1): 69–91.

Fawaz, Leila Tarazi, and C. A. Bayly, eds. 2002. *Modernity and Culture: From the Mediterranean to the Indian Ocean*. New York: Columbia University Press.

Field, Henry. 1959 [1985]. *An Anthropological Reconnaissance in West-Pakistan*. Karachi: Indus Publications.

Forbes, Andrew. 1981. Southern Arabia and the Islamicisation of the central Indian archipelagoes. *Archipel* 21: 55–92.

———. 1983. The mosque in the Maldive Islands: A preliminary historical survey. *Archipel* 26: 43–74.

Franke, Richard W. 1992. Land reform versus inequality in Nadur village, Kerala. *Journal of Anthropological Research* 48 (2): 81–116.

Fraser, Hastings. 1885. *Memoir and Correspondence of General James Stuart Fraser.* London: Oriental Press.

Freeman-Grenville, G. S. P. 1962. *East African Coast: Select Documents*. Oxford: Oxford University Press.

Freitag, U., and W. G. Clarence-Smith, eds. 1997. *Hadhrami Traders, Scholars and Statesmen in the Indian Ocean, 1750s–1960s*. Leiden, New York & Köln: Brill.

Friedman, Yohanan, ed. 1984. *Islam in Asia*. Vol. 1, *South Asia*. Jerusalem: The Magnes Press.

Fuglesang, Minou. 1994. *Veils and Videos: Female Youth Culture on the Kenyan Coast*. Stockholm: Stockholm University.

Fuller, C. J. 1975. The Internal Structure of the Nayar Caste. *Journal of Anthropological Research*, 31 (4): 283–312.

———. 1976. *The Nayars Today*. Cambridge: Cambridge University Press.

———. ed. 1997. *Caste Today*. Oxford: Oxford University Press.

Gardner, Katy. 1995. *Global Migrants, Local Lives: Travel and Transformation in Rural Bangladesh*. London: Oxford University Press.

Gazetteer of the Bombay Presidency. 1896. *History of Gujarat*. Vol. 1. Part 1. Bombay: Government Central Press.

———. 1901. *Gujarat population. Hindus*. Vol. IX. Part I. Bombay: Government Central Press.

Geiger, Susan. 1997. *TANU Women: Gender and Culture in the Making of Tanganyikan Nationalism, 1955–1965*. Portsmouth, NH: Heinemann.

Geijbels, M. 1978. Aspects of the veneration of saints in Islam: With special reference to Pakistan. *The Muslim World* 68: 178–86.

Gellner, Ernest. 1972. *Doctor* and Saint. In *Scholars, Saints and Sufis: Muslim Religious Institutions since 1500*, ed. Nikkie Keddie, 307–326. Berkeley: University of California Press.

Ghosh, Amitav. 1988. *The Shadow Lines*. New Delhi: Ravi Dayal.

———. 1992. *In An Antique Land*. Delhi: Ravi Dayal.

Gilbert, Erik. 2002. Contending modernities: Dhows, steamers and cloves in colonial Zanzibar. Paper presented to the International Conference on Cultural Exchange and Transformation in the Indian Ocean World, University of California-Los Angeles.

Giles, Linda L. 1995. Sociocultural Change and Spirit Possession on the Swahili Coast of East Africa. *Anthropological Quarterly* 68 (2): 89–106.

———. 1999. Spirit possession and the symbolic construction of Swahili society. In Behrend and Luig 1999, 142–64.

Gillion, K. L. 1968. *Ahmedabad: A Study in Indian Urban History*. Berkeley: University of California Press.

Gilroy, Paul. 1993. *The Black Atlantic: Modernity and Double Consciousness*. Cambridge, MA: Harvard University Press.

Gladstone, J. W. 1984. *Protestant Christianity and People's Movements in Kerala: A Study of Christian Mass Movements in Relation to Neo-Hindu Socio-Religious Movements in Kerala, 1850–1936*. Trivandrum, Kerala: Seminary Publications.

Gopikuttan, G. 1990. House construction boom in Kerala: Impact on economy and society. *Economic and Political Weekly* 25, September 15: 2083–88.

Gough, Kathleen. 1961. Nayar: Central Kerala. In Schneider and Gough 1961, 298–384.

Graebner, W. 2002. An account of sound: Swahili Taarab and the musical imaginary of the western Indian Ocean. Paper presented to the International Conference on Cultural Exchange and Transformation in the Indian Ocean World, University of California-Los Angeles.

Grant, N. P. 1839. Journal of a route through the western part of Makran, performed in 1809. *Journal of the Royal Asiatic Society* 5: 328–40.

Gregory, Robert G. 1971. *India and East Africa: A History of Race Relations within the British Empire, 1890–1939*. Oxford: Clarendon Press.

———. 1993. *South Asians in East Africa: An Economic and Social History, 1890–1980*. Boulder: Westview Press.

Grönhaug, R. 1974. *Micro-Macro Relations: Social Organization in Antalya, Southern Turkey*. Bergen: Bergen Studies in Social Anthropology.

———. 1978. Scale as a Variable in the Analysis. In *Scale and Social Organization*, ed. F. Barth, 78–121. Oslo: Universitetsforlaget.

Gupta, Akhil, and James Ferguson, eds. 1997. *Culture, Power, Place: Explorations in Critical Anthropology*. Durham and London: Duke University Press.

Gupta, Anirudha, ed. 1991. *Minorities on India's West Coast: History and Society*. Delhi: Kalinga.

Hannerz, U. 1992. *Cultural Complexity: Studies in the Social Organization of Meaning*. New York: Columbia University Press.

Harries, L. 1962. *Swahili Poetry*. Oxford: Clarendon Press.

Harris, Joseph. 1971. *The African Presence in Asia: Consequences of the East African Slave Trade*. Evanston, IL: Northwestern University Press.

———. 2002. The Segmentation of the Indian Ocean Region: Arabs and the Implementation of Immigration Regulations in Zanzibar and British East Africa. In Deutsch and Reinwald 2002, 21–38.

Herskovits, M. 1966. *The New World Negro*. Ed. F. Herskovits, Bloomington: Indiana University Press.

Hodgson, Marshall G. S. 1993. *Rethinking World History: Essays on Europe, Islam, and World History*. Cambridge: Cambridge University Press.

Hollingsworth, L. W. 1960. *The Asians of East Africa*. London: Macmillan & Co.

Horton, Mark, and John Middleton. 2000. *The Swahili: Social Landscape of a Mercantile Society*. Oxford: Blackwell Publishers.

Hourani, G. F. 1951. *Arab Seafaring in the Indian Ocean in Ancient and Early Medieval Times*. Princeton: Princeton University Press.

———. 1990. *Voyages, Vol. III: Inde, Extrême-Orient, Espagne et Soudan*. Paris: Editions La Découverte.

Ibn Battuta. 1994. *The Travels of Ibn Battuta,* AD 1325–1354. Translated by C. F. Beckingham. Vol. 4. Cambridge: Hakluyt Society.

Inda, Jonathan X., and R. Rosaldo, eds. 2002. *The Anthropology of Globalization*. Oxford: Blackwell.

Indrapala, K. 1986. The role of peninsula Indian Muslim trading communities in the Indian Ocean trade. In Shukri 1986, 113–27.

Irshard, Al-Haj Saeed Mohamed. 1984. Impact of Madras education on the lives & times of Muslims of Weligama. In *Mishkathul Baari Souvenir, 1884–1984*, 51–52. Weligama: Sri Lanka Madurasathul Baari Arabic College.

Isaac, T. M. T. 1993. Economic consequences of the Gulf crisis: A study of India with special reference to Kerala. In *The Gulf Crisis and South Asia*. ed. P. Wickramasekara, 59–102. New Delhi: UNDP/ILO.

Jacobson, Doranne.1979. The veil of virtue: Purdah and the Muslim family in the Bhopal region of central India. In *Family, Kinship and Marriage among Muslims in India,* ed. Imtiaz Ahmad. Delhi: Manohar.

Janzen, John M. 1992. *Ngoma: Discourses of Healing in Central and Southern Africa*. Berkeley: University of California Press.

Jarwan, M. R. al-. 1985. *Risalat ila Waladi*. Sharjah: Al-Khaleej.

Jayasuriya, Shihan de Silva, and Richard Pankhurst, eds. 2003. *The African Diaspora in the Indian Ocean*. Trenton, NJ: Africa World Press.

Jefferey, Patricia.1979. *Frogs in a Well*. London: Zed Press.

Jeffrey, Robin. 1993. *Politics, Women and Well-Being: How Kerala Became a Model*. Delhi: Oxford University Press.

Kakar, S. 1996. *The Colors of Violence. Cultural Identities, Religion and Conflict*. Chicago: University of Chicago Press.

Kamerkar, Mani, and Soonu Dhunjisha. 2002. *From the Iranian Plateau to the Shores of Gujarat: The Story of Parsi Settlements and Absorption in India*. Mumbai: Allied Publishers Private Limited.

Kamioka, K., and H. Yajima. 1979. *The Inter-regional Trade in the Western Indian Ocean: The Second Report on the Dhow Trade*. Tokyo: Institute for the Study of Languages and Cultures of Asia and Africa.

Karaka, Dosabhai Framji. 1977 [1884]. *History of the Parsis, including their manners, customs, religion, and present position*. New York: AMS Press.

Khalidi, Omar. 1993. African diaspora in India: The case of the Habashis of the Dakan. *Hamdard Islamicus* 11 (4): 3–21.

Kiribamune, Sirima. 1986. Muslims and the trade of the Arabian Sea with special reference to Sri Lanka from the birth of Islam to the fifteenth century. In Shukri 1986, 89–112.

Kirk, W. 1962. The N. E. monsoon and some aspects of African history. *Journal of African History* 3: 263–67.

Knappert, Jan. 1982. Swahili oral traditions. In *Genres, Forms, Meanings: Essays in African Oral Literature*. ed. V. Görög-Karady, 22–30. Oxford: JASO.

Kramer, Fritz. 1987. *Der rote Fez*. Frankfurt am Main: Syndikat.

Krishnaswamy, S. 1966. A riot in Bombay, August 11, 1893: A study in Hindu-Muslim relations in western India during the late nineteenth century. Ph.D. Diss., University of Chicago.

Kulasuriya, Ananda. 1976. Regional independence and elite change in the politics of 14th century Sri Lanka. *Journal of the Royal Asiatic Society*. 2: 136–55.

Kulke, Eckehard. 1974. *The Parsees in India: A Minority as Agent of Social Change*. Munchen: Weltforum Verlag.

Kurien, Prema A. 2002. *Kaleidoscopic Ethnicity: International Migration and the Reconstruction of Community Identities in India*. New Brunswick, NJ: Rutgers University Press.

Kutty, A. R. 1972. *Marriage and Kinship in an Island Society*. University of Saugar Monographs in Anthropology and Sociology, ed. S. C. Dube. Delhi: National Publishing House.

Lambek, M. 1993. *Knowledge and Practice in Mayotte: Local Discourses of Islam, Sorcery and Spirit Possession*. Toronto: University of Toronto Press.

———. 2000. Localising Islamic Performances in Mayotte. In Parkin and Headley 2000, 63–98.

Larsen, Kjersti. 1998. Spirit possession as historical narrative: The production of identity and locality in Zanzibar town. In *Locality and Belonging*, ed. Nadia Lovell, 125–46. London: Routledge.

Larson, Pier M. 2000. *History and Memory in the Age of Enslavement: Becoming Merina in Highland Madagascar, 1770–1822*. Portsmouth, NH: Heinemann.

Lawrence, Bruce 1984. Early Indo-Muslim saints and conversion. In Friedman 1984, 109–45.

Leonard, Karen. 1978. *Social History of an Indian Caste: The Kayasths of Hyderabad*. Berkeley: University of California Press.

———. 2002. South Asians in the Indian Ocean world: Language, policing, and gender practices in Kuwait and the UAE. Paper presented to the Conference Cultural Exchange and Transformation in the Indian Ocean World, University of California-Los Angeles.

Leur, J. C. van. 1955. *Indonesian Trade & Society*. Hague: W. van Hoeve.

Levy, R. 1965. *The Social Structure of Islam*. Cambridge: Cambridge University Press.

Lewis, Ion M. 1971. *Ectstatic Religion: A Study of Shamanism and Spirit Possession*. London: Routledge.

———. 1986. *Religion in Context: Cults and Charisma*. Cambridge: Cambridge University Press.

Lewis, Martin W., and Karen E. Wigan. 1997. *The Myth of Continents: A Critique of Metageography*. Berkeley: University of California Press.

Lodhi, Abdulaziz Y. 2000. Oriental Influences in Swahili: A Study in Language and Culture Change. Ph.D. diss. Goteborg.

Lokhandwalla, M. 1970. *An Arabic History of Gujarat of ad-Dabir*. Baroda: Oriental Institute.

Lorimer, J. G. 1908–15. *Gazetteer of the Persian Gulf, Oman and Central Arabia*. Calcutta.

Luhrmann, T. M. 1996. *The Good Parsi*. Cambridge and London: Harvard University Press.

Maharaj, H., and V. P. Dwivedi. 1949. *Shri Uderaalaal Aakyaan*. Mumbai: Vichaarshil Prakaashan.

Malekandathil, P. 2001. *Portuguese Cochin and the Maritime Trade of India*, 1500–1663. Delhi: Manohar

Mallah, Issam el-, ed. 1994. *The Complete Documents of the International Symposium on the Traditional Music in Oman*. Wilhelmshaven: F. Noetzel, Heinrichshofen Books.

Mangat, J. S. 1969. *A History of the Asians in East Africa*. Oxford: Clarendon Press.

Markovits, Claude. 2000. *The Global World of Indian Merchants, 1750–1947: Traders of Sind from Bukhara to Panama*. Cambridge: Cambridge University Press.

Martin, E. B. & C. P. Martin. 1978. *Cargoes of the East*. London: Elm Tree Books.

Martin, E. B. 1982. The present-day dhow trade of India. *Great Circle*. 4: 105–18.

———. 1986. Mombasa dhow trade during the past ten years. *Kenya Past and Present*. 18: 47–53.

Mathew, K. S., ed. 1995. *Mariners, Merchants and Oceans: Studies in Maritime History*. Delhi: Manohar.

———. 1997. *Indo-Portuguese Trade and the Fuggers of Germany*. Delhi: Manohar.

Mayer, A. C. 1952. *Land and Society in Malabar*. London: Oxford University Press.

———. 1958. The dominant caste in a region of central India. *Southwestern Journal of Anthropology* 14, 407–27.

Mazrui, Ali A. 1997. Comparative slavery in Islam, Africa and the West: Background to Black reparations. Paper presented at the Istanbul Conference on Islamic Thought.

Mbilinyi, M. L. 1979. Experience in schooling and teacher training. In *Education for Liberation and Development: The Tanzanian Experience*, ed. H. Hinzen and V. H. Hundsdorfer, 76–87. Hamburg: UNESCO Institute for Education.

McGregor, R. S. 1997. *The Oxford Hindi-English Dictionary*. Oxford: Oxford University Press.

McPherson, Kenneth. 1993. *The Indian Ocean: A History of People and the Sea*. Oxford: Oxford University Press.

———. 2002. Port cities as nodal points of change: The Indian Ocean, 1890s–1920s. In Fawaz and Bayly 2002, 75–95.

Mencher, Joan P. 1965. The Nayars of south Malabar. In *Comparative Family Systems*, ed. M. F. Nimkoff, 163–91. Boston: Houghton Mifflin.

———. 1974. "The Caste System Upside Down, or the Not-So-Mysterious East." *Current Anthropology* 15 (4): 469–93.

Middleton, John. 1992. *The World of the Swahili*. New Haven: Yale University Press.

Miller, Roland E. 1992. *Mappila Muslims of Kerala: A Study in Islamic Trends*. Rev. ed. Madras: Orient Longman.

Milner, Murray Jr. 1994. *Status and Sacredness: A General Theory of Status Relations and an Analysis of Indian Culture*. New York: Oxford University Press.

Minda, Ababu. 2004. *An African Indian Community in Hyderabad: Siddi Identity, Its Maintenance and Change*. Goettingen: Cuvillier Verlag.

Mines, Diane P., and Sarah Lamb. 2002. *Everyday Life in South Asia*. Bloomington: Indiana University Press.

Mirzai, Behnaz A. 2002a. African identity in Iranian society. Paper prepared for the International Conference on Blacks and Asians: Encounters through Time and Space, Boston University, 12–14 April, 2002.

———. 2002b. *Zar* in the context of the African diaspora: An overview. Paper presented to the International Conference on Cultural Exchange and Transformation in the Indian Ocean World, University of California-Los Angeles.

Misra, S. C. 1964. *Muslim Communities in Gujarat: Preliminary Studies in Their History and Social Organization*. Bombay: Asia Publishing House.

Moçambique, 1971.

Mohan, Vasundhara. 1985. *Muslims of Sri Lanka*. Jaipur: Aalekh Publishers.

Mollat, M. 1980. The importance of maritime traffic to cultural contacts in the Indian Ocean. *Diogenes* 111: 1–18.

Moore, Melinda A. 1986. A New Look at the Nayar Taravad. *Man* 20: 523–41.

———. 1988. Symbol and meaning in Nayar marriage ritual. *American Ethnologist* 15 (2): 254–73.

Moosvi, S. 1992. The Gujarat ports and their hinterland: The economic relationship. In Banga 1992, 121–29.

Moyer, Eileen Marie. 2002. Dancing a geographic imaginaire: Explorations of the trans-Indian Ocean movements of Bombay Bar girls. Paper presented to the International Conference on Cultural Exchange and Transformation in the Indian Ocean World, University of California-Los Angeles.

———. 2003. In the shadow of the Sheraton: Imagining localities in global spaces in Dar es Salaam, Tanzania. Ph.D. diss., University of Amsterdam.

Mukherjee, Rudrangshu, and Lakshmi Subramanian, eds. 1998. *Politics and Trade in the Indian Ocean World: Essays in Honour of Ashin Das Gupta*. Delhi: Oxford University Press.

Nagar, Richa. 1995. Making and breaking boundaries: Identity politics among South Asians in postcolonial Dar es Salaam. Ph.D. diss, University of Minnesota.

Nanavutty, Piloo. 1977. *The Parsis*. New Delhi: National Book Trust.

Nandy, Pritish. 2002. Love and longing in Mumbai: An illicit drug circuit, police interrogation and loneliness. *The Times of India, Bombay Times*, 11 June.

Nicholls, C. S. 1971. *The Swahili Coast*. London: George Allen & Unwin.

Oldenburg, Veena Talwar. 1992. Lifestyle as resistance: The case of the courtesans of Lucknow. In *Contesting Power: Resistance and Everyday Social Relations in South Asia*, ed. Douglas Haynes, and Gyan Prakash, 23–61. Berkeley: University of California Press.

Osella, Filippo, and Caroline Osella. 2000. *Social Mobility in Kerala: Modernity and Identity in Conflict*. London: Pluto Press.

Palsetia, Jesse S. 2001. *The Parsis of India: Preservation of Identity in Bombay City*. Leiden, Boston, Koln: Brill.

Pandhi, M. B. 1976–77. Naukashastra, nauka sthapatya-no prachin gauravanvit itihas dharavtun—Kachchn-nun vahanvatun. In *Museum Bulletin: Special issue to Honour the Centenary Celebrations of Kutch Museum*, ed. S. K. Bhowmik, 141–72. Museum and Picture Gallery: The Department of Museums, Gujarat State.

Pankhurst, Richard. 2003. The Ethopian Diaspora to India: The Role of Habshis and Sidis from Medieval Times to the End of the Eighteenth Century. In Jayasuriya and Pankhurst 2003, 189–222.

Parkin, David. 2000. Inside and outside the mosque: A master trope. In Parkin and Headley 2000, 1–22.

Parkin, David, and S. C. Headley, eds. 2000. *Islamic Prayer across the Indian Ocean: Inside and Outside the Mosque*. Richmond: Curzon.

Pastner, Carroll, and Stephen Pastner. 1972. Agriculture, kinship and politics in southern Baluchistan. *Man* 7 (1): 128–36.

Patel, J. K. 1991. African settlements in Gujarat. In Anirudh Gupta 1991, 17–24.

Pearson, M. N. 1976. *Merchants and Rulers in Gujarat: The Response to the Portuguese in the Sixteenth Century.* Berkeley: University of California Press.

———, ed. 1981. *Coastal Western India: Studies from the Portuguese Records.* New Delhi: Concept Publishing.

———. 1985. Littoral society: The case for the coast. *Great Circle*, 7/1: 1–8.

———. 1998b. Indians in East Africa: The early modern period. In Mukherjee and Subramanian 1998, 227–49.

———. 2000. Consolidating the faith: Muslim travellers in the Indian Ocean world. *UTS Quarterly: Cultural Studies and New Writing* 6 (2): 6–13.

———. 2003. *The Indian Ocean*. London: Routledge.

Peters, Emrys L. 1990. *The Bedouin of Cyrenaica: Studies in Personal and Corporate Power.* Cambridge: Cambridge University Press.

Pfleiderer, Beatrix. 1981. Mira Datar dargah: The psychiatry of a Muslim shrine. In *Ritual and Religion among Muslims in India*, ed. Imtiaz Ahmad, 195–234. Delhi: Manohar.

Phalaksha, N. 1989. *Political and Cultural History of Karnataka.* Tiptur: Sashi Prakashana.

Pipes, Daniel.1981. *Slave Soldiers and Islam: The Genesis of a Military System.* New Haven: Yale University Press.

Pocock, D. F. 1957. Difference in East Africa: A study of caste and religion in modern Indian society. *Southwestern Journal of Anthropology* 13 (4): 289–300.

Polanyi, K., C. M. Arensberg, and H. Pearson, eds. 1957. *Trade and Market in the Early Empires*. New York: Free Press.

Pollock, S. 1993. Ramayana and political imagination in India. *Journal of Asian Studies* 52 (2): 261–97.

Pouchepadass, J. 1990. The ecological history of the central Western Ghats in the modern period: A preliminary survey. Pondicherry: Pondy Papers in Social Sciences, 6.

Prins, A. H. J. 1965. *Sailing from Lamu*. Assen: Van Gorcum.

———. 1965–66. The Persian Gulf *dhows*: Two variations in maritime enterprise. *Persica* 2: 1–18.

Purpura, Allyson. 2000. Portrait of Seyyid Silma from Zanzibar: Piety and subversion in Islamic prayer. In Parkin and Headley 2000, 117–36.

Rai, Kauleshwar. 1979. *Indians and British Colonialism in East Africa, 1883–1939*. Patna: Associated Book Agency.

Ramesh, R. V. 1970. *A History of South Canara (from the Earliest times to the Fall of Vijayanagara)*. Dharwar: Karnatak University, Research Publications Series, no. 12.

Rao, Damodara 1996. Towards a spatial approach (A speculative exercise with special reference to paaddanas). In *Coastal Karnataka*, ed. U. P. Upadhyaya, 163–75. Udupi: Rastrakavi Govinda Pai Samshodana Kendra.

Ray, A. 1992. Cambay and its hinterland: Early eighteenth century. In Banga 1992, 131–52.

Redfield, R. 1955. The social organization of tradition. *The Far Eastern Quarterly* 15 (1): 13–21.

Reid, Struan. 1993. *The Silk and Spice Routes: Exploration by Sea*. London: UNESCO.

Risso, P. 1995. *Merchants and Faith: Muslim Commerce and Culture in the Indian Ocean*. Boulder: Westview Press.

Roberts, Allen. 2002. The Indian Ocean world and area studies. Opening address to the International Conference on Cultural Exchange and Transformation in the Indian Ocean World, University of California-Los Angeles.

Ryahi, Ali. 1977 [1356]. *Zar va bad va Baloch* [Zar, wind and the Baloch]. Tehran: Tahuri.

Sakarai, L. J. 1980. Indian merchants in East Africa, part one: The triangular trade and the slave economy. *Slavery and Abolition* 1 (3): 292–38.

———. 1981. Indian merchants in East Africa, part two: British imperialism and the transformation of the slave economy. *Slavery and Abolition* 2 (1): 2–30.

Saletore, B. A. 1936. *Ancient Karnataka: History of Tuluva*. Poona: Oriental Book Agency.

Samaraweera, Vijaya. 1986. Aspects of the Muslim revivalist movement, 1889–1915. In Shukri 1986, 113–27.

Sampat, D. D. 1935. Seth Liladhar Morrarji Bhimani. *Bhaatiya Yuvak*, Divali, 131–32.

Schimmel, Annemarie. 1975. *Mystical Dimensions of Islam*. Chapel Hill: The University of California Press.

Schneider, David M., and Kathleen Gough, eds. 1961. *Matrilineal Kinship*. Los Angeles: University of California Press.

Sengers, Gerda. 2003. *Women and Demons: Cult Healing in Islamic Egypt*. Leiden, Boston: Brill.

Severin, T. 1982. *The Sindbad Voyage*. London: Hutchinson.

Sharma, K. L., ed. 1994. *Caste and Class in India*. New Delhi: Rawat Publications.

Sheriff, Abdul. 1987. *Slaves, Spices and Ivory in Zanzibar*. London: James Currey.

Shroff, Beheroze. 2004. Sidis and Parsis: A Filmmaker's Notes. In Catlin-Jairazbhoy and Alpers 1994, 159–77.

Shukri, M. A. M., ed. 1986. *Muslims of Sri Lanka: Avenues to Antiquity*. Beruwala, Sri Lanka: Jamiah Naleemia Institute.

Siddiqi, Akhtar Husain. 1991. *Baluchistan (Pakistan): Its Society, Resources and Development*. Lanham-New York-London: University Press of America.

Singh, D., and A. B. Rajshirke. 1992. The merchant communities in Surat: Trade, trade practices and institutions in the late eighteenth century. In Banga 1992, 181–98.

Singh, S. Niham. 1923. *The Nizam and the British Empire*. Calcutta: New Press.

Sinopoli, C. M., and Morrison, K. D. 1995. Dimensions of imperial control: The Vijayanagara capital. *American Anthropologist* 97 (1): 83–96.

Smith, Llyn F. 1997. Islamic ideology and religious practice among Muslims in a southern Sri Lankan town. Ph.D. Diss., University of London.

Spooner, Brian. 1964. Kuch u Baluch and Ichthyophagi. *Journal of the British Institute of Persian Studies* 2: 53–67.

Spodek, H. 1976. Urban-rural integration in regional development: A case study of Saurashtra, India. Department of Geography, University of Chicago.

Srinivasan, Padma. 2001. Indians in the East African slave trade during the nineteenth century. *Indica*, 38 (1 & 2): 229–36.

Steiner, R. L., and J. Weiss. 1951. Veblen revised in the light of counter-snobbery. *Journal of Aesthetics and Art Criticism* 9 (3): 263–68.

Subramanian, L. 1985. Capital and crowd in a declining Asian port city: The Anglo-Banian order and the Surat riots of 1795. *Modern Asian Studies* 19 (2): 205–37.

———. 1987. Banias and the British: The role of indigenous credit in the process of imperial expansion in western India in the second half of the eighteenth century. *Modern Asian Studies* 21 (3): 473–510.

———. 1992. Western India in the eighteenth century: Ports, inland towns and states. In Banga 1992, 153–79.

———. 1998. Power and the weave: Weavers, merchants and rulers in eighteenth century Surat. In Mukherjee and Subramanian 1998, 52–82.

Sullivan, B. N. 2003. *Dhow Chasing in Zanzibar Waters*. London: The Gallery Publications.

Sultana, Farhat. 1996. Gwat and Gwat-i-leb: Spirit healing and social change in Makran. In Titus 1996, 28–50.

Swidler, Nina. 1996. Beyond parody: Ethnography engages nationalist discourse. In Titus 1996, 168–90.

Tambs-Lyche, H. 1997. *Power, Profit and Poetry: Traditional Society in Kathiawar, Western India*. Delhi: Manohar.

Taylor, Meadows. 2002 [1873]. *Confessions of a Thug*. New Delhi: Rupa.

Temple, Richard. 1868. *Report on the Administration of the Government of H.H. the Nizam in the Deccan*. Calcutta: Government Publications.

Thangal, Al'Haj Rifai Moulana Nalla Koya. 1978. Message from His Eminence Al-Haj Rifai Moulana Nalla Koya Thangal. In *Refayee Feast Souvenir, 1889–1978*. Kapuwatta, Weligama: Jama-Athul Akram Refayee Ratheeb Association.

Thawfeeq, M. M. n.d. *Muslim Mosaics*. An 'El Eslam' publication. Colombo: Moors Islamic Cultural Home.

Thompson, Tony. 2003. Revealed: Bollywood craze that is fuelling London's vice rackets. In *The Observer*, 27 July.

Tibbetts, G. R. 1956. Pre-Islamic Arabia and South-east Asia. *Journal of the Malayan Branch of the Royal Asiatic Society*. 24 (3): 182–208.

Timberg, T. A. 1978. *The Marwaris: From Traders to Industrialists*. Delhi: Vikas.

Tinker, Hugh. 1993. *A New System of Slavery: The Export of Indian Labour Overseas*. London: Hansib Publishing.

Titus, P., ed. 1996. *Marginality and Modernity: Ethnicity and Change in Post-Colonial Balochistan*. Karachi: Oxford University Press.

Topp, Janet. 1994. A history of Taarab music in Zanzibar: A process of Africanisation. In *Continuity and Autonomy in Swahili Communities: Inland Influences and Strategies of Self-Determination*, ed. D. Parkin, 153–65. London: SOAS.

Torri, M. 1982. In the deep blue sea: Surat and its merchant class during the dyarchic era. *The Indian Economic* and *Social History Review* 19, (3–4): 267–301.

———. 1990. Trapped inside the colonial order: The Hindu bankers of Surat and their business world during the second half of the eighteenth century,. In Borsa 1990b, 47–80.

Toussaint, Auguste. 1966. *History of the Indian Ocean*. Translated by June Guicharnaud. Chicago: University of Chicago Press. French edition first published 1961.

Toynbee, A. J. 1981. *The Greeks and Their Heritages*. Oxford: Oxford University Press.

Turner, Victor. 1974. *Dramas, Fields, and Metaphors: Symbolic Action in Human Society*. Cornell University Press: Ithaca and London.

Vaidya, K. B. 1945. *The Sailing Vessel Traffic on the West Coast of India and Its Future*. Bombay: Popular Book Depot.

Varadarajan, L. 1991. Perspectives on maritime activity in Gujarat. In Anirudh Gupta 1991, 1–16.

Vasantha Madhava, K. G. 1991. *Western Karnataka: Its Agrarian Relations, 1500–1800*. Delhi: Navrang.

Vassanji, M. G. 1991. All worlds are possible now. In *Uhuru Street*. Nairobi: Heinemann.

———. 1996. *The Book of Secrets*. London: Picador.

Villiers, Alan. 1940. *Sons of Sinbad*. New York: Charles Scribner's.

———. 1952. *The Indian Ocean*. London: Museum Press Limited.

Vincent, D. D. 1805. *The Periplus of the Erythrean Sea*. 3 Parts. London: A. Straham for T. Cadwell Jnr. & W. Davies.

Vink, M. 1995. The Dutch East India Company and the pepper trade between Kerala and Tamilnad, 1663–1795: A geo-historical analysis. In Mathew 1995, 273–300.

Vivekananda, Swami. 1978. *What Religion is: In the Words of Swami Vivekananda*. Edited by Swami Vityatmananda. Calcutta: Avaita Ashrama.

Von Grunebaum, G. E. 1988. (1951) *Muhammadan Festivals*. London: Curzon Press.

Watson, Helen. 1994. Women and the veil: Personal responses to global process. In *Islam, Globalization and Postmodernity*, ed. Akbar S. Ahmad and Hastings Donnan, 141–59. London: Routledge.

Weber, Max. 1958. *The Religion of India*. New York: Free Press.

Weiner, Annette B. 1992. *Inalienable Possessions: The Paradox of Keeping-While-Giving*. Berkeley: University of California Press.

Wikan, Unni. 1990. *Managing Turbulent Hearts: A Balinese Formula for Living*. Chicago: University of Chicago Press.

Wink, André. 1999. *Al-Hind: The Making of the Indo-Islamic World*. 2 vols. Vol. 1, *Early Medieval India and the Expansion of Islam*, 7th–11th Centuries. New Delhi: Oxford University Press. First published by E. J. Brill, Leiden, 1990.

Wright, Marcia. 1993. *Strategies of Slaves and Women: Life-Stories from East/Central Africa*. New York/London: Lilian Barber Press/James Currey.

Zachariah, K. C., E. T. Mathew, and S. Irudaya Rajan. 1999. *Impact of Migration on Kerala's Economy and Society*. Working paper no. 297. Thiruvanathapuram, Kerala: Centre for Development Studies.

Contributors

Sabir Badalkhan, Ph.D. in folklore, teaches at the University of Naples, L'Orientale. He has also taught folklore courses as a Visiting Professor at the Ohio State University, Columbus. His research interests include oral tradition in Baluchistan (both in Pakistan and Iran), the Luri itinerary musicians, singers, and storytellers in southwest Asia; seafaring and fishing activities on the Baluchistan coast; and general folklore and folklife in Baluchistan. He has widely published in international journals and conference proceedings on topics related to Baluchi folklore and folklife. He has carried out extensive fieldworks in the Iranian and Pakistani parts of Baluchistan, collecting valuable material on the folklore of the Med fishermen of Makran and on Baluchi folklore in general.

Helene Basu is Professor of Social Anthropology at Westfaelische Wilhelms-Universitaet Muenster. She has worked on several fieldwork projects in India, Pakistan and Tanzania and published extensively on the history, religious performances and social constructions of identities of Sidis. She has co-edited a book (with Pnina Werbner) on the vitality of Sufism in South Asia, *Embodying Charisma. Modernity, Locality and the Performance of Emotion at Sufi Shrines* (1998). Another major research project of hers (2004) focuses on gendered social memory, female asceticism and aesthetic productions of Charan bards in Kacch (*Von Barden und Königen. Ethnologische Studien zum Gedächtnis und zur Göttin in Kacch (Indien)*. She is currently working in Tanzania on themes related to the African diaspora in India and Indian diasporas in East Africa.

Ned Bertz is an Assistant Professor in the Department of History at the University of Hawaii at Manoa. He teaches courses on South Asia in addition to African and Indian Ocean world history. His doctoral dissertation from the University of Iowa is on race, nationalism, and the Indian diaspora of Tanzania framed within the history of the Indian Ocean world. He conducted fieldwork for this project in Dar es Salaam and Zanzibar (Tanzania) and New Delhi, Bombay, Punjab and Gujarat (India) during 2000–2003.

Marine Carrin, anthropologist, is Director of Research with the CNRS at the Centre d'Anthropologie, Toulouse. She has worked among the Santals for many years and is the author of *La Fleur et l'Os: Symbolisme et rituel chez les Santal* (1986) and *Enfants de la Déesse: Prêtrise et dévotion féminine au Bengal* (1997) as well as a large number of articles. She is the editor of *Managing Distress: Therapeutic cults in South Asia* (1999). A book on Santal ritual discourse is in preparation. She has recently published several articles on the Bhuta cults and related themes in South Kanara, India.

Elizabeth L. H. Chettur is Ph.D. candidate in the Anthropology Department at Boston University and Adjunct Instructor at Rhode Island College. She is currently in the final phase of her dissertation, Globalization, Consumption, and Status: A Multi-Caste Study of Changing Perceptions of Social Distinction and Prestige in Kerala, South India. Her research interests include South Asia, religion and economy, social identity, globalisation, and theories of social change.

Ababu Minda is a social anthropologist born in Ethiopia. He received his Ph.D. from Georg-August-University of Goettingen in 2004. His dissertation is based on his field research among the African Indian community of Hyderabad. He has also conducted fieldwork among the Rastafarian community of Ethiopia about whom he published in his piece "Rastafarians in the Promised Land" (2004). His research interests include ethnicity, identity, migration and diaspora. Dr Minda has been teaching several courses at Alemaya University, Ethiopia.

Kerrin G. von Schwerin, received her Ph.D. from the University of Heidelberg. She taught South Asian history at the South

Asia Institute in Heidelberg and at Free University Berlin. Her main interests are directed at Indian Muslims. Her publications include *Indirekte Herrschaft und Reformpolitik in Hyderabad, 1653–1911*. She has also published several articles on Sufi institutions in India.

Abdul Sheriff was born and educated in Zanzibar. He studied at the University of California at Los Angeles, and the School of Oriental & African Studies, University of London. He taught history at the University of Dar es Salaam from 1969 to 1993. In 1993 he was appointed Advisor & Principal Curator of the Zanzibar Museums. He has been a Visiting Professor at various universities in the US and in Germany and a Fellow at the Wissenschaftskolleg zu Berlin in 2002–3. Professor Sheriff has published and edited a number of books, including *Slaves, Spices & Ivory in Zanzibar* (1987), *Zanzibar under Colonial Rule* (1991), *The History & Conservation of Zanzibar Stone Town* (1995), *The Architecture of the Stone Town of Zanzibar* (1998), as well as numerous scholarly articles. His current research interest is on the Dhow culture of the Indian Ocean.

Beheroze Shroff received an M.A. in English at the University of Bombay, and later at UCLA she obtained an M.A. in English and an M.F.A. in Film and T.V. Production. She went on to make independent documentary films. *Sweet Jail: The Sikhs of Yuba City* explores issues of immigration and gender in the pioneering Sikh community of California. *Reaching For Half the Sky* documents the fourth national conference of autonomous women's groups in India. *A Life Before Death* explores the sexual and social exploitation of joginis in Andhra Pradesh. *Voices of the Sidis-Part One*, Shroff's latest documentary, raises dilemmas of hybrid identities that confront the Sidis of Gujarat. Shroff presently teaches part time at the University of California, Irvine.

Edward Simpson is a Lecturer in Social Anthropology at Goldsmiths College, London. He is author of the monograph *Muslim Society and the Western Indian Ocean: The Seafarers of*

Kachchh (2006). More recently, his research has focused on the politics of post-disaster reconstruction in South Asia.

Llyn Smith is currently Chair of Anthropology at Humboldt State University, California. She has previously undertaken research on transgender issues, Islamic cosmology and the constitution of Islamic community in South Asia, and has an enduring interest in the field of economic development. She is currently investigating the growth of "sail training" on "tall ships" as a response to transformations in global capital and the restructuring of the conditions of labour.

Harald Tambs-Lyche is Professor of Ethnology at the University of Picardie—Jules Verne, Amiens. He has worked on Indian immigrants in Britain (*London Patidars: Case Study in Urban Ethnicity,* 1980) and on religion and society in Saurashtra, Gujarat (*Power, Profit and Poetry: Traditional Society in Kathiawar, Western India,* 1997; *The Good Country: Individual, Situation and Society in Saurashtra,* 2003). He has edited *The Feminine Sacred in South Asia* (1999), and is currently working on South Kanara, Karnataka, particularly on the Konkani community of Gauda Saraswat Brahmins.

Index